CANADIAN
Copyright
LAW
3RD EDITION

The indispensable
guide for publishers,
web professionals,
writers, artists,
filmmakers, teachers,
librarians, archivists,
curators, lawyers
and business people

Lesley Ellen Harris

McGraw-Hill
Ryerson

Toronto Montréal Boston Burr Ridge, IL Dubuque, IA Madison, WI New York
San Francisco St. Louis Bangkok Bogotá Caracas Kuala Lumpur Lisbon London
Madrid Mexico City Milan New Delhi Santiago Seoul Singapore Sydney Taipei

**McGraw-Hill
Ryerson Limited**
A Subsidiary of The McGraw-Hill Companies

ISBN: 0-07-560369-1

234567890 W 045678901
Printed and bound in Canada.

Canadian Cataloguing in Publication Data

Harris, Lesely Ellen
  Canadian copyright law: the indispensible guide for publishers, web professionals,
writers, artists, filmmakers, teachers, librarians, archivists, curators, lawyers and
business people

3rd ed.
Includes index.
ISBN 0-07-560369-1

1. Copyright — Canada — Popular works. I. Title.

KE2799.2.H37   2000   346.7104'82   C00-932379-1
KF2980.H37   2000

Publisher: **Joan Homewood**
Editorial Co-ordinator: **Catherine Leek**
Production Co-ordinator: **Susanne Penny**
Editor: **Katherine Coy**
Interior Design and Electronic Page Composition: **Heidy Lawrance Associates**
Cover Design: **Greg Devitt**

To my husband, Ken

CONTENTS

PREFACE TO THE THIRD EDITION ix
ACKNOWLEDGEMENTS xi
A NOTE ON THE TEXT xiii
INTRODUCTION xv

Chapter 1: UNDERSTANDING INTELLECTUAL PROPERTY 1
   What Is Copyright? 1
   Overview of Intellectual Property 2
Summary 11

Chapter 2: COPYRIGHT LAW IN CANADA 12
   History of Canadian Copyright Law 12
   Government Responsibility for Copyright in Canada 15
   The Concept of Copyright Law 15
Summary 16

Chapter 3: IS YOUR CREATION ELIGIBLE FOR COPYRIGHT PROTECTION? 17
   Criteria for Copyright Protection 17
   Originality 18
   Fixation 20
   Nationality and Place of Publication 23
   Sound Recordings, Performances and Broadcasts 25
Summary 26

Chapter 4: ARE FORMALITIES REQUIRED TO OBTAIN COPYRIGHT PROTECTION? . . 27
   Automatic Protection 27
   Marking Your Creations 28
   Registration With the Canadian Government 30
   Registration or Deposit Other Than With the Canadian Government 38
Summary 43

Chapter 5: **HOW DOES INTERNATIONAL COPYRIGHT PROTECTION WORK?** ... **44**
 The Concept of International Copyright Protection 44
 International Copyright Conventions 45
 The Berne Convention 46
 The Universal Copyright Convention 47
 The Rome Convention 48
 New Digital Copyright Treaties 49
 Other International Copyright-Related Conventions 49
 International Trade Agreements and Copyright Law 50
 In Which Country Do You Enforce Your Rights? 50
 How to Enforce Your Rights in Foreign Countries 51
 The Protection of Foreigners in Canada 53
 Member Countries of the Berne Convention, UCC and WTO 53
 Summary 53

Chapter 6: **WHAT IS PROTECTED BY COPYRIGHT?** **54**
 The Meaning of "Works" and "Other Subject-Matter" 54
 Works Protected by Copyright 55
 Literary Works 57
 Dramatic Works 63
 Audio-Visual Materials 64
 Choreographic Works 66
 Musical Works 66
 Artistic Works 68
 Folklore 73
 Government Materials 73
 Other Works 73
 Other Subject-Matter 78
 Summary 79

Chapter 7: **WHO OWNS COPYRIGHT?** **80**
 Owning Copyright 80
 The General Rule 81
 Specific Works 82
 Specific Situations 88
 Moral Rights 93
 Summary 94

Chapter 8: **THE DURATION OF COPYRIGHT** **95**
 A Limited Duration 95
 General Rule For Works 95
 Moral Rights 98
 Specific Works 99
 Specific Situations for Works 100
 Other Subject-Matter 102
 Corporate Ownership 103
 Public Domain Works 103
 Summary 104

Chapter 9: **RIGHTS PROTECTED BY COPYRIGHT** **105**
  The Nature of Rights Granted by the *Copyright Act* 105
  Economic Rights in Literary, Dramatic, Musical and Artistic Works 107
  The Right to Prohibit Importation 112
  The Right of Authorization 113
  Economic Rights in Specific Works 113
  Moral Rights 118
  Neighbouring Rights 121
  Rights Not Currently in the *Copyright Act* 123
Summary 125

Chapter 10: **LIMITATIONS ON RIGHTS** **126**
  What are Limitations on Rights? 126
  Limitations for Specific Purposes 126
  Exceptions for Specific Works 130
  Exceptions in Specific Situations 133
  Other Exceptions 149
  Exceptions From Moral Rights 150
Summary 150

Chapter 11: **HOW CAN RIGHTS BE EXPLOITED?** **151**
  How the *Copyright Act* Works 151
  Who Can Exploit a Work or Other Subject-Matter? 153
  How to Exploit a Work 153
  Testamentary Dispositions 157
  Copyright in Future Works 158
  The Value of Rights 158
  Assignment Must Be In Writing 159
  Moral Rights 161
  Neighbouring Rights 162
  The Collective Administration of Copyright 162
Summary 165

Chapter 12: **HOW IS COPYRIGHT VIOLATED?** **166**
  What is a Violation of Copyright? 166
  Terms Used to Describe Violations of Copyright 167
  Copyright 168
  Moral Rights 171
Summary 171

Chapter 13: **WHAT ARE THE REMEDIES FOR THE VIOLATION OF COPYRIGHT?** ... **172**
  Remedies in General 172
  Border Remedies 172
  Civil Remedies 175
  Criminal Remedies 187
  Spotting Illegal Works 189
Summary 189

Chapter 14: **USING COPYRIGHT MATERIALS** **190**
    The "Use" of Copyright Materials 190
    When Is Permission Required? 191
    Obtaining Permission 191
    Copyright Collectives 195
    Obtaining Permission for Specific Works 195
    Using Crown Works (i.e. Government Material) 207
    Unlocatable Copyright Owners 209
    Moral Rights 211
  Summary 213

Chapter 15: **CANADIAN AND AMERICAN COPYRIGHT LAWS: A COMPARISON** .. **214**
    The Relevancy of American Copyright Law to Canadians 214
    Works Protected in the United States 214
    Rights Granted in the United States 215
    Fair Use and Exceptions 215
    Length of Protection 216
    Registration and Copyright Notice Requirements 217
    Employment Situations and Assignments of Copyright 218
    Moral Rights 219
    New American Digital Legislation 219
    How to Obtain Further Information on American Copyright Law 220
  Summary 221

Chapter 16: **DIGITAL COPYRIGHT AND ELECTRONIC RIGHTS** **222**
    Introduction 222
    Old Law, New Technology 223
    Terminology 224
    Current Copyright Law and Digital Media 225
    How Can Digital Rights be Exploited? 233
    Enforcing Copyright on the Internet 236
    Copyright Protection in Other Countries 238
    Old Law, Net Technology Revisited 238

Appendix I: **COPYRIGHT ACT** **239**
Appendix II: **APPLICATION FOR REGISTRATION OF**
        COPYRIGHT AND CERTIFICATE OF REGISTRATION **302**
Appendix III: **MEMBER COUNTRIES OF BERNE CONVENTION,**
        THE UCC AND THE WTO **312**

ENDNOTES **316**
INDEX **319**
ABOUT THE AUTHOR **329**

PREFACE
TO THE
THIRD EDITION

It is hard to believe that almost a decade has passed since the first edition of this book was published. In 1991, I had not heard of the Internet. In 1995 when the second edition of this book was being written, I had my very first email account on the Ottawa Freenet. I had never "surfed" the Web though I was familiar with the Internet as it then existed, which consisted of Archie and Veronica and Gopher. Today, I claim my address is on the Web (at **http://copyrightlaws.com**) and I truly have a virtual office. Almost all my correspondence with clients is online, including invoices which clients access at a private Web site. I no longer carry business cards but merely hand-out my URL and tell people to click on my photo to access me (via email). I've cancelled my telephone line and use only a cellular phone. The world has truly changed.

So how has Canadian copyright law fared during the initial stages of the Digital Age? Very well, as you will soon see in this book. The Canadian *Copyright Act* has proven itself to be flexible in its application to the rapidly changing technology. In preparing the third edition of this book, I have updated the chapter on digital media, and have added many examples throughout the book which relate to digital media, and have included Web site and email addresses wherever relevant.

The changes in this edition are not, however, limited to digital media. Recent amendments to the Canadian *Copyright Act* are discussed throughout this book. These changes are important for those who create and own copyright protected materials, as well as for those who distribute and otherwise use these materials. Non-profit libraries, archives, museums and educational institutions have many new "free" uses of protected materials under the new law. There is a new levy on blank audio tapes and cassettes to be collected and paid to performers, producers and authors for private copying of their works. There are new guaranteed minimum awards for copyright infringement. There is an extension of rental rights to composers, lyricists and performers of musical works. In addition, there is a change in the perpetual copyright protection in unpublished works to a term of life of the author plus 50 years, and a change in the term of copyright in photographs to life of the author plus 50 years

If you have any comments for improving the accuracy, accessibility and comprehensiveness of information in this edition, please contact me at **ccl@copyrightlaws.com**.

Lesley Ellen Harris
October 2000

ACKNOWLEDGEMENTS

I would like to thank the numerous people who generously gave their time and shared their expertise and knowledge in helping me write this edition. They include Bruce Couchman, John Stuart Dick, Allen Israel, Claude Majeau, Wanda Noel, Gisèle Tassé-Goodman, Michael Shapiro, and my researchers Lynn Burshtein, Danny Ciraco and Rachel Rajput, as well as people from copyright collectives, organizations, associations, unions and government agencies listed in this book. I would also like to thank my publisher, Joan Homewood, and others, including Cathy Leek and my editor, Katherine Coy, at McGraw-Hill Ryerson.

A NOTE
ON THE TEXT

I wrote this book for the lay reader. It is in no way a treatise on Canadian copyright law or a survey of case law, but a simplified description of a complex area of the law. The examples I have chosen in the text are merely examples. Each particular case must be examined on its own facts. My intention was to produce an information guide — not to offer legal advice. If you face a legal problem, seek professional advice.

The book can be read from cover to cover or used, as required, for reference purposes. You might wish to first read the entire book before using it as a reference since the nature of copyright is such that understanding one area of copyright law is often necessary to understanding other areas of the law.

I have quoted cases or specifically referred to them only to illustrate a point that reference to a particular case makes clearer. An unofficial version of the consolidated Canadian copyright statute is reproduced at the end of the book for reference purposes. You should take caution in reading the *Copyright Act* without being familiar with legal jargon and without access to the court cases that interpret the *Act*.

You might find certain sections of the book oversimplified — others overly complex. I have tried to find a balance between explaining the law simply yet providing enough detail for you to understand its intricacies.

I have avoided technical terms or legal jargon as much as possible. Words like "work," "creation," "copyright materials," or "other subject-matter" refer to something protected by copyright law. "Creators" create copyright works and the word "creator" is used interchangeably with the word "author." "Creator" and "user" are two words often used when talking about items protected by copyright law. The creator is the person who creates the work. However, the creator is not necessarily the owner of copyright in that work. The user is the person who uses copyright materials; he or she is also called a "consumer" of copyright material.

Copyright is not an area of law that can be seen in black and white. Terms like "arguable," "probable," "likely" and "most likely" are necessary to address the many grey areas of copyright law. When you come across these words, take extra caution in applying the law to your particular circumstance.

This book is comprehensive in that it covers, or at least mentions, most provisions in the Canadian *Copyright Act*. However, I have omitted a small number of provisions because they apply in such a minuscule number of cases and are too complex for a general guide.

I have dealt only with copyright law, and briefly other areas of intellectual property law. I may touch on, but I do not specifically deal with related legal issues such as personality rights, privacy, contract, libel and slander, passing off, tax and bankruptcy. All of these areas may be of some interest to those who create, own or use copyright materials, and most of these topics could be books themselves.

The law I describe in this text is the law as it stands at the time of writing: October 1, 2000. Legislative changes and court cases interpreting the law may change some of the law as described. Technological developments may also impact upon some of the information set out in this book.

INTRODUCTION

Copyright is the Cinderella of the law. Her rich old sisters, Franchises and Patents, long crowded her into the chimney corner. Suddenly the Fairy Godmother, Invention, endowed her with mechanical and electrical devices as magical as the pumpkin coach and the mice footmen. Now she whirls through the mad mazes of a glamorous ball.[1]

One of the basic problems in understanding copyright is that we cannot see it. Perhaps that is why people who would not dare steal a towel from a hotel room would, without a second thought, photocopy a book or reproduce a computer program.

Copyright affects everyone. Anyone who has ever written a letter or email message, made a sketch, or taken a photograph is a "creator" of copyright material. And anyone who has ever photocopied an article, taped a CD or television program, or downloaded a document from the Internet is a "user" of copyright material.

Copyright law, however, is very complicated, and my purpose in writing this book is to demystify it and set out its fundamental principles in everyday language. This book is written not only for those who create copyright materials, but also for those who use copyright materials. Those in the cultural, entertainment, education, information and computer industries are particularly affected by copyright law. However, the Internet makes copyright everyone's business.

Intellectual property, and especially copyright, is a growth industry.

Not too long ago, we lived in a time and age when intellectual property laws were ignored. Software programs were pirated. Entire books were reproduced. Hollywood films were copied. Times have changed. Not only is the average citizen and business now much more aware of the rights of owners of intellectual property, the owners themselves are much more aware of their own rights, and more willing to enforce them around the world. Why the change?

The change has been coming about for a number of years, but it was accelerated when intellectual property recently burst onto the front pages of newspapers as the final issue in the General Agreement on Tariffs and Trade (GATT) talks. And with the burgeoning of digital media, it hasn't left the front pages.

Copyright law has been struggling with technology ever since the invention of the printing press. With each new technology — like photocopiers and VCRs and the Internet — consumers find it easier to reproduce copyright materials. At the same time, creators find it harder to control such reproduction and thereby lose control over the use of their creations. Writers lose royalties from book sales as large excerpts or entire books are photocopied or scanned into a computer, instead of being purchased. Musicians lose royalties from CD sales due to people taping them or exchanging them over the Internet. Creators cannot afford to forego compensation for the use of their creations and, as they more intensely exercise their rights, people who duplicate their works are becoming much more conscious of encroaching or misappropriating those rights. The content on the Internet is primarily copyright material — inevitably both creators and users will be facing new copyright law challenges.

The second reason for this new awareness of copyright is the change in the law at a domestic level as well as its prominence in international trade agreements. The Canadian *Copyright Act* was written in 1921 and enacted in 1924. It remained substantially unchanged until 1988. In 1987, when the changes to the *Act* were introduced into the House of Commons, there seemed to be a new awareness of copyright law. People now thought twice when they touched the button on the photocopier.

Copyright became a regular subject in the media. Articles suggesting that children may be committing their first criminal act by sitting in on reading hour in the library, or that a teacher may require permission to hang a finger painting in the classroom, brought copyright issues to the public's attention as never before. Intellectual property issues began appearing in international trade agreements like the Canada-U.S. Free Trade Agreement, and the North American Free Trade Agreement, and the agreement on Trade-Related Aspects of Intellectual Property as part of GATT.

This new awareness made creators think about enforcing and benefitting from their legal rights: rights that they might have been lax about in the past; users began to feel guilty about using copyright materials without clearing permission. A new era in copyright had begun.

In this new era questions such as "How do I protect my poem from copyright infringement?"; "Do I have to register my work?"; "Is computer code protected by copyright?"; "What are electronic and digital rights?"; "How do I clear copyright in a book?"; "Is a CD-ROM protected by copyright?"; "Is it legal to download music from a Web site?"; and "How do I stop someone who's using my work without my permission?" have become of concern to all of us. I wrote *Canadian Copyright Law* to help answer these questions and correct the misinformation that is all too frequent. I hope I have succeeded.

Chapter 1

UNDERSTANDING INTELLECTUAL PROPERTY

I want to impress upon honourable gentlemen who are not lawyers the fact that the question of copyright is of importance not only to lawyers, but to many people in this country.

Honourable George G. Foster, Senate, March 27, 1919

WHAT IS COPYRIGHT?

Literally, copyright means the "right to copy." The Canadian *Copyright Act* grants copyright owners the sole and exclusive right to reproduce, perform or publish a work. These rights give copyright holders control over the use of their creations, and an ability to benefit, monetarily and otherwise, from the exploitation of their works. In addition, copyright protects the reputation of creators.

Copyright law is one area of a larger body of law called "intellectual property." The word "intellectual" is used to distinguish it from "physical" property. Intellectual property law refers to and protects the intangible or intellectual nature of an object, whereas physical property law refers to and protects the tangible or physical aspect of an object. For example, there is both an intellectual and physical property component to a book or refrigerator. The physical component of the book or refrigerator is the object itself, the book which you can hold in your hand, or the refrigerator whose door you can open and close. The intellectual component of the book is the words that appear on the page and the expression of any ideas contained in those words. The intellectual component of the refrigerator is the material that led to its creation, such as sketches containing its design or plans for its motor, and even the name of the refrigerator. The physical and intellectual components of any creations are separate. By owning the physical or intellectual property in a creation, you do not necessarily own the other sort of property in it. In other words, purchasing or owning a book does not mean that you own the copyright in that book. You are limited in what you can do with that book, and you cannot make any uses of the book that only the copyright owner may make.

There are traditionally five areas of intellectual property:

- patents
- trade-marks
- industrial designs
- confidential information and trade secrets
- copyright

In addition, since 1990, a new area of intellectual property has been recognized in a Canadian statute for integrated circuit topography protection. The protection of databases that are not protected by copyright law is currently being discussed around the world as a new sort of intellectual property. Database protection is further discussed in Chapter 6: What is Protected by Copyright?

By examining the various types of intellectual property, you will gain a better understanding of how copyright fits into this body of law. You will also realize, as we go through various examples under each area of intellectual property, that each type of intellectual property protects a different kind of creation or a different aspect of a creation, and that each type provides its own special set of rules of protection.

Note that the term intellectual property is sometimes interpreted in a narrow sense to apply to copyright and neighbouring rights, and the term industrial property is used to refer to patents, trademarks, industrial designs, confidential information and trade secrets, as well as integrated circuit topography protection.

OVERVIEW OF INTELLECTUAL PROPERTY

"Can I patent my book?" or "Can I copyright my idea for a new mouse-trap?" These are examples of questions a copyright lawyer is frequently asked. Such questions demonstrate a general knowledge of intellectual property, in that patents or copyright protect inventions or creations, but they also show a lack of comprehension of the distinction between the various areas of intellectual property. This section of the book will explain the different kinds of intellectual property and examine whether something you have created, or someone else's creation that you may want to use, is protected by one of the areas of intellectual property, and if so, under which type of intellectual property. This section will also briefly describe the nature of protection given by each area of intellectual property.

Patent Law

A patent is a document issued by the government that describes an invention. According to the federal statute that governs patent law in Canada, the patent legally protects an inventor, or patent owner, and allows him or her to prevent others from making, using and selling that invention within Canada for twenty years after an application for a patent is filed.

Examples of things protected by patents:

- articles such as a washing machine
- compositions such as a chemical composition used in a lubricant for that washing machine
- apparatus, for example, the machine used for making the washing machine
- processes, for example, the method used to make the washing machine
- any improvement on any of the above

Ninety percent of patents are for improvements to existing patented inventions.[1]

A patent is granted only for the physical embodiment of an idea, or for a process that produces something saleable or tangible. New medicines, communications systems, energy sources and electric can openers are all patentable. However, you cannot patent a scientific principle, an abstract theorem, an idea, a method of doing business, a computer program, a medical treatment, or any inventions having illicit or immoral purposes.

In order for an article, composition, apparatus or process to be patentable, it must meet all of the following criteria:

- it must be new (i.e., the same such invention must not exist)
- it must be useful (i.e., functional and operative)
- it must be "unobvious" (to someone skilled in that area)

Preparing and prosecuting a patent application is a complex, tedious task and is usually done by a registered patent agent. It can take approximately three years from the date of application to obtain a patent.

If you obtain a patent, you may then sue anyone who makes the patented product or uses the patented process without your permission. However, there are certain situations where "compulsory licences" exist and you must let others use your patented invention, provided they make royalty payments to you. For example, firms in Canada that manufacture new foods or pharmaceutical products come under this category. A compulsory licence will also apply where you do not make your invention commercially available, without good reason, within three years after the patent is granted.

The law does not require a patented object to be marked as "patented" or an awaited patent as "patent pending," though doing so may remind others of your rights, or pending rights, in the object. It is illegal to mark an article as patented where a patent has not yet been granted.

If you plan on securing patent protection, you should be careful not to disclose your invention before filing an application with the Patent Office because it may preclude you from obtaining a valid patent. If you must disclose your invention, for example, to evaluate potential commercial interest, you should only do so on a confidential basis and require the party to whom you are disclosing it to sign a confidentiality agreement that states that he will not disclose your invention to anyone else. You will not be able to obtain a valid patent if you disclose your invention more than one year prior to filing a patent application in Canada. In many countries such disclosure results in an absolute bar to obtaining a valid patent.

If you are granted a patent in Canada, that protection is good throughout Canada. To get patent protection in other countries, you must apply separately in each country, or apply through the treaty called the Patent Co-operation Treaty (PCT). This treaty provides a standardized international filing procedure for many of our principal trading partners including the United States, Japan and most European countries. Just as a Canadian patent is not automatically valid in other countries, a foreign patent has no effect in Canada unless a separate Canadian patent has been obtained.

The use of the patent system is not currently being fully utilized in certain industries such as high technology. This is due to the rapid change of technology, the relatively long period of time it takes to obtain a patent (normally three years) and the high cost to prosecute, maintain and protect a patent.

Some owners of "patentable" inventions have found adequate alternative protection in other areas of the law such as trade secrets or contracts.

Trade-Mark Law

A trade-mark is a word, symbol, picture, logo, design or shaping of goods, or a combination of these elements, used to distinguish the goods or services of one person or organization from those of another in the market-place. A trade-mark allows its owner exclusive use of that mark to be identified with certain goods or services.

Examples of trade-marks are the word and logo "Coca Cola" and the distinctive shape of the Coke bottle.

The following marks are not registrable under the Canadian *Trade-marks Act*:

- names and surnames of living persons even if they are the applicants' own names or surnames (for example, LESLEY ELLEN HARRIS)
- words which are descriptive of the goods or services associated with the trade-mark (for example, CAFFEINE for coffee or INK SET for pens)
- words which clearly describe the place of origin of wares or services (for example, VANCOUVER for shoes or NEPAL for backpacks)
- words which describe the goods or services in any language (for example, VIN, VINO or WINE for wine)
- coats of arms of the Royal Family, badges and crests of the RCMP and the Canadian Armed Forces, the Red Cross and national symbols
- any mark that is obviously immoral or offensive
- deceptively misdescriptive marks

Certification marks can also be trade-marks if the certification mark is used to distinguish goods or services which meet a defined standard. An example of a certification mark is the "cotton mark" on clothing used to indicate the presence of cotton.

A trade name, that is, a business name of a corporation, partnership or individual is not necessarily a trade-mark, but may be registered under the *Trade-marks Act* if it is used as a trade-mark.

A trade-mark may be protected in two manners. It may be protected through use (common law protection); that is, by using the mark in connection with a service or product. This protection is perpetual so long as use of the mark is not abandoned. Also, common law protection is only in the geographic area in Canada in which a reputation for the mark has been acquired through use. Alternatively, the mark may be protected by registering it under the *Trade-marks Act*. Registration provides *prima facie* evidence of ownership of the mark and provides stronger protection than that provided by the mere usage of a mark. Registration entitles the registered owner to exclusive use of the mark throughout Canada even in geographic areas where use of the mark has not occurred. At the time of writing this book, registration normally takes twelve to eighteen months if no major difficulties are encountered. Registered protection lasts for fifteen years, renewable indefinitely for fifteen-year periods.

It is not mandatory to use the symbol ® for registered trade-marks, or for common law marks, to identify trade-marks. Likewise, it is not obligatory to complement a trade-mark with an asterisk followed by a footnote that describes the trade-mark as such and the owner of it. Identifying trade-marks does, however, inform others that the mark is a trade-mark, and can provide information of the origin of the mark. Trade-mark notices can also help to identify the source of the wares/services associated with the mark and inform a consumer as to who is responsible for their character and quality.

If you have a registered trade-mark, you have the exclusive right to use that mark throughout Canada in respect of such wares or services. If anyone else sells, distributes or advertises wares or services in association with your mark or a similar confusing one, you may enforce your rights against that person.

Your Canadian trade-mark registration is good throughout Canada, and separate registration must be obtained, if necessary, in other countries. Similarly, foreign trade-marks are not protected in Canada unless they have been registered here, though some may be protectable in Canada through use in Canada, or by massive spillover advertising, acquired reputation and goodwill in Canada.

Industrial Design

An industrial design is any original shape, pattern or ornamentation applied to a useful article of manufacture. The functional or utilitarian features of that article are not protected by industrial design, but may be protected by a patent. It is the "visually appealing" part of the design, and not the article to which it is applied that is protected as an industrial design.

The shape of a table, a telephone, or a decoration on a plate are examples of industrial designs.

Registration of a design is mandatory under the federal *Industrial Design Act* within twelve months of the publication of the design in Canada. Registration generally takes nine or ten months to secure. If registered after January 1, 1994, the protection lasts for ten years, beginning on the date of registration of the design. However, before the expiry of five years from the date of the registration of the design, you must pay a maintenance fee or your protection will expire. For designs registered before January 1, 1994, registration lasts for a period of five years and is renewable for a further five years.

It is not mandatory to mark a product to indicate that it is registered as a design but marking will give you certain benefits both regarding remedies in an infringement suit and notice to the public that the design is registered and you are its owner. The marking should consist of a capital "D" inside a circle and the name, or abbreviated name, of the design's owner, on the article, its label or packaging. Because of a recent change in the marking procedures in the law, you may see older designs with a mark consisting of the name of the design owner, the letters "Rd." and/or "Enr." and the year of registration.

The owner of the design has the right to make, use, rent or sell a product incorporating the design. The owner may sell or license some or all of those rights.

Protection in foreign countries must be separately obtained.

The relationship between creations protected by copyright and those protected by industrial design is further discussed in Chapter 6: What Is Protected by Copyright?

Confidential Information and Trade Secrets

Traditionally, ideas have been called the "orphans" of intellectual property. Ideas, *per se*, are not recognized as protectable subject matter of patents, trade-marks, industrial designs, topography protection or copyright. The closest thing to protecting an idea would be through an agreement or contract that treats that idea as confidential information or as a trade secret.

Thus what is unique to the intellectual property area of confidential information and trade secrets is that it protects concepts, ideas and factual information. For example, an idea for computer software, or a television show, or machinery to build cars may be considered confidential information. Further, a customer list, or knowledge of a recipe, say, for a certain soda pop, obtained by working at a soft drink company, may be considered trade secrets.

Unlike the other areas of intellectual property, confidential information and trade secrets are not governed by a statute (except in the province of Quebec where trade secrets fall under the *Civil Code*), but are based upon common law.

Generally, a duty to maintain confidential information or trade secrets arises from a certain relationship. The relationship puts you under a legal obligation not to divulge the information to others. That relationship can be established because of the association of people, as in an employer-employee situation, or due to the nature of the information conveyed, as in a discussion of an idea. In order to be protected, the information conveyed must not be common knowledge and it must be communicated in such a way, whether implicit or explicit, to instill an obligation of confidence.

One of the best ways to protect confidential information or trade secrets is through written contractual arrangements. Such a contract should describe in sufficient detail the type of information, the length of protection—if it is a limited one—geographical limitations on divulging the information and any allowable uses of the information. The more specific and limited the terms and conditions in the contract, the more likely a court of law would uphold such an agreement.

In certain extreme circumstances one may disclose confidential information; for instance, when it is in the public interest. Otherwise, such information may only be used within the limits of an agreement. If no agreement exists, you may disclose confidential information where no competitive edge can be gained from the use of the information, and the information will not be used in a way that will detrimentally affect the originator of the information. A court may be requested to grant an order to stop the continuing use of information, or may order monetary compensation to be paid by a person who unlawfully uses confidential information.

Copyright Law

Copyright law protects many different elements in the cultural, information and technology industries. It protects such diverse things as inter-office memorandums, books, computer programs, CD-ROMs, Web site content, sculptures, and films. It does not, however, protect ideas, but only the embodiments of these ideas.

Copyright protection is automatic, upon the creation of a work (i.e., once the work is in some sort of tangible form) and the protection lasts for fifty years after the creator's death. The protection gives creators exclusive use of their works, and protects the paternity and integrity (the "moral rights") of the creator. Protection in Canada ensures protection in more than one hundred and forty countries around the world.

In discussing copyright protection, reference is sometimes made to "neighbouring rights." Neighbouring rights protect the rights of performers (for example, actors and musicians), record producers and broadcasters. Neighbouring rights are rights akin to copyright, but are distinct from copyright. They are discussed in further detail in Chapter 9: Rights Protected by Copyright.

Integrated Circuit Topography Protection

Since 1990, Canada has had intellectual property protection for the topography of integrated circuits. These integrated circuits, referred to as "microchips," are tiny electronic devices found in everything from common appliances such as VCRs and washing machines to robots. Since the traditional areas of intellectual property do not provide adequate protection for microchips, at least twenty countries have recognized this newest kind of intellectual property by establishing protection in a separate statute.

The Canadian statute granting protection to topographies protects the original design of a registered topography on its own or when embodied in a product like a VCR. A topography is considered original if it is developed through the application of intellectual effort and is not the mere reproduction of a substantial part or whole of another topography.

Some integrated circuit products may be entitled to protection under other areas of intellectual property. For example, Random Access Memories (RAMs), and Read Only Memories (ROMs), which may be used to store sets of instructions for electronic processors, may be entitled to microchip protection for the topographies embodied in such circuits, and the sets of instructions they store may be subject to copyright protection as literary works, and may be entitled to patent protection as industrial methods.

Owners of registered topographies may prevent others from the following activities with respect to a protected topography or any substantial part of the topography:

- reproducing it
- manufacturing a product incorporating it
- importing or commercially exploiting it or a product or industrial article incorporating it (commercially exploiting could be, for example, sale, lease, offering or exhibiting for sale or lease or other commercial distribution)

A topography must be registered in order to be protected and the application for registration must be filed within two years of the first commercial exploitation of the topography. Registered integrated circuit topographies are protected for up to ten years from the date of filing the application for registration. The term expires on December 31st on the tenth year after the year of the first commercial exploitation, or the year of the filing date, whichever happens first.

The rights of an owner of a topography are limited by the following three exceptions. After the first authorized sale of a product embodying a registered microchip, the registered owner has no right to control its use, rental, resale or redistribution (unless expressly reserved through a contractual arrangement). Also, a protected topography may be freely copied for the sole purpose of analysis or evaluation, or for the sole purpose of research or teaching with respect to topographies. Further, the topography may be taken apart to design a new and original one. This new topography must meet the originality requirements in the statute if it is exploited commercially without the authorization of the original owner of the rights.

It is not obligatory to identify products embodying registered microchips. However, failure to do so may be a valid defence in an infringement lawsuit if a defendant can prove that he had no knowledge of the registration of the topography. The voluntary notice may include the registered title, or similar wording, used to identify the topography in the registration application.

Protection under the federal statute protecting microchips is extended to nationals of other countries on a reciprocal basis. Canada currently has reciprocal agreements with the United States, Switzerland, Japan and Australia.

Overlap of Intellectual Property Protection

In some circumstances, you will find that a particular creation, or aspects of it, qualifies for more than one type of intellectual property protection. Where more than one type of protection is possible, you should consider the nature of protection(s) that most appropriately fits your needs. For instance, consider such things as the use to be made of the creation and which type of protection(s) would cover that use, the various durations of protection, and the costs and procedures required for protection.

Further Information and Registration Forms

With the exception of confidential information, each of the above areas of intellectual property has an office within the Canadian Intellectual Property Office (CIPO) and further information and registration forms can be obtained by contacting:

Canadian Intellectual
    Property Office (CIPO)   T: 819.997.1936
Place du Portage, Phase I   F: 819.953.7620
50 Victoria Street   **E: cipo.contact@ic.gc.ca**
Hull, Quebec K1A 0C9   **⦿ : cipo.gc.ca**

Address the specific office within the CIPO, such as the Patent Office, Trade-marks Office, Industrial Design Office, Copyright Office or Integrated Circuit Topographies Office.

    Industry Canada also has regional offices from which information on intellectual property may be obtained.

SUMMARY

At the beginning of the section on the areas of intellectual property, two questions were asked: "Can I patent my book?" and "Can I copyright my idea?" You should now be able to answer these questions. To help you, the six areas of intellectual property are set out in the following chart.

Table 1.1 – The Six Areas of Intellectual Property

	PATENTS	TRADE MARKS	INDUSTRIAL DESIGNS	CONFIDENTIAL INFORMATION	COPYRIGHT	INTEGRATED CIRCUIT TOPOGRAPHY PROTECTION
TYPES OF PROTECTABLE WORKS	article, composition, apparatus, process, improvement	word, symbol, picture	shape, pattern, design applied to a useful article	idea, concept, factual information	literary, dramatic, musical, artistic works	"microchips"
LAMP EXAMPLE	remote control for lamp	name of lamp	design on lamp shade	idea for an improved lamp	instruction guide	microchip in the lamp
BASIS OF PROTECTION	federal statute	federal statute + common law (unregistered marks)	federal statute	common law	federal statute	federal statute
FOREIGN PROTECTION	must apply in each country or through the treaty	must apply in each country	must apply in each country	depends on agreement	international protection	on a reciprocal basis
TERM OF PROTECTION	20 years	if registered 15 years + 15 year renewable periods; if unregistered, perpetual protection	10 years (but must pay a maintenance fee after 5 years)	depends on agreement	life + 50 years	up to 10 years
REGISTRATION	necessary	not necessary	necessary	n/a	not necessary	necessary
MARKINGS	no	no	yes	n/a	no	no

Chapter 2

COPYRIGHT
LAW IN
CANADA

> "*I am excited about the opportunities presented by the Internet because it allows artists to communicate directly with fans. But the bottom line must always be respect and compensation for creative work. I am against Internet piracy and it is wrong for companies like Napster and others to promote stealing from artists online.*
>
> Elton John

HISTORY OF CANADIAN COPYRIGHT LAW

In Canada, copyright law falls under federal jurisdiction. The law, then, does not vary from province to province but is consistent throughout the country. This is because the Parliament of Canada was given exclusive jurisdiction to deal with the matter of "copyrights" under subsection 91(23) of the *Constitution Act of 1867*.

The current Canadian copyright legislation is found in one statute, called the *Copyright Act*.[1] This piece of legislation, based on the *United Kingdom Copyright Act, 1911*, came into force on January 1, 1924. Since that time, it has remained the governing copyright legislation in Canada, along with its schedules, annexes and rules, and including various amendments made to it.

A copy of the Canadian *Copyright Act*, consolidated with amendments made to it since its enactment in 1924, is included in Appendix I. The *Act* and regulations may also be found on the Web at: **canada.justice.-gc.ca/STABLE/EN/Laws/Chap/C/C-42.html**.

Before the 1924 *Act* came into force, the governing legislation consisted of various pre-Confederation provincial legislation, post-Confederation federal statutes, British statutes and the Berne Convention (an international convention on the protection of copyright works).

Since 1924, there have been a number of minor amendments made to the *Copyright Act* and, in 1988, the *Act* was substantially modified. The bill introduced in the House of Commons that resulted in the 1988 amendments was numbered "Bill C-60" and is also known as "Phase I" of the amendments in the current copyright revision process. Nine issues were dealt with in the 1988 modifications:

- the protection of choreographic works
- the protection of computer programs
- the right to exhibit an artistic work at a public exhibition
- the clarification between industrial design and copyright protection
- the abolition of the compulsory licence for the making of sound recordings
- the collective administration of copyright
- the role of the Copyright Board
- the enhancement of rights to protect the reputation of a creator
- fines for the violation of copyright

Since 1988, the 1924 *Act* has been amended a number of times. It was amended in order to comply with the Canada-United States Free Trade Agreement and the North American Free Trade Agreement (NAFTA). The definition of "musical works" was amended by Bill C-88 and certain administrative provisions were amended by the *Intellectual Property Improvement Act*. As of January 1, 1996, amendments to the *Copyright Act* became effective to comply with aspects of Canada's obligations for the Trade—Related Intellectual Property Rights (TRIPs) of the General Agreement on Tariffs and Trade (GATT).

A further major reform to the Canadian *Copyright Act* took place on April 25, 1997 with the Royal Assent of Bill C-32, also known as "Phase II" of the copyright revision process. These revisions include the following:

- new rights for performers and producers, including royalty payments when their sound recordings are broadcast or performed in public

- a levy on blank audio recording media, such as audio tapes and cassettes, to be collected and paid to performers, producers and authors for private copying of their works (such copying was made legal)
- exceptions for nonprofit educational institutions, libraries, archives and museums to use copyright protected materials in specific ways without payment or authorization
- an exception to allow broadcasters to make a temporary copy of an event or performance to be broadcast at a later time
- enhanced protection for exclusive distributors of books in Canada
- guaranteed minimum awards for copyright infringement
- an extension of rental rights to composers, lyricists and performers of musical works
- a change in the perpetual copyright protection in unpublished works to a term of life of the author plus fifty years
- a change in the term of copyright in photographs to life of the author plus fifty years

As is evident, the Canadian *Copyright Act* remains a statute originally enacted in 1924, subject to major and minor amendments. The basic structure and many of the provisions in the statute remain the same as in 1924, which is remarkable considering the law was enacted in an era before computers, photocopiers, VCRs and the Internet. Many would agree that the *Act* has done very well to deal with modern technology. For instance, prior to the amendments made in 1988, the 1924 statute, which obviously did not deal with computers, was interpreted to protect computer software (the 1988 amendments legislated this decision by the courts). A further test of the elasticity of the copyright law is ongoing with its application to the Internet and other digital media. Despite the *Act*'s flexibility, there are outstanding issues that require review and which will be addressed in future amendments to the *Copyright Act*, including revisions relating to the Internet and other digital media.

This book deals with the Canadian copyright law as it exists today. It does not consistently point out whether provisions were originally found in the 1924 *Act*, or have since been added, except for information purposes or when the date of a provision or an amendment has relevance on its comprehension and its practical effect. Also, the book does not examine possible future amendments in detail but may make references to Canadian government and international policy concerning such changes to the law.

GOVERNMENT RESPONSIBILITY FOR COPYRIGHT IN CANADA

There are two departments within the federal government that are primarily responsible for copyright matters in Canada. Industry Canada (**www.ic.gc.ca**) is responsible for the administration of the *Copyright Act*; for example, the registration of copyright works. To be specific, the federal agency responsible for registering copyrights in Canada is the Copyright Office, directed by the Registrar of Copyrights. The Copyright Office is part of the larger agency of the Canadian Intellectual Property Office (CIPO) (**www.cipo.gc.ca**) that comes under the jurisdiction of Industry Canada.

Industry Canada and Canadian Heritage (**www.pch.gc.ca**) are jointly responsible for developing policy for the revision of the *Act*.

In addition, there is an independent tribunal known as the Copyright Board (**www.cb-cda.gc.ca**) that, among other things, sets royalties in certain circumstances for the use of copyright works. The role of the Copyright Board is discussed, where appropriate, throughout this book.

The government does not have a role *vis-à-vis* enforcing the rights set in the *Copyright Act*. The *Act* sets out private rights for citizens to enjoy. As such, it is not the responsibility of the government to monitor the use of copyright materials and to ensure that such uses are within the parameters of the law. Although individuals must generally enforce their own rights, there are certain cases where "criminal remedies" as set out in the *Act* are appropriate to deal with a violation of copyright and the Crown may institute an action. Criminal remedies are further discussed in Chapter 13: What are the Remedies for the Violation of Copyright?

THE CONCEPT OF COPYRIGHT LAW

There are two very important concepts in Canadian copyright law that must be appreciated for a full understanding of the law, and consequently, much of the information provided in this book. These concepts relate to property rights in a creation, and to copyright protection and how it relates to ideas.

Property Rights in a Creation

When you have a creation, you have two property rights in this creation. First, you have the right in the physical property, in the creation itself. Second, you have the right in the intangible property, attracting certain rights that govern the use of the creation. Copyright protects this intangible right. Thus, if you own a book, you may read it, display it on your coffee table and even lend it to a friend. However, you may not do anything that only the copyright owner has the exclusive right to do. For example, by virtue of owning the physical book, you may not reproduce or translate it.

Copyright Protection and Ideas

It cannot be over-emphasized that ideas are not protected by copyright law. What the law protects is the expression of these ideas. This is based on the notion that ideas are part of the public domain and that no one can have a monopoly in them. This basic copyright principle applies no matter how novel or great an idea.

What this concept implies is that anyone can follow an idea set out in a book or an instructional video, or create a work based on the same idea, without violating copyright. It also means that there can be copyright in two works expressing the same idea since it is the original expression of the idea that is protected by copyright. For example, two people may independently make sketches of the same tree, each sketch being protected by copyright and neither of them violating the copyright in the other one.

Unlike the Canadian *Copyright Act*, the American *Copyright Act* is very explicit in stating items to which copyright protection does not extend. Section 102 of the American *Copyright Act* states the following: "In no case does copyright protection for an original work of authorship extend to any idea, procedure, process, system, method of operation, concept, principle, or discovery, regardless of the form in which it is described, explained, illustrated, or embodied in such work." Although this definition has no binding impact on Canadian law, it illustrates the notion concerning the lack of copyright protection in ideas and the like.

SUMMARY

Current Canadian copyright legislation is found in a federal statute called the *Copyright Act*, which came into force in 1924 and has been subject to numerous amendments. Revision of the *Act* is an ongoing process.

In general, individuals are responsible for enforcing their rights under the *Copyright Act*, while the government is responsible for the administration and revision of the *Act*.

Canadian copyright law protects the intangible aspect of a creation. It does not protect an idea, but protects the expression of an idea.

Chapter 3
IS YOUR CREATION ELIGIBLE FOR COPYRIGHT PROTECTION?

Take away from English authors their copyrights, and you would very soon take away from England her authors.

Anthony Trollope, *Autobiography*, 1883

CRITERIA FOR COPYRIGHT PROTECTION

The first part of this chapter discusses the three criteria for the protection of traditional copyright materials known as "works;" the second part focusses on the protection of non-traditional material like performers' performances, sound recordings and broadcasts.

Copyright protection exists as soon as a creation is created or comes into existence. However, in order for a creation to be eligible for this protection, the creation must be a "work" within the meaning of the *Copyright Act*.

A "work" within the meaning of copyright law will be protected by copyright upon its creation provided three criteria are met. These criteria and basic requirements for copyright protection relate to:

- originality
- fixation
- nationality of creator and place of publication

This chapter will explain these three criteria. In doing so, the chapter will also answer, in a broad sense, the question of who can obtain copyright protection in Canada. This latter question is revisited from a number of points of view in later chapters, for instance, when discussing who can register a work, and who can sue for violation of copyright.

Specific types of works protected by copyright are discussed in Chapter 6: What Is Protected By Copyright?

ORIGINALITY

In order for a work to be protected by copyright, it must be original in the copyright sense of the word. The *Copyright Act* emphasizes this prerequisite for protection by stating that "copyright shall subsist in Canada for the term hereinafter mentioned, in every original literary, dramatic, musical and artistic work." The definition section defines "every original literary, dramatic, musical and artistic work" to include "every original production in the literary, scientific or artistic domain, whatever may be the mode or form of its expression." Thus, if a work is otherwise qualified to be protected by copyright, and it is original, then it will be protected by copyright.

What Does Originality Mean?

Although the term "original" is used in the *Copyright Act*, this term is not defined in the *Act*. In order to fully understand the meaning of originality, one must first examine the criterion of "originality." To do so, one must return to the basic copyright principle that protection extends to the expression of an idea and not to the idea itself. Thus, original in the copyright sense must also relate to the expression of an idea and the effort exerted to express that idea, and not to the originality of the idea, the thought itself, or the novelty of the words used.

Second, one must examine the standard of originality in the copyright law. The first thought that comes to most people's minds is that the criterion of originality means that a creation must be completely novel (as in patent law) and also possess some aesthetic, artistic or literary quality. This is not true. In fact, the standard of originality is very low, at least in relation to our expectations.

The term "original" in the copyright sense has been described to apply where the work has not been copied from another work. One "originality test" which has been adopted on numerous occasions by Canadian courts is the following:[1]

... the Act does not require that the expression must be in an original or novel form, but that the work must not be copied from another work—that it should originate from the author.

Whether a creation is original in the copyright sense is always a factual question and one of degree that ultimately a court must decide. The court will apply the circumstances and facts of a particular case to the law as it is set out in previous court decisions. For example, it will apply the facts to the originality test as set out above.

In addition to the originality test set out above, courts have considered a number of other factors in determining the originality of a work. The factors below have been extracted from these court cases and can act as guidelines to help you determine whether a court might consider your work original in the copyright sense of the word.

Court cases have interpreted the criterion of originality to possess the following qualities:

- the work must originate with the author
- the work must not be a copy of another work
- the work must be the fruit of an independent, creative effort rather than a mechanical or automatic arrangement
- the author must use skill, experience, labour, taste, discretion, selection, judgement, personal effort, knowledge, ability, reflection and imagination

With these guidelines in mind, the type of materials which may be protected by copyright include print and electronic books, songs, paintings, tables, compilations, (for example, in a Web site), directories, translations, adaptations and dictionaries, as well as a new arrangement of a work in which copyright protection has expired.

Original thought or great literary skill is not mandatory for a work to be protected by copyright. But independent creation and effort are necessary. Thus, originality refers to the expression and independence of effort.

The low threshold of originality means that anyone can create a similar or identical work provided he or she does so independently. As a result, in theory, two identical works may exist, each one being separately protected by copyright, as long as each of them was created independently of the other one. For example, two books on patent law written at the same time, published at the same time and intended for the same audience may each be original in the copyright sense of the word. Each would enjoy separate copyright protection, provided each book's author wrote it independently of, and without access to, the other. This example also points out that a work may be original where common knowledge has been drawn upon. Further, a work may be original even if an author received suggestions for parts of it.

Databases and Other Compilations

Similar to other copyright protected works, in order for databases and other compilations to be protected by copyright, they must meet one of the general criterions for copyright protection—sufficient originality. This means that there must be a sufficient degree of skill, judgement and labour involved in the arranging and selecting of the content in the database or other compilation. Based on this reasoning, a Canadian court recently decided that the telephone listings contained in the "Yellow Pages" was not a protectable database. It is possible that other cases involving the protection of compilations may rely on this decision and examine the protection of other compilations based on factors such as whether that particular compilation is sufficiently original depending on the degree of skill, judgement and labour involved in arranging and selecting the content in that compilation. This is a question of fact and must be determined based on the specific circumstances in any particular case. The protection of databases is further discussed in Chapter 6: What is Protected by Copyright?

FIXATION

You now know that in order for a work to be protected by copyright, it must be original; that is, not copied from another work. In order for an original work to be protected by copyright, it must also meet the criterion of "fixation."

Fixation is not defined in the *Copyright Act*. In fact, the concept of fixation is not something explicitly discussed in the *Act* as a general criterion for copyright protection (except in the case of dramatic works as discussed below). It is a criterion that has, for the most part, developed through court cases.

The term "fixation" is used in copyright parlance around the world. In fact, Article 2 of the Berne Convention uses this very expression, leaving it open to member countries to deal with the issue of whether works should be protected only if "they have been fixed in some material form."

The court cases in which the concept of fixation has arisen have determined that copyright subsists only in works that are "expressed . . . in some material form, capable of identification and having a more or less permanent endurance."[2] This criterion reinforces the principle that copyright protects the "form" in which an idea is expressed and not the ideas contained within that form.

Although fixation is not as a rule explicitly mentioned in the *Act*, the concept of fixation is seen through various provisions in the copyright statute that denote this concept. For instance, all works falling under the definitions of artistic and literary works do possess a material existence.

Fixation may have important functions outside the copyright law. For example, fixation may provide proof of the existence of a work and perhaps evidence with respect to the author of that work. It may provide a means of preserving and maintaining a historical record, and it may provide some valuable insight into the author of the work and the process of the creation of it.

Dramatic Works

As mentioned above, fixation with respect to dramatic works is specifically mentioned in the *Copyright Act*. When reading the chapter on creations protected by copyright, you will discover that dramatic works is one subject-matter of copyright protected materials. The *Copyright Act* defines a dramatic work to include "any piece for recitation, choreographic work or mime, the scenic arrangement or acting form of which is fixed in writing or otherwise. . . ." It is interesting to note that fixation with respect to dramatic works was included in the *Act* prior to the court case making the concept of fixation a necessary criterion for the copyright protection of all works.

As set out in the definition of dramatic works, fixation of dramatic works is not limited to writing. According to the provision in the *Act*, and the inclusion of the word "otherwise," there are other possible methods of fixation. So, it was most likely known even when the *Act* was written in 1921 that there is no one and only precise method of transcribing dramatic works. The wording of the *Act* implies that a sketch of a dramatic work may qualify as being fixed, or perhaps a visual reproduction of the dramatic work by a video, or a combination of these and/or other methods. Also, the wording of the legislation indicates that fixation is required only of the "scenic arrangement or acting form" and therefore not of every specific detail. What need be captured in any fixation of a dramatic work are the movements and general characteristics of the dramatic work in question.

Musical Works

The meaning of musical works is discussed in Chapter 6: What is Protected by Copyright?, however, it is important to understand that in this section, musical work refers to a song and not to a recording of a song.

Until recent amendments made to the law in 1993, there was some debate as to what would be considered fixation of a musical work. The discussion centred on the question of whether the musical work must be notated in some manner to constitute a fixation or whether a recording of that musical work would by itself be sufficient to meet the requirement of fixation. The debate was due to the definition then in the *Copyright Act* that defined a musical work to mean "any combination of melody and harmony, or either of them, printed, reduced to writing or otherwise graphically produced or reproduced." Musical notation obviously fit within this definition. However, since the definition defined being fixed in terms of being printed, reduced to writing or otherwise graphically produced or reproduced, it was more than arguable that a recording of the musical work would not constitute fixation of it.

The current copyright law defines a "musical work" to mean "any work of music or musical composition, with or without words, and includes any compilation thereof." Thus, the requirement to have the melody and/or harmony printed, reduced to writing or otherwise graphically produced or reproduced no longer exists. It is now clear that any sort of fixation of a musical work such as musical notation, audio or video recording, or other means by which the music is expressed in material form capable of identification and having a more or less permanent endurance, is sufficient to meet the criterion of fixation.

Examples of "Fixed" Works

A simple illustration of a fixed work is a book manuscript, in handwriting, on paper. This work would probably be considered fixed if it was in draft form—even point form—and probably even if the handwriting is illegible. The final form of the manuscript as well as its published editions would probably all be considered fixed as well. A typed version of the manuscript, or one on a computer hard drive or diskette, or printed from a word processor, would, in all likelihood, also be considered fixed for purposes of the *Copyright Act*.

The manuscript example set out above is fairly straightforward. There are a number of other situations that are not as obvious. In order to examine other situations of fixed works, one must return to the definition of fixation as developed by case law, which is that a work "must be expressed to some extent at least in some material form, capable of identification and having a more or less permanent endurance." From this definition, one can see that fixation is not necessarily restricted to something put down in writing. For example, a computer program embedded in a CD-ROM may qualify as fixation of a copyright work.[3] Further, fixation of a choreographic work may be through sketches, by special dance notation (Laba notation or Benesh notation) or computer notation, or by a simple recording of the work on video or film, even though these records are "interpretations" of the choreography and not the "work" itself. Another example is that a work may be fixed simultaneously with its communication to the public, for instance in the case of a broadcasted work. In general, the medium of a work will not restrict its ability to be considered fixed for purposes of the copyright law.

Examples Where There Is No Fixation

Now that we have examined examples of fixed works, let us look at examples where a work may not be considered fixed for copyright purposes. One such example may be lectures, speeches, addresses and sermons that have not been written down or recorded in some manner prior to their presentation (however, there is some thought that this may be an exception to the fixation requirement; this is discussed in Chapter 6). The same may be true of an improvised comedy skit, a jam session or an improvised tune. An image or text on a computer screen (that has not been saved) may not be considered fixed. A work transmitted by broadcast or cable without being recorded prior to, or simultaneously with, its transmission may not be considered fixed.

In some cases, protection may be obtained through a confidential relationship with the audience of the improvised work or lecture in a seminar, through audience members signing a waiver agreeing not to reproduce the work.

NATIONALITY AND PLACE OF PUBLICATION

In order for a work to be protected by copyright, it must meet the criteria of originality and fixation. It must also meet certain conditions concerning the nationality of the author and the place of first publication of the work. In summary, virtually everyone living in Canada enjoys automatic copyright protection. The details are set out below.

In order to be eligible for copyright protection, the author of any published or unpublished work, including a cinematograph (i.e., audio-visual work), must, at the date of the making of the work, be a citizen or resident (including a landed immigrant or refugee claimant) of Canada or another treaty country. A treaty country includes any Berne Convention (Berne) country, any country adhering to any level of the Universal Copyright Convention (UCC), and any country member of the World Trade Organization (WTO).[4] To further understand the eligibility requirements and how the international system of copyright works, see Chapter 5: How Does International Copyright Protection Work?

Recently, the *Act* eliminated references to "British subject" and "Her Majesty's Realms and Territories," that is, British subjects and residents within Her Majesty's Realms and Territories, were eligible authors. However, these previously eligible authors are protected for any copyright or moral rights that subsisted in Canada before September 1, 1997.

In addition, the Canadian government can extend copyright protection to other countries where that country provides similar protection to Canadians even where the remedies for enforcing rights or restrictions on the importation of works differs from Canadian law.

There are two ways in which a cinematograph may be eligible for copyright protection. One, if the maker of the cinematograph is, at the date of the making of it, a corporation with its headquarters in a treaty country. Second, if the maker is a natural person, and is, at the time of making the cinematograph, a citizen or resident of a treaty country. For a cinematograph, its maker is the individual or company who makes the necessary arrangements to make the cinematograph. Note that the concept of "maker" is relatively new to the Canadian *Copyright Act* and it is possible that courts of law may interpret it in an unexpected manner, however the intent of the maker qualifying (as opposed to the author) was to have an additional way for a cinematograph to be eligible for copyright protection without affecting the status of who is the author of a cinematograph.

You are also entitled to automatic copyright protection if your work was first published in a treaty country (even if you were not a citizen or subject of Canada). The first publication must be in a quantity as to satisfy the reasonable demands of the public, which depends on the nature of the work, and this first publication must occur within a treaty country. If a work is initially not published in an eligible country but a second publication in an eligible country occurs within thirty days (or a longer period as fixed by order-in-council) that would be sufficient.

Although corporations are not specifically mentioned as being protected "persons," they are recognized as being protected by copyright in certain circumstances, and it is most likely that corporations incorporated in any of the eligible countries would be protected in Canada.

Protection of these persons is according to the Canadian *Copyright Act* when copyright protection is claimed in Canada.

SOUND RECORDINGS, PERFORMANCES AND BROADCASTS

Sound recordings may be protected in three manners. First, a sound recording may be protected if its maker is a citizen or permanent resident of Canada or a Rome Convention (Rome), Berne, or WTO country at the time the record was first fixed. Second, a sound recording may be protected if its maker is a corporation, and the corporation's headquarters are in Canada, a Rome, Berne or WTO country when the record was first fixed. If neither of these conditions is met, the sound recording may be protected if it was first published in a Rome, Berne or WTO country in a quantity sufficient to meet reasonable public demand.

Performers are eligible for protection of their performances for different rights depending on how they are eligible for protection in Canada. As of January 1, 1996, a performer has rights in his or her live performances in Canada or another WTO country. Note that the performance itself need not take place after January 1, 1996. However, the retroactive protection against pre-1996 "bootleg" audio recordings, which goes back fifty years, is not absolute and is subject to certain limitations. As of September, 1997, performances that occur in Canada or another Rome country, or that are simultaneously broadcast from Canada or from another Rome country by a broadcaster headquartered there, are protected. Protected performances fixed on sound recordings are those where the maker of the record is headquartered in Canada or another Rome country or is a citizen or a permanent resident of Canada or another Rome country, or first publication takes place there. To be entitled to the blank audio recording media levy, the performer must be a citizen or a resident of Canada.

Broadcasters headquartered in Canada or a Rome or WTO country have a copyright in signals broadcast from that country.

The Minister of Industry may expand the category of protected performances, sound recordings and broadcasts to other NAFTA countries, or to other countries, on a reciprocal basis.

SUMMARY

In order for a "work" to be protected in Canada by Canadian copyright law, it must be original in the sense that it was not copied from another work, it must be fixed in some material form with a more or less permanent endurance, and the copyright holder must be a citizen or resident of Canada or another treaty country, and/or any published work must be first published in a treaty country. Other subject-matter like performers' performances, sound recordings and broadcasts must meet their own specific requirements in order to be eligible for protection.

Chapter 4

ARE FORMALITIES REQUIRED TO OBTAIN COPYRIGHT PROTECTION?

Hands up all of you who have sung the song Happy Birthday to You ... The music publishing division of Warner Bros. bought the rights to that particular song for a reported sum of $25 million and have been charging a five-figure [$12,500] licensing fee for its use in films. Though some producers have balked— Richard Donner, upon hearing of the fee, dropped the song from the birthday scene in the movie Lethal Weapon II .... Not bad for a tune written in 1893 by two kindergarten teachers in Kentucky.

Marquee, Vol. 15, No. 1, February 1990

AUTOMATIC PROTECTION

Under the Canadian *Copyright Act*, there are no formalities requisite to obtaining copyright protection. Copyright protection is automatic. It exists upon the creation of a work or sound recording, or when a performance or broadcast signal occurs. There is no requirement, for example, to register a work or other subject-matter, mark it with the copyright symbol or deposit it with a deposit registry for copyright purposes. Also, adding phrases like "All Rights Reserved" does not entitle you to any further protection than you would have had without the inclusion of such a phrase. You have copyright protection in your work or sound recording upon the creation of it, or when a performance or broadcast signal occurs, without doing any of these things, once the criteria for protection (discussed in Chapter 3) have been met.

Although copyright protection in Canada is not dependent upon any formalities, registering, marking, and depositing a work or other subject-matter may help you enforce your rights. Because such "formalities" are optional under Canadian law, you must decide whether you want to register, mark or deposit your creation, and if so, the best method to use. Options include the Canadian government voluntary registration system, the American government registration and deposit scheme—which is open to Canadians—and non-governmental organizations where you can register and deposit a work or other subject-matter. This chapter will discuss advantages and procedures of voluntarily marking, registering and depositing materials protected by copyright.

MARKING YOUR CREATIONS

The Copyright Symbol

The copyright symbol, ©, used to mark materials protected by copyright, is a universal symbol. In fact, it appears in one of the international copyright conventions, the Universal Copyright Convention. Although using this symbol, or otherwise marking your creations as protected by copyright, is not mandatory under Canadian copyright law, there are certain advantages of marking a work. First, it is a reminder to the world at large that copyright exists in the work. As such, it provides evidence in a court action that the alleged violator should have known that copyright existed in the work. Second, it may help people who want to use the work to locate the copyright owner and obtain permission to use it. Third, marking is beneficial if a court case is pursued in the United States since the American *Copyright Act* precludes an alleged violator from submitting that he or she did not know that copyright existed in a work where a proper copyright notice has been placed on the work.

There are three elements to a copyright notice. First, the "c in a circle"—©—or the abbreviation "Copr." or the word "Copyright" should be presented. Second, the name of the copyright owner (not necessarily the author) should be included in the notice. Third, the year of first publication should be set out. These elements need not necessarily appear in this sequence.

One form of marking a work is the following:
    © Name of Copyright Owner Year of First Publication
or   © 2000 Lesley Ellen Harris

This notice should be clearly placed in a manner and location best suited to alert the user of the work in question to the fact that copyright subsists in the work. This can vary depending on the type of work involved. For a Web site, a suitable location for the copyright notice may be on the home page, or on a page that appears by clicking through to a specified copyright or legal notices page, or both. For instance, you may include a simple copyright notice on your home page and perhaps on other pages of your Web site, with a click through to a more detailed copyright and legal notices page.[1]

As a general rule, place the notice in a manner and location that gives reasonable notice of the claim of copyright, so that it appears in a conspicuous position on a work that will not be missed by a casual observer.

The year to include in a copyright notice should be the year of first publication, or the year in which substantial revisions to a work occurred. For constantly evolving Web sites, the year in the notice would be updated whenever more than trivial revisions or additions are made to the site. While earlier years can remain as part of the notice, the date of the latest substantial revisions must be included. If only one year is to appear in the notice, it should be the oldest year—the year associated with the oldest elements in the work. It is best to err on the side of omitting newer years as opposed to omitting older years. Alternatively, you could include a range of years (e.g., 1996-1999, or 1995-2000), starting from the date of the oldest elements in the work and ending with the date of the newest elements in the work.

The Sound Recording symbol

Often you will see the symbol ℗ on a sound recording. This is a symbol found in the American copyright legislation. The ℗ is used like the ©, but only with respect to sound recordings. The advantages of marking a work with ℗ are similar to those for marking a work with ©. The form of the notice for a sound recording is the following:

    ℗ Name of Copyright Owner   Year of First Publication

The notice should be placed on the label attached to the recording, or on the cover or container accompanying the recording, or both.

REGISTRATION WITH THE CANADIAN GOVERNMENT

Is It Necessary?

The Canadian government provides a registration system for works and other subject-matter protected by copyright. The Copyright Office is part of the Canadian Intellectual Property Office (CIPO), which falls under the jurisdiction of the federal government department, Industry Canada. Since copyright is automatic in Canada, registration with the Copyright Office does not confer copyright protection nor does it guarantee the existence of it. In other words, a work or other subject-matter need not be registered to be protected.

There are certain advantages to voluntarily registering a copyright work or other subject-matter with the Canadian government. The *Copyright Act* sets out some of these advantages. According to the *Act*, a certificate of registration creates the following two presumptions:

- that copyright subsists in a work or other subject-matter
- that the person registered, i.e., the name appearing on the certificate of registration, is the owner of the copyright in that work or other subject-matter

These presumptions are helpful in a court action since a copyright owner of a registered work or other subject-matter need not prove that copyright subsists, and that the person registered is the owner. The copyright owner need only provide evidence to these points if the alleged violator argues otherwise; that is, that copyright does not subsist in the work or other subject-matter, and that the person registered is not the owner of the copyright.

Further, registration may be advantageous in a court action since it creates a presumption that the alleged violator knew of the existence of copyright in the work in question. Thus, it is up to the alleged violator to show that he or she was unaware that the work was subject to copyright protection. It would be difficult for someone to defend the existence of copyright and to sustain the argument that he or she was unaware that a work was subject to copyright protection if the work was registered with the Canadian Copyright Office. This is because the alleged violator could have checked the Registers of Copyrights for copyright information on the work, for example, the owner of copyright in the work. However, since mere registration does not give copyright protection, an alleged violator could argue, notwithstanding registration, that a work lacked copyright protection.

Registration may, in some circumstances, entitle a copyright owner to certain remedies other than merely stopping the violator from continuing the illegal acts. Where a work is not registered with the Canadian Copyright Office, a copyright owner may only get a court order to prevent further violations of copyright. However, where the work or other subject-matter is registered, the copyright owner may be entitled to stop further violations as well as be eligible for a range of other remedies including monetary compensation. Remedies are further discussed in Chapter 13: What are the Remedies for the Violation of Copyright?

In addition to registering a copyright work, the Canadian registration system allows for the registration of any "grant of interest" or change in ownership in copyright, or in a part of the copyright. If you become a subsequent owner of copyright, you should consider registering this interest. Doing so will give you priority over a similar grant of interest if that other interest has not been registered. In other words, if A and B are both granted an interest in a copyright work and only B registers this interest, B may have priority over A with respect to his or her rights in the work.

Despite the advantages of registering copyright with the Canadian government, many copyright owners choose not to register, or at least not immediately upon the commencement of copyright protection. This is for two reasons. First, registration can be made at any time prior to the commencement of a lawsuit. Note, however, that lack of registration at the time of a violation of copyright may limit a copyright owner's recourse to a court order to stop the violating act from continuing, as opposed to other recourse such as being monetarily compensated. Also, since registering helps establish the date of creation of that work, it may be advantageous to register it immediately upon creation. An earlier date of creation may be necessary if others claim that they created the work before you and that your work or sound recording is a copy of their work or sound recording.

The second reason that some copyright owners do not register their works with the Canadian Copyright Office is that they use alternative registration/deposit methods to establish proof of ownership of copyright and date of creation.

There are no "disadvantages" of registering with the Canadian government, except perhaps the time and fee involved. There are, however, certain problems or concerns with the Canadian government registration system of which you should be aware. One of the main concerns is that registering does not provide authenticity with respect to that registration. An applicant is asked to provide limited information on the registration form and it is not validated by the Copyright Office or supported by a deposit of the protected material. Since the Copyright Office does not examine applications, there may be more than one work registered under the same title. Also, there is no publication that lists all registered copyrights in Canada and there is no publication that notifies the public on an ongoing basis of new works or other subject-matter registered at the Copyright Office. However, the Copyright Office does keep records of all copyrights in its registers.

NATIONAL LIBRARY DEPOSIT

There is often some confusion with the deposit of copyright material with the Copyright Office and the deposit requirement with respect to the National Library. The *National Library Act* requires Canadian publishers to send them two copies of all books, pamphlets, serial publications, microforms, spoken word sound recordings, video recordings, electronic publications in physical formats such as CD-ROM, DVD, computer disks, and one copy of published musical sound recordings and multimedia kits. This legal deposit is not related to copyright. Further information on the National Library legal deposit may be obtained by contacting:

Canadiana Acquisitions and Legal Deposit Office
National Library of Canada
395 Wellington Street
Ottawa, Ontario K1A 0N4

T: 819.997.9565
F: 819.953.8508
E: **legal.deposit@nlc-bnc.ca**
(WEB) **www.nlc-bnc.ca**

INTERNATIONAL STANDARD BOOK NUMBER (ISBN)

Another confusion with copyright is the universal book numbering system known as the ISBN (international standard book number). The

ISBN is not related to copyright. The ISBN is a number used for publishing purposes to provide a unique identification number for all books published in Canada and abroad from one specific publisher. Books, pamphlets, educational kits, microforms, CD-ROMs, and Braille publications have an ISBN. The Canadian ISBN Agency is part of the National Library of Canada and further information about the ISBN can be obtained from:

> Canadian ISBN Agency
> National Library of Canada
> 395 Wellington Street
> Ottawa, Ontario K1A 0N4
>
> T: 819.994.6872
> F: 819.997.7517
> E: **isbn@nlc-bnc.ca**
> **www.nlc-bnc.ca**

You may also want to contact the National Library of Canada regarding the international standard serial number (ISSN), a unique code for identifying serial publications, such as periodicals, newspapers, annuals, journals and monographic series, and the international standard music number (ISMN), a unique code for the identification of printed music publications.

How to Register Copyright with the Canadian Government

REGISTRATION FEES
The current fees for registering a copyright are:

$65.00 CDN	For registering a work or other subject-matter, including receiving a certificate of registration.
$65.00 CDN	For registering an assignment, licence, etc., including receiving a certificate of registration.
$130.00 CDN	For accelerated action on the above two services.

Registration is valid for the full term of copyright protection and no additional registration fees are required during this term.

WHO CAN REGISTER?

Any author, publisher, owner or "other person interested in the copyright" can register copyright material in the name of the owner. A creator or copyright owner can register by him- or herself, or have a publisher, lawyer or other representative do so on his or her behalf. If registration is pursued after an author's death, it can be registered by the author's heirs or legal representatives.

IN WHOSE NAME?

Registration establishes the owner and not necessarily the author of copyright in a work. The person whose name is registered is presumed, in the absence of any contrary evidence, to be the owner of the copyright in the work or other subject-matter. The name of both the copyright owner and the author of the copyright material must be included on the registration application. The name of the author will help establish the duration of copyright protection. The name of the author is also important with respect to moral rights that, as you will soon see, attach to an author of a work protected by copyright notwithstanding that the author is not the owner of copyright in that work.

If the author uses a pseudonym it may be set out in the application, but the full legal name of the author must also be indicated. Otherwise, it will be impossible to determine the term of copyright. The same is true in an employer/employee situation. The employer may register in his or her name as owner of the copyright, but the employee's name must be indicated as the author.

Even though you must include your legal name on a copyright application, if you use a pseudonym, you may ask the Copyright Office to keep the legal name information on file only and not in the Register, which is open for public inspection. Note, however that certain "interested" parties (such as an exclusive licensee though not a journalist) may have access to your application upon request.

PROCEDURE

In order to register a copyright with the Canadian government, you must file the information required under the Canadian *Copyright Act* or complete the suggested application for registration, and pay the registration fee. A sample registration application is included in Appendix II, available from CIPO, and on its Web site. Note that there are different forms for registering a "work" such as a book or computer software, and for registering "other subject-matter" such as a performer's performance, sound recording or communication signal.

Online registration is possible, secure and works extremely well. When you file electronically with the Copyright Office, the official filing date of your application is the date the electronic application is received in the Office of the Registrar of Copyrights.

To obtain copyright forms, information circulars or further information, contact:

> Canadian Intellectual Property Office
> Client Service Centre
> Copyright Office
> Place du Portage Phase I
> 50 Victoria Street
> Room C-229, 2nd Floor
> Hull, Quebec K1A 0C9
>
> Business hours: 8:00 to 16:45
>
> T: 819.997.1936
> F: 819.997.6357
> E: **cipo.contact@ic.gc.ca**
> *cipo.gc.ca* (The site contains excellent information to guide you through the registration process, as well as an online registration option.)

It is not possible to register with a regional office of Industry Canada. You can, however, obtain information booklets on copyright and registration forms from any Industry Canada regional office. You can also deposit completed registration forms at regional offices. The forms will then be forwarded to the CIPO in Hull.

WHAT INFORMATION IS REQUIRED ON THE REGISTRATION APPLICATION?

Basically, the registration application is a declaration that the applicant is the copyright owner, the author or an agent for the applicant of the registered work or other subject-matter, and that it has or has not been published (if published, date and place when it was first published by the issue of copies to the public must also be specified), and that registration is requested.

The form is straightforward and requires the following information:

- title of work is mandatory for a literary, artistic, musical or dramatic work, but is optional for other subject-matter (no description is necessary nor desired, but if one is added, it should not exceed 118 characters. Since the information provided on the registration application is so limited, it may be difficult to connect a certain work with a copyright registration if that work is untitled.)
- type or category of work or other subject-matter
- name of author
- name and address of copyright owner
- applicant information
- date
- declaration from the author, owner, assignee or licensee
- agent for applicant (if applicable)

LARGER BODIES OF WORKS

Larger bodies of works such as encyclopedias, newspapers, reviews, magazines or other periodical works, or work published in a series of books or parts, may be registered as one work. Also, a book of poems, or a book of photographs of sculptures, may be registered under one title. When doing so, insert the words "a book of . . ." within brackets, following the nature of the work.

Multimedia

Multimedia including a Web site is registrable as a single work since it is considered a "compilation." The registration application for the multimedia work should indicate the predominant category (i.e., literary, dramatic, artistic, musical) that describes the work.

Do not deposit copies

Copies of the work or other subject-matter should not be sent to the Copyright Office. The Copyright Office does not have any depository system or facilities to store these items. Any copy of a work sent to the Copyright Office will be sent back to the applicant, without any examination of the work or verification of its relation to the application with which it was sent.

THE ROLE OF THE COPYRIGHT OFFICE AND THE REGISTRAR OF COPYRIGHTS

The Copyright Office does a cursory examination of the application. It will not undertake an extensive examination of the application. The Registrar of Copyrights will not examine the veracity of the applicant's declaration and takes no responsibility for the veracity of the entries made in the Registers. The responsibility of the Copyright Office is to make sure the information required under the Canadian legislation is provided before registration.

The Copyright Office keeps records, called the Registers of Copyrights, in which "names or titles of works and other subject-matter and the names and addresses of authors, owners and of any agents for the applicant, and such other particulars as may be prescribed" are entered. Once the entry is made in the Registers, the Registrar of Copyrights or another Copyright Office employee will sign a certificate containing a registration number and affix the seal of the Copyright Office. This certificate will be issued to the registrant. This certificate provides evidence that the person registered is the copyright owner and can be used in court to establish ownership as well as the date of creation of the work. A sample registration certificate is included in Appendix II.

The Registers are kept at the Copyright Office and are open to inspection by the public. Any person may take copies of information entered in the Register, or make extracts from, any Register.

All registration applications must be done in writing or via the Internet. Correspondence with the Copyright Office may only be by an applicant or his or her agent.

The Copyright Office will not provide any advice on matters concerning the interpretation of the *Act* or any other question of law.

If the Copyright Office makes an error while preparing a registration document, it may fix this error without obtaining further authority. A new certificate of registration is issued bearing the same registration number, and the one with an error has to be destroyed.

The Copyright Office's power to amend a registration document is limited. It has no authority to alter a registration after a registration certificate has been issued. For example, it cannot make a correction to the title or type of work unless ordered to do so by a court. The Registrar of Copyrights or any "interested person" may apply to the Federal Court for such an order. The procedure of obtaining a court order is outlined in the Federal Court Rules.

UNPUBLISHED WORKS

If an unpublished work is registered, it need not be re-registered once it is published since proof of ownership and creation has been established by the first registration.

DO YOU NEED TO REGISTER DIFFERENT DRAFTS OR VERSIONS OF THE SAME WORK?

You do not need to register different drafts or versions of the same material. Generally, you should register the final draft or version—the one that you will be circulating. Once you register copyright material and you prepare a subsequent draft or version of it, consider registering the new version if you feel that it is substantially different from the earlier registered version.

HOW LONG DOES REGISTRATION TAKE?

According to the Copyright Office, the registration process usually takes less than four weeks. Furthermore, the Canadian Copyright Office commits to deliver service on request for accelerated action within three days.

Registration takes effect when the application is accepted by the Copyright Office, whether at the time of filing or after any required amendments are made by the applicant. The sort of amendments discussed here refer to information needed to complete an application or to correct spelling mistakes.

WHAT IF YOU HAVE A CHANGE OF ADDRESS?

A change of address need not be registered with the Copyright Office. If notified, the Copyright Office will note the change in the names' indexes for the convenience of searchers, but not in the Copyright Registers.

REGISTRATION OR DEPOSIT OTHER THAN WITH THE CANADIAN GOVERNMENT

Due to the voluntary nature of the Canadian copyright registration system and the fact that no deposit is required, some copyright owners use other methods of "registering" or "depositing" their materials either as the sole method of registration or in conjunction with the Canadian government registration system. Using an alternative method is no substitute for registration under the Canadian *Copyright Act*, though in practice it may provide some proof in a courtroom. However, a copyright owner would not be entitled to the advantages in the *Copyright Act* that benefit creators and copyright owners who register with the Copyright Office. Thus, a copyright owner not registered with the Canadian government would have to prove in a court proceeding that copyright existed in a work and that he or she is the owner of that copyright. On the other hand, using an alternative method in conjunction with the Canadian government registration system may provide additional proof to that obtained from merely using the Canadian registration system.

All registration/deposit systems have the same underlying purpose: to provide evidence that you are the copyright owner in a specific work and the date of creation of the work. Different creators' and copyright owners' associations and lawyers recommend different methods of registering and/or depositing a copyright work, depending upon the intended exploitation of a work, the possible violation of copyright by others, and the value of the work. Another factor in choosing one or more methods is the cost involved with each method. In deciding whether to register a work, keep in mind that you need not do so at the time of creation, but the earliest date possible at which you can prove the creation of your work will be advantageous in court proceedings. Needless to say, if registration and deposit are not undertaken immediately upon creation of the work, you are not barred from doing so at a later date. However, also keep in mind that lack of registration at the time of a violation of copyright may limit your recourse to a court order to stop the violating act from continuing, as opposed to other recourse such as monetary compensation.

Mailing a Copy to Yourself

This method of copyright "registration/deposit" is sometimes referred to as "poor man's copyright."[2] It is one of the least complicated, least time-consuming and least expensive ways to "register/deposit" a work or other subject-matter.

This method is straightforward. Put your manuscript, photographs of sculptures, lead sheet or any other reproduction of your work in an envelope and mail it to yourself by registered mail. When you receive the envelope/package, put the registered mail slip and envelope/package in your files (or safety deposit box or give it to your lawyer). DO NOT OPEN IT under any circumstances, unless and until you are before a court of law. Once opened before a judge, the envelope and its contents will act as evidence in establishing a date of creation, and ownership of copyright, in that protected material.

Alternatively, you can mail the envelope/package to a friend, who may, if necessary, later be called as a witness regarding the envelope/package.

Registering with the American Copyright Office

Once you have copyright protection in Canada, you automatically have protection in the United States. It is not mandatory to register in the United States in order to have protection there.

There are, however, important benefits for Canadians as well as American citizens to register in the United States. One benefit is the American Copyright Office's requirement of depositing copies of the work when you file a copyright registration application. This deposit can provide further proof of copyright ownership beyond that obtained from voluntary registration with the Canadian Copyright Office, where no such deposit is necessary or possible. Note that the American law also requires deposit of foreign (e.g., Canadian) works if they are published in the United States through the distribution of copies that are imported or are part of an American edition.

There are additional advantages of registering in the United States. For example, if a copyright infringement suit is initiated in an American court, American registration provides certain advantages in court proceedings. These additional advantages are especially important for copyright holders who exploit their works in the United States and are further explored in Chapter 15: Canadian and American Copyright Laws: A Comparison. Registration may be made at any time during the duration of copyright protection.

To register in the United States, you must mail the completed appropriate application form to the American Copyright Office. Although there is a pilot project for filing applications online, it is unlikely to be generally available in the near future. With the completed form, you must include the non-refundable filing fee of $30 U.S. per application, and submit a non-returnable deposit of the work being registered. Deposit requirements may vary depending on the nature of the work. For example, the American Copyright Office realizes that a painting or sculpture cannot be given as a deposit, and provides guidelines for substitute items of deposit. Deposit requirements for motion pictures are particularly complex, and like most American copyright law issues, are the subject of free Copyright Office information circulars, available upon request.

At the time of writing this book, you could expect a certificate of registration within about eight months of your filed application.

To obtain copyright forms, free information circulars, or further information, contact:

Copyright Office
Publications Section, LM-455
Library of Congress
Washington, D.C. 20559-6000 U.S.A.

T: 202.707.3000 (information specialists are on duty 8:30 to
17:00 ET, Monday - Friday)

Forms hotline (24 hours) T: 202.707.9100
F: 202.707.6859 (indicate person or section)
Fax-on-demand: 202.707.3000
E: **copyinfo@loc.gov**
 www.loc.gov/copyright

Registering with a Non-Governmental Organization

There are "specialized" registration and deposit places. This book refers to them as "specialized" since they generally only deal with specific types of materials. Certain artists' organizations and/or unions have set up these "specialized" systems to deal with the type of materials that they represent. The systems are generally open to organization/union members, as well as to non-members at a slightly higher fee. These "specialized" systems may provide evidence of ownership and proof of creation on a particular date, but they do not confer any copyright protection or give you the benefits of registering with the Canadian or American Copyright Offices.

The addresses of some of the existing specialized registration and depositories are given below. You may wish to contact arts organizations in your discipline to find out about other non-governmental systems. One caution in depositing your materials with any of these depositories is that there are no specific formalities or regulations that govern them. You will want to ensure that any depository you use is legitimate and can guarantee that your work will be kept in safe storage for the necessary period of time.

A second caution relates to the time period that the depository will keep your protected materials. When you register with the Canadian or American

Copyright Office, that registration is good for the full term of copyright. When you deposit your material with one of these non-governmental depositories, the deposit may be valid for a limited number of years, subject to a renewal (at an additional fee). The depository may, without notifying you, dispose and destroy your material within a certain time period following the expiration of the time of deposit. It is your responsibility to renew the registration.

Lastly, similar to the Canadian government registration system, these "specialized" agencies do not verify any registrations or deposits of your materials.

One example of a non-governmental service is that set up by the Writers Guild of Canada and a separate one by the Writers Guild in the United States. These services will hold in deposit any draft and final scripts, treatments, and related materials for radio, feature films, television, videos and interactive media.

For further information, contact:

> Writers Guild of Canada (WGC), Registration Service
> 123 Edward Street, Suite 1225
> Toronto, Ontario M5G 1E2
> Attention: Script Registration
>
> T: 416.979.7907 or 1.800.567.9974
> F: 416.979.9273
> E: **info@writersguildofcanada.com**
> **writersguildofcanada.com**

Note that the WGC Registration Service also accepts book manuscripts, poetry, short stories, stageplays and periodical articles.

> Writers Guild of America, West (WGAw), Registration Department
> 7000 West 3rd Street
> Los Angeles, California 90048-4329 U.S.A.
>
> T: 323.782.4500
> F: 323.782.4803
> E: n/a
> **www.wga.org**

The WGAw Registration Office also accepts stageplays, book manuscripts, short stories, poems, commercials, lyrics and drawings.

At the time of writing this book, the Writers Guild of Canada fees were $20 CDN for registering works of non-members and $10 CDN for members. The registration is valid for five years, subject to a five-year renewal.

The Writers Guild of America, West fees were $20 U.S. for registering works of non-members and $10 U.S. for members. Registration is valid for five years, subject to a five-year renewal.

SUMMARY

Copyright is automatic in Canada upon creation of a work or sound recording, or when a performance or broadcast signal occurs, provided certain criteria have been met. Notwithstanding automatic protection, one may mark a copyright work with ©, name of copyright holder, and year of first publication, and deposit and register copyright material using various government and non-government procedures and depositories.

Chapter 5

HOW DOES INTERNATIONAL COPYRIGHT PROTECTION WORK?

Some 500,000 pages are photocopied every minute throughout the world, and this phenomenon is growing every day thanks to the possibilities offered by new reproduction technology. . . . that is 260 billion pages per year. (Taken from the European Report of the European Commission, March 1991.)

Mrs Tarja Koskinen, Chairman,
International Federation of Reproduction
Rights Organizations (IFRRO), Helsinki,
in a paper entitled "Reprography, Electrocopying,
Electronic Delivery and the Exercise of Copyright"
for the WIPO Worldwide Symposium on the
Future of Copyright and Neighboring Rights,
Le Louvre, Paris, June 1 to 3, 1994.

THE CONCEPT OF INTERNATIONAL COPYRIGHT PROTECTION

International copyright protection does not, *per se*, exist. There is no one international copyright law. Each country has its own copyright laws. However, you can have protection in other countries under that country's copyright law through the copyright relations countries share with each other.

This chapter focusses on international copyright law from a Canadian point of view. Details of international copyright conventions and trade agreements are discussed followed by specific information on how Canadian authors are protected in other countries and how foreign authors are protected in Canada. Specific aspects relating to international copyright issues are also included in other chapters.

INTERNATIONAL COPYRIGHT CONVENTIONS

There are two principal international copyright conventions, the Berne Convention and the Universal Copyright Convention. Canada is signatory to both of them. These conventions do not by themselves provide copyright protection. Their purpose is to provide minimum standards that member countries include in their domestic copyright legislation. This establishes a minimum level of copyright protection around the world. Based on the principle of national treatment, these conventions ensure that authors are protected in countries other than their own.

National Treatment

In copyright conventions, national treatment means that each country signatory to the convention must give citizens or permanent residents of other signatory countries at least the same copyright protection that it gives its own nationals. For example, a Canadian author is entitled to the same copyright protection in Australia as any Australian citizen, by virtue of both countries being members of the Berne Convention. Likewise, an Australian author is entitled to copyright protection in Canada in the same manner as any Canadian author. This protection includes duration of copyright, rights of the author, as well as remedies available for the violation of these rights.

An important exception to national treatment is "the rule of the shorter term." The Berne Convention provides a minimum term of protection for most types of works of life-plus-fifty. If countries grant a longer term than life-plus-fifty, they have the choice of granting that longer term to works from all treaty partners or only to works from those treaty partners that grant the longer term. For example, both the United States and the European Union countries have a life-plus-seventy duration whereas Canada (and many other countries) has a life-plus-fifty duration. The United States grants national treatment to all of its treaty partners. Therefore, Canadian works are protected for life-plus-seventy in the United States. However, the European Union countries use the rule of the shorter term. Therefore, Canadian works are protected for life-plus-fifty years in European Union countries.

THE BERNE CONVENTION

The Berne Convention, formally called the International Union for the Protection of Literary and Artistic Works, is the older, and probably more important, of the two copyright conventions. The Berne Convention was concluded in 1886 and has been revised a number of times, most recently in 1971, often to reflect technological changes. Effective June 26, 1998, Canada became a member of the most recent version (1971) of the Berne Convention. Prior to that time, Canada was a member of the 1928 version of Berne. Recent amendments to the Canadian *Copyright Act* ensure that Canada meets the minimum levels of protection required in the 1971 level. Canada protects creators from Berne Convention countries that belong to any level of the Convention. As of July 19, 2000, there are 146 member countries of Berne.

Notwithstanding Canada's membership in the Berne Convention, the Convention has no legal effect in Canada. It is, however, sometimes referred to by Canadian courts to interpret the *Act*. As well, jurisprudence from other Berne member countries is used to interpret the Canadian *Copyright Act*.

The Berne Convention is administered by the World Intellectual Property Organization (WIPO, or OMPI in French— **WEB www.wipo.int**). WIPO is an intergovernmental organization based in Geneva, Switzerland and is one of the sixteen specialized agencies of the United Nations' system of organizations. Its function is to promote the protection of intellectual property internationally through co-operation among its member states, and to administer treaties on intellectual property, including copyright. WIPO encourages the establishment of new international treaties and the updating of national legislation, provides technical assistance to developing countries, and collects and disseminates information.

Minimum Standards

The Berne Convention sets minimum standards of protection that member countries are required to include in their domestic law; some of these provisions are optional. These minimum standards relate to the categories of works protected, scope of protection and duration of the protection. For example, member countries must provide copyright protection for most types of works for at least fifty years after an author's death. Countries must provide moral rights protection, "the author shall have the right to claim authorship of the work and to object to any distortion, mutilation or other modification of, or other derogatory action in relation to, the said work, which would be prejudicial to his honor or reputation." In addition, with respect to the right of reproduction, Berne states that members may only include exceptions in their laws where the reproduction does not conflict with the normal exploitation of the work and does not unreasonably prejudice the legitimate interests of the author.

Automatic Protection in Berne Convention Countries

Once copyright protection is secured in one's own country, provided that it is a Berne Convention country, protection is automatic in all other countries that are also signatories to the Convention. There are no prerequisite formalities to the protection like registering a work, or marking it with the copyright symbol. In fact, Berne Convention countries are not allowed to require any formalities; protection must always be automatic upon the creation of a work. The degree of protection and available remedies for violation of copyright are governed solely by the laws of the country where protection is claimed.

Membership in the Berne Convention

Certain countries could not join the Berne Convention because their domestic laws did not conform to Berne Convention standards, or because they had fundamentally different legal systems. The United States and Russia were examples. The United States could not join the Berne Convention because its domestic law used to contain formalities prerequisite to copyright protection (e.g., registering a work and marking it with the copyright symbol). In order to have more formal legal relationships between Berne and non-Berne countries, a new, less demanding convention, the Universal Copyright Convention (UCC) was drafted, and came into force in 1955.

The United States is a member of the UCC. As of March 1, 1989, the United States is also a member of the Berne Convention. Thus, Berne member countries may claim protection in the United States through the Berne Convention and need not comply with the UCC formalities necessary in countries that merely adhere to the UCC.

Canadians claiming protection in non-Berne countries may be entitled to protection in other countries by virtue of that country's adherence to the UCC.

THE UNIVERSAL COPYRIGHT CONVENTION

The Universal Copyright Convention was concluded in 1952 and was revised in 1971. Canada is a member at the 1952 level.

Minimum Standards

Like the Berne Convention, the UCC sets minimum standards of protection that member countries are required to include in their domestic law. These minimum standards relate to the categories of works protected, scope of protection and duration of the protection. For example, member countries must provide copyright protection for at least twenty-five years after an author's death; and contracting states must provide "adequate and effective protection" to copyright holders including the exclusive right of reproduction by any means and the broadcasting and public performance rights. Moral rights are not provided for in the UCC.

No Automatic Protection

Unlike the Berne Convention, copyright protection is not automatic in UCC countries upon protection in one's own country. Authors from UCC countries are only protected on a national treatment basis in other UCC countries if they comply with certain conditions. One of the principal conditions is the copyright notice. The UCC requires that, from first publication, all copies of a work published with the authority of the author or other copyright proprietor bear the symbol ©, accompanied by the name of the copyright proprietor, and the year of first publication, placed in such manner and location as to give reasonable notice of claim of copyright.

© Name of Copyright Owner Year of First Publication
or © Lesley Ellen Harris 2001

If you include this copyright notice, you are considered to have complied with other formalities such as "deposit, registration, notice, notarial certificates, payment of fees or manufacture or publication in that Contracting State." However, you must also check the formalities required by the country where you claim protection because contracting states are still free to require further formalities or conditions for the acquisition and enjoyment of copyright within those countries.

THE ROME CONVENTION

Concluded in 1961, the International Convention for the Protection of Performers, Producers of Phonograms and Broadcasting Organizations (Rome Convention) protects neighbouring rights of performers, producers of sound recordings and broadcasters. Effective June 4, 1998, Canada became a member of the Rome Convention. The Rome Convention sets out a remuneration right for performers and producers of sound recordings when their recordings are either performed in public or broadcast in countries that have acceded to the Rome Convention. As of February 11, 2000, there are sixty-five member countries of the Rome Convention.

NEW DIGITAL COPYRIGHT TREATIES

On December 20, 1996, negotiators from 160 countries reached agreement on two new treaties, the WIPO Copyright Treaty and the WIPO Performances and Phonograms Treaty. This was after three weeks of discussions in Geneva under the auspices of WIPO, at a Diplomatic Conference on Certain Copyright and Neighbouring Rights Questions. These treaties deal with copyright needs in the digital era and changing international copyright norms in light of new technologies. The text of the two treaties as adopted is at **www.wipo.int**.

The international treaties are binding only on those countries that actually join them. Countries must have their laws in conformity with the treaties at the time they join.

Each treaty may only come into force after being ratified by thirty countries. As of July 15, 2000, nineteen countries have joined the WIPO Copyright Treaty; and sixteen countries have joined the WIPO Performances and Phonograms Treaty. At the time of writing, Canada is not a member of either new treaty.[1]

OTHER INTERNATIONAL COPYRIGHT-RELATED CONVENTIONS

Besides the Berne Convention and the UCC, there are other international conventions concerning copyright law and copyright-related issues. Canada is not currently a member of these other conventions. Some of these conventions are described below.

- the Geneva Convention for the Protection of Producers of Phonograms Against Unauthorized Duplication of Their Phonograms (1971) (Geneva Phonograms Convention) provides international protection against the piracy of sound recordings. Each member nation must protect nationals of other member nations against the unauthorized manufacture, importation and distribution of copies of sound recordings.

- the Brussels Satellite Convention combats the misappropriation of satellite signals on an international level (required because satellite transmission was thought to be inadequately treated in the major international copyright conventions). This convention does not create new rights for programs transmitted by satellite, but focuses on the unauthorized distribution of signals themselves (and not the content of the material sent by the signals).

In addition, individual countries may have agreements with other countries for the protection of works in each other's countries.

INTERNATIONAL TRADE AGREEMENTS AND COPYRIGHT LAW

Until recently, international copyright relations were through international copyright conventions and bilateral agreements. However, in the past several years, Canada has signed three international trade agreements that have provisions for intellectual property including copyright. These trade agreements are the Canada-United States Free Trade Agreement (FTA), the North American Free Trade Agreement (NAFTA) and the agreement on Trade Related Aspects of Intellectual Property Rights (TRIPs), which is part of the Uruguay Round of the General Agreement on Tariffs and Trade (GATT). Countries that signed the GATT are members of the World Trade Organization (WTO).

These trade agreements are separate from the copyright conventions and are not intended to replace conventions like Berne or the UCC. In fact, the trade agreements sometimes require that countries provide as a minimum the protection required by the copyright conventions. The purpose of including intellectual property in trade agreements is to strengthen intellectual property rights and encourage foreign investment by combating piracy, enhance standards for the protection of copyright around the world, and strengthen the enforcement of rights both internally and at the borders.

Changes made to the Canadian *Copyright Act* by virtue of the FTA, NAFTA or TRIPs are discussed, where appropriate, throughout this book.

IN WHICH COUNTRY DO YOU ENFORCE YOUR RIGHTS?

Under the international system of copyright, a copyright owner enforces his or her rights in the country where the alleged violation of copyright takes place. For instance, if your book were photocopied in Australia, then you would claim your rights under the Australian copyright statute.

With the Internet, it is often difficult to establish where a work is used. Is it used where the work is uploaded onto a Web site, or where it is downloaded, or perhaps in other countries along the way?

As recent court cases suggest, the question of which country has jurisdiction over the Internet is a source of much debate among legal scholars, law associations and courts in Canada and around the world. Like much of the law relating to Internet-related issues, the leading cases and commentaries are American.

Overall, the position on jurisdiction on the Internet seems to be based on a number of factors:

- Is there a connection between the location where the activity is taking place and the place where the infringement has occurred?
- Is either of the countries of origin in which the sender or receiver of the impugned Internet activity is located signatories to an international agreement that would regulate this activity?

The answer, if there is one, appears to be that a jurisdictional analysis based on existing international law principles should be done to determine which country has jurisdiction over a particular Internet activity. Until a specific international agreement deals with the question of jurisdiction on the Internet and/or further court cases deal with the issue, there is no definitive answer regarding which country has jurisdiction over the Internet.

HOW TO ENFORCE YOUR RIGHTS IN FOREIGN COUNTRIES

When your copyright works are used in a foreign country, your rights are governed by the copyright laws of that country.

If you enjoy copyright protection in Canada, you automatically have protection in all Berne Convention countries, and as of January 1, 1996, in all WTO countries. You may claim protection in a WTO country for a work still protected by copyright as of January 1, 1996, notwithstanding when that work was created or published. In order to secure protection in UCC countries, you must mark the work from the time of first publication with the word "copyright," "copr." or ©, the year of first publication, and the name of the owner of the copyright.

If the country in which you claim protection belongs either to Berne, the UCC, or the WTO, then you can claim protection in that country by virtue of one of these memberships. That country need not be a member of Berne and the UCC and the WTO. Therefore, if you claim protection in a country that is both a member of Berne and/or the WTO and the UCC, and you have not complied with the UCC copyright notice requirement from the time of first publication, you can claim protection under Berne or the WTO, which do not have the notice requirement. Almost all UCC members are also members of Berne and by the terms of the conventions Berne governs relations between members of both conventions. If you are claiming protection in a country that is not a member of either of the copyright conventions or the WTO, you may still be able to obtain protection under specific provisions of that country's national laws. If this situation applies to you, consult a copyright expert before first publication, in order to ensure that you comply with any requirements prerequisite to copyright protection that depend on the facts existing at the time of first publication. Eligibility for copyright protection is also discussed in Chapter 3: Is Your Creation Eligible for Copyright Protection?

The above discussion simplifies the nature of international copyright protection. If you are distributing and marketing your work in foreign countries, be aware that copyright laws vary greatly from country to country and different rights and remedies may apply to you in foreign countries. In some cases, these rights and remedies will be greater than, and sometimes lesser than, your rights and remedies in Canada. Also be aware that foreign countries do not always recognize special rules concerning authorship or first ownership of copyright that may exist in the country of origin of the work. Instead, these countries will apply their own domestic law to determine the author or first owner of copyright rather than the law of the country of origin. For instance, certain European countries do not recognize the American work-for-hire rule when an American work is in their territory. Further, some countries apply their own rule regarding the author of an audio-visual work, rather than the rule in the country of origin of the work. This is a conflict of laws issue. A copyright lawyer can help determine your rights and remedies in the foreign country where you claim protection and infringement and, in the case of infringement, whether you should proceed with enforcing those rights in Canada or in the country involved.

Claiming protection in the United States is explored in further detail in Chapter 15: Canadian and American Copyright Laws: A Comparison.

THE PROTECTION OF FOREIGNERS IN CANADA

Foreign creators who meet the criteria of nationality and place of publication (as well as originality and fixation), as discussed in Chapter 6: What is Protected by Copyright?, are automatically protected in Canada under Canadian copyright law. Foreigners who are initially protected by copyright in their own country, a country that is a member of Berne, the UCC, or as of January 1, 1996, the WTO, are automatically protected and entitled to most of the rights and remedies set out in the Canadian *Copyright Act* when their works are used in Canada. It is not necessary to register one's work or mark it with the copyright notice.

If you are using foreign copyright materials in Canada, see Chapter 14: Using Copyright Materials for information on how to obtain permission to use these materials.

MEMBER COUNTRIES OF THE BERNE CONVENTION, UCC AND WTO

Certain provisions in the *Act* refer to and apply to a "treaty country," which means a Berne, UCC, or WTO member country.

Member countries of the two international copyright conventions and the WTO are indicated in Appendix III.

SUMMARY

There is no such thing as international copyright protection. However, Canadians have automatic copyright protection in Berne and WTO countries, and have protection in UCC countries if the copyright notice has been properly used. Protection is according to the domestic laws of the country where the work is being used. Sound recording producers may also be protected in Rome countries.

Foreigners initially protected in Berne, WTO, UCC and Rome countries enjoy automatic copyright protection when their works are used in Canada and are entitled to the rights and remedies in the Canadian *Copyright Act*.

There are two new digital copyright treaties that may help pave the way for establishing global minimum protection of rights on the Internet and in other digital media.

WHAT IS PROTECTED BY COPYRIGHT?

As you know, you can't copyright an idea . . .
Michael Douglas' character in the film *Fatal Attraction*
from the screenplay by James Dearden

THE MEANING OF "WORKS" AND "OTHER SUBJECT-MATTER"

You may have already noticed that this book uses the term "work" when referring to material protected by copyright. The term "work" is the word used in the Canadian *Copyright Act*, the Berne Convention and the copyright legislations of many other countries to describe literary, artistic, musical and dramatic creations protected by copyright. In addition, the Canadian *Copyright Act* protects "other subject-matter" which includes sound recordings, performances and communication signals (collectively referred to as neighbouring rights). Works and other subject-matter are both protected under the Canadian *Copyright Act* but enjoy somewhat different protection and are distinguished in the *Act*. Some refer to works as traditional copyright material and to other subject-matter or neighbouring rights as non-traditional copyright material. For purposes of clarification, this book often uses the word "materials" to cover both works and other subject-matter.

Ideas

One important point to remember in determining what is protected copyright material is that copyright protects the expression of an idea and not the idea itself. Thus, the material that is protected by copyright law is the expression of an idea, creation or thought. For instance, a book on how to build a backyard shed is protected by copyright, but anyone can use the ideas in the instructions to build a shed or write their own book on building sheds (of course, without copying the other book).

Facts

Similar to ideas, facts or factual information (for example, historical details) are not subject to copyright protection. Note, however, that other areas of the law may protect facts and restrict the use of information; for example, if facts are obtained on a confidential basis. The lack of protection in facts and the like must be distinguished from the expression of the facts or information in a particular format. If original, and expressed in some material form, there may be copyright protection in the expression of facts. For example, there may be copyright protection in a book setting out the history of the film industry in Canada. However, there is no copyright protection in the facts concerning the film industry in Canada that are set out in the book; there is merely copyright protection in the expression of those facts.

Real-life Events

With the popularity of reality-based television shows and docudrama movies, the issue of obtaining rights from the people involved in these real-life events has become the focus of much discussion. Like facts and information, real-life events are not *per se* protected by copyright. However, if you are producing a docudrama and there is an article or book about the real-life event, obtaining permission from the author of the article or book would ensure that the author does not later make a claim of copyright infringement against you. Also, the author may have valuable research materials you can use. In addition, producers of projects based on real-life events often obtain releases or rights to the stories from involved people to protect themselves against other legal claims such as defamation, privacy and publicity. Further, having exclusive rights to a story from the people involved can give the producer an advantage over other producers basing a project on the same story.

WORKS PROTECTED BY COPYRIGHT

Copyright law was originally concerned with the protection of printed material, but has, over the years, been expanded, either explicitly or by interpretation, to extend to a large variety of works and media. Although the

Copyright Act does specify all the types of works protected by copyright, you will soon see that most creations, whether an inter-office memorandum, a sculpture, film, computer program or Web page do qualify and fall within one of the main categories of works and are protected by copyright, provided they meet the other necessary criteria for copyright protection, such as originality and fixation. As one court case has put it, "there remains the rough practical test that what is worth copying is *prima facie* worth protecting."[1]

It is not out of line to say that the *Copyright Act* is very generous in the types of works it protects. A "work" is eligible for copyright protection notwithstanding the mode or form of that work. The creation could be in draft or final form, or it could be a sketch for a larger work such as a painting or the painting itself, or even a poem written on a napkin. The *Act* protects a work prepared for commercial or non-commercial purposes. It protects published and unpublished creations, and creations produced by amateurs or professionals. It protects print and analogue works as well as digital content. It protects works in any language, even non-human languages. It protects humorous, common or crude works. It may even protect indecent, obscene or immoral works though the rewards upon suing for violation of copyright in such works may be somewhat limited.

General Rule

Although the *Copyright Act* extends protection to a wide variety of creations, it does set out specific categories under which these creations must fall. The *Copyright Act* states that copyright subsists "in every original literary, dramatic, musical and artistic work." It further states that "every original literary, dramatic, musical and artistic work includes every original production in the literary, scientific or artistic domain, whatever may be the mode or form of its expression, such as compilations, books, pamphlets and other writings, lectures, dramatic or dramatico-musical works, translations, illustrations, sketches and plastic works relative to geography, topography, architecture or science." Note that the examples given at the end of this definition are merely examples to illustrate the meanings of the words. Protection is by no means limited to these creations.

The categories of protected works are helpful in terms of providing some order to the large amount of items protected by copyright. As well, they are important, and referred to, in terms of duration and ownership of copyright, and the rights attaching to works protected by copyright. If a creation fits within one of the categories of works protected by copyright, and that creation meets the general criteria necessary for copyright protection—originality, fixation, nationality and place of first publication—then the creation will be protected by copyright.

Courts have interpreted the *Copyright Act* in specific cases to protect new types of works not specifically mentioned in it. In some cases, these "new" types of works are a result of new technology and as such were not contemplated by the drafters of the original law in 1921. This was the case with respect to computer software. The *Copyright Act* was interpreted to extend to computer software without any specific mention of computer software in the legislation. Chapter 16 deals with the manner in which the current law may be interpreted to deal with digital media.

The remainder of this chapter will look at specific examples of works under each of the categories, followed by a discussion of what is protected as other subject-matter or neighbouring rights. The works listed below are merely examples of protected works. It would be impossible to include an exhaustive list of works protected by copyright. If your work is similar to one of the examples given, it is likely that it is a work protected by copyright.

For the sake of clarity, different or additional headings than those used in the legislation are used in this chapter. Also, when going through the list of protected works under specific headings, you may recognize that some works fall into more than one category. For example, a book could be a book of short stories and be protected as a literary work. Further, these books could be collections and therefore also be protected as collective works or could be works of joint authorship and be protected as such.

You may also note that some works incorporate other works and that some works enjoy more than one layer of copyright protection. For example, a magazine may enjoy separate copyright from the articles in it, or a choreographic work may enjoy distinct copyright from the set of musical works that are a part of it. Finally, a film may enjoy separate copyright from the underlying screenplay. This is also true for all of the underlying copyright protected materials in a multimedia work like a CD-ROM or a Web site.

When looking for the protection of a certain work, look under the category that most logically or prominently applies to that work.

LITERARY WORKS

The *Copyright Act* defines a "literary work" to include tables, computer programs and compilations of literary works. These are merely examples of creations protected as literary works and do not, by any means, represent the full scope of works protected as literary works. In fact, this definition would be deceiving if you followed it as setting out the only types of literary works protected by copyright. Much to the contrary, the types of works protected by copyright as literary works are quite extensive, as you will see below.

The term "literary" with respect to literary works should not be taken in its literal sense. For one thing, the work need not necessarily be "written" in the ordinary sense of the word to be protected as a literary work. Also, the work need not possess particular literary merit to be protected.

Generally, a literary work exists if the author has used labour, skill and ingenuity to arrange his or her thoughts. A court case protecting exam papers as literary works set out quite succinctly the meaning of literary with respect to literary works:

> . . . it seems to be plain that it is not confined to "literary work" in the sense in which that phrase is applied, for instance, to Meredith's novels and the writings of Robert Louis Stevenson. In speaking of such writings as literary works, one thinks of the quality, the style, and the literary finish which they exhibit. Under the Act of 1842, which protected "books," many things which had no pretensions to literary style acquired copyright; for example, a list of registered bills of sale, a list of foxhounds and hunting days, and trade catalogues; and I see no ground for coming to the conclusion that the present Act was intended to curtail the rights of authors. In my view the words "literary work" cover work which is expressed in print or writing, irrespective of the question whether the quality or style is high.[2]

With this sort of description of literary works, a legal contract would constitute a literary work, as would a letter written on the inside of tree bark. Most items that afford information, instruction or pleasure in the form of literary enjoyment would also qualify as literary works. For example, poems, short stories, magazines, newsletters, instruction manuals, exam papers, game rules and advertising material may also be literary works, even if they are only in a digital form. Specific examples are set out below.

Books, Pamphlets, Letters, Memoranda

BOOKS

As already suggested, a book need not have any "literary" merit to be protected as a literary work. An instruction manual for your dishwasher is protected as much as a book of poems by e.e. cummings; a book explaining Einstein's theory has protection equal to a book by Margaret Atwood.

Under the *Copyright Act*, the term "book" may have a different meaning than the traditional sense of the word. For instance, the *Act* defines a "book" to include every volume, part or division of a volume, pamphlet, sheet of letter-press, sheet of music, map, chart or plan separately published. These are only illustrations of what may constitute a book for purposes of the copyright law, but it does suggest some examples that may not usually occur to us.

Although most people would define a book as a literary work, that is not necessarily true under the copyright law. If the book contains poems or tables, then it would be protected as a literary work. However, certain books may also be protected under other categories of protection. For instance, a book of photographs could be protected as an artistic work or as a compilation of artistic works.

LETTERS

All letters, whether business or personal, are protected by copyright. This includes e-mail.

OTHER "WRITTEN" DOCUMENTS

All "written" documents, whether prepared for internal or external purposes, whether in draft or final form, whether in print or in digital form, are protected by copyright. In fact, each draft of a document may be separately protected by copyright. This includes papers and dissertations, and other school assignments prepared by students as part of course and degree work.

Titles, Names, Slogans, Words

As a general rule, copyright does not protect words, slogans, titles, short phrases, pseudonyms, names of people, goods, services, business associations, domain names and the like. In some cases, trade-mark or other forms of protection may be available.

The *Copyright Act* makes specific mention of the copyright protection of titles. This is in relation to the definition of a work. The *Act* defines a "work" as including the title of it when such title is original and distinctive. Thus, even though titles are not protected independently from a work, a title may be protected as part of a work. Although the *Act* is not as specific with respect to slogans, short phrases and the like, as it is with titles, one may be able to argue that the same type of protection may apply.

There may be an exception to the general rule of titles not being protected by copyright. A judge in one court case said, "This Hour Has Sixty Minutes is a title which could not be considered as original and distinctive, whereas This Hour Has Seven Days is a title which probably could be considered as original and distinctive, because normally no one expects to hear that an hour is composed of seven days."[3]

Lectures, Addresses, Speeches, Sermons

A lecture is protected as a literary work. In general, a lecture must be fixed in some form in order to be protected. For example, if you give a lecture on "Irony in Atom Egoyan Films," and the lecture is not written down or otherwise "fixed," then you have no copyright in that lecture, despite it being a type of work protected by copyright law.[4]

A lecture may be an address, speech or sermon, or other similar work such as lessons or pleadings.

News

Like ideas and facts, news has, *per se*, no copyright protection. However, once the news is put in some material form, copyright protection may persist in that particular expression of the news. For example, a news article in a print newspaper, or a news article on a newspaper's Web site, is protected by copyright since the article is a form or expression of that news.

Editions

Editions *per se* are not protected by copyright. That is, the way a work is typographically arranged (format, type fonts and layout) is not currently protected by the law. Thus, anyone can photographically copy or reset an edition of Shakespeare's *King Lear* (which is no longer protected by copyright), and thereby benefit from the expense and labour of the original publisher.

Copying an edition, however, should be done with caution. This is because even though an edition of a book is not, as a whole, protected by copyright, certain elements of the edition may be protected by the law. For instance, art work on the cover, the table of contents, the foreword, editorial comment(s) and marginal notes may all be protected by copyright, if they meet the criteria for copyright protection. These protected portions are all "new" or added elements to an original work and it is only these portions that are protected, not the entire edition. If you copy an entire edition of a work, with any new or added elements, you may be violating copyright in these additions to the edition. Also, if you reproduce an "edition" which is an adaptation of a work in the public domain, that adaptation may have copyright protection whereas the protection in the original work has expired.

Translations

Translations are protected by copyright. Any translated work is considered a "new" work and is separately protected from the original work. The justification for this protection is that a translator does more than merely reproduce another copy of the original work. However, if a translator makes a great many changes, the resulting work may not be considered a translation.

If you are translating a work, you must obtain permission to do so from the copyright owner in the original work.

There may be two copyrights where there is a translated work. Copyright exists in the original work as well as in the translated work. Thus, if you translate a play from French to English, the original French version is protected by copyright and the translated English version is separately protected by copyright as a translation. A third party performing the translated version of the play must obtain permission from both the copyright owner of the original work and the copyright owner of the translated play.

Even if copyright has expired in a work that has been translated, there may be copyright protection in that translation. Thus, if you translate a play by Henrik Ibsen into Hebrew, even though copyright has expired in the original work, there is copyright protection in the Hebrew version of the work.

Computer Programs

Computer programs are protected by copyright law. The *Copyright Act* defines a computer program as "a set of instructions or statements, expressed, fixed, embodied or stored in any manner, that is to be used directly or indirectly in a computer in order to bring about a specific result." This definition was added to the *Act* in 1988, following court decisions. Types of programs protected by copyright may include an operating system, word processing program, a computer game or an accounting program.

With respect to a computer program, what is protected is the computer program itself and not the language used to write that program (since languages are not protected by copyright). Also, the idea of the program is not protected. Anyone can reach the same end result by creating his or her own program, as long as the other program was not used in doing so. Since copyright cannot protect the idea of a program, trade secrets or confidential information may be other areas of the law to examine when dealing with the protection of computer software.

Note that information displayed on a computer screen is probably not protected by copyright since the work is ephemeral and not in any permanent form, therefore the criterion of fixation is not met.

DISKETTES, CD-ROMS,—DVDS
(DIGITAL VIDEO DISKS) AND WEB SITES

Computer programs are protected notwithstanding the physical object or type of physical object that embodies them. A computer program on a diskette, CD-ROM, DVD and other new technology are equally protected by the law. Also protected is a computer program that resides on a Web site (for example, which you may be able to download onto your computer).

PUBLIC DOMAIN SOFTWARE OR SHAREWARE

Those of you familiar with computers and computer software have probably come across the term "public domain software" and "shareware." Public domain software is protected by copyright, but can be copied without obtaining permission from, or making a payment to, the copyright owner. The copyright owner of public domain software has decided to waive his or her rights in the software and is allowing the public to freely use it.

Shareware software is copyright protected but with an unusual distribution twist. Instead of asking users to pay for the software before they use it, shareware authors urge users to try it and to voluntarily pay a modest amount directly to the copyright holder if the user continues to use that software beyond a trial period.

Tables

Tables are protected by copyright as long as original thought, labour, selection and so on were involved in the making of the table. For instance, a table of statistics may be protected by copyright.

Games

A game, as a specific item, is not explicitly protected by copyright. However, various elements of the game may be protected by the law. For instance, the instruction manual may be protected as a literary work and the game board may be protected as an artistic work. If it is a computer game, there may be an additional underlying copyright work: the game's software.

DRAMATIC WORKS

Dramatic works is a second category of works listed in the *Copyright Act*. The term "dramatic work" is defined in the *Act* as including "any piece for recitation, choreographic work or mime, the scenic arrangement or acting form of which is fixed in writing or otherwise," and any cinematograph work and any compilation of dramatic works. It is evident from this definition that the term dramatic works encompasses a number of forms of expression including verbal and non-verbal, purely physical and musical elements.

Basically, a dramatic work entails the representation of a dramatic element. Many things that may appear to be a literary work—mainly because they are written down—may be a dramatic work (or may be considered both a literary and dramatic work). In order for a work to be considered a dramatic work, there must be some dramatic action. These dramatic elements need be "fixed" in some form in which the dramatic elements are recognized. Every precise element need not be in that fixation.

A dramatic work may be protected whether the work extends to amateurs or professionals, and may be protected wherever the performance takes place, be it a park, theatre, synagogue or church.

Note that some dramatic works may lend themselves more to protection through the law of confidentiality as opposed to copyright since often what is being protected are ideas. This may be true with respect to an idea for a television series.

Scripts for Radio, Television, Film, CD-ROMs, etc.

Scripts and sketches for radio, television, film, CD-ROMs and other media may be protected as dramatic works. The script need not be an exact portrayal of the actual performance or dramatic event.

In one case, a court held that a sketch for a television show was a dramatic work even though the script was departed from on a daily basis. The criteria set in the case for the protection of the sketch was that the sketch need only be "fixed in writing sufficiently to say it was a dramatic composition capable of being published or performed and in which the dramatic element was present."[5]

Plays

The element of a play that is eligible for copyright protection is some sort of fixed description of the play. A script or any other descriptive material that captures the dramatic element of the play would probably be eligible for copyright protection.

For a work to be eligible for copyright protection, the end result need not necessarily be a play, as the common usage of that word connotes. In general, "any piece for recitation" may be protected by copyright if the general criteria necessary for protection are met.

Note that the different elements in the play may also have copyright protection by themselves. For example, any choreography, musical works or sets used in the dramatic work may enjoy copyright protection on their own.

Radio Programs

Impromptu radio programs, talk shows, and the like are not automatically protected by copyright, since the general criterion of fixation may not always be met. If, however, these shows were previously or simultaneously recorded with their broadcast, that recording would constitute a fixation of the work. The criterion of fixation would also be met where there is some sort of script, or similar material, which captures the dramatic element of the radio program. For example, a radio sketch set out on paper may be protected. The same is true of a radio commentary that is read from a printed sheet of paper.

Operas, Musicals and Comedies

Operas, comedies, and musical dramas and plays, and the like may be protected by copyright as dramatic works as long as the criteria for such protection have been met; that is, a dramatic element is captured in a fixed form.

AUDIO-VISUAL MATERIALS

The *Copyright Act* does not use the term "audio-visual material," however it does protect audio-visual materials as "cinematographs." Cinematographs are protected as dramatic works. For purposes of the *Copyright Act*, there are two different ways in which audio-visual material is protected. This is dependent upon the nature of the work, that is, whether the work possesses an "original character." The distinction between the two kinds of audio-visual works or cinematographs is relevant with respect to other areas of copyright protection, such as ownership of the work and duration of protection.

For purposes of this book and ease of comprehension, the terminology "scripted" and "non-scripted" audio-visual works or cinematographs will be used. These words have no legal significance and may not, in fact, be 100% accurate.

"Scripted" Audio-visual Materials such as Films and Television Programs

Scripted works, for purposes of this book, are audio-visual works that possess an "original character." This "original character" is derived from the arrangement or acting form or the combination of incidents represented. Audio-visual works with "original character" may be films or videos that follow a script, are overseen by a director, and are subject to an edit.

"Non-scripted" Audio-visual Materials such as Improvised Works, Home Videos and News Coverage

"Non-scripted" audio-visual works are those without "original character" and include improvised works, a film of a news item, a film of a dog walking around a yard and home videos. "Non-scripted" works have no scripts, are not subject to much editing and there is no control over any "dramatic" event in them. As mentioned above, it is possible that some so-called improvised works qualify as having an "original character" and would therefore fall under the above category of works arbitrarily called scripted works.

Expression by a Process Analogous to Cinematography

Whether the audio-visual work is scripted or non-scripted, in order for it to be protected by copyright, it must have been "expressed by any process analogous to cinematography." This criterion is broad and allows for different types of technologies that are arguably analogous to cinematography. It does not require that the work be made on film (with a negative) or on magnetic tape.

Sound Tracks

The sound track of a film is protected as a film or cinematograph where it accompanies the film or cinematograph.

CHOREOGRAPHIC WORKS

Choreographic works are protected by copyright. They are protected under the category of dramatic works, but are dealt with separately here because they are subject to different criteria for protection than other dramatic works.

The *Copyright Act* defines a "choreographic work" as including any work of choreography, whether or not it has a story line. This definition was added to the *Copyright Act* in 1988. Prior to this definition, choreographic works required, because they fell within the category of dramatic works, a plot or at least a sequence of action, to be protected by copyright. Many choreographic works do not, however, possess a plot or sequence and are simply visually aesthetic patterns. For instance, pantomimes, or certain works of performance, and some modern dance, jazz and abstract ballet, do not necessarily possess a plot.

The protection of a choreographic work extends to the choreographer's arrangement and selection of steps into a choreographic work and not to individual steps within that work. Because of the nature of a choreographic work, it must be notated, sketched, recorded on film or video, etc., to be eligible for copyright protection. Otherwise, there is no fixation of the work.

It is likely that a choreographic work would include figure skating. However, it is unlikely that a sporting event would be considered a choreographic work because it is not preconceived or fixed in any manner.

MUSICAL WORKS

The *Copyright Act* defines a "musical work" to mean "any work of music or musical composition, with or without words, and includes any compilation thereof." A musical work, for copyright purposes, is a composition or song, but not a CD or other object that embodies the composition. CDs and other sound recordings are separately defined in the law and are discussed below under specific headings.

As always, the general criteria of copyright works must be met with respect to musical works. The criterion of originality is an interesting one. This is because many musical compositions have similar tone succession or slight variations in rhythm or harmony. Some originality or creative work in creating the song will help establish its originality. Whether a musical work is original is a determination to be made based upon the facts of each individual case. With respect to the criterion of fixation, a fixation of a musical work could be a musical notation or recording.

The type of musical works protected by the law is broad and includes beer commercials and opera and hiphop.

As stated in its definition, a musical work can be a musical composition with or without words. However, there is some confusion as to whether there are two copyrights where there are lyrics accompanying that music. If there are two copyrights, the music would be protected as a musical work and the lyrics would be protected as a literary work. The legal quandary is not as relevant where the same person creates the tune and lyrics since a court case has held that where a single author has written a song, the song was subject to a single copyright.[6] However, this view has been criticized, and in practice, not always adhered to. These issues are important when permission is being sought to use a musical work.

Sheet Music

Musical scores are protected by copyright. This is true with respect to individual songs and compilations of songs.

If you write your own music, it is protected by copyright as soon as it is "fixed" in some permanent form, for example, on staff paper. If you write music on a computer, you should be aware that it is generally believed that there is no copyright in what appears on your computer screen since what you see is ephemeral; a copy saved on your hard drive or on a disk, or a print-out of the music would satisfy the fixation requirement.

Arrangements, Adaptations

The issue of arrangements and adaptations is relevant to all copyright works, however, it is dealt with here because of the frequency of the arrangements of musical works.

An arrangement or adaptation may attract copyright protection provided it meets the general criteria for copyright protection including originality in the form of sufficient skill and labour. One example might be an arrangement of a Vivaldi piece. Another might be a new adaptation, that is, the piano arrangement for the orchestral score of the opera, *The Merry Wives of Windsor*.[7]

An arranged or adapted work has two layers of copyright protection. There is protection in the original work and there is protection in the arranged or adapted version. Thus, if you use an arrangement or adaptation, you must clear copyright in both the original and the arranged or adapted version. And if you are adapting a work, and the original work is protected by copyright, you must obtain permission to adapt it from the owner of the original work.

Sound Recordings

Sound recordings are *not* a sub-category of musical works and are discussed below under Other Subject-Matter.

ARTISTIC WORKS

Artistic works is a further category of works provided for in the *Copyright Act*.

Just as a literary work does not need to have particular literary merit or standard to be protected by copyright, an "artistic work" is generally not judged by its artistic or aesthetic nature. The real test of an artistic work is whether the work is original; that is, an original expression from its creator and not copied from somewhere else.

The term "artistic work" is a generic term applying to works in a "visual medium." In fact, it has been suggested that a more appropriate name for this category of works may be "works of the visual arts and other artistic works" as this would more accurately define works that fall under this category.

The definition section of the *Copyright Act* sets out a number of examples of artistic works. These include paintings, drawings, maps, charts, plans, photographs, engravings, sculptures, works of artistic craftsmanship, architectural works and compilations of artistic works. These and other artistic works are described below.

Paintings and Drawings

All paintings and drawings, whether on canvas or on the back of a chocolate bar wrapper, are protected by copyright. Also, a painting by a three-year-old is protected as is one by a well known artist such as Robert Bateman. A painting used in the set for a play may also be protected by copyright.

Engravings

Engravings are protected by copyright. The term "engraving" is not specifically defined in the *Act*. However, the *Act* sets out certain examples of items that may be considered engravings including "etchings, lithographs, woodcuts, prints and other similar works, not being photographs." Since the definition is an illustrative one, other engravings may be protected if produced by a process analogous to the exemplary list of engravings included in the *Act*.

"Original prints" made in a numbered limited edition and signed individually, in accordance with the standards of the arts community, are each considered an artistic work under the *Copyright Act*. Unnumbered and unsigned prints are also considered to be artistic works. The legal rights attached to prints (as a type of engraving) are identical whether the print is a limited or unlimited edition, signed or unsigned, numbered or unnumbered. All prints which are protected as engravings have, in addition to the other rights of a copyright owner in other copyright works, an exhibition right and an "absolute" right of integrity.

Works of Artistic Craftsmanship

Works of artistic craftsmanship is the one sub-category of artistic works where the "artistic" nature of the work is relevant. Thus, the meaning of the word "artistic" when employed in the expression "works of artistic craftsmanship" is different than when employed in the term "artistic work." The meaning of "artistic" in relation to a work of artistic craftsmanship is that the work must be original, and that it must possess a certain artistic character.

In determining the meaning of "artistic" with respect to a work of artistic craftsmanship, it seems that items that "look nice" to the public may not be considered to have artistic appeal. However, a work which is genuinely admired and valued for its appearance, and which gives pleasure or satisfaction, whether emotional or intellectual, may be an artistic work even if some people think it "meaningless or common or vulgar."[8]

Since there must be some craftsmanship involved in the making of a work of artistic craftsmanship, it follows that such a work should not be created by a mere technician, but should be an item produced by a craftsperson. An example of such a work may be a lamp or a piece of jewellery.

Photographs

Photographs are protected by copyright. A photograph is defined in the *Act* to include "photo-lithograph and any work expressed by any process analogous to photography." Photographs made with a negative as well as instant or polaroid photographs and electronic photos are equally protected by copyright. This is true for any photograph that is currently protected by copyright, notwithstanding when the photograph was taken and the fact that prior to January 1, 1994, only photographs with a negative were protected.

Sculptures

Sculptures are protected by the *Copyright Act*. The *Act* defines "work of sculpture" as including casts and models. According to this definition, a finished sculpture, and any and all casts, moulds and models employed to create that sculpture are protected by copyright.

A Henry Moore sculpture or one you create in a pottery class may be protected by copyright.

Sketches and Illustrations

Sketches and illustrations and the like are protected by copyright law. Sketches and illustrations used to create other copyright works are separately protected by copyright from the work created with the aid of these sketches and illustrations.

Geographical, Topographical, Architectural and Scientific Plastic Works

Plastic works relative to geography, topography, architecture or science are specifically mentioned in the law as being protected by copyright. An example might be a globe or a model of a building.

Architectural Works

Architectural works are protected by copyright. These works are defined in the *Act* as "any building or structure or any model of a building or structure." Before 1988 and the legislative changes to the *Copyright Act*, in order for an architectural work to be protected by copyright, it required an "artistic character and design." Thus, it was necessary to judge the quality and merit of architectural works in order to determine their eligibility for copyright protection. Under the current law, these works need only meet the requirement of originality to which all works are subject.

Examples of protected architectural works may be a building, or a structure such as a tower, gate, bridge or parking garage. The copyright protection in a building, structure or model is separate from the copyright protection in the plans and sketches made with respect to that building, structure or model.

Maps, Charts and Plans

Maps, charts and plans are protected by copyright. Copyright in plans is distinct from the copyright in a structure based on that plan.

Comic Strips

Comic strips are protected by copyright. The written part of the comic strip is protected as a literary work and the drawings are protected as artistic works.

Fictional Characters

Fictional characters, such as Bart Simpson or Garfield (the cat) are not, by themselves, protected by copyright, but may have components that are subject to copyright protection. The different elements of fictional characters must be examined on their own. First, the name of a character is not protected by copyright as copyright does not protect names. Second, a physical portrayal of a character may attain some copyright protection. For instance, if the character is represented in a drawing in a comic strip, the drawing may be protected as an artistic work. Third, if a copyright work contains a character as a substantial part of it, and includes highly distinctive characteristics of the character, the character may be subject to copyright protection (for example, if copied accurately and in detail, it might constitute a violation of copyright).

In one court case, the illicit reproduction of the cartoon character Popeye the Sailor in the form of brooches, charms and plastic dolls was held to violate a substantial part of the original copyright work.[9]

In any legal suit dealing with the violation of copyright of a fictional character, a successful defence must show:

- a similarity in the expression of the idea of the character in the original and copied versions of the character
- the character has significant importance to the original work
- the character possesses original and distinctive characteristics
- the character has a certain popularity, including one in the eyes of the violator that entices a deliberate appropriation of the character

Industrial Designs

We have already seen, in Chapter 1, that industrial design constitutes one of the five traditional areas of intellectual property. Until the 1988 legislative changes, there was much confusion concerning the relationship between the *Copyright Act* and the *Industrial Design Act* because of the overlapping protection provided by copyright and industrial design law. Under the current law, the *Copyright Act* carves out certain works, which, under certain circumstances, are no longer subject to copyright protection, but are protected under the *Industrial Design Act* (provided they meet the requirements including the registration ones in the *Industrial Design Act*).

In simplified terms, certain artistic works such as designs that are "applied to useful objects" that in turn are created in quantities of more than fifty units, or plates, engravings or casts used to produce more than fifty units of such useful articles, are not protected by copyright but instead come within the realm of industrial design protection.

These artistic works that may be protected as industrial designs must fall into at least one of the following categories: shape, configuration, pattern or ornament (which are appreciated solely by the eye). The design must not represent a purely utilitarian function or the method of construction of an article. The design itself will be protected by the law, but the functional part of the article to which the design is applied is not subject to protection. Examples of industrial designs are the pattern on wallpaper or the shape of a lampshade.

The exceptions to the general rule are set out in the *Copyright Act*. In the following circumstances, a design is protected by copyright even if it is applied to useful articles that are reproduced in quantities of more than fifty units:

- "a graphic or photographic representation that is applied to the face of an article"
  Example: decoration on a calendar, a painting on a plate, posters

- items relating to "character merchandising"
  Example: representation of a real person (the prime minister), a fictitious being (Bart Simpson), event (the Olympic games) or place (the National Gallery), which is "applied to an article as a feature of shape, configuration, pattern or ornament" (i.e., a mug with a picture of Bart Simpson)

- a trade-mark or label used in conjunction with products reproduced in quantities of more than fifty

- "material that has a woven or knitted pattern or that is suitable for piece goods or surface coverings or for making wearing apparel"
  Example: printed wallpaper or woven draperies

- buildings that qualify as architectural works of art

- "articles that are sold as a set, unless more than fifty sets are made"
  Example: golf clubs, set of dishes

The Governor-in-Council has the authority to specify other types of works or articles that may come under this exception and be protected by copyright.

The law as set out above is very complicated and expert advice should be sought if you think your work may cross the line between industrial design and copyright protection.

FOLKLORE

According to *The Funk & Wagnalls Standard Dictionary Comprehensive International Edition* (1968), folklore is "The traditions, beliefs, customs, sayings, stories, etc., preserved among the common people." Examples of folklore are oral stories, songs, dances and dance steps. In some cases, folklore may fit within one of the categories protected by copyright. However, items classified as folklore do not always fit the criteria necessary for protection of copyright materials (for instance, they are not fixed) and, as such, are not protected by copyright. Since Canadian law does not deal specifically with the protection of such folklore, situations will remain where folklore is not protected by copyright law.

GOVERNMENT MATERIALS

Government materials, also called "Crown works," are protected by copyright. This includes the works of federal, provincial and territorial governments. Generally, municipal governments are not considered Crown works because municipal governments are not emanations of the Crown.

OTHER WORKS

Works described under this subheading refer to, and include, many of the above-mentioned works when they are compiled or collected in a specific way or where more than one author is involved.

Collective Works

A collective work is "any work written in distinct parts by different authors, or in which works or parts of works of different authors are incorporated." Examples of collective works are an encyclopedia, dictionary, year book or similar work, a newspaper, review, magazine or similar periodical—whether in print or in a digital form. Collective works need not, however, be limited to literary works. A collective work may be a book of photographs or musical works. Also, a protected collective work need not be comprised of works that are protected by copyright. There can be copyright in a collective work when elements, or all of the portions, making up the collective work are in the public domain. Further, there may be copyright in a collective work comprised of previously published materials. For example, there may be copyright in a collection of "Best Canadian Short Stories of 2000" containing short stories by different authors that have previously been published in magazines and literary journals.

In order for a work to qualify as a collective work, there must be originality in the making of the work. In this sense, the originality relates to the skill and labour exerted to make the collective work. For example, a mere joining of two individual works will probably not constitute a collective work. Whether there is sufficient skill and labour in the making of a collective work is a question that must be examined based upon the circumstances in each individual case.

It is important to understand that two copyrights may exist where there is a collective work. First, there is copyright in the collective work itself, and second, there is copyright in each individual work included in the collection, provided that copyright already exists in those individual works and the individual works are not in the public domain. For example, in the case of a newspaper, there is copyright in the newspaper as a whole. As well, there is copyright in each individual article in the newspaper.

Compilations

A compilation, in copyright parlance, is very close to the everyday meaning of the word. Basically, a compilation is the result of the gathering of materials from other sources. For example, an encyclopedia, dictionary, Web site or CD-ROM may qualify as a compilation. It does not matter if the sources from which the data or information is gathered are protected by copyright, easily accessible or in the public domain. However, if the sources are protected by copyright, the compiler must clear copyright in these works before including them in the compilation.

The *Copyright Act* defines a compilation as "a work resulting from the selection or arrangement of literary, dramatic, musical or artistic works or parts thereof, or a work resulting from the selection or arrangement of data." Whether a compilation is a compilation of literary, artistic or other type of work is a matter of fact to be determined in each particular situation. It is difficult to predict how a court of law might determine the category of work in which to classify the compilation. For example, is a compilation containing five literary works, one musical work and three artistic works, a compilation of literary work? It is possible that the test would be based on the duration of the works, that is, if there is a musical work seven minutes long and three readings of literary works each one minute long, the compilation could be classified as a musical work rather than a literary work. And what if the compilation was a combination of text and photographs or text and sounds and moving images? With text and photographs, the comparison could be the number of square inches or the number of bytes although again this is impossible to predict. It is most likely to be determined on a quantitative basis where a single large work, whether in duration or bytes or square inches, could outweigh more numerous works in a different category. The categorization of a compilation is important for purposes of voluntary registration with the Canadian government, duration of copyright, rights protected, and so on.

A compilation is protected by copyright if certain elements went into the making of it. Whether a work would be considered a compilation is a matter of fact, which must be decided based on the circumstances in each individual case. Some factors a court might take into account in making this factual determination would be the compiler's knowledge, experience, judgement, research, skill, time, labour, thought, arrangement and selection put into the making of the compilation.

Generally, there is only one copyright in a compilation; that is, the copyright in the compilation itself. However, if the materials that form the compilation enjoy copyright protection, they will continue to enjoy copyright and moral rights protection on their own. If there is a collection of compilations, that collection may qualify as a collective work.

DATABASES

Simply put, a database is an assembly or compilation of facts, data, content or information in an organized format and whose individual components may be individually accessed. A database may be as simple as a collection of names and phone numbers, or as complex as a listing of every article ever written on astrology or a library catalogue.

In copyright parlance, a database would be considered a compilation, as it is a compilation of information. Thus, databases are protected by copyright. The fact that the database is in electronic or print format is irrelevant to its protection. In order for a database to be protected by copyright, it has to meet the general criteria of compilations, for instance, there must be sufficient original skill and labour put into the selection and arrangement of data.

Note that it is the database itself, the collection of data, and not the information contained in the database that is protected by copyright. This is similar to the concept that an idea is not protected by copyright, only the expression of it. The components in a database are separate from the database and if they are protected by copyright (for instance, they are eligible for protection or the duration of their protection has not expired), they continue to be protected as a separate copyright work from the database. If these components are not protected by copyright, when compiled as a database, they do not by themselves acquire a separate copyright in them. However, whatever the copyright status of its underlying individual components, the database itself may have its own copyright protection.

Under Canadian copyright law, some databases, whether digital or not, are not protected by copyright. This is because these databases do not meet one of the general criterions for copyright protection—sufficient originality—which means that the degree of skill, judgement and labour involved in the arranging and selecting of the content in the database is too low. For example, a recent case held that telephone listings contained in the "yellow pages" was not a protectable database under Canadian law. The Court held that there was insufficient skill, judgement and labour involved in the overall arrangement of the compiled information and its arrangement according to headings.

BLANK FORMS

Blank forms—that is, forms with grids or boxes into which information can be placed—may be protected by copyright. For copyright purposes, these forms may be classified as compilations (e.g., they could be compilations of literary or artistic works). As compilations, these forms must possess some literary information in the copyright meaning of this phrase. For instance, if the forms are more than mere copies of other forms, and sufficient judgement, skill and labour are used in making them, they may be protected by copyright. In one case where accounting forms were held to be protected by copyright, the judge said that for copyright to subsist in a "compilation of the commercial type here" there must be "a literary sense of functionally assisting, guiding, or pointing the way to some end."[10]

Works of Joint Authorship

A work of joint authorship is sometimes confused with a collective work. However, the definitions of these two works as they appear in the *Copyright Act* help to distinguish them.

The *Copyright Act* defines a work of joint authorship as a "work produced by the collaboration of two or more authors in which the contribution of one author is not distinct from the contribution of the other author or authors." Thus, in order for a work to qualify as one of joint authorship, two conditions must be met:

- the work must be created by two or more authors
- the contribution of each author must not be distinct from the contribution of any of the other authors

The above definition of a work of joint authorship should help dissolve the confusion between a collective work and a work of joint authorship. Although in both cases, works are created by more than one author, it is only in the case of a work of joint authorship that the contributions of each author are not separable and indistinguishable from that of the other author. In some cases, a collective work may also be a work of joint authorship, that is, where more than one person was responsible for compiling the individual works that comprise the collective work.

An example of a work of joint authorship is the song "Revolution" which was composed by John Lennon and Paul McCartney. This does not mean that all songs are works of joint authorship, especially if the words and music are credited separately. In each case, the law, as set out above, must be applied to the particular facts at hand.

Some of the factors that might be considered in determining whether a work is one of joint authorship is that each contribution must be substantial, though not necessarily equal, and that there must be "joint labour in carrying out a common design." Providing ideas or inspiration, or involvement in the expression of ideas is not enough, especially if such a contribution did not include any research, compilation or writing necessary to create a work. In addition, the contributions need not be made simultaneously.

A court recently held in a case involving Canadian singer Sarah McLachlan that whether the contribution of a co-author is significant for a co-authorship depends on both quantitative and qualitative factors, including the relation of the contribution to the work as a whole. The Court decided that in order to be considered joint authors, each author must have contributed significant original expression to the work, intended that his or her contribution be merged with that of the other author into a unitary whole, and intended the other person to be a joint author of the work.[11]

One case has held that "a person who merely suggests certain ideas without contributing anything to the literary or dramatic form of the copyright is not a joint author."[12] However, where two people jointly write a book or screenplay, for example, and only one of them is actually putting the ideas, etc., on paper, both persons would most likely be considered joint authors.

Since there is only one work created when there are two or more authors of a work, there is only one copyright in a work of joint authorship. (However, if a collective work is also a work of joint authorship, there may be more than one copyright by nature of it being a collective work.)

OTHER SUBJECT-MATTER

Performers' performances, sound recordings and communication (or broadcast) signals are non-traditional copyright materials referred to as "other subject-matter" in the *Copyright Act*. They are protected on a different basis than works, and issues like authorship and originality, which are discussed in various parts of this book, do not apply to these non-traditional copyright materials.

Performers' Performances

For purposes of copyright law, a "performer's performance" refers to live performances such as a musician performing a song, a person reading a novel or poem, or an actor acting in a play. It also includes a performance of a work in the public domain or one that has not been recorded, an improvisation of a dramatic, musical or literary work such as a jam session—and a recorded performance of an actor, author, singer, musician and dancer on a variety of media including tape, CD-ROMs, video and film, and compilations of these recordings.

Note that copyright protection in a performer's performance is different than and separate from the right of public performance, which is the right to perform a copyright work as opposed to a right in the performance itself.

Sound Recordings

The *Copyright Act* defines a sound recording as "a recording, fixed in any material form, consisting of sounds, whether or not of a performance of a work" and it specifically excludes a soundtrack of a film where the soundtrack accompanies the film. Examples of sound recordings include a recording of a bird chirping, music, an acted-out drama, a lecture and recorded seminars. Even recordings of works that are in the public domain such as a Bach *Prelude*, may be protected as a sound recording. Also included are compilations of sound recordings, for example, on a CD. The sound recording would be protected on any sort of media including vinyl, tape, CD, DAT (digital audio tape), and on the Web.

An important and difficult concept to grasp is that three copyrights may exist when a sound recording is involved. First, there is copyright protection in the sound recording. Second, there may be copyright in any protected works embodied on the sound recording. Third, there may be a copyright in a performer's performance. Therefore, if a musical work is recorded, there is protection in the musical work, the sound recording and the performer's performance. These are important concepts to keep in mind when determining what rights attach to a work reproduced on a sound recording.

Music Videos

Although not contemplated when the *Copyright Act* was written in 1921, music videos are protected by the *Act*. Different components of a music video may be protected in different manners. For instance, the sound track to a music video may be separately protected, arguably as a sound recording, though the category under which it would be protected is subject to debate. The visual aspect of the video may be protected in the same manner as other audio-visual works, which are discussed above.

Communication Signals

The *Act* defines a communications signal as "radio waves transmitted through space without any artificial guide, for reception by the public." Protected broadcasts include television broadcasts and pay-per-view broadcasts, but not satellite or cable retransmitted signals. A radio signal is also protected.

SUMMARY

Canadian copyright law protects, explicitly and implicitly, a broad variety of creations or "works" under the categories of literary, dramatic, musical and artistic works. Collective works, compilations and works of joint authorship are also protected by copyright. In addition, copyright protects other subject-matter like performers' performances, sound recordings and broadcast signals. The classification of a work or other subject-matter protected by copyright is important with respect to duration of protection, ownership and the rights of copyright owners.

Chapter 7

WHO
OWNS
COPYRIGHT?

*Because copyright is the mechanism for establishing
ownership, it is increasingly seen as the key to wealth
in the Information Age.*

Charles C. Mann,
"Who Will Own Your Next Good Idea?,"
The Atlantic Monthly, September 1998

OWNING COPYRIGHT

In determining the ownership of copyright materials, recall that every creation has two rights. There is a right in the physical property of the creation and there is a separate and distinct right in its intangible property. The right in the physical ownership of a book is separate and distinct from copyright and, for instance, the right to adapt that book into a film. This chapter will focus on the second right—the intangible right—which you now know is copyright.

The ownership of copyright is important because it determines who has control over, and who is entitled to remuneration from, that protected material. The owner, who may or may not also be the author of a work, is the sole and exclusive person with the right to say yes or no to a particular use of that work. He or she is the one who benefits from the exploitation of a copyright work, and the one to be contacted in order to clear permission to use the work.

THE GENERAL RULE

The general rule of ownership is stated in the *Copyright Act* as the following: "Subject to this Act, the author of a work shall be the first owner of the copyright therein."

Who Is the Author of a Work Protected by Copyright?

According to the general rule of ownership of copyright works, the author of a work is the work's first owner. This raises the question, who is the author of a work? There is no one definite definition of "author" in the *Act*. Court cases have helped interpret the meaning of author in the copyright sense.

According to these cases, the author is the person who creates the work, or the first person to express the idea in a tangible form; for example, the person who puts the work on paper or otherwise "fixes" it. A person who writes a book is its author; a person who draws a painting is its author; a person who composes a musical work is the author of the song, and a person who designs graphics for a Web page is the author of those graphics. A stenographer, however, would not be considered an author. But a ghost writer would probably be considered an author.

In determining the author of a work, remember the general copyright principle that copyright does not protect ideas but only the expressions of those ideas. It follows from this principle that the author is not the person who merely supplies ideas, but the person who expresses those ideas. However, if two people are jointly writing a screenplay, for example, and only one of them is actually putting the ideas in a tangible form (i.e., on paper), these persons would most likely be considered joint authors. But someone who comments, edits or suggests changes to a work would not necessarily be a co-author of that work, unless the contributions were concrete enough to be a tangible part of the expressed idea. Also, where an author originally puts down an idea in a rough form and a second writer rewrites it, these authors would probably be considered co-authors of the finished work.

Some provisions in the *Copyright Act* are specific about the "author" of certain copyright works. Where there is no such provision, the guidelines set out above must be applied to your particular case to determine the author of the work.

It is relevant to mention again that this book uses the term author and creator interchangeably.

Although the author and owner of a copyright work may be the same person, this is not necessarily the case. Different provisions in the *Copyright Act* distinctly speak of author and owner. For example, duration of copyright is based on the life of the author. Exploitation of copyright works can only be by copyright owners. Moral rights only protect authors of copyright works. The distinction between author and owner is referred to throughout this book.

There are no authors of other subject-matter, just owners, as discussed later in this chapter.

The Second and Subsequent Owners of Copyright

Although the general rule is that the author is the first owner of copyright, the *Act* is careful in stating that this rule applies "subject to the *Act*." The *Act* contemplates a number of specific circumstances where this general rule does not apply. The rule may not apply with regard to specific works and with regard to specific situations. Before assuming that the general rule of ownership applies in your particular case, check the discussion below in light of your specific circumstances.

Keep in mind that the owner of the copyright in a work can, and often does, change. This subject is further discussed in Chapter 11: How Can Rights be Exploited?

SPECIFIC WORKS

Specific works that do not follow the general rule of ownership, or to which the general rule is difficult to apply, are discussed below.

Where your situation falls within one of the specific works, also check that one of the specific situations in the subsequent section does not override the principle set out with respect to the specific work.

Letters

When you write a letter, whether it is a personal or business letter, you are the owner of copyright in that letter. This holds true unless, for instance, in the case of a business letter, the letter was written as part of a job (in which case the employer will own the copyright in it). Even after a letter has been mailed or otherwise sent to someone else, the author of the letter retains the ownership of copyright in it. Thus, only the author of the letter has the right to reproduce it in any form whatsoever. The same rules apply to e-mail.

Photographs

The author of a photograph is the person who owns the initial negative or other plate at the time when that negative or other plate was made. If there is no negative or other plate, the author is the owner of the initial photograph at the time when that photograph was made. The author is the first owner of copyright in the photograph. Even though a photographer may be the person principally responsible for the composition of a photograph, he or she will not automatically own that photograph unless he or she is the owner of the negative or plate from which it was made, or the owner of the initial photograph. Also see the discussion below on portraits and on commissioned works.

The *Copyright Act* specifically refers to corporations owning photographs. Where a corporation is the owner of a photograph, it is deemed to reside within a treaty country if it has a place of business therein.

Portraits

Ownership of a portrait vests in the creator of that portrait. However, where the portrait is commissioned or made in the course of employment or apprenticeship, copyright will belong to the person who commissioned the portrait or employer, unless there is an agreement to the contrary. Commissioned portraits are discussed further below.

There are two non-copyright concerns with respect to photographers of portraits. First, a photographer who owns copyright in a portrait should be cautious of using the portrait in any manner that may perturb the person who is the subject of the portrait. Second, photographers who take photographs of people, though not necessarily in the form of portraits, might want to consider obtaining "model releases" from these persons to protect themselves with respect to legal areas other than copyright.

Engravings

The creator of an engraving is the first owner of the copyright in it. This is true unless the engraving was commissioned or made in the course of employment or apprenticeship, and there is no agreement that stipulates otherwise. Also, see the discussion on commissioned works below.

Audio-visual Works

Audio-visual works are subject to the general rule of ownership, however it is not always straightforward who is the author and therefore first owner of copyright in audio-visual works.

SCRIPTED WORKS

The author or first owner of copyright in a scripted audio-visual work is not expressly provided for in the *Act*. This is a matter of controversy. Some argue that the author is the producer of the film (i.e., the one principally responsible for the arrangements undertaken for the making of the film), while others argue that a film's director, or even a screenwriter, is its author. It is further arguable that the producer is the owner, and the author is the director (by him or herself or along with other contributors to the film). There is no Canadian case law on this point. Unlike ownership of copyright, authorship is a matter of law and cannot be changed by contractual arrangements. Once one decides who is the author of an audio-visual work, then the general rule—author as first owner—is applied. Notwithstanding who owns the copyright in a film, the author of the film owns the moral rights in it and duration of protection is based on the author's life. Because the duration of a scripted audio-visual work is based on the life of the work's author, a corporation could not be the author of the work.

Although the author or first owner of copyright in a scripted audio-visual work is not specifically mentioned in the *Act*, the *Act* states that the maker of a cinematographic work is "the person by whom the arrangements necessary for the making of the work are undertaken." The maker is referred to in other parts of the legislation.

Although a film is a copyright work itself, the screenwriter, music composer, stage designer and others continue to have copyright in the works they created for the film.

NON-SCRIPTED WORKS

Like scripted works, the author of a non-scripted work is not expressly provided for in the *Act* and is a matter of controversy. Where a production company hires and is the employer of a director and producer, the company is the first owner of copyright in the non-scripted work (e.g., instruction video) however, this does not help determine who is the author of the work.

Non-scripted works made before January 1, 1994

For non-scripted works made prior to January 1, 1994, the author and first owner is the owner of the medium of fixation regardless of whether it is a negative or magnetic tape.

Musical Works

The law is unclear with respect to the ownership of musical works. This is because of the confusion over whether musical works are subject to two copyrights—one in the music as a musical work and a second one in the lyrics as a literary work. Where the same person creates the tune and lyrics, ownership in that song, as tune and lyrics, vests in that one person. Also, where two or more people together write a tune and lyrics and the contribution of each person is indistinguishable from that of the other person, then those two or more persons are joint authors of the song. However, the situation is not as straightforward where one author writes the lyrics and another person composes the tune. It is arguable that each contributor owns copyright in his or her contribution or that they jointly own copyright in the song as a whole.

In practice, most copyrights in musical works are assigned to a music publisher who then acts on behalf of the authors of the musical works. Thus, the vast majority of copyright permissions can be cleared through the music publisher, without concern to the manner in which the *Copyright Act* denotes the authors of the musical works. Where there is no music publisher, and one person writes the lyrics and another person composes the tune, permission to use the song may be required from both authors as there may be two separate copyrights, the lyricist and music composer each owning copyright in their individual and distinct contributions. Where the contribution of each person is indistinguishable from that of the other person(s), then permission to use the song would be required from both of the joint authors. The right of public performance in a musical work is almost always cleared through SOCAN, a copyright collective, which is discussed in detail in Chapter 14: Using Copyright Materials.

Newspaper, Magazine or Periodical Contributions

This subheading refers to any contributions to newspapers, magazines or periodicals, including contributions by writers and photographers. Recall that copyright does not exist in news, facts and information, but in the manner in which these things are conveyed. As such, the contributions referred to in this section are not news, facts or information, but expressions in any format of the news items, facts or information. For purposes of this discussion, newspaper, magazine and periodical contributors will be divided into two categories: freelancers and staff persons.

FREELANCERS

As a general rule, freelancers are authors and first copyright owners of their individual contributions to newspapers, magazines or periodicals, unless they have agreed otherwise. For purposes of clarity and because of on-going American and Canadian lawsuits, it is prudent as a freelancer or when working with one, to clarify in writing what specific uses may be made of the freelancer's contribution. For instance, may the work be published in the print edition of the newspaper or magazine, in addition to the elec-tronic edition, or would separate rights need to be obtained, and payment made for use in the electronic edition?

STAFF PERSONS

Staff persons are also authors of their contributions, but are in a different position than freelancers with respect to copyright ownership. Generally, staff persons or "employed" persons have no copyright in their distinct contributions to newspapers, magazines or periodicals. In these cases, the employer of the staff person owns the copyright in that work, but this is a limited type of ownership. The author still retains the right to prohibit the work's publication outside of a newspaper, magazine or similar periodical. For instance, a staff journalist has no right to prevent an article from being first published in the newspaper of his or her employer, then subsequently in the employer's magazine, but the journalist can stop it from being repro-duced in a book or adapted to a film. These rules apply unless there is an agreement to the contrary.

Collective Works

If you recall, a "collective work" is "any work written in distinct parts by different authors, or in which works or parts of works of different authors are incorporated." Examples of collective works are a newspaper, an anthology and an encyclopedia. Two or more separate copyrights may exist in a collective work and therefore there may be two or more copyright owners in a collective work. Copyright exists in the collective work itself, and separately in each individual work that is a part of that collection.

With respect to the collection as a whole, the person who selects or arranges the works that go into the collection is the author and first owner of the copyright in it. This means that the authors of the individual contri-butions are not joint owners of the copyright in the collection. There may be circumstances where there is more than one owner of copyright in a collective work. This may occur where more than one person was responsible for "collecting" the individual works that comprise the collection. In this case, these persons may be considered joint authors and co-owners of the collection.

With respect to the individual contributions that make up a collective work, the individual copyright holders of these contributions continue to hold copyright in them.

An example will illustrate the concept of ownership in collective works. This example will look at a collection of poems. In our example, prior to the collection being compiled, each poet has copyright in his or her poems (and none is in the public domain). When a collection is made of these poems, there are two different layers of copyright ownership. Each individual poet will continue to own copyright in his or her contribution; the compiler of the collection of poems will own copyright in the collection as a whole. The same principles apply in the case of a magazine. There is copyright in the entire magazine that may, for example, belong to the publisher, and there may also be copyright in each individual article in that magazine, belonging to the author of each article (provided the authors are freelance writers and are not employees of the publisher).

Compilations

A compilation is a selection or arrangement of parts or wholes of copyright works or data, resulting in a new work such as a dictionary or database. The person responsible for making the compilation is the author and first copyright owner of that compilation. If copyright existed in any of the works from which the compilation was made, the copyright owners of those works would continue to hold copyright in them. The compiler must clear copyright in any copyright-protected underlying works.

Adaptations and Arrangements

An adaptation or arrangement may be a change in format from a book to a screenplay, or scoring a musical work composed for a violin, or a piano. The author and first copyright owner in these "new" works is the person who adapts the work, for instance, the screenwriter or person who created the new musical score.

Note that permission must be sought from the copyright owner of the original work before adapting it. Also, use of an adaptation may require copyright permission from both the copyright owner of the original work and the copyright holder of the adaptation. Further, not every adaptation is a new copyright work; as explained in the previous chapter, the adaptation must possess sufficient skill and labour to qualify as a copyright protected work.

Translations

The author and first copyright owner of a translation is the person who produces the translation.

Permission must be obtained from the copyright owner of the original work before a translation is begun. If a third person wants to use the translation, for example, for broadcast, permission must be obtained from both the copyright owner of the original work and the copyright holder of the translation.

Papers, Dissertations and Other School Work

The author and first owner of any paper, dissertation or other work prepared for school courses and degree programs is the author of the work, i.e., the student preparing the paper, dissertation, etc.

SPECIFIC SITUATIONS

Commissioned Works

The general rule of ownership applies to many situations of commissioned works. However, there is a special rule that applies to commissioned engravings, photographs or portraits. The *Copyright Act* states that where the work being commissioned is an engraving, photograph or portrait, the person ordering that work is "deemed" to be the first owner of the copyright in it, provided the following conditions are met:

- the person ordering the work has offered and paid "valuable consideration" such as money or services
- the work was created because of the order and was not created prior to the order being made

This is true provided there is no agreement between the commissioner and the creator stating that copyright subsists with the creator of the work.

The importance of the provision for commissioned works is highlighted in the following example. A family portrait is taken by a commercial photographer. The photographer is the owner of the initial negative of the portrait when that negative was made and therefore is the author of the photograph (and therefore normally the copyright owner). The family wants to make extra copies of the portrait. Without the commissioned works provision, the family cannot make these extra copies unless they have the permission of the photographer. Thus, the provision ensures that the family is the owner of the family portrait, notwithstanding ownership of the initial negative at the time the negative was made.

Just because this provision only applies to certain works—engravings, photographs and portraits—it does not mean that the copyright in all other types of commissioned works is owned by the creator of the work, and not the commissioner of it. In situations involving works other than engravings, photographs and portraits, the commissioner may obtain copyright by making an agreement to that effect with the creator of the work.

Works Made in the Course of Employment

Many of the principles concerning ownership of specific works may be overridden where these works are made in the course of employment.

Works made in the course of employment may include anything from letters to internal memoranda to computer software to film scripts to photographs. Some employees are employed for the purpose of creating copyright works, such as scriptwriters, Web site designers and photographers, where others incidentally create copyright works while performing their regular tasks, for example, lawyers or policy analysts. The discussion here applies equally to all types of employment situations.

The general principle regarding works made in the course of employment is that copyright ownership in such works initially belongs to the employer. There are three criteria that must be met in order for a work to be owned by an employer:

- the employee must be employed under a "contract of service"
- the work must be created in the course of performing this contract
- there must not be any contract or provision in a contract that states that the employee owns the copyright (such a contract need not be in writing)

The *Copyright Act* does not set out exactly what constitutes an employment relationship and each situation must be determined according to the facts of that particular situation. These are some of the factors and questions a court may examine when determining whether there is an employment relationship:

- Did the employee conceive the work during employment?
- Did the employer give orders to create the specific work?
- Did the employer give orders on how the work was to be done?
- Was the work carried out under the supervision of the employer?
- Did the employer have control over the author's work?
- Was the work created as an integral part of the workings of the business?
- Was the work created as part of the ordinary duties of the creator?
- Was the work created in the course of the employment or employment contract?
- Was the work created during the normal hours of employment?
- Was the work created on the employer's premises?
- Was the work created for the business (as opposed to being created for personal use)?
- Is the work closely related to the type of business of the employer?
- Was the work created for the exclusive use of the business?

Where the majority of answers to the above questions are in the affirmative, then you are leaning towards an "employment" situation.

An example where copyright belongs to an employer is the case where a math teacher writes examination papers to be used with the teacher's students. On the other hand, if this same teacher writes a work of fiction during the weekends, he or she would own copyright in that fiction work.

Copyright conditions in any employment situation may be reversed by a contract. A contract granting copyright to employees for works made in the course of employment may be done individually for each work, or generally for all works made during the term of employment. All items in such an agreement are negotiable.

Because an employment situation always depends on the particular facts of the case, it is best to have a written agreement that sets out whether or not it is an employment situation, at least for purposes of ownership of copyright materials.

Note that even where employers own copyright in their employees' creations, the employees are still the authors of these creations. This is important with respect to the duration of copyright protection, and also with respect to moral rights.

WORKING IN OTHER COUNTRIES

If you are working in other countries or are working in Canada with a foreign company, you may be subject to different laws and contractual relationships concerning the ownership of copyright works. Be sure to check your contracts and also read Chapter 5: How Does International Copyright Protection Work?, which sets out principles relating to international copyright. Chapter 15 contains specific information on how the United States deals with works created in the course of employment.

Works Created During an Apprenticeship

Works created during an apprenticeship are subject to the same rules as works created during the course of employment.

Professionals, Consultants and Independent Contractors

Consultants and independent contractors are the authors of, and generally own the copyright in, their works, unless they have agreed otherwise. Thus, a lawyer or self-employed statistician will own the copyright in any documents prepared by them, even if prepared on behalf of a client, unless they have agreed otherwise. Whether you are an employed person is a question of fact that can only be determined by examining your particular circumstances. In order to help determine whether you qualify as a consultant or as an independent contractor, go through the questions listed under the subheading "Works Made in the Course of Employment," as these are the questions a court would consider when determining the same.

Works Made for or Published by the Government

The *Copyright Act* states that where any work is, or has been, prepared or published by or under the direction or control of any government department, the copyright in that work belongs to the government. This is subject to any agreement to the contrary.

Government employees include those employed in federal or provincial government departments as well as Crown corporations.

Even where the government owns copyright in works prepared by or under its direction or control, the creators of these works are their authors.

Works Made by Two or More Authors

There are two types of works that may be made by two or more authors. One type is a collective work, which is discussed above under specific works, and the second, discussed here, is a work of joint authorship.

A work of joint authorship is a work produced by the collaboration of two or more authors in which the contribution of one author is not distinct from the contribution of the other author or authors.

There is only one copyright in the case of works of joint authorship. Co-authors of "works of joint authorship" are co-owners of the work. They must jointly exercise their rights in the specific copyright work. Neither author is an exclusive owner of the copyright in the work and neither author can authorize the use of his or her work without the other author's approval. For example, neither co-writer of a screenplay can license the right to a producer to produce the screenplay without the permission of the other co-writer.

A work of joint authorship may also be a collective work if the joint authors produced the resulting work from other sources or works. In this situation, there will be two copyrights and two copyright owners—the joint authors will own the copyright in the collective work, and each individual author will own copyright in his or her individual contribution (provided copyright still exists in the contribution).

Corporations

The *Act* specifically allows for corporations to be "authors," and therefore owners, of copyright in photographs and sound recordings. Corporations may also be owners of copyright materials where an author has assigned copyright to them or in the case of employed, apprenticed or commissioned creators. Corporations may also be able to use copyright materials through contractual arrangements with the creator or copyright owner.

Works Generated by, and with the Aid of, Computer Software

The *Copyright Act* does not specifically address the situation of works generated with the aid of computers and computer programs. In general, if you create, control and manipulate an image or other copyright material with the help of a computer or computer program, you are the author of the new work. Whether you own that creation depends on the factors discussed in this chapter that are set out for the determination of ownership of creations. By creating works with the help of a computer program, you will never acquire rights in that computer program. Also, keep in mind that you require permission to scan a copyright work into a computer and to adapt or manipulate it.

Where a copyright work is generated by a computer in a circumstance where there is no human author, the author would probably be the person who made the necessary arrangements (i.e., controlled or manipulated the computer in order to create the copyright work).

OTHER SUBJECT-MATTER

The above rules relating to who is the author and owner of a work do not apply to other subject-matter. Specific rules for other subject-matter are set out below.

Performers' Performances

The performer owns the copyright in his or her performance.

Sound Recordings

The "maker" of a sound recording owns the copyright in it. A "maker" is defined as "the person by whom the arrangements necessary for the first fixation of the sounds are undertaken," which in lay language is the producer of the sound recording.

Communication Signals

The broadcaster who broadcasts a signal owns the copyright in it. The *Act* defines a broadcaster as "a body that, in the course of operating a broadcasting undertaking, broadcasts a communication signal in accordance with the law of the country in which the broadcasting undertaking is carried on." It excludes a body whose primary activity regarding communication signals is their retransmission.

MORAL RIGHTS

This section will look at ownership of moral rights. You may wish to first read the full description of moral rights set out in Chapter 9: Rights Protected By Copyright, then return to this portion, which discusses the ownership of these rights.

The purpose of moral rights is to protect the honour and reputation of an author. Since moral rights protect the author directly and are "personal" rights, it is felt that they cannot be exercised except by authors themselves or by their heirs. It follows that even after copyright has been assigned in a work, moral rights remain with the author. Thus, the holder of moral rights is always the author of a work, even where the author is not the holder of the copyright in the work. This is also true in employment situations. Even where an employer is, by virtue of employment, the owner of copyright in a work, the employee retains the moral rights in his or her creations. In Canada, the only way that an author can forfeit moral rights is by "waiving" them (agreeing not to exercise them), or by passing them on upon death (see more on assigning and waiving moral rights in Chapter 11: How Can Rights Be Exploited?).

An example will illustrate the concept of ownership of moral rights. Mr. Smart purchases a painting of a lady and when doing so also purchases the copyright in that painting. Because Mr. Smart owns the copyright in the painting, he can do anything with the painting that only the copyright owner may do. For example, he can reproduce the painting (e.g., photograph it or scan it into a computer) or exhibit it in public. However, notwithstanding that he owns copyright in the painting, he cannot do anything with that painting that might violate the author's moral rights (unless he has obtained a waiver of the moral rights). For example, Mr. Smart cannot put a moustache on the lady's face or use the painting in association with a service, cause or institution in a manner that may be prejudicial to the honour or reputation of the artist.

Other Subject-Matter
There are no moral rights in other subject-matter.

SUMMARY
The general rule of ownership in copyright is that the author of a work is the first owner of the copyright therein. The author is the person who first fixes the work. There are a number of exceptions to this general rule that apply with respect to a number of specific works, and in a number of specific situations. Further, copyright ownership can change through contractual arrangements.

There are special rules for ownership of other subject-matter.

Notwithstanding the ownership of copyright in a work, moral rights always belong to the author of the work. Moral rights cannot be assigned, but they can be waived or passed on upon death.

Chapter 8
THE DURATION
OF COPYRIGHT

> *Her heirs [Margaret Mitchell's] decided to allow a*
> *sequel of [*Gone With the Wind*] while they still*
> *controlled the property. Mitchell's copyright expires*
> *in 2011.*
>
> "Scarlett's fate revealed in long-awaited sequel,"
> *The Globe and Mail*, August 10, 1991

A LIMITED DURATION

Unlike physical property, ownership in copyright protected material has a limited duration. Whereas you can own your house for an indefinite amount of time, you can only own the copyright in your book or sculpture for the period of time stipulated in the *Copyright Act*.

GENERAL RULE FOR WORKS

There is a general rule concerning the duration of copyright. The general rule applies unless specific provisions exist in the *Act* for that type of work or situation. These specific provisions are outlined below and should be read along with the general rule.

General Rule

The *Copyright Act* provides the general rule for the length of copyright protection for published works as "the life of the author, the remainder of the calendar year in which the author dies, and a period of fifty years following the end of that calendar year." Those familiar with copyright often refer to this duration as the life-plus-fifty rule. According to the life-plus-fifty rule, an author will enjoy copyright in a work he or she creates throughout his or her lifetime, and his or her heirs or assignees will enjoy copyright for a period of fifty years until the calendar year end after the author's death. In certain circumstances, the life-plus-fifty rule does not apply. Departures from the general rule are discussed below.

AUTHOR VERSUS OWNER OF A WORK

It is very important, in terms of duration of copyright, to distinguish between the author and the owner of a copyright work. The term of copyright is generally determined by the life of the author, and not by the life of the owner of copyright. This is extremely relevant where copyright has been transferred, or when certain provisions of the law such as the provision dealing with creations made during the course of employment grant copyright to someone other than the creator of the work. In these situations, duration of copyright is still determined by the life of the author. Where duration is tied to the life of the author, the date when the work was created or first published is irrelevant with respect to the term of copyright protection.

The determination of the author of a copyright work is discussed in the previous chapter on ownership of copyright works.

CALCULATION OF THE DURATION

Calculation of the duration of copyright is based on the calendar year plus fifty years, as opposed to the actual date of the author's death. For instance, if a writer died on November 26, 1970, copyright in his books expires on December 31, 2020. In fact, most creations of the same author (unless any creations are subject to a specific provision other than the general rule of copyright) will be protected for the same amount of time. Therefore, all of our exemplified author's published books will be protected until December 31, 2020.

Not long ago, copyright expired fifty years after the exact date of the author's death, and not at the end of the calendar year. Thus, in the above example, copyright in our writer's books would expire on November 26, 2020. The "calendar year" duration applies to all works protected by copyright as of January 1, 1994 (i.e., they were not then in the public domain), no matter when they were created.

Unexploited Works

With regard to the term of copyright protection, works that were not exploited have until very recently been treated differently than exploited works. The term "exploit" in this situation refers to publication, performance in public (which includes delivery of a lecture) and communication to the public by telecommunication. Published does not mean published in the sense of a book publisher publishing a book. In copyright parlance, "published" is a broader concept that includes making copies of the work available to the public in quantities that satisfy the reasonable demands of the public, taking into account the nature of the work in question. Performance in public means a performance outside a family or quasi-family circle. The meaning of publication, performance in public and communication to the public by telecommunication are further explored in Chapter 9: Rights Protected by Copyright.

OLD LAW

Prior to Bill C-32, the general rule with respect to the duration of copyright in unexploited works was that they were protected in perpetuity, or until published or performed in public. This was true with respect to unpublished works of a living author and unpublished works at the time of an author's death. Once a work was published or performed in public, the general rule of copyright for published works applied.

The purpose of perpetual copyright protection in unexploited works was to protect authors and copyright owners from derogations of their private rights. For instance, there may be a desire not to publish certain letters, diaries, sketches and manuscripts. It was believed that if perpetual copyright did not exist, that some authors would destroy their works rather than have them ever fall into the public domain. Perpetual copyright in unpublished works has been a major cause of frustration to historians and researchers who can have access to these works, but may not use them in the copyright sense; for example, they may not reproduce or publish them.

CURRENT/NEW LAW

Recent changes to the *Copyright Act* phase out perpetual copyright protection in unexploited works and eventually all works including unexploited ones will be subject to the general rule of life-plus-fifty. As of December 31, 1998, the general rule of duration applies to works not published or performed or communicated to the public by telecommunication (or in the case of lectures, delivered) during the life of an author. This applies to any literary, dramatic or musical work and any engraving. For example, if an author dies after December 31, 1998 with an unpublished manuscript or book, the manuscript or book is protected until the calendar year end in which the author dies and for a period of fifty years following that year end.

There are three exceptions to the above:

- crown or government works are protected until published and for an additional fifty years from the date of publication
- artistic works (except engravings) have always been protected for life-plus-fifty of the artist regardless of whether the work was published during the artist's lifetime
- works with specific durations of protection are not subject to this, that is, works like sound recordings, communications signals, certain cine-matographic works and some photographs – all of which are protected for fifty years after their making

TRANSITIONAL PROVISIONS

The *Copyright Act* provides a number of transitional provisions relating to unexploited works by deceased authors as of December 31, 1998. In the case of an author who died with an unexploited work that her heirs or estate exploited prior to December 31, 1998, the work would be protected for fifty years from the date it is exploited. Where an author died on or after December 31, 1948 and whose works remained unexploited as of December 31, 1998, the work is protected until December 31, 2048. Finally, in the case of an author who died before December 31, 1948 with an unexploited work that remained unex-ploited as of December 31, 1998, the work would be protected until December 31, 2003.

MORAL RIGHTS

The *Copyright Act* specifically states that moral rights subsist for the same term as the copyright in a work. Accordingly, the general rules and specific provisions set out in this chapter apply equally to the moral and economic rights. Thus, moral rights endure for the life of the author plus fifty years from the calendar year of the author's death. Such a term allows heirs to sue on behalf of a deceased author where it seems that a modification to a work resulted in prejudice to the author's honour or reputation, or to protect any other of the moral rights.

The durations of copyright set out in this chapter refer to the "term of copyright," but this expression encompasses the moral rights as well. Thus, any durations of copyright are also the length of protection for moral rights.

SPECIFIC WORKS

Literary, Artistic, Musical, Dramatic and Choreographic Works

The general rule of life-plus-fifty applies to these works, unless specifically provided for otherwise below.

Photographs

Prior to the 1997 amendments, the *Copyright Act* provided that copyright subsisted for fifty years from the end of the calendar year of the making of the initial negative or other plate from which the photograph was directly or indirectly derived or, if there was no negative or other plate, from the making of the initial photograph. The 1997 amendments abolished this special rule for photographs so that the general rule of life-plus-fifty applies to photographs. This helps ensure equal treatment. The changes do not apply to any photographs that have fallen into the public domain prior to January 1, 1999.

The 1997 changes provides two different rules for the duration in photographs depending on who the author is, and if that author is an individual or "natural person" or if the author is a corporation (in which the majority of voting shares are not owned by a natural person.)

AUTHOR AS INDIVIDUAL OR NATURAL PERSON (BEHIND CORPORATION)

If the author/photographer is an individual (as opposed to a corporation), protection lasts for fifty years following the calendar year end of the photographer's death. Also, if the corporation has a natural person as its majority shareholder, copyright in photographs will last for fifty years following the end of the year in which this majority shareholder dies.

AUTHOR AS CORPORATION (NOT OWNED BY A NATURAL PERSON)

If a corporation is deemed to be the author of the photograph and a natural person does not hold the majority of its voting shares, the duration of copyright is fifty years following the end of the year the initial negative or plate was made, or if there is no plate or negative, from the date the photograph was taken.

Audio-visual Works

SCRIPTED AUDIO-VISUAL WORKS

Scripted audio-visual works are subject to the general rule of duration, until the calendar year-end fifty years after the death of the author.

NON-SCRIPTED AUDIO-VISUAL WORKS

Non-scripted audio-visual works made since 1944 are protected for fifty years following the end of the calendar year in which they are first published or made available to the public. If copies are not made available to the public (i.e., they are not published) before the expiration of fifty years following the end of the calendar year of their making, they are protected for fifty years from the calendar year-end of their making.

Non-scripted audio-visual works made before 1944 are subject to protection for fifty years from the date of making.

SPECIFIC SITUATIONS FOR WORKS

Works Made by Two or More Authors

COLLECTIVE WORKS

Recall that examples of collective works are anthologies such as encyclope-dias or magazines. Two copyrights may exist with respect to collective works. In the case of a magazine, for instance, there is copyright in the magazine as a whole, and there is also copyright in each individual article in the magazine. Thus, there may be two different durations of copyright. In order to determine the term of copyright in each component of the collective work, first determine the owner of the copyright in each one, then apply the general rule of duration on one of the specific provisions. Note that because there are two layers of copyright in a collective work, one copyright may expire while the other one continues to run.

WORKS OF JOINT AUTHORSHIP

Works of joint authorship refers to works where there is a single copyright in a work that has been created by more than one author and the contribution of any one author is indistinguishable from that of the other author(s). Copyright in this situation is based on the death of the last living author and for fifty years thereafter until the end of the calendar year.

Authors who are nationals of countries other than Canada, the United States and Mexico that grant a duration of copyright protection shorter than the one above for works of joint authorship cannot claim a longer term in Canada. See the discussion under "Works of Unknown Authors" where the identity of one of the authors in a work of joint authorship is unknown.

Works Exploited after an Author's Death

The *Act* no longer has specific terms of copyright protection for posthumous works, however, for certain works or subject-matter unpublished, or not performed in public or broadcast prior to March 19, 1998, consult the *Copyright Act* (section 7) for details about their term of copyright.

Works of Unknown Authors

Since January 1, 1994, the Canadian *Copyright Act* sets out the term of copyright in works by anonymous and pseudonymous authors. Copyright in anonymous and pseudonymous works lasts for the shorter of fifty years from first publication of the work, or seventy-five years from the making of the work. However, if during the above term, the identity of one or more of the authors becomes commonly known, copyright subsists for the life of whichever of those authors dies last and for fifty years until the end of that calendar year.

Works Prepared in the Course of Employment

The term of copyright protection for works prepared in the course of employment is subject to the life-plus-fifty rule. The life-plus-fifty rule is based on the life of the author, and not the life of employer or copyright owner.

Works Owned by the Government

The *Copyright Act* provides that where a work is, or has been, prepared or published by or under the direction or control of the federal, provincial or territorial government, the copyright in the work continues for a period of fifty years to the calendar year-end from the date of the first publication of the work.

If the work is not published, then it is protected until publication plus fifty years. Some government works are never published and therefore have perpetual copyright protection.

Arrangements, Adaptations and Translations

When determining the duration of copyright in a particular work, you should keep in mind that a new work based on a work in the public domain (i.e., copyright protection has expired), may be subject to a "new" term of copyright protection. For example, a translation of a George Walker play or an adaptation of a Mozart concerto would acquire a "new" term of copyright protection. When a work has been arranged, adapted, translated or the like, the general rule of life-plus-fifty applies to the arranged, adapted or translated work. However, if there is insufficient skill and labour in that adaptation, there will be no new copyright work, and therefore no duration of copyright in that adaptation.

Reversionary Interest Proviso (Twenty-five Years After the Author's Death)

Where the author of a work is the first owner of the copyright in it (it is not a situation of employment, Crown works, commissioned engraving, photograph or portrait), any copyright acquired by contract becomes void twenty-five years after the author's death. This does not mean that the term of copyright is affected. It means that any subsequent owner of copyright will lose his or her rights (provided the conditions apply) twenty-five years after the author's death. At this time, the copyright becomes part of the author's estate and only the estate has the right to deal with the copyright.

There is no reversion where the author disposes of the copyright by will for the period following the twenty-five-year limit. Thus, the section may be avoided by bequeathing copyright for the period between twenty-five and fifty years after the author's death. It also does not apply where a work has been assigned as part of a collective work, or a work or part thereof, that has been licensed to be published in a collective work.

Where a literary, dramatic or musical work or engraving was not published, performed or delivered in public prior to an author's death, the date of calculation for the "twenty-five years after the author's death" runs from the date of publication, performance or delivery in public—twenty-five years from that date.

OTHER SUBJECT-MATTER

Sound Recordings

The *Act* provides that copyright subsists in a sound recording for fifty years from the calendar year end in which the first fixation of the sound recording occurred. According to the *Act*, a "plate" includes "any stereotype or other plate, stone, block, mould, matrix, transfer or negative used or intended to be used for printing or reproducing copies of any work, and any matrix or other appliance used or intended to be used for making or reproducing sound recordings, performers' performances or communication signals." This fifty-year term applies to the original and to various copies pressed from the original.

When determining whether copyright still exists in a sound recording, remember that if a literary, dramatic or musical work is embodied in the sound recording, there may be two different lengths of copyright to consider. For example, a musical work (composed in 1933) is recorded in 1941. The composer of the musical work dies in 1984. Copyright in the sound recording lasts for fifty years from the fixation of the recording—from 1941 to December 31, 1991. Copyright in the musical work subsists for fifty years after the author's death—until December 31, 2034. The same scenario would apply to any dramatic or literary work on a sound recording.

Performer's Performance

Performances are protected for fifty years until the calendar year end of its first fixation in a sound recording, or its performance if it is not fixed in a sound recording.

Communication Signals

Communication signals are protected for fifty years after the end of the calendar year in which the signal is first broadcast.

CORPORATE OWNERSHIP

There are no special rules for determining duration of copyright where a corporation owns copyright in a work or sound recording. As always, the duration of copyright is determined according to the life of the author of the protected material unless the duration of copyright for that kind of work is otherwise determined, for instance in the case of sound recordings and photographs.

PUBLIC DOMAIN WORKS

Once copyright has expired in a work, the work is said to be in the "public domain." The work is no longer protected by copyright and can be used freely, without obtaining permission from, or compensating, the copyright owner. For example, works of Mozart and Shakespeare are in the public domain and can be copied freely (provided the works are not adaptations). The duration of copyright cannot be extended or renewed.

Works may be copied freely even where the copyright protection granted by the *Copyright Act* has not expired, if the copyright owner chooses to let people freely use the work. For example, creators of computer programs sometimes decide not to exercise the copyright in their programs and allow others to freely copy them. Web site owners often allow certain content from their sites to be freely copied. From time to time, authors of scholarly papers may decide not to collect copyright royalties for the use of their works. You should never assume that these or any other creations can be copied freely unless you know this for a fact; for instance, when it is clearly indicated on the work. Even when it is indicated that a work may be freely copied, determine for what purposes this is permitted. For instance, you may be able to print out a page from a Web site for personal purposes, but not include it in a print book or make 100 copies for your colleagues.

SUMMARY

In general, the duration of copyright is according to the life of the author and not owner of a work. The general rule is that copyright and moral right protection in a work endure for fifty years until the calendar year end after the author's death. The general rule applies unless there is a specific provision providing otherwise. In addition, there are specific durations for other subject-matter.

Chapter 9

RIGHTS PROTECTED BY COPYRIGHT

My personal belief is, of course, that no one should be able to tamper with any artist's work in any medium against the artist's will . . .

Woody Allen, Subcommittee on Technology
and Law of the United States Senate
Judiciary Committee, May 12, 1987

THE NATURE OF RIGHTS GRANTED BY THE *COPYRIGHT ACT*

Rights are actions that only a copyright owner may do, or authorize others to do, with protected material. Anyone who exercises a right without the copyright owner's permission is violating copyright and may be subject to a number of remedies that the *Copyright Act* provides to a copyright owner, including monetary compensation for the violation, stopping the violating act and preventing any further infringement. This chapter will examine three kinds of rights set out in the *Copyright Act*: economic rights, neighbouring rights and moral rights. Copyright protects the economic interests of the creators and owners of literary, dramatic, musical and artistic works. Moral rights protect the integrity and personality of a creator of a work. Neighbouring rights protect the economic rights of performers, broadcasters and makers of sound recordings.

Copyright versus Moral Rights

Moral rights must be distinguished from copyright. In order to do this, think of copyright as economic rights; that is, those rights that can be exchanged for money. An example of economic rights is where an author grants to a publisher the right to publish his or her book in exchange for a royalty payment. These economic rights, or copyright, include a myriad of rights, or a "bundle of rights" such as the right to publish, reproduce, perform in public, broadcast, translate and so on, as well as the right to authorize any of these actions. An author has the right to "exploit" these rights in any manner he or she chooses, and the right to be monetarily compensated for such exploitation.

Moral rights have a different value than copyright. The purpose of moral rights is to protect the honour and reputation of a creator and, as such, are very closely related to the personality of an author. Moral rights cannot be exercised by any person other than the author (or an heir), and therefore cannot be exchanged for money.

Often when the term "copyright" is used, it refers to both copyright, i.e., economic rights, moral rights and often also neighbouring rights. Sometimes, however, there is a distinction between these rights that is necessary when discussing certain aspects of the law. The context in which the word copyright appears will usually indicate the scope of its meaning. Once you understand the concepts of the different rights, you will probably have no difficulty in determining the exact reference when you see the term copyright.

The Rights Set Out in the *Copyright Act*

The way rights are set out in the *Copyright Act* is very complex. Although the bulk of these rights is set out in one section of the *Act*, the wording is somewhat complicated. As such, this chapter does not follow the exact order of the rights as they appear in the *Act* and does not always use the *Act*'s terminology. Nonetheless, in order to be true to the legislation it is sometimes necessary to have wording and organization that are somewhat awkward. This is an important chapter and care should be taken in understanding the concepts in it.

The rights set out in this chapter are set out as "full" rights and do not always take into account specific provisions in the *Act* that may be limitations on, or exemptions from, these rights. The next chapter will deal with these limitations or exemptions.

As a final note, as you begin to discover the rights set out in the law, you may be surprised to find that certain rights are, in fact, included in the law, and others, that you might have thought were rights, are not actually so. This chapter will examine both these "rights."

ECONOMIC RIGHTS IN LITERARY, DRAMATIC, MUSICAL AND ARTISTIC WORKS

This section deals with economic rights in literary, dramatic, musical and artistic works. In general, copyright owners of literary, dramatic, musical and artistic works enjoy the same rights. However, there are some specific rights attaching to specific works, for example, the exhibition right in artistic works, and the commercial rental right for computer programs and sound recordings. These are separately discussed below.

The economic rights set out in the *Act* are the sole and exclusive rights of the copyright owner. Only the copyright holder has the right to exercise these economic rights or to authorize others to do so. No one else can exercise them without the permission of the copyright holder.

Every economic right is independent of any other right. For example, the right to publish a work is distinct from the right to perform a work in public. Likewise, the right to translate a work is distinct from the right to broadcast a work. A copyright holder is entitled to a "bundle" of these distinct rights.

The Right of Reproduction

A copyright owner has the sole and exclusive right to "produce or reproduce the work or any substantial part thereof in any material form whatever." This means that a copyright owner has the initial right to bring a work into existence by producing it, and to make subsequent reproductions of the work. Reproduction refers to the reproduction of the same work in the same format or in another format. For example, you can reproduce a play script by photocopying it or by copying it out by hand or by digitizing it (e.g., scanning it). In addition, reproducing a road map in a different size and format, for example, to be included in a calendar, would be considered a reproduction for copyright purposes[1] (and it may also be considered an adaptation). Further, digital reproductions are reproductions for purposes of copyright law.

WHAT IS A SUBSTANTIAL PART?

The right to produce or reproduce a work applies to copying an entire work or a "substantial part" of the work. Anything less than a substantial part may be copied without authorization. This raises the question, "what is a substantial part"? This concept is not defined in the *Act*. Many court cases have, however, looked at its meaning.

Basically, there are two factors a court of law would consider when determining whether a certain use of a copyright work constitutes using a substantial part of it. First, the court will examine the quantity of the work, that is, how much of the original work has been copied. Second, the court will examine the quality of the work, that is, was the portion copied "qualitatively" a substantial portion of the work copied. Even the reproduction of a small amount of a copyright work, which is an "important" part of it, may be considered a substantial part of a work. In one case concerning a musical work, twenty-eight bars of a song were played (which equalled twenty seconds of a four-minute song) and these twenty-eight bars were held to "contain what is the principal air of the 'Colonel Bogey' march—the air that every one who heard the march played through would recognize as being the essential air of the 'Colonel Bogey' march."[2]

As you can see, there is no hard and fast rule to determine whether a "substantial" part of a work is being copied. In each situation, you must consider the part of the work being copied and ask whether it is qualitatively and quantitatively a substantial part of a work.

WHAT IS A MATERIAL FORM?

There is another issue you must consider with respect to the right of reproduction. The reproduced portion of the work must be in "any material form whatever." If the reproduction is not in a material form, then the copyright holder has no right to prevent the reproduction, or to authorize it.

The term "any material form whatever" is very broad and would encompass a variety of formats depending on, and appropriate to, the type of work in question. Photocopying is a prime example. As a general rule, photocopying a copyright work, or a substantial part of it, is not permitted under the law since it is a reproduction in a material form. Copying computer software may be a reproduction for copyright purposes, as may be inputting data into a computer (provided it is "saved" in some form and does not merely appear on screen). Another example of reproduction is photographing a copyright work such as a painting.

The Right of Public Performance

The right to perform a work in public, or the "performing right," gives the copyright holder the sole and exclusive right to perform the work in public, visually or acoustically. The performance can be live or by means of a mechanical instrument or a receiving set such as a radio or television.

This right of public performance and the neighbouring right in a performer's performance are two distinct rights that are separately defined in the copyright law. Neighbouring rights including rights in a performer's performance, are discussed later in this chapter.

Similar to the reproduction right, the right to perform a work in public is not limited to the performance of an entire work. The copyright owner has the right to authorize the public performance of a "substantial part" of the work. Anything less than a substantial part may be publicly performed without authorization. The question as to what constitutes a "substantial part," is explored above.

Unlike the right of reproduction, the right to perform a work only refers to the "public" performance of the work. Thus, a book may be read aloud at home or a video played in your living room, but if the same occurs in public (whether or not a fee is charged), permission of the copyright holder is necessary.

The term "public" is not defined in the *Copyright Act*, but has been discussed in a number of court decisions. It seems that when the audience is by nature domestic or quasi-domestic (a family or those living under the same roof), the performance is less likely to be considered a "public" performance. One proposed definition of public is to "include situations where individuals share living quarters by reason of their work, education, vacation or detention."[3]

If the performance takes place in a "non-domestic" setting, it may be considered a "public" performance whether or not an admission fee is charged, or whether there is a small or large audience. In fact, there need not be an audience listening to the performance, as long as the performance is meant for an audience. Note that certain performances for specific audiences, as outlined in Chapter 10: Limitations on Rights, are allowed under the law.

Examples of a public performance of a copyright work are the presentation of a play at a community centre, the reading of a poem during a rally, the showing of a television program or rental video in a store, and the playing of music on the radio in a restaurant.

The Right of Publication

The copyright holder has the sole and exclusive right to first publish a work (i.e., an unpublished work), or any substantial part thereof, and to initially make that work available to the public. Once an author has authorized a work's publication, he or she has no rights on subsequent sales; for example, on resales or rentals, unless reserved by contract or unless it is a commercial rental of computer software or sound recordings. Resales and rentals are further discussed below.

WHAT IS "PUBLICATION" IN COPYRIGHT LAW?

The right to publish a work is not explicitly defined in the *Act*, but the *Act* does state that publication is "in relation to any work, making copies of the work available to the public." According to this provision, publication is not restricted to the publishing of a work in the sense of, for example, a book publisher publishing your next novel. It does include this concept, but goes further than that. Since copies must be made available to the public in order for publication to occur, the fact that many copies of a particular work have been made does not by itself constitute publication of that work. These works (or at least more than one copy of the work) must be available to the public, though the public need not necessarily be in the possession of any of the copies of the work. In this context, the term "public" might be defined to refer to those outside a closed circle such as family, friends, a company, or a restricted group of people.

For purposes of the *Copyright Act*, publication includes the construction of an architectural work as well as the incorporation of an artistic work into an architectural work.

The following acts do *not* constitute publication for purposes of copyright law:

- the performance in public of a literary, dramatic, musical or artistic work or a sound recording
- the communication by telecommunication of a literary, dramatic, musical or artistic work or a sound recording
- the exhibition in public of an artistic work, and the issue of photographs and engravings of works of sculpture and architectural works where associated with the exhibition of such artistic works

A work or other subject-matter will not be considered to be published, performed in public, or communicated to the public by telecommunication if done without the consent of the copyright owner.

Note

The introductory portion of the legislative provision in the *Copyright Act* dealing with rights basically mentions the above rights, the right to produce or reproduce a work, to perform a work in public, and to publish an unpublished work. Following this introduction is a listing of other rights that seem to be sub-categories of these three basic rights. This information is given to help you understand why some of the rights listed individually below were not included above.

The Right of Adaptation

The copyright holder has the right to adapt, or authorize the adaptation of, a work. An example is the adaptation of a play into a film. Also, an author has the right to convert a dramatic work "into a novel or other non-dramatic work"; for example, a film into a book, or even an artistic work. Further, the author has the explicit right to convert a novel or other non-dramatic work, or artistic work, into a dramatic work. For example, a novel or magazine article could be converted into a film. A painting could be adapted into a dramatic work through a performance. Or the adaptation could be reproducing any literary, dramatic, musical or artistic work into a film.

The Right of Translation

A copyright owner has the sole and exclusive right to translate, or authorize others to translate, a work. A translation might be a translation of a book from French to English. Since the copyright owner has this right, you must obtain his or her permission before translating the work.

The Right of Telecommunication to the Public

A copyright owner has the sole and exclusive right to authorize the use of a work on radio or television, and the transmission of a work via cable, satellite and telephone wires. More specifically, the *Act* allows the copyright owner "to communicate the work to the public by telecommunication." Thus, any form of telecommunication requires the permission of the copyright owner. Such telecommunications would include any radio or television broadcast including transmissions by microwave over the airwaves as well as cable transmissions. As defined in the *Copyright Act*, telecommunications is "any transmission of signs, signals, writing, images or sounds or intelligence of any nature by wire, radio, visual, optical or other electro-magnetic system."

The right to communicate to the public by telecommunication extends to communicating works to people who view them in "apartments, hotel rooms or dwelling units situated in the same building" by means of an internal transmission system.

The copyright holder has the right to initial telecommunications of copyright materials, as well as the right with respect to subsequent telecommunications of the same materials. This latter right is commonly called the "retransmission right." Any "retransmitters" of "distant signals" (ones that cannot normally be received off-air because the community is located well beyond that signal's good quality reception area) have to pay a royalty to the respective copyright owners. These retransmitters may be cable TV companies, a master antenna system, a low-power television station and a direct-to-home system delivering television signals by satellite. Retransmitters may also retransmit signals from radio stations.

One important element of the retransmission right is that individuals do not actually authorize this right, but are merely entitled to a royalty payment when their works are used. Further, this payment cannot be collected on an individual basis, but only through a "collective" that collects such royalties on behalf of many copyright holders. The subject of "collectives" is discussed in Chapter 14: Using Copyright Materials.

Copyright owners of works who benefit from the telecommunications rights include producers of television programs and movies; copyright holders of recorded sports events; and copyright holders of musical works that are played on radio stations or on television.

THE RIGHT TO PROHIBIT IMPORTATION

There are two distinct elements of this right. First, a copyright holder has the right to ensure pirated copies of his or her work are not imported into Canada. By obtaining a court order, a copyright owner may enlist the assistance of Canadian customs officials to prevent the importation of such copies. The right only applies where the importer had knowledge that his or her activity violated copyright.

Second, there is a right against parallel imports. Parallel imports refers to both works in general and to books that were legally published elsewhere (i.e., outside of Canada) but have been imported into Canada without the consent of the Canadian rights holder. Both authors of books, and book distributors, can prevent parallel importation of their works, or works they represent through exclusive distribution arrangements. The provision against parallel importation for books is clearer and stronger than for other types of works.

The parallel imports provision for other types of works than books is subject to conflicting interpretations. One interpretation is that a copyright owner can keep out a parallel import produced by a foreign exclusive licensee but that an exclusive licensee cannot keep out a work produced by a foreign copyright owner, but may be able to keep out a work by a foreign exclusive licensee.[4]

THE RIGHT OF AUTHORIZATION

You have already seen the term "authorization" used a number of times in this chapter. This is because the right of authorization is one of the exclusive rights of the copyright owner. Thus, only the copyright holder may authorize the use of any of the exclusive rights set out in the *Act*. It follows that if these rights are used and have not been authorized by the copyright holder, then copyright has been violated.

A person other than the copyright owner should never authorize others to "use" a work in a copyright sense. Even if you have authorization to use a copyright work, you cannot authorize someone else to use it. For instance, if you have permission to reproduce a book, you do not automatically have permission to authorize someone else to reproduce it, or to perform it in public (for example, to do a public reading of the book).

If a work is used without the permission of the copyright owner, the "user" of that material does not acquire copyright in it, nor does the copyright owner lose any of his or her rights set out in the law.

ECONOMIC RIGHTS IN SPECIFIC WORKS

The rights described above apply to literary, dramatic, artistic and musical works, provided it is possible for such rights to apply. For instance, it may not be possible for the translation right to apply to an artistic work such as a painting. In addition to those rights listed above, there are further rights, which apply to specific works like artistic works, musical works and computer programs. This section discusses further rights as well as the specific rights for sound recordings.

Exhibition Right in Artistic Works

Before examining this particular right, it is important to look at its history in order to understand why the right only exists with respect to artistic works. The exhibition right has existed in the *Copyright Act* since 1988. Prior to that time, creators of paintings, sculptures and the like claimed that because of the nature of their works, they could not benefit from many of the rights set out in the *Act*. For example, a sculpture could not be translated. Creators of artistic works professed that a right should be included in the *Act* that recognized the unique nature of an artistic work. Thus, the exhibition right was added to the law. It gives creators the right to control the use of an artistic work and to be entitled to a royalty payment each time an artistic work is exhibited in public.

Prior to the exhibition right being added to the *Copyright Act*, it was not a novel concept in Canada. Prior to 1988, most major public art galleries and museums voluntarily followed an exhibition fee schedule for loaned and donated works, which was established by Canadian Artists' Representation/Le front des artistes canadiens (CARfac).

The exhibition right is set out in the *Copyright Act* as the right "to present at a public exhibition, for a purpose other than sale or hire, an artistic work created after June 7, 1988, other than a map, chart or plan." As such, the exhibition right applies to:

- artistic works, which you will recall, include paintings, sculptures, drawings, photographs and engravings if these artistic works were created after June 7, 1988

The right does *not* apply to:

- maps, charts and plans
- artistic works created before or on June 7, 1988
- artistic works that are presented for the purpose of "sale or hire" (for example, sales by commercial galleries, art dealers or museum sales shops or rentals by the Canada Council Art Bank, though the exhibition of a rental work would be subject to the exhibition right)

The right applies to "presentations at a public exhibition." Neither "presentations" nor "public exhibitions" is defined in the *Copyright Act*. Whether a particular situation would constitute a presentation at a public exhibition depends on the facts in each particular case. Some of the factors that a court might take into account when deciding this are:

- the physical location of the work (Is it in a gallery or the office of an accountant?)
- the exhibitor's intention to attract attention to the work (Are there incentives in the form of lighting, segregated space, posters and information and/or invitations drawing people to the exhibition?)
- purpose of exhibition (To show works or mere decoration?)
- the attention given to the exhibit (Did people stop to look or did they just walk by?)
- the audience of the exhibit ("Public" does not have to include all members of the public, but can include members of a smaller public connected by a common event, interest or characteristic: is the audience related to the exhibitor?)
- the size of the audience
- the charging of an admission fee (Free admission is not conclusive that it is public; would the audience pay to see the exhibit if it were held at another venue?)
- compensation to the artist

With the above elements of an exhibition in mind, an "exhibition" would probably not include a painting hanging on a living room wall. However, a show at the National Gallery of Canada would be an exhibition.

There are a number of grey areas where it is not always possible to easily determine whether an exhibition is taking place. For instance, an exhibition at a bank may or may not be a public exhibition. Other examples include corporate collections, professional offices, public buildings such as the Parliament buildings, or the corridors of a public library, hotel rooms and restaurants. Whether an exhibition occurred in these situations would depend on the circumstances in each particular case.[5]

Commercial Rental Right in Computer Programs and Musical Works in Sound Recordings

Until January 1, 1994, once a copyright work had been purchased, the copyright owner had no further rights in the physical property itself, unless the copyright owner and purchaser had agreed otherwise. Therefore, a copyright owner could not prevent the public renting of a copyright work. This meant that every time you rented a musical work or computer program on a CD from a store, the copyright owner did not receive any royalties from the rental of that musical work or computer program. Since January 1, 1994, a new right exists in the *Copyright Act* for the commercial rental of a musical work embodied in a sound recording and computer programs (regardless of when the sound recording or computer program was created). As a result, rental stores have either closed or must obtain permission from copyright holders to rent sound recordings and computer programs. All other copyright works can be rented without permission from, or payment to, the copyright holder.

When the rental right was first introduced in 1994, its beneficiaries were authors of computer programs and producers of sound recordings. With recent amendments to the Canadian *Copyright Act*, the rental right in musical works in sound recordings now benefits composers, lyricists and performers of any musical works in these musical works.

The commercial rental right applies where there is a "motive of gain" in the overall operations of the person who rents out the computer program or sound recording embodying a musical work. For instance, the activities of a public library would probably not in substance constitute a rental nor would they be considered to have a motive of gain; libraries are able to rent computer programs and musical works in sound recordings without the permission of the copyright owner, even if an administrative fee or other cost is charged. Also, since a court would look at the overall operations for a motive of gain, there could be a gain where the rental is a "loss leader" to the rental store. In general, there is no motive of gain where no more than costs, including overhead, are recovered. Of course, if an infringement of this right is claimed, a court of law would look at all of the surrounding circumstances.

For purposes of the commercial rental right, the right applies to any sort of protected musical work embodied on a sound recording. However, only certain computer programs are subject to the rental right. Generally, the right is for stand-alone computer programs like word processors and accounting programs. The *Copyright Act* refers to eligible computer programs as ones that can be reproduced in the ordinary course of their use other than by a reproduction during their execution in conjunction with a machine, device or computer, such as an elevator or car. Also, the right does not apply to "copy-protected" software, that is, software that cannot be reproduced in the ordinary course of its use. Since most of the cartridge-type computer games currently being sold are copy-protected, they would not enjoy a rental right.

When you rent copyright works, you must still respect the rights of the copyright holder. For instance, you cannot reproduce any rented copyright work or show it in public without the permission of the copyright holder.

Violation of the rental right is subject only to civil remedies and not to criminal remedies. Civil and criminal remedies are discussed in Chapter 13: What Are the Remedies for the Violation of Copyright?

Right to Make a Sound Recording
Due to the complexity of the right to make a sound recording, it is separately dealt with in this section.

MECHANICAL RIGHT
A copyright holder has the right to make an audio recording of a work, or authorize others to do so. According to the *Copyright Act*, a copyright holder has this right, "in the case of a literary, dramatic or musical work, to make any sound recording, cinematograph film or other contrivance by means of which the work may be mechanically performed or performed." For example, the copyright owner of a song or play has the right to make or authorize the making of a sound recording of that song or play. The music industry often refers to this right as the mechanical right.

Where a work is in the public domain, anyone may make a sound recording of that work. Thus, anyone may make a recording of Vivaldi's "Four Seasons."

SYNCHRONIZATION RIGHT
The right to make a sound recording includes the "synchronization right." The synchronization right is not specifically mentioned in the *Copyright Act*, but is a term used worldwide in the film and television industry. This term describes the rights used when, in the making of a film or television program, music is synchronized with the picture in the film or television program. The synchronization right does not concern itself with the making of a sound recording *per se*, but comes into play when sound is matched with pictures. The pictures on a film are on the video track of the production and the sound is recorded on what is called the sound track of a production. The two elements must be matched, so if someone is playing a violin, the sound of the violin is heard, and the auditory and visual action correspond. Permission of the copyright holder of the musical work is necessary when synchronizing it with a film or television program.

The synchronization right is usually dealt with by contractual arrangements and is perceived as a right separate from the mechanical right. Separate permissions must be obtained for the use of the mechanical and synchronization rights.

MORAL RIGHTS

Since moral rights are an integral part of the *Copyright Act*, there are portions throughout this book dealing with moral rights. See, for example, Chapters 7, 8 and 11 through 14. This section will set out a full description of the various components of moral rights.

Moral rights protect the personality or reputation of an author. Because these rights attach to the personality of an author, an author retains them even after he or she has assigned the copyright in a work. This is a very important concept. An older English case described the moral rights concept in the following phrase "to protect the copy after publication."[6] Another case described the same concept stating that "after the author has parted with his pecuniary interest in the manuscript, he retains a species of personal or moral right in the product of his brain."[7] Since moral rights are so personal to an author, they cannot be assigned for subsequent copyright owners to exercise, except upon the death of an author.

Notwithstanding that moral rights cannot be assigned, authors can agree not to exercise their moral rights.

Moral rights can be divided into three categories:

- right of paternity
- right of integrity
- right of association

Right of Paternity

An author has the right, "where reasonable in the circumstances, to be associated with the work as its author by name or under a pseudonym and the right to remain anonymous." An author has this right whenever he or she has economic rights in a work, and this right applies in relation to uses covered by those economic rights. For example, when reproducing a magazine article, the author of the article has the right to have her name appear on the article.[8]

According to this section, an author has the following rights:

RIGHT TO CLAIM AUTHORSHIP

An author has the right to have his or her name associated with a work. For example, a writer has a right to have her name appear on the cover of her book.

RIGHT TO REMAIN ANONYMOUS

An author has the right to remain anonymous with respect to a work. Thus, an author could request that his or her work could be presented to the public without any name appearing on it as its author.

RIGHT TO USE A PSEUDONYM

An author has the right to use a pseudonym or a pen name.

The above three elements of the right of paternity are subject to the condition "where it is reasonable in the circumstances." It would be reasonable to have a book published with the author's name on it; however, a court may not consider it "reasonable in the circumstances" to have a composer's name mentioned when music incidental to a broadcast is played within that broadcast. The question of "reasonableness" is a matter for a court to decide, depending upon the circumstances of each case.

Right of Integrity

A second component of moral rights is the right of integrity. According to the *Copyright Act*, the author's right to the integrity of a work is violated if the work is, to the prejudice of the honour or reputation of the author, distorted, mutilated or otherwise modified.

RIGHT TO PREVENT CHANGES TO A WORK

An author has the right to prevent any distortion, mutilation or other modifications to his or her work. This right is subject to the distortion, mutilation or other modification being prejudicial to the honour or reputation of the author. Whether something is prejudicial in this manner is a question of fact that can be determined through the testimony of witnesses. For example, painting a moustache on the Mona Lisa (provided the Mona Lisa were still protected by copyright) may be a violation of Da Vinci's moral rights. Also, manipulating a scanned photograph may also possibly be a violation, provided it is prejudicial to the honour or reputation of the author of the photograph.

One of the more well known Canadian moral rights cases concerns the artist Michael Snow's sculpture *Flight Stop* of sixty geese hanging in the Toronto Eaton Centre.[9] In this case, the Eaton Centre had tied ribbons around the necks of the sixty geese in the sculpture as a Christmas decoration. The artist, Michael Snow, had no knowledge of this and did not consent to this decoration. The Court said "the plaintiff is adamant in his belief that his naturalistic composition has been made to look ridiculous by the addition of ribbons and suggests it is not unlike dangling earrings from the Venus de Milo. While the matter is not undisputed, the plaintiff's opinion is shared by a number of other well-respected artists and people knowledgeable in his field." The Court held that the attachment of the ribbons to the sculpture was prejudicial to the artist's honour or reputation and ordered that the ribbons be removed.

Special Treatment of Artistic Works

As mentioned above, the right of integrity, with respect to distortions, mutilations or other modifications of a work is always subject to the factual question as to whether there is a resulting prejudice to the honour or reputation of the author. There is one exception to this "prejudicial" condition. This exception applies in the case of a painting, sculpture or engraving. With respect to these works, the prejudice is "deemed to have occurred as a result of any distortion, mutilation or other modification of the work." Thus, there need be no proof of the prejudice.

The reason that paintings, sculptures and engravings are given this preferential treatment is because the legislators of the *Copyright Act* felt that because these specific works are often unique, one-of-a-kind works, any change to them would be prejudicial to a creator's honour or reputation.

RIGHT TO PREVENT USE OF A WORK IN ASSOCIATION WITH A PRODUCT, SERVICE, CAUSE OR INSTITUTION

A further component of moral rights is the right of association. An author has the right to prevent anyone else from using his or her work "in association with a product, service, cause or institution." This right is subject to the distortion, mutilation or other modification being prejudicial to the honour or reputation of the author. Whether something is prejudicial in this manner is a question of fact that can be determined through the testimony of witnesses.

An example of this right might be an art exhibit sponsored by a tobacco company where the artist's reputation rides on the fact that he is a no-smoking advocate.

Other "Moral Rights"

As is evident, the Canadian *Copyright Act* does not specifically deal with such things as the right to withdraw a work (once being exhibited, performed, etc.), or the right to revoke a licence to use a copyright work where a licensed right has not been exercised. It also does not explicitly deal with the right to prevent the destruction of a copyright work, though this is arguably a "modification" that is prejudicial to the honour or reputation of a creator, or could be protected by other areas of law.

Certain rights that may or may not be considered moral rights may be secured by contract in order to ensure certainty in a particular situation. These include the situations set out in the above paragraph. Another example may be a choreographer who wants to protect her integrity by contracting in advance the right to approve casting, costumes, stage designs, settings and lighting for a particular choreographic work.

NEIGHBOURING RIGHTS

Neighbouring rights protect the rights of performers (actors, singers and the like), record producers and broadcasters. Neighbouring rights are rights akin to copyright, but are distinct from copyright. In basic terms, copyright can be described as those rights granted to creators of copyright works whereas neighbouring rights are rights granted to users of those copyright works. For example, copyright protects the composer of a song whereas neighbouring rights would protect the performer of the song. Another way of putting it is that a performer performs music to produce a "neighbouring" work called a performer's performance. Neighbouring rights can sometimes be obtained through contractual agreements. This book sometimes refers to neighbouring rights as non-traditional copyright material, while the *Copyright Act* refers to neighbouring rights as "other subject-matter."

As is evident from discussions throughout this book, most of the neighbouring rights are relatively new to the Canadian *Copyright Act*. These new rights include a right in performers' performances, expanded rights in sound recordings, and rights in broadcasts. In addition, there is a new right for performers to enforce contractual obligations.

Performer's Performance

Performers who perform in Canada are entitled to a number of rights. Performances that do not take place in Canada but that would qualify for protection in Canada due to international relationships via the WTO or Rome Convention may have more limited protection in Canada. The rights granted to performers for performances in Canada and other countries is dependent on whether the performance took place in a WTO or Rome Convention country.

For performances in Canada and in WTO countries, since January 1, 1996, the Canadian *Copyright Act* protects performers against unauthorized fixation (i.e., recording) of their live performances, as well as reproduction or broadcast of their live performances. Thus, a performer has the right to authorize any recording of his or her live performance (including improvisations and performances of public domain works), any reproduction of the audio or video recording, as well as any broadcast of it on radio or television. Eligible performances are discussed in Chapter 3: Is Your Creation Eligible for Copyright Protection?

Since September 1, 1997, performances in Canada or in a Rome Convention country have the above rights plus wider rights that include rental, public performance, broadcast and authorizing any of these rights. Eligible performances are discussed in Chapter 3.

Performers Enforcing Contractual Obligations

Performers in cinematographic works experience a unique problem. These performers have had extreme difficulty enforcing their rights in contractual agreements where the rights are no longer owned by the person or company who signed the original agreement. These contractual arrangements lose their power when assigned to others than the original producer because these others do not "assume" the original obligation to performers. For example, performer Lawford signs an agreement to appear in producer Ken's film. Subsequently, Ken sells his rights to distributor Shelley. Lawford has no agreement with Shelley and therefore cannot obtain payment when the film is shown.

A new provision in the *Act* specifically provides performers the right to exercise their contractual right to remuneration against the original producer, assignees of the original agreement, and subsequent rights holders.

Rights for Performers and Producers in Sound Recordings

PUBLIC PERFORMANCE AND BROADCAST

Sound recording performers and producers are entitled to receive royalty payments from those who use their sound recordings for public performance or broadcast. The responsible party for paying these new royalties are the radio broadcasting industry and commercial establishments that use sound recordings. The royalties are collected by a single copyright collective established in 1997, The Neighbouring Rights Collective of Canada (NRCC), which is discussed in Chapter 14: Using Copyright Materials. However, the NRCC will not distribute these royalties to individuals, rather, they are distributed to its five member collectives.

Canadian performers and producers are also eligible to receive royalties when their sound recordings are performed or broadcast in the more than fifty other countries that have agreed to abide by the Rome Convention. The United States is not a member of the Rome Convention and thus its performers and producers are not entitled to collect these royalties in the United States or from other countries, nor are Canadian performers and producers able to collect these royalties from the United States.

PRIVATE COPYING

Authors (composers and lyricists), producers and performers of musical works in sound recordings are entitled to monies collected as a blank audio recording media levy. This is compensation for private copying of sound recordings, which is permissible under Canadian copyright law but subject to a levy on blank audio media like cassettes and digital formats, made or imported, and sold in Canada. Eligible copyright holders receive their portion of the levy from their designated professional association or copyright collective.

Broadcasts

Broadcasters have the right to "fix" their transmissions, to enforce reproduction rights on unauthorized fixations, to performance rights in television programs played in premises where the public pays an entrance fee to view them, the right to authorize any of these rights, and a right to authorize simultaneous retransmission by other broadcasters. Further, broadcasters have the right against unauthorized distribution and importation of fixed communication signals.

RIGHTS NOT CURRENTLY IN THE *COPYRIGHT ACT*

Public Lending Right

A public lending right in the *Copyright Act* would compensate authors when their books are lent to the public in a library. Without such a right, authors receive no royalty when a book is loaned by a library (although the author does receive a royalty from the sale of the book to the library). The under-lying principle for a public lending right is that a book is borrowed from a library instead of being purchased and therefore an author loses out on royalties from sales each time that book is loaned.

Under the current Canadian copyright law, there is no public lending right. This is because the government felt that copyright was not the best way to achieve the goal of compensating authors for the public lending of their works by libraries.[10] However, a compensation scheme outside the *Copyright Act* has been instituted.

In 1986, the Public Lending Right (PLR) Commission was established to "administer a program of payments to Canadian authors for their eligible books catalogued in libraries across Canada." The PLR Commission oper-ates under the administrative aegis of the Canada Council. The scheme compensates writers, translators, illustrators and the like for the "free and unlimited use of their works by the public in Canadian libraries." PLR payments are determined by a sampling of holdings of a particular book in a representative number of libraries; the greater the number of libraries that shelve a book, the larger the PLR payment. For the year ending in February, 2000, the average payment to an author was $663. In that same year, 12,148 authors received a payment from the PLR and the total author budget was $8,052,114. Books of poetry, children's or young adult literature, drama, fiction and nonfiction are potentially eligible works.

> For more information on the PLR, contact:
>
> Public Lending Right Commission
> 350 Albert Street
> P.O. Box 1047
> Ottawa, Ontario K1P 5V8
>
> T:613.566.4378
> F:613.566.4332
> E: **plr@canadacouncil.ca**
> 🌐 **www.canadacouncil.ca/archival/plr-dpp/page.htm**

The Web site includes detailed and helpful information concerning the eligibility for the PLR by authors, editors, translators, contributors to anthologies, illustrators and photographers. It also includes information on the percentage of the PLR payment that an eligible person will receive from the PLR.

Right of Resale

The *Copyright Act* does not have a right of resale. Therefore, a copyright holder has no rights in the resale of a work, unless such rights have been reserved by contract.

An example of this concept occurs when an author cannot stop the resale of a book in a used book store and an author is not entitled to any royalties from the resale of a book. Keep in mind, however, that the author still has copyright in that book notwithstanding the fact that it is physically owned by its original purchaser or by a subsequent purchaser. Thus, the author can claim any rights under the *Copyright Act* and can, for example, prevent the reproduction of the book, or the use of it in association with a service, product, cause or institution, if that use is prejudicial to the honour or reputation of the author.

Droit de Suite

A *droit de suite* is the right of an artist to follow or participate in any proceeds from a resale of the "physical" (as opposed to the copyright) aspect of a work. Thus, a *droit de suite* would enable creators of original artistic works to share in the proceeds from resales and to claim a share of the increases in the value of a work of art such as a painting as it is resold. The current *Copyright Act* does not contain a *droit de suite*. An artist, however, may negotiate a term in a purchase and sale agreement of a piece of art that is similar to a *droit de suite* and that would enable the artist to benefit from increases in the value of a work.

SUMMARY

Copyright holders are entitled to a bundle of rights, such as the right to publish, reproduce and perform in public a copyright work, or to authorize others to do so. Authors of copyright works also have moral rights in their creations. In addition, there are limited rights in performers' performances, sound recordings and broadcasts. The rights described in this chapter are subject to limitations set out in the next chapter.

Chapter 10
LIMITATIONS
ON RIGHTS

*It is therefore highly important to preserve the literature
of a nation, and it is preserved by the copyright laws
which give the necessary encouragement to its authors.*
Mr. W. G. Raymond, House of Commons, May 29, 1925

WHAT ARE LIMITATIONS ON RIGHTS?

In the previous chapter, we dealt with the rights of authors and copyright holders. This chapter covers limitations on, or exceptions from, these rights. Basically, these limitations are certain provisions in the *Copyright Act* that allow people to use copyright materials without obtaining the permission of, and/or paying compensation to, the copyright holder.

LIMITATIONS FOR SPECIFIC PURPOSES

Fair Dealing for Purposes of Research, Private Study, Criticism, Review or News Reporting

One of the more familiar limitations on rights in Canadian copyright law is called "fair dealing." The concept of fair dealing is often compared, or used interchangeably, with the American concept of "fair use." Caution should be taken when talking about "fair dealing" and "fair use" as the American fair use notion is a broader concept than the Canadian fair dealing provision. The American provision allows many more free uses of copyright materials than fair dealing.

WHAT IS FAIR DEALING?

The fair dealing provision was originally included in the Canadian *Copyright Act* in 1921, at a time when reproducing copyright materials meant copying out by hand. At the time, the fair dealing provision applied to the use of quotes and "small" passages for purposes of private study, research, criticism, review or newspaper summary. Of course, the concept of photocopiers, computers, computer scanners and the Internet was not envisioned. However, like other terms and provisions used in the *Copyright Act*, fair dealing has adapted to meet the technology of the time.

The term "fair dealing" is not defined in the *Copyright Act*. The wording used in the *Act*, which may seem straightforward, cannot be interpreted on its face. Some court cases have dealt with this concept, but no case has clearly established what exactly constitutes fair dealing. In fact, there remains much confusion as to which activities may be considered fair dealing. Because of the uncertain nature of fair dealing, users of copyright material such as librarians, teachers and researchers, who are not copyright experts, must sometimes decide for themselves as to whether their activities would be considered fair by a judge.

Although the law in this area is difficult to apply, there is some guidance as to what constitutes fair dealing. For instance, in order for something to constitute fair dealing, it must fit under one of the purposes listed in the fair dealing section of the *Act* (i.e., research, private study, criticism, review or news reporting). In addition, the overall use of the copyright material must be "fair."

Whether or not a certain activity might constitute fair dealing can be analyzed in the following way. First, consider whether a substantial part of a work is being copied. One must first establish this factor because all the rights in the *Act* apply to using a substantial part of a work. If anything less than a substantial part of a work is being used, then the copyright owner has no right to prevent its use. Remember that what constitutes a substantial part of a work is not defined in the law; it depends on the nature of reproduction and is also a matter of degree, in terms of both the quality and quantity of the work used.

If a substantial part of a work is being copied, one must then consider whether that copying would be considered fair. Fairness is determined in terms of quality (the value of the amount taken in comparison to the rest of the work) and in terms of quantity used (the amount copied). A court may take into account other factors such as the competition between the infringing copy and the original work. As you can see, whether a specific use of a copyright work would be considered fair dealing is a determination of fact.

As one court case expressed, "you must consider first the number and extent of the quotations and extracts. Are they altogether too many and too long to be fair?" The case went on to consider the proportions of the work taken. "To take long extracts and attach short comments may be unfair. But, short extracts and long comments may be fair. Other considerations may come to mind also. But, after all is said and done, it must be a matter of impression."[1] In the end, it is the impression left with the court that determines whether a use is considered fair.

In a recent case involving the use of a book by Barbara Hager on Shania Twain published by ECW Press, the judge stated in relation to the fair dealing claim by ECW Press that

> . . . it was not often *verbatim* copying, but rather the rearranging of sentences, with additional material interspersed, while following the same concepts, thought patterns and sometimes sentence structure. Ms. Hager's reaction on reading the ECW book was that it appeared as though someone had scanned her work onto the computer and then switched the words and sentences around a bit, using a thesaurus to change some words. I doubt that the changes were sophisticated enough to require the use of a thesaurus but the conclusion I draw from the facts is that in terms of quantity, a substantial amount of her work was taken. In addition, the parts of her book that are most valuable to her were taken: the direct quotes from Shania Twain. I conclude that qualitatively a very valuable and significant part of her work was taken.[2]

Finally, the use of the copied portion must be for one of the five purposes set out in the fair dealing provision: research, private study, criticism, review or news reporting. These five purposes are not further elaborated in the *Act*, but seem to be interpreted narrowly. For instance, private study or research does not seem to extend to multiple copies for classroom use. Criticism usually refers to quotes and extracts from a work to illustrate a commentary on it. One court case has stated, "a critic cannot, without being guilty of infringement, reproduce in full, without the author's permission, the work which he criticizes."[3] However, a critic writing about a particular painting may argue (without legal precedence to support the argument) that reproduction of the entire painting in a newspaper article is necessary for review purposes. A 1995 court case held that the reproduction of a magazine cover by a newspaper where a photograph on the cover was predominant is not fair dealing of the photograph.[4]

If you are using a work under the fair dealing provision for purposes of criticism, review or news reporting, in your use you must mention the source and the author's name if it is given in the source. The performer must be mentioned in the case of a performance, the maker in the case of a sound recording, and the broadcaster in the case of a broadcast signal.

There is some judicial precedent supporting that it is not fair to deal with a work that has never been published (in the copyright sense).

Because the application of the law concerning fair dealing is dependent upon a court's assessment of the facts in a case, a common sense approach might be that if a "very small" portion of a copyright work is being used and the use is clearly for the purposes of research, private study, criticism, review or news reporting, then it is probably acceptable to use that work. Otherwise, and if there is any doubt, you should obtain copyright permission for the use of a work, or a portion thereof.

Parody

Parody is not specifically mentioned in the *Copyright Act*, however, certain parodies would be allowed under the Canadian law, depending on the particular circumstances. There have been some Canadian cases dealing with the parody of copyright works. In one court case, a parody of various graphical representations of the St. Hubert stylized head of a rooster was held to violate copyright.[5] In another case, where an advertising agency prepared a parody of the words of the musical work "Downtown" and used it for radio advertising purposes in Ottawa, it was held to violate copyright.[6] In the United States, parody is considered a form of criticism and falls under the fair use provision.

Public Recitation of Extracts

It is not illegal for a person to read or recite in public any reasonable extract from any published work. Without this exception, such a reading would violate the right of public performance in the work.

Legislative, Judicial and Administrative Proceedings

The *Copyright Act* does not explicitly provide any exceptions for the use of copyright materials during legislative, judicial or administrative proceedings, or for the use of the reports of such proceedings. However, as discussed in Chapter 14, you may reproduce certain works owned by the federal government and provincial governments such as legislation and court decisions, without obtaining permission or paying a fee.

EXCEPTIONS FOR SPECIFIC WORKS

Computer Programs

There are two specific provisions in the *Copyright Act* that allow owners of legal copies of computer programs to make a single reproduction of these programs. These provisions apply to owners of programs, whether original or subsequent owners, and not to borrowers of programs, whether borrowed from a friend or office, or for a rental fee from a store. These two provisions are discussed below.

BACK-UP COPY

An owner of a legitimate copy of a computer program may make one back-up copy of that program or a modified version of that program (modifications are further discussed below). The person must be able to prove that the back-up copy is destroyed as soon as he or she ceases to be the owner of the copy of the computer program from which the back-up was made.

COPYING FOR PURPOSES OF ADAPTATION, MODIFICATION, CONVERSION OR TRANSLATION

An owner of a legitimate copy of a computer program may make a single copy of that program by "adapting, modifying or converting the computer program or translating it into another computer language," provided that the person can prove the following:

- the reproduction is essential for the compatibility of the program with a particular computer
- the reproduction is solely for the person's own use
- the copy is destroyed when the person ceases to be the owner of the copy of the program from which the copy was made

OTHER COMPUTER SOFTWARE USES

Any other copyright uses of computer programs than those mentioned above require permission from the copyright holder. Thus, if you buy a program and want to reproduce it on several different computers in your office, you require permission for each individual reproduction. Sometimes a computer company will give you a special licence, often referred to as a "site licence," which will allow you to use a purchased program on a network of computers. Also, when you purchase customized software, you may sign an agreement that allows for a variety of uses of that software, including making various copies of the software for use in different machines. Generally, however, if you buy mass distributed software, your use of that software is subject to the "shrinkwrap" licence included in the sealed plastic packaging in which the software appears, or the "web-wrap" or "click-through" licence for software purchased and delivered online. Whether these licences are binding depends on the law of the relevant jurisdiction (i.e., likely the jurisdiction of the purchase of the software). Although each manufacturer of software products will have its own licence agreements, usually the agreement only allows you to use the software on a single computer (or on your own laptop and desktop) and to make a back-up copy (which, as you know, is allowed under the *Copyright Act*).

Using public domain or shareware software is not an "exception" under the *Copyright Act*. In these cases, the particular copyright owners are allowing the use of these programs, either for free or subject to a "voluntary" payment. This is a choice made on an individual basis by copyright holders.

There is no exception to allow you to copy a substantial part of a computer program for purposes of evaluating that program to determine whether you wish to purchase it. This is not to say that you cannot borrow or loan computer programs for evaluation purposes. You can loan or borrow programs for any purpose, but you are not allowed to do anything with that program that is contrary to the *Copyright Act* (e.g., reproduce the program without permission).

Private Copying of Sound Recordings

With audio recorders increasingly in homes over the past few decades, authors (composers and lyricists) and producers of sound recordings have been unable to enforce their rights and collect royalties for private or home copying of sound recordings. Recent changes to the copyright law recognize the problem of enforcing these rights by now permitting home taping. A levy has been placed on all blank audio media—like cassettes and tapes—made or imported, and sold in Canada. The proceeds of this levy are distributed to eligible composers, lyricists, performers and producers of sound recordings through their professional associations or copyright collectives. This is further discussed in Chapter 14: Using Copyright Materials.

The *Copyright Act* grants one exemption to paying this levy, to associations representing persons with perceptual disabilities.

Time-Shifting of Television Broadcasts

There are no specific provisions for "private" reproductions, or for time-shifting purposes, of home taping of television. (Time-shifting means taping something to watch at a later time.)

Re-using Moulds, Casts, etc., of Artistic Works

An author may re-use any mould, cast, sketch, plan, model or study used to make an artistic work, even if the author no longer owns the copyright in the artistic work, as long as the author does not thereby "repeat or imitate the main design of that work."

Works Permanently Situated in a Public Place

Certain works that are permanently located in public places may be reproduced in certain manners without violating copyright. A painting, drawing, engraving, photograph or cinematographic work can be made of any sculpture or work of artistic craftsmanship if the sculpture or work of artistic craftsmanship is permanently situated in a public place or building. The painting, drawing, engraving or photograph may also be published. Always keep in mind that this provision refers to works permanently situated in public places or buildings. A painting that travels from one public art gallery to another would probably not be permanently situated in a public place.

This provision also extends to architectural works. You can publish and reproduce paintings, drawings, engravings or photographs of architectural works in public places as long as the paintings, drawings, etc., are not architectural drawings or plans.

The purpose of the provision for works permanently situated in a public place is to allow tourists to photograph a statue or monument in a public place, or to allow a person to sketch the outside of a building.

Incidental Uses of Copyright Materials

There is a new exception in the *Act* for the incidental inclusion of copyright protected material in other copyright protected material. However, in order for this use not to violate copyright, it must be incidental and not deliberate. For example, this would allow a news camera crew to incidentally and not deliberately film a street scene in which music is playing in the background.

Importation of works

Any person may import two copies of a work or other subject-matter for personal use. Any number of copies of a work or other subject-matter may be imported for use by a federal or provincial or territorial government department. In addition, any number of used books may be imported into Canada. A single copy of a book, or any number of copies of a work or other subject-matter, may be imported for use by any non-profit library, archive, museum or educational institution at any time before the work is made in Canada. See below for the definition of non-profit library, archive, museum or educational institution.

EXCEPTIONS IN SPECIFIC SITUATIONS

The exceptions described below under the headings schools, libraries, and so on, are exceptions in the *Act* that specifically refer to these headings. Other provisions, for example, fair dealing or specific exceptions such as the ones for computer programs may also apply with respect to schools, libraries or in any other of the specific situations listed below.

Meaning of "premises," "commercially available" and "motive of gain"

There are certain terms that specifically arise in many of the school and library, archive and museum exceptions. One is "premises," which is defined as a place where education or training is provided, controlled or supervised by the educational institution.

Another term is "commercially available," which is defined as "available on the Canadian market within a reasonable time and for a reasonable price and may be located with reasonable effort," or where there is a licence available from a copyright collective such as CANCOPY or COPIBEC (see discussion below) "within a reasonable time and for a reasonable price and may be located with reasonable effort."

"Motive of gain" is defined as recovering no more than the costs including overhead costs, associated with doing the specified act.

Schools

Until recently, schools have had very few exceptions in the Canadian *Copyright Act*. However, the *Act* now includes many exceptions specifically for non-profit educational institutions at all levels including pre-school, elementary, secondary and post-secondary education, as long as they are licensed or recognized by or under federal or provincial legislation. The exceptions also apply to continuing, professional or vocational education or training where the institution is directed or controlled by a board of education regulated by or under provincial legislation. They also apply to any government department or agency or non-profit body that controls or supervises the education or training mentioned above. Further, the government may include other non-profit institutions to this list by regulation. In addition, the exceptions apply to any library, archive or museum that forms part of an educational institution. Each of the exceptions is described below. At the time of writing this book, there have been no court cases interpreting these specific provisions and whether a particular circumstance falls within a specific exception depends on the facts in the particular situation.

INSTRUCTION

Educators may make a "manual reproduction of a work onto a dry-erase board, flip chart or other similar surface intended for displaying hand-written material," or may make "a copy of a work to be used to project an image of that copy using an overhead projector or similar device." A slide projector or computer projection may arguably be considered a similar device. This must be done for the purposes of education or training on the premises of the educational institution. Except in the case of manual reproduction (e.g., by physically drawing an image or writing text with a marker), the exceptions do not apply if the work is commercially available in an appropriate medium. There must be no motive of gain.

TESTS AND EXAMS

Educators may reproduce, translate or perform in public or broadcast a work or other subject-matter on a school's premises "as required" for a test or exam. This is provided the work or other subject-matter is not commercially available in an appropriate medium. There must be no motive of gain.

PERFORMANCES

Certain performances for or by students are allowed. The performance must take place on the school's premises for education or training purposes and not for profit. The audience must consist primarily of students of the school, instructors or any person who is directly responsible for setting a curriculum for the school. This would not therefore include a school play in which the audience consisted primarily of family and friends. There must be no motive of gain. Allowable performances are:

- live performances in public, primarily by students, of a work such as a play or music
- playing sound recordings

- playing radio or television programs live while being broadcast or transmitted by cable (this is arguably true for Web casts as well)

This provision would probably allow school libraries to conduct children's story hours (however, there is no equivalent provision for non-school libraries to do so).

TAPING RADIO AND TELEVISION PROGRAMS

An educator may tape off-air a single copy of a news program or a news commentary program, excluding documentaries on radio or television, at the time the program is aired. This must be done for the purposes of playing the copy to students for educational or training purposes. This is subject to some conditions. The copy may be shown any number of times within one year after it is made to an audience primarily composed of students of the school on its premises and for educational or training purposes. After one year, the copy must be destroyed or royalties must be paid and there must be compliance with certain terms and conditions. These royalties are set by the Copyright Board.

In addition, an instructor may tape a single copy of any other type of work (other than a news program or news commentary program) from a radio or television broadcast at the time the program is aired, and keep it for up to thirty days to determine whether or not to play the copy for educational or training purposes. At the end of the thirty days, the copy must be destroyed, or royalties paid as set by the Copyright Board, and use is then subject to the Board's terms and conditions.

In both of the above situations, the copies must be lawful ones. For instance, if you receive a pay-per-view signal via illegal means, then the off-air taping exceptions do not apply.

PUBLIC PERFORMANCE OF MUSICAL WORKS

A college or school, religious, charitable or fraternal organization may publicly perform a musical work in furtherance of a religious, educational or charitable object without paying royalties to the copyright holder of the musical work. In order for this provision to apply, the performance must be closely connected to the "object." For example,

> . . . singing or performing music in and as part of a church service is directly furthering that service, itself a charitable object; an educational meeting with musical interpolations is carried on in a charitable sense and is itself such an object;

and in the relief or amelioration of poverty, the accompaniment of the music of an orchestra at a Christmas dinner given to the poor through the means of voluntary contributions is equally so.[7]

The provision would probably also apply to playing a record (and the embodied music) in a classroom for purposes of studying the music, or a to college music class that is learning the score to a piece of music by performing it in the classroom. However, the provision will not apply where the music is performed in a school for purposes of entertainment, for instance, at a school dance, though it may apply with respect to an assembly undertaken for educational purposes.

Note that this provision merely exempts the payment of royalties. The copyright owner still has the right, by obtaining a court injunction, to stop the performance in question.

PUBLICATION OF SHORT PASSAGES IN A COLLECTION

The *Copyright Act* allows the publication of short passages in collections for school use without violating copyright. However, a number of conditions apply:

- the collection must be mainly composed of non-copyright matter
- the collection must be intended for the use of schools and must state this in the title and in any advertisements issued by the publisher
- the passages must be from published literary works not themselves published for the use of schools
- not more than two passages from works by the same author may be published by the same publisher within five years
- the source from which the passages are taken must be acknowledged
- the name of the author, if given in the source, must be mentioned

COPYRIGHT COLLECTIVES

Because the use of copyright materials is so widespread in schools and often immediate access is required with respect to those materials, copyright collectives (groups of copyright holders that administer their copyrights as a whole) can provide much of the access necessary for schools. Collectives are also discussed in Chapter 11 and contact information for various copyright collectives is in Chapter 14. Collectives exist for many different types of rights and works including the public performance of music and artistic works. Schools will most likely have the greatest contact with the reprography collectives (that license photocopying and related reproduction).

CANCOPY, also known as the Canadian Copyright Licensing Agency, is the collective for Canadian users of print materials outside of Quebec, and COPIBEC is the collective for users of print materials within Quebec. CANCOPY and COPIBEC have reciprocal agreements with each other and if your school has a licence with either collective, they will be licensed for English and French print materials throughout Canada. It is not therefore necessary to have a licence with both CANCOPY and COPIBEC.

In late 1999, CANCOPY negotiated a single blanket licence for photocopying published print materials in all elementary and secondary schools outside Quebec. The licence also covers school boards, where they exist, and ministries of education. This pan-Canadian licence was negotiated through the Council of Ministers of Education, Canada (CMEC). The licence is in effect beginning in 1999 and ending in 2004. The licence allows copying up to ten percent of a book, journal, magazine or newspaper. This ten percent limit may be exceeded if, for example, a teacher offering a course needs to copy: an entire chapter comprising twenty percent or less of a book; an entire short story, play, essay, or poem from an anthology; a newspaper, magazine or journal article; an entry from a reference work; an illustration or photograph from a publication containing other works; and in limited circumstances specified in the licence, out-of-print books. In addition, the licence allows works published in Canada to be copied into large print format. Schools may copy a class set, including two copies for the teachers, and they may make a reasonable number of copies for library use. Systematic, cumulative copying from the same published work beyond the above limits for one course of study or program in one academic year, or over time for retention in files, is explicitly not permitted. The licence does not permit copying of excerpts from more than three sources that together total more than nineteen pages for inclusion in a course pack. It does not permit copying of tests, exam papers, workbooks and activity books, instruction manuals and teachers' guides; government publications (except those of the Quebec government); print music and works by authors, artists and publishers on CANCOPY's exclusions list. See Figure 10.1 relating to the pan-Canadian licence.

In addition, CANCOPY has a model agreement negotiated with the Association of Universities and Colleges of Canada (AUCC) which covers specified copying within colleges and universities. CANCOPY's postsecondary licence covers limited photocopying by students, faculty and other university staff for classroom use, and in university libraries and oncampus copy shops. See Figure 10.2 for details.

Figure 10.1: The Pan-Canadian Licence

The Pan-Canad

Every publicly funded school outside the Province of Québec has a licence to copy through CANCOPY -- the same licence. The licence also includes school boards, where they exist, as well as ministries and departments of education. It was developed by CANCOPY* in co-operation with ministers of education, the Ontario school board associations and the Council of Ministers of Education, Canada, and is in effect until August 2004.

Copying Guidelines

The licence gives educators permission to copy from a vast repertoire of commercially published books, magazines and newspapers - in advance. As long as you adhere to the copying guidelines, your copying is legal and will not infringe copyright. Please note, the licence extends to copying done in support of educational purposes only.

You can photocopy

Fax, type and word process (without adaptation), make slides and overheads, duplicate from a stencil, copy onto microform (for research and archival purposes)

Excerpts from published books, magazines and newspapers

Except for these types of publication, which are not covered

X Print music
X Workbooks and other publications intended for one-time use
X Work cards
X Instruction manuals and teachers' guides
X Tests and assignment sheets

Published in Canada and these foreign countries

Australia, Denmark, France, Germany, Iceland, Ireland, Italy, Liechtenstein, Malta, Netherlands, New Zealand, Norway, South Africa, Spain, Switzerland, UK, US

Up to 10% of any work

For any course of study or program over any school year, or over time for retention in files, or more, if required to copy:

✓ A whole short story, play, essay or poem from an anthology
✓ A whole article from a newspaper, magazine or journal
✓ A whole entry from a reference work
✓ An entire artistic work from a publication containing other works
✓ A whole chapter from a book, as long as that chapter does not comprise more than 20% of the book

Is there a credit to the author and the source on at least one page of your copies?

*CANCOPY is a non-profit organization established by Canadian creators and publishers to administer copying rights and facilitate access to published works. The *Copyright Act* protects creators and publishers who rely on royalties from the use of their works including photocopying.

ian Licence:
Are you covered?

Exclusion of Digital Uses
This licence applies to paper publications only. It does not apply to non-paper publications of any kind. The licence authorizes copying of print publications using a number of digital processes, but for the purposes of generating a paper copy only. Files generated in the course of copying must not be transmitted over a computer network or duplicated electronically in any way.

Prohibition Against Assembly of Course Packs for Students
The licence prohibits the inclusion of copies in course packs for students. A course pack is a set of materials, compiled at once or over time, which is designed to support a course or unit of study and substitute for a learning resource that might otherwise have been purchased. A compilation that includes copies taken from fewer than 4 sources and totaling fewer than 20 pages is not a course pack for the purposes of the licence.

Prohibition Against Sale of Copies
The licence prohibits recovery of more than the direct cost of production and distribution of copies.

Students with Perceptual Disabilities
Teachers and others involved in educating the perceptually disabled have permission to copy into large print for these students. As long as they were published in Canada, you may copy work cards, assignment sheets, tests and examination papers, and material intended for one-time use such as workbooks and activity books. And any Canadian work covered by the licence may be copied in its entirety.

A Special Note About Copying Visual Materials
If you wish to make a slide from an artistic work of a living artist, there is a restriction. The slide must also include material in addition to the artistic work, above and beyond a caption, unless you have confirmed that no slide of that work is available for purchase.

Limited Permission to Copy Work Cards, Tests and Assignment Sheets
The licence permits copying of up to 10% over time from work cards and tests and assignment sheets, where the portion to be copied was not intended for one-time use and you have obtained written confirmation from CANCOPY that it is no longer commercially available.

Copying Government Publications
The licence does not apply to publications of the Government of Canada or any provincial or territorial government, except the Province of Québec. Check the permissions statement on these publications before you copy.

Special Permissions for Libraries
Libraries may copy in excess of the proportional limits, copying as many pages as required, to:
- prevent deterioration of a rare and fragile work in their collection
- repair a damaged copy of a work in their collection, or
- replace a copy of a work that has gone missing from their collection.

This permission applies to out-of-print works only. Librarians must first obtain written confirmation of print status from CANCOPY.

Toll-free Access to CANCOPY Expertise and Additional Licensing
If you have questions, or require permission to copy outside the scope of the licence, you may contact CANCOPY toll-free.

An exclusions list of specific copyright holders and specific works may be issued by CANCOPY in advance of September 1 of any year of the Pan-Canadian licence. It is the responsibility of signatories to the licence to bring any such list to the attention of all personnel authorized to copy. ❖ The Pan-Canadian licence includes an indemnity. All claims are to be brought to CANCOPY's immediate attention. ❖ The Pan-Canadian licence does not restrict, hinder or prohibit copying otherwise permitted by law. ❖ This document does not encapsulate all terms and conditions of the Pan-Canadian licence.

CAN©OPY
Canadian Copyright Licensing Agency
(416) 868-1620 / 1-800-893-5777
Fax: (416) 868-1621
www.cancopy.com

Figure 10.2: CANCOPY — Association of Universities and Colleges of Canada (AUCC) Poster

Under Canada's Copyright Act, it is illegal to copy most published materials without permission. Under a CANCOPY Post-Secondary Licence, you are allowed to make photocopies under the following restrictions.

Volume

No copying shall exceed 10% of a published work or the following, which ever is greater:
© an entire chapter, which is 20% or less of a book
© an entire newspaper article or page
© an entire single short story, play, poem, essay or article from a book or periodical issue containing other works
© an entire single item of print music from a book or periodical containing other works
© an entire entry from an encyclopaedia, dictionary, annotated bibliography or similar reference work
© an entire reproduction of an artistic work from a book or periodical issue containing other works.

Number of Copies

The licence authorizes the making of one copy for each student in a class and two for each professor. It also authorizes the institution to make copies for administrative purposes.

Authorized Uses

The Agreement authorizes making copies for the purposes of education or recreation only. It does not extend to copies made for use in association with political activities or commercial products and services.

Excluded Works

The licence does not cover:
© Crown publications
© Most print music
© "Consumables", works intended to be used and replaced i.e. workbooks
© Letters to the editor and advertisements in newspapers, magazines or periodicals
© Publications containing commercially valuable proprietary information, such as newsletters
© Works on the exclusions list (a copy is available from your institution's administration)

Permission to copy is subject to certain limits.
Please take care to keep within these limits.

© Works containing a notice expressly prohibiting copying under licence with a Reproduction Rights organization.

Fair Dealing

Some of the photocopying done by universities may be covered by a concept in copyright law known as "fair dealing". No permission is needed for copying done as "fair dealing" for the purposes of private study, research, criticism, review, or newspaper summary. However, "fair dealing" isn't defined in the current law and knowing just what you may do isn't easy. (For the AUCC's interpretation of "fair dealing", contact Steve Wills, AUCC's Senior Policy Analyst by telephone at (613) 563-1236, ext. 234, or by e-mail at "swills@aucc.ca.)

In the past when students, faculty and staff wanted to make copies that didn't fall under "fair dealing," they were required to contact individual copyright holders and obtain permission. That process was often onerous and time-consuming. Many individuals didn't even know where to start.

Thanks to the licence your university has signed with CANCOPY, much of the guesswork has been taken out of this process. With the CANCOPY licence and "fair dealing," you should be able to copy the materials you need in the course of your day-to-day activities.

Prohibition Against Sale

The sale of copies is prohibited unless reported and paid for through the university.

CAN©OPY®

Canadian Copyright Licensing Agency
1 Yonge Street, Suite 1900 • Toronto, ON, M5E 1E5
416 868 1620 • Fax 416 868 1621 • Toll Free 1 (800) 893 5777
www.cancopy.com

In Quebec, the Société Québécoise de Gestion Collective des Droits de Reproduction, known as COPIBEC, manages photocopying rights. COPIBEC was founded in 1997 and plays a similar role to its predecessor L'union des Écrivains Québécois (UNEQ). UNEQ and the Quebec Department of Education have had an agreement since 1984 with regard to the reproduction of copyright works in CEGEPs, primary and secondary schools. At the current time, COPIBEC licenses pre-school, primary, secondary and higher education institutions that provide photocopying permissions for teachers and administrators in such works as books and newspaper and magazine articles. For all levels of education, copying is permitted up to ten percent or up to twenty-five pages of a work in COPIBEC's repertoire. Specific details on copying under COPIBEC's agreement are available on its Web site.

In general, agreements with COPIBEC and CANCOPY do not cover unpublished works.

Licence agreements with copyright collectives have a limited duration. You should follow the "copyright news" in order to ensure you always have up-to-date information on the licence agreements that cover you. Also, when renewed, it is possible that a licence may contain different terms and conditions and allow for different amounts of photocopying than the previous agreement. Brochures and posters on your school's agreement with CANCOPY or COPIBEC may be available upon request. In addition, CANCOPY and COPIBEC have Web sites with helpful information, or you may contact them by telephone if you have specific questions and/or request written information. Contact information for CANCOPY and COPIBEC are set out in Chapter 14: Using Copyright Materials.

How the Exceptions Interplay with Collectives
A question that often arises with the new exceptions in the *Copyright Act* is the interplay between the exceptions and a collective. If you do not have a CANCOPY or COPIBEC licence, the exceptions may permit you to copy certain things without obtaining permission. If you do have a licence, the exceptions may still be helpful for copying not covered in the licence. For example, even though a newsletter may not be covered by your licence, you may be able to copy a small amount that would fall under the fair dealing provision, or to reproduce it for purposes of a test or exam. In some situations, a licence with CANCOPY or COPIBEC will permit you to copy much more than the *Copyright Act*.

If certain copying is allowed under a CANCOPY or COPIBEC licence, then there may be no need to claim that same copying as covered by the exceptions. By copying under your licence as opposed to the exceptions, you would not be obligated to abide by the record-keeping required in relation to some of the exceptions.

LIBRARIES, ARCHIVES AND MUSEUMS

Until recently, libraries and archives had very few exceptions specifically intended for them, and museums had none. However, recent changes to the *Copyright Act* provide a number of exceptions. Except for some additional exceptions for archives as set out below, these exceptions are grouped together for any eligible library, archive or museum. An eligible library, archive or museum ("LAM") is one that is not established or conducted for profit, and not part of, not administered, and not directly or indirectly controlled by, a body that is established or conducted for profit—such as a special library like the library at IBM. Also, the LAM must hold and maintain a collection of documents and other materials that is open to the public or to researchers. The government may include other non-profit institutions by regulation.

In addition to the discussions below, see the previous two sections on copyright collectives.

MANAGEMENT AND MAINTENANCE

The LAM exceptions are divided into a number of headings. The first one allows a LAM to make a copy of a work or other subject-matter for the maintenance or management of its permanent collection. This applies to both published and unpublished works. It applies to works in the LAM's permanent collection or the permanent collection of another LAM. This exception applies in the following circumstances:

- if the original is rare or unpublished and it is deteriorating, damaged or lost, or at the risk of deteriorating or becoming damaged or lost (if a copy is not commercially available)
- for on-site consultation purposes if the original cannot be viewed, handled or listened to because of its condition or because of the atmospheric conditions in which it must be kept (if a copy is not commercially available)
- in an alternative format if the original is in an obsolete format or the technology required to use the original is unavailable (if a copy is not commercially available)

- for internal record-keeping and cataloguing
- for insurance purposes or police investigations
- "if necessary for restoration"

Any intermediate copies made for making the above preservation copies must be destroyed as soon as they are no longer needed.

FAIR DEALING

A LAM may reproduce on behalf of a patron anything that the patron would be permitted to copy under the fair dealing provision. There must be no motive of gain. Note that this is restricted to reproduction and not other rights in the *Copyright Act*. Therefore, if a patron may broadcast a part of a work under the fair dealing provision, this does not permit a library to do so on behalf of that patron. If the copy is made after December 31, 2003, there are no record-keeping requirements when making this copy; otherwise, the record-keeping requirements described below under "Single Copies of Articles," apply to such copying.

Any copying done under this section must have text printed on the copy or a stamp applied to the copy or by other suitable means stating "that the copy is to be used solely for the purposes of research or private study" and "that any use of the copy for a purpose other than research or private study may require the authorization of the copyright owner of the work in question."

SINGLE COPIES OF ARTICLES

Certain articles from magazines and periodicals may be copied under the new LAM provisions. The exception applies to an article in a "scholarly, scientific or technical periodical"—a term that is not defined in the *Act*. It also applies to an article in a newspaper or periodical if that newspaper or periodical was published more than one year before the copy was made. Therefore, on May 1, 2000, you may not use this exception to copy an article in a newspaper published on January 1, 2000, but you may use it to copy an article in a newspaper published on January 1, 1999. "Newspaper or periodical" is not specifically defined in the *Act* but is one other than a scholarly, scientific or technical periodical. An article in a newspaper or periodical does not include a work of fiction, poetry or a dramatic or musical work.

For copying to take place under the above exception, a number of conditions must exist:

- the person requesting the copy (i.e., the patron) must satisfy the LAM that he or she will not use the copy for a purpose other than research or private study

- the library may only provide the patron with a single copy of the article
- the copy must be made by "reprographic reproduction," which is generally photocopying and does not include, for example, scanning the article into a computer
- there must be no motive of gain

To copy under this provision, certain records must be kept. The LAM must record the following information for each copy of each article made under this provision. Note that if the LAM has a licence with CANCOPY or COPIBEC and that licence covers this kind of copying, the LAM may copy under the licence and therefore would not be required to keep these records. Records required are:

- the name of the LAM making the copy
- if an interlibrary loan, the name of the requesting LAM (see below)
- the date of the request
- sufficient information to identify the work being copied such as title, ISBN, ISSN
- if applicable, the name of the newspaper, periodical, or scholarly, scientific or technical periodical in which the work is found
- if applicable, the date or volume and number of the newspaper, periodical, or scholarly, scientific or technical periodical
- the numbers of the copied pages

The LAM must keep a copy request form with the above information or may keep the information in any other manner that may be accessed in a readable form within a reasonable time, for example, in an electronic database. Such records must be kept for at least three years. The records must be accessible to the copyright owner, his or her representative, or a copyright collective in manners specified in the regulations.

INTERLIBRARY LOAN
One LAM may make a single copy of an article as described above for a patron of another LAM. The article being copied must be in a "printed form." Also, the copy given to the patron may not be in a digital form.

Use of Copyright Warnings
There is a new provision in the law that states that a non-profit educational institution, library, archive or museum does not infringe copyright if a copyright warning is posted near a photocopying machine on its premises. For this provision to apply, the following conditions must be met:

- the photocopier is installed by or with the approval of the school or LAM on its premises for use by students, instructors or staff at the school, or by persons using the LAM
- the school or LAM has a licence with CANCOPY or COPIBEC or is in the process of negotiating one, or the school or LAM is paying a collective under a certified tariff or the collective has filed a proposed tariff with the Copyright Board
- a notice warning of infringement of copyright is affixed to, or within the immediate vicinity of, every photocopier in a place and manner that is readily visible and legible to persons using the photocopier
- the notice must contain at least the following information:

WARNING!
Works protected by copyright may be copied on this photocopier only if authorized by

(a) the *Copyright Act* for the purpose of fair dealing or under specific exceptions set out in that *Act*;
(b) the copyright owner; or
(c) a licence agreement between this institution and a collective society or a tariff, if any.

For details of authorized copying, please consult the licence agreement or the applicable tariff, if any, and other relevant information available from a staff member.

The Copyright Act provides for civil and criminal remedies for infringement of copyright.

The *Act* does not provide a similar provision for other equipment such as VCRs or scanners, or computers with Internet access, on a school or LAM premise, which may be used to infringe copyright. As such, following the above is no guarantee that a school or LAM may be exempt from infringement for illegal copying taking place on this equipment. However, it may be prudent to post similar warnings near such equipment.

Archives Only

In addition to the above provisions for LAMs, there is a special provision for archives to copy an unpublished work that is deposited in the archive. In order for this exception to apply, a number of conditions must be met:

- the copyright owner must not have prohibited copying the work
- the archive is satisfied that the person using the copy will only use it for research or private study
- the archive may only make one copy of the work
- any fees for copying must be limited to the archive's costs including overhead but the archive may not profit from this copying
- there must be no motive of gain

In addition, if the work is deposited in the archive after September 1, 1999, then the archive must notify the person depositing the work in the archive that the archive may copy the work under this provision.

Any copying done under this section must have text printed on the copy or a stamp applied to the copy or by other suitable means stating that "the copy is to be used solely for the purposes of research or private study" and that "any use of the copy for a purpose other than research or private study may require the authorization of the copyright owner of the work in question."

Where an author of a work in an archive is still living or where he or she died on or after January 1, 1949, an archive may have further obligations regarding copying that work, if he or she has not already consented to copying by the archive. In these situations, the archive must try to obtain the permission of the copyright owner of the work (i.e., not necessarily the author or depositor of the work). If he or she consents, the archive may copy the work; if the owner does not provide permission to copy the work, then the archive may not copy the work. However, if the archive cannot locate the copyright owner after reasonable efforts to do so, the archive may make a single copy of the work provided the archive is satisfied the patron will use the copy only for research or private study and is not making a profit from that copy. The archive must keep a record of any copying done under this exception in the prescribed format.

Note that donors can deposit works with archives even if they do not own the copyright in the works. This is because it is the physical property that donors give to the archives, and not the authorization to make any copyright uses with the materials. If a donor does own copyright, he or she can grant it to the archives. Whether or not the donor owns copyright in the deposited materials, the donor can request a deposit agreement with the archives that limits copyright and non-copyright uses by the archives. Thus, the *Copyright Act* does not always govern the use to which copyright material deposited with an archive may be put.

In addition, there are some specific provisions in the *Act* for copying by the National Archives of Canada.

News Reporting and Summary

Recall that copyright does not protect ideas, facts or news as such, but only the expression of these items. News reports or summaries may , at least under copyright law, report these items. There are many cases, however, where, in preparing a report or summary, materials are used that are protected by copyright. Like other users of copyright materials, those preparing news reports and summaries must clear copyright in any protected material to be included, subject to the three provisions discussed below.

CRITICISM, REVIEW OR NEWS REPORTING

Fair dealing applies to criticism, review or news reporting. See the above section on fair dealing for an explanation of fair dealing.

PUBLIC LECTURES

There is a provision in the *Act* that allows a person, for purposes of news reporting or news summary, to report a public lecture without clearing copyright permission. The following conditions must be met for this provision to apply:

- the lecture must be delivered in public (broadcast to the public is probably not acceptable)
- there must be no conspicuous written or printed notices prohibiting the report affixed before and maintained during the lecture at or about the main entrance of the building where the lecture is given, and in a position near the lecturer

POLITICAL SPEECHES

Any person may publish a report for purposes of news reporting or news summary of an address of a political nature delivered at a public meeting.

Broadcasters

In addition to the general exceptions in the *Copyright Act* that may arguably apply to broadcasters, there is a specific exception for broadcasters for "ephemeral recordings." Under the ephemeral recordings exception, broadcasters may make a temporary copy of a performance, or an event, for later broadcast without payment to or authorization from the copyright owner. A broadcaster may, for example, tape a live figure-skating competition that includes musical accompaniment. For a thirty-day period following the making of the copy, it may be used as many times as desired by the broadcaster. Further, the exception allows a broadcaster to transfer a sound recording to a format more technically suitable for broadcasting. For example, a broadcaster may copy a CD-ROM onto a computer hard drive; this may be kept and used an indefinite amount of times during the thirty days after the making of the copy. In both of the above circumstances, with the permission of the copyright owner, the broadcaster may retain the copy for more than thirty days following its making. In both instances, the exception will not apply where broadcasters can negotiate blanket licence agreements with a copyright collective for all types of reproductions.

Another exception that may be beneficial to broadcasters is the incidental use one discussed above. For all other uses, broadcasters must clear copyright for the use of any rights necessary to broadcast a program, or to include any works, like music, in a broadcast.

Persons with Perceptual Disabilities

Under the *Copyright Act*, perceptual disability is defined as "a disability that prevents or inhibits a person from reading or hearing a literary, musical, dramatic or artistic work in its original format" and includes disabilities from: severe or total impairment of sight or hearing or the inability to focus or move one's eyes; the inability to hold or manipulate a book; or an impairment relating to comprehension.

If a person with a perceptual disability or a non-profit organization acting on his or her behalf, requests it, a person may make a copy or sound recording of, and/or translate, adapt or reproduce in sign language, a literary, musical, artistic or dramatic work (though not a cinematographic work) in a "format specially designed for persons with a perceptual disability." Also, if so requested, a person may perform in public a literary or dramatic work (though not a cinematographic work) in sign language, either live or in a "format specially designed for persons with a perceptual disability." These exceptions do *not* allow the making of a large print book. Also, the exceptions do *not* apply where the copyright protected material is commercially available in a format specially designed to meet the needs of the requesting person.

For any other uses of copyright materials (e.g., large print book version) for persons with perceptual or other disabilities, permission must be obtained from the copyright owner to produce special format materials.

Places of Worship

The only provision in the *Act* that relates to using copyright works in places of worship is a provision that allows a religious organization to perform a musical work in public if in furtherance of a religious, educational or charitable object. In this situation, compensation is not owing to the copyright owner of the musical work. This provision is discussed in further detail under exceptions for schools.

Non-profit Organizations

There are no explicit provisions in the *Copyright Act* for the use of copyright materials by non-profit organizations, clubs or associations. However, a number of exceptions in the *Copyright Act* are for specific non-profit organizations such as non-profit educational institutions, libraries, archives and museums.

Agricultural Fairs

The *Act* specifically allows playing live music or a sound recording, or broadcasting a signal with a live performance of a musical work or a sound recording of music "without motive of gain at any agricultural, agricultural-industrial exhibition or fair that receives a grant from or is held by its directors under federal, provincial or municipal authority." The courts have interpreted this provision in a very restrictive manner. The Supreme Court of Canada has held that there should be no motive of gain on the part of either the promoters or the musicians.[8] By holding this, the Supreme Court has effectively eliminated any practical application of the provision since, once promoters and musicians are paid (which they usually are), then the exception regarding the payment to composers no longer applies.

OTHER EXCEPTIONS

Cultural Property Export and Import Act

Permission of the copyright holder is not needed to make a copy of an object referred to in section 14 of the *Cultural Property Export and Import Act.*, for deposit in an institution provided for in that section.

Access to Information Act

Permission of the copyright holder is not needed to disclose, under the *Access to Information Act*, "a record within the meaning of that *Act*, or to disclose, pursuant to any like *Act* of the legislature of a province, like material."

However, this section does not authorize any person to whom a record or information is disclosed to do anything that only a copyright owner has the right to do. For example, the person has no right to reproduce or publish the disclosed information.

Privacy Act

Permission of the copyright holder is not required to disclose, under the *Privacy Act*, "personal information within the meaning of that *Act*, or to disclose, pursuant to any like *Act* of the legislature of a province, like information." However, this section does not authorize any person to whom a record or information is disclosed to do anything that only a copyright owner has the right to do.

Broadcasting Act

Permission of the copyright holder is not necessary to make a fixation or a copy of a work or other subject-matter if necessary to comply with the *Broadcasting Act* or any rule, regulation or other instrument made under it. However, that copy must be destroyed immediately when it is no longer required. For example, if the *Broadcasting Act* required that a copy of every broadcast be kept for thirty days, permission of the copyright owner would not be necessary for the making of this copy, and that copy would have to be destroyed at the expiration of the thirty days.

EXCEPTIONS FROM MORAL RIGHTS

In addition to the exceptions from copyright discussed above, which likely also apply to moral rights, the *Copyright Act* provides some specific exceptions from moral rights. These are listed below. The following acts do not, by that act alone, constitute a distortion, mutilation or other modification of the work:

- a change in the location of a work
- the physical means by which a work is exposed or the physical structure containing a work
- steps taken in good faith to restore or preserve a work

SUMMARY

The *Copyright Act* grants copyright holders a number of rights, however, the law places certain limitations on these rights that act as exceptions for those using copyright materials. These exceptions, as set out in the *Act*, are for specific purposes and specific situations.

Chapter 11

HOW CAN RIGHTS BE EXPLOITED?

Copyright is, of course, the enshrinement in law of the essential right of the creator to control the productions of his or her mind, and to be rewarded for them.

Notes for a statement by the
Honourable Flora MacDonald, M.P.,
at a press conference announcing the tabling of a
bill on copyright, Ottawa, Ontario, May 27, 1987

HOW THE *COPYRIGHT ACT* WORKS

One of the main purposes of copyright law is to grant rights to copyright holders, which they may then exchange for money. This is how the *Copyright Act* works. Take the example of the author of a book. The author negotiates with a publisher to publish the book. In exchange for the right to publish the book, the publisher pays the author royalties, which are a percentage of the selling price of the book. If the author then sells the rights to make a film adaptation of the book, the purchaser of those rights pays the author for their acquisition. The same is true if the author authorizes the translation of the book, and so on. The same scenario applies with respect to all works protected by the *Copyright Act* and all rights granted to copyright owners of works.

Now that you know the types of materials protected by copyright law, and you know the sort of rights that belong to copyright owners, you must learn how, as a creator and/or owner, you can exploit these rights and benefit from that exploitation, and how, as a consumer of copyright materials, you can obtain the required access to copyright materials.

If you are involved in exploiting rights or obtaining permission to use rights, you must understand certain fundamental concepts about the nature of the rights granted by the *Copyright Act* and the type of exploitation permissible by the law.

Rights Are "Distinct" and "Exclusive"

One of the most important concepts concerning the nature of the rights set out in the *Copyright Act* is that these rights are exclusive and distinct. "Exclusive" means that the copyright owner has the "sole right" to do what he or she chooses with a work. No one else may use a copyright work without the permission of the copyright owner. "Distinct" means that each right is separate or independent from any other right and therefore may be dealt with separately by the copyright owner. The concept of "distinct" allows a writer to assign the right to publish a book to a publisher, and the right to make a film of the book to a film producer, and the right to a third person to translate the book.

Since a creator has the sole rights in his or her creations, even where a publisher or film producer has the right to publish a book or make a movie of a book, that publisher or film producer has no subsequent rights, such as making a translation of the book or including that book in a CD-ROM or a Web site. The copyright owner must consent to each and every copyright use of a work.

Copyright Is Separate from the Physical Object

Another important concept to keep in mind is that copyright is separate from the physical object in which copyright exists. This means that ownership of copyright does not necessarily follow the physical embodiment of that copyright. For instance, the sale of a painting does not necessarily entail the abandonment of copyright by the copyright holder. Similarly, the purchase of a video does not necessarily entail that any use can be made of that video. If that video is to be shown in public, the right to perform it in public must be cleared from its copyright owner.

Copyright and Moral Rights Are Separate

Remember that copyright and moral rights are separate. Thus, a contract dealing with one does not automatically deal with the other, though in certain circumstances this may be implied from the contract.

WHO CAN EXPLOIT A WORK OR OTHER SUBJECT-MATTER?

In order to authorize someone to use a copyright work, you must have the right to do so. The general rule is that you should be an owner of copyright (see Chapter 7: Who Owns Copyright?), or have been granted permission by the copyright owner to deal with the authorization of any right set out in the *Copyright Act*.

The following people may have the right to grant others to use copyright works:

- the author of a work, provided this author is also the first owner of the copyright in the work
- a copyright owner other than the author, by virtue of one of the provisions in the *Act* granting this status, where, for example, there is an employment situation, a commissioned engraving, photograph or portrait or where the work is made for the Crown (see Chapter 7: Who Owns Copyright?)
- the owner of other subject-matter
- a legal representative which includes "heirs, executors, administrators, successors and assigns, or agents or attorneys who are thereinto duly authorized in writing." In other words, someone to whom the author or copyright owner has given such rights in writing
- a "duly authorized agent." The *Act* does not specify that a duly authorized agent must have authority in writing as is the case for a legal representative

HOW TO EXPLOIT A WORK

Licences and assignments are two ways to allow others to use a copyright work.

In an assignment situation, you "assign" your rights thereby permanently giving your copyright, or a part thereof (see divisibility of copyright, below), to someone else. The *Act* provides that the person who receives the assignment, the assignee of rights, is treated as a copyright owner with respect to those assigned rights. The assignee may use those acquired rights in the same manner as a copyright owner, within the limitations of the agreement setting out the assignment. A full or partial assignee may also take any legal action that would be open to an owner of copyright to protect those rights.

The person who is giving away certain rights, or the assignor, is treated as a copyright owner for any rights that have not been assigned. Thus, the assignor can continue to exercise copyright in certain manners.

Whereas an assignment is like a sale or transfer of rights, a licence is comparable to a lease of rights. In a licence situation, you "license" a piece of your copyright thereby temporarily permitting someone else to use your copyright material.

Using the words "assignment" or "licence" will not by themselves guarantee the type of grant of rights you wish to make. The wording of a licence agreement could be such that, in practice, it has a similar effect to an assignment. The important concept to understand is that the rights set out in the *Copyright Act* may be exploited without necessarily being sold.

In the case of an assignment, you grant an interest in the copyright material or in a specific right in that material. This interest is exclusive and cannot be granted to anyone else. In the case of a licence, there could be a grant of an interest, or the licence could be a mere permission to allow someone to use your copyright material. Where the licence entails a grant of interest, the licence must be exclusive; that is, only one person may benefit from it. Where the licence is a mere permission, one or more persons may benefit from it with respect to the exact same use of the work during the same period of time, unless of course, there is an agreement otherwise.

When the same right is licensed to more than one person at a time, it is, in technical terms, called a non-exclusive licence. For example, a non-exclusive licence may be given to many movie theatres to show a particular film. Another example is an author of an article providing the right to three different Web sites to post his article on those sites. A licensee should be aware when he or she is obtaining a non-exclusive licence that others may make the same use of the material. Several people may exercise the same rights in a licence situation (as opposed to an assignment situation) because there is no grant of interest, merely a permission to use the material.

Copyright may be assigned or licensed in a number of ways. Below is a list of ways that are specified in the *Copyright Act*. Although the discussion below may specifically refer to an assignment of copyright, the same rules generally apply to a licence.

By Rights

The *Act* states that the copyright owner of a work may assign a right "either wholly or partially." Thus, rights such as publication, reproduction and performance in public can be divided up for purposes of authorizing others to use the work. What this means is that an artist may assign the right to reproduce a painting to X, and may assign the right to exhibit the painting to Y, and perhaps retain all other rights.

The rights can be divided even more specifically. For instance, an artist may assign the right to reproduce a painting in a book to X, to reproduce the painting in a video to Y, to exhibit the painting in gallery ABC to Z, to exhibit the painting in gallery XYZ to A, to include it in a digital form in a CD-ROM, and so on.

Or a writer could give her publisher the right to publish, translate, make magazine serializations of portions and an audio version, of a book, but she may retain the right to make an electronic or a film version.

In a further example, the right of translation of a book into French could be granted to Jacques, the right to translate it into Italian to Maria, and the right to translate it into Hebrew to Mordecai. All other translation rights could be retained by the copyright owner for the time being.

There are virtually no limits in the *Copyright Act* on how rights are divided. This leaves open the possibility of negotiating the division of rights to be customized to the situation.

When dividing rights, it is not necessary to use the exact wording found in the *Copyright Act*. In one court case, an assignment included the right to "manufacture, produce, advertise, publicize, sell, distribute, license or otherwise use or dispose of the copyright material."[1] These words are not all specifically used in the copyright legislation.

By Time

The *Copyright Act* states that a copyright owner may assign copyright for the whole term of copyright, or for any part of the duration of copyright. Obviously, the longest length of time that an assignment may endure is for the full length of the copyright protection, that is, fifty years until the calendar year-end after the author's death. There is no minimum length of time for which an assignment may endure.

Different assignments can last for varying lengths of time. For instance, an assignment to X to exhibit a work can last for fifteen years, after which time Y may exhibit the work for the next fifteen years; at the same time, Z may have the right to reproduce the work for twenty-five years.

REVERSIONARY INTEREST

There is one statutory limitation on the assignment of copyright that is commonly referred to as the reversionary interest. This provision limits certain assignments to a maximum period of twenty-five years. Where an author of a work is the first owner of the copyright in it (that is, it is not a situation of employment, Crown works, commissioned engraving, photograph or portrait), any copyright acquired by contract becomes void twenty-five years after the author's death. Thus, any assignee or licensee of copyright loses his or her rights twenty-five years after the author's death. At this time, the copyright becomes part of the author's estate and only the estate has the right to deal with the copyright. Note that there is no reversion where the author disposes of the copyright by will for the period following the twenty-five-year limit to the assignee who is already assigned the copyright. Thus, the section may be avoided by bequeathing copyright for the period between twenty-five and fifty years after the author's death (but only if the bequeath is to the assignee and not some other person). It also does not apply where a work has been assigned as part of a collective work or a licence has been granted to publish a work or part thereof in a collective work.

By Territory

A copyright owner may assign a right either generally or subject to territorial limitations. This means that an author may grant a right "worldwide" (for use in the entire world) or "globally," or subject to certain territories. Examples of territorial limitations are North America, Canada or The West Indies. The size of the territory is irrelevant. Also, there are no restrictions on the segmentation of geographical location to which a copyright can be assigned. In practice, it is rare to divide copyright among a jurisdiction smaller than a country, although "English Language throughout Canada" or "French Language throughout Canada" is a commonly seen exception to this practice.

Note that the territorial grant of a right does not by itself give the right to control the distribution of legally made copies once these are available in the marketplace. Such protection is made through the specific provisions of the *Act* that prevent the importation or sale of certain foreign editions.

Registering a Grant in Interest

The *Copyright Act* allows for the (voluntary) registration of any "grant of interest" or change in ownership of copyright, or a part of copyright. This registration is through the same registration system for the initial registration of a copyright work, at the Canadian Copyright Office. The registration of a subsequent owner of a whole or part of a work protected by copyright can be extremely important to a grantee of a right in copyright. This is because any grantee who has registered a grant of interest will have priority over any other similar grantee of interest if that other interest has not been registered. For instance, if X and Y are both granted an interest in a work protected by copyright and only Y registers this interest, Y may have priority over X with respect to his or her rights in the work. The same is true if A is granted an interest on January 1, B is granted the same interest on February 1, C is granted the same interest on March 1 and D is granted the same interest on April 1, all in the same year. If only C registers this interest, C will have priority over all other claimants in that interest.

TESTAMENTARY DISPOSITIONS

Like "tangible" property, intellectual property—namely copyright—can be passed on, upon death, to other persons through a will. A person inheriting the physical property (e.g., real estate, furniture and jewellery) of an author will not necessarily inherit the intangible rights of copyright. However, if there is no specific inclusion or exclusion of copyright in a will, then upon the death of a copyright owner, copyright would pass to the heirs of the copyright owner's tangible property.

A copyright holder who, upon his or her death, would like copyright in some or all of his works to pass on to specific persons, should specify this in his or her will. Such copyright holders should consider appointing a copyright executor, that is, someone with special knowledge in the area and someone who understands the copyright holder's desires. It is important that the copyright executor be in a position that enables him or her to exercise the desires of the copyright holder, and is not in any position that may give rise to a conflict of interest. For example, a publisher may be in an awkward position to be an executor for a writer who publishes with that publisher's firm. A copyright holder is not limited to specifying one specific copyright executor. For instance, two people may jointly be the executor, or there may be different executors for different works or with respect to different rights in the same work.

COPYRIGHT IN FUTURE WORKS

The current *Copyright Act* only deals with the granting of rights in existing works. There is no specific mention of assignments or licences of creations to be made in the future. One case has held that there can be an assignment in future works in the form of an agreement to assign.[2]

In practical terms, assignments in future works often take place. For example, a writer signs a publishing contract with a publishing house for a yet unwritten book. The same is true with respect to music publishing contracts.

"Future" Rights

Because electronic and digital rights are relatively new and the use and value of these rights is still being determined, current licence and assignment agreements may request the rights for any medium whatsoever whether currently existing or as yet to be "discovered." Copyright owners should carefully think about giving away such broad rights. For instance, a copyright holder who published a book twenty years ago may still have the electronic rights to that book, however, if twenty years ago he signed an agreement to publish the book in any medium whatsoever whether then existing or in the future, he probably already gave away his electronic rights.

If a copyright holder is given an offer to assign future rights to a work, the copyright holder should consider whether the sum of money is worth the value of "unknown" rights and whether he or she should retain and negotiate those rights at a later date. Copyright holders must always keep in mind that each right has a value attached to it. Persons obtaining electronic rights should, on the other hand, ensure that they have all the necessary rights to be able to create and distribute an electronic product. Digital copyright, electronic rights and licensing are discussed in greater detail in Chapter 16: Digital Copyright and Electronic Rights.

THE VALUE OF RIGHTS

Like most things in an agreement concerning the use of copyright materials, the value of permission to use the materials is a matter of negotiation to be agreed upon by the involved parties. The *Copyright Act* does not set out the amount of money or other compensation for which a work may be negotiated. The *Act* sets out the rights of a copyright holder, then it is up to that copyright holder, or a representative, to place a value on that right when permitting particular uses in particular circumstances.

The value of a right will depend on many factors including the nature of the copyright material, the popularity of the creator, the use(s) to which the material is to be made and the demand in the marketplace. A copyright holder and anyone wishing to use copyright material must come to terms on the value of any assignment or licence. In some circumstances, artists' organizations may have information on compensation rates, which may be helpful for both creators and users when determining such rates in particular cases.

When the value of a right is based on monetary compensation, the copyright holder may receive a one-time flat fee or ongoing payments based upon the quantity of copies sold, or more often, based upon the revenue received, from the use of the copyright material. These ongoing payments are referred to as royalties.

A "royalty advance," which is usually "recoupable" against future earnings, can also be negotiated. For instance, a writer may get a lump sum payment upon signing a contract with a book publisher. This is called a royalty advance. When the book is published and sold in the marketplace, the writer may be entitled to royalties based upon a percentage of the sale price of the book. Before paying the writer any royalties, the publisher will first deduct any royalty advances made to the writer. In that sense, the advance is recoupable. The manner in which royalties and advances are set out in an agreement vary in each industry such as film, book publishing, e-media and the visual arts. Specific industry associations may be able to guide you on these matters.

ASSIGNMENT MUST BE IN WRITING

The *Copyright Act* specifically states that no assignment or grant is valid unless it is in writing and signed by the owner of the right in respect of which the assignment or grant is made. Thus, where there is an assignment of copyright or a licence granting an interest in copyright, there should be a written agreement to this effect signed by the copyright owner and the person obtaining any rights. A verbal agreement is not adequate unless it is confirmed in writing. If there is no written agreement regarding the assignment of copyright, ownership of copyright is determined by the rules set out in the *Act*.

Both exclusive and non-exclusive licences that do not entail a proprietary interest may be granted orally. The fact that a written agreement is not mandatory should not prevent the making of one. A written agreement can clearly set out the terms and conditions of any agreement and can provide clarity and proof in any situation.

What Is a Valid Contract?

In any agreement, whether in the form of a licence or assignment, the basic requirements of a valid contract must be present. As a basic rule, a valid contract or agreement has three components:

- offer
- acceptance of the offer
- consideration

An offer is a proposal, and manifestation of willingness, by one person to enter into a contract with another person, based on certain terms and conditions. The offer must be communicated and the other person must have the chance to be able to reject or accept it. The offer must be one that is capable of being accepted. Acceptance of the offer means that the person to whom an offer was made has agreed to enter into the contract. The acceptance can be in the form of conduct or by words.

A valid contract must include the element of consideration. Consideration is something that is of some value in the eyes of the law. Money is one example of consideration. *Black's Law Dictionary* defines consideration as "The inducement to a contract . . . [s]ome right, interest, profit or benefit accruing to one party, or some forbearance, detriment, loss, or responsibility, given, suffered, or undertaken by the other."

A contract is valid only between the parties who agreed to it. Any terms and conditions to which the parties agree, provided they do not contravene any specific laws, may be included in the contract. A contract need not take a specific form or be drafted by particular people. It can be written on a napkin by the parties involved or be prepared by a lawyer. In most situations, there is no requirement that the contract be in writing; note the exception in the case of an assignment or grant of interest in copyright. Although an oral contract may be valid in many circumstances, it is always a good idea to have a written contract since, if the parties to the agreement ever end up in court, a written agreement will be easier to prove than an oral agreement.

Contracts vary from industry to industry and in each particular circumstance depending on the negotiated terms and conditions. Standard contracts, for example for book publishing, screenplay options, art exhibitions, CD-ROM and Web site content, etc., are available in various books and publications and through professional organizations. These contracts will highlight points you need to address in your own situation, however, they should be thoroughly examined and customized to meet your particular circumstances.

MORAL RIGHTS

Assigning Moral Rights

Moral rights cannot be assigned. This is because moral rights protect the reputation of an author and it would be illogical for a subsequent copyright owner to protect the reputation of an author, provided the author was still alive.

Waiving Moral Rights

Although moral rights cannot be assigned, an author can decide not to exercise these rights, and may waive the exercise of them. Moral rights may be waived in whole or in part. An author, then, may agree not to exercise certain rights and can still retain other moral rights. For example, an author could waive the moral right to have his or her name appear in association with a work, but retain the right to have a work used in association with a service, cause or institution. Further, there is nothing in the *Act* to prevent an author from waiving rights in favour of one person in one arrangement and not waiving them in agreements with other persons.

If an author chooses to waive a moral right in a work, it should be expressed clearly and the author should understand what he or she is doing. The mere fact that an author is assigning copyright in a work does not mean that the author is also waiving the moral rights. If you waive moral rights, you will not be able to stop any changes or manipulations to images, text, music, etc., including those in digital formats. The *Act* does not specify that a moral rights waiver need be in writing, and a waiver may therefore be in writing, oral, express or implied.[3]

Where an author waives his or her moral rights in a work in favour of an assignee or licensee of copyright, any new copyright owner or licensee may also be privy to a previous waiver of moral rights. This is true unless the author in connection with the original waiver has indicated something to the contrary in the original waiver; for instance, that the waiver did not extend any further than the owner or licensee on behalf of whom the waiver was originally made.

Testamentary Dispositions

There are specific rules in the *Copyright Act* dealing with moral rights upon the death of the author of a copyright work. The *Act* states that when an author dies, his or her moral rights pass to the person to whom those rights are specifically left. Where there is no specific provision dealing with moral rights in a will and an author dies with a will that deals with copyright in the work, moral rights pass to the person to whom that copyright is left. If neither of the above two situations occur, moral rights pass to the person entitled to any other (tangible) property belonging to the author. If a person is bequeathed moral rights, he or she in turn may bequeath those same moral rights to another person.

Note

Since copyright can be divided in a variety of ways, be very specific about the rights set out in any agreement concerning copyright and/or moral rights. Specificity is required with respect to the particular rights, duration of assignment or licence, territorial limitations and royalties. As a copyright owner, make sure you only license or assign those rights that are necessary for that particular exploitation. As a licensee or assignee, make sure you obtain all the necessary rights to allow you to exploit the material in the manner you wish. Also, always keep in mind that moral rights cannot be assigned or licensed and are treated separately from copyright.

NEIGHBOURING RIGHTS

Similar to economic rights in works as discussed above, the owner of a performer's performance, sound recording and broadcast signal, may assign or license the right in whole or in part. For example, a performer may license the use of his performance for purposes of broadcasting or fixation. (However, this does not apply if the performer authorizes the use of a performance in a cinematograph.)

The blank audio recording media levy may also be licensed or assigned.

THE COLLECTIVE ADMINISTRATION OF COPYRIGHT

There is nothing in the *Copyright Act* that states that a copyright owner must exercise copyright on an individual basis. In fact, in some circumstances, copyright holders cannot collect royalties unless they do so as a "group." There are a number of copyright holder groups, or copyright collectives, that administer different rights in the *Act*. Collectives, also known as "societies" or "licensing bodies" are specifically referred to in the *Act* and, in many respects, are governed by it. In certain respects, these collectives operate under their own rules. This section will discuss various aspects of collectives.

The collective exercise of copyright has been used effectively in the Canadian music industry for over seventy years. It is also used, domestically and internationally, with respect to the administration of other rights, such as the right to reproduce (as in photocopying). When a copyright holder joins a collective, the copyright holder permits the collective to negotiate royalties on his or her behalf. These royalties are collectable from consumers of copyright materials, and once collected by the collective are distributed back to the appropriate copyright owners.

There are generally two types of licences that a collective can negotiate with users of copyright materials:

- blanket licences
- specific use licences (also known as individual licences or transactional licences)

A blanket licence covers all the materials that a collective represents. These materials are known as the collective's repertoire. A blanket licence will allow a user to do specified things with any and all materials in the repertoire. Blanket licences are paid for in advance for a specified period of time and allow unlimited use, for example, copying or performing in public, within the terms of the licence. For instance, a licence to perform music in a certain bar may cost $1,000, which covers a one-year period for the performance of all music in that bar.

The other type of licence does not give "blanket" permission to use all of the copyright materials in a collective's repertoire. For example, a specific use licence requires clearance and payment each time material is used. A specific use licence requires clearance and permission for each type of material. Thus, material could be cleared to be used several times and in different media.

One of the primary reasons for the establishment of collectives under the *Copyright Act* is for them to issue blanket licences, thereby eliminating the need for a multitude of permissions to clear copyright. However, another important role of certain collectives is to collect royalties or levies payable under the *Copyright Act* that are only payable to collectives and not directly to individual rights holders. The collectives would collect and distribute the royalties or levies to appropriate rights holders. In the following situations, rights holders may only receive payments through a collective:

- retransmission right of telecommunication signals
- performance in public or broadcast of a sound recording
- blank audio recording tape levy
- off-air taping of radio and television programs by educational institutions

Collectives have proven themselves to work well for the administration of certain rights, but do not lend themselves to all rights. However, where they exist, collectives may be advantageous over the individual exercise of copyright for a variety of reasons. For example, technology like photocopiers make it impossible for an individual creator to monitor the unauthorized use of copyrights. Collectives can ensure that creators are compensated for the use of their materials. Collectives can save creators time and aggravation. They eliminate the creators' role in giving individual copyright permission and replying to numerous letters and phone calls requesting permission to use their copyrights, and from negotiating royalties. The collective replies to requests by potential users of copyright materials, negotiates a royalty with them, collects the money and distributes it to the copyright holder.

In addition to dealing with royalties, some collectives may take appropriate action to defend a violation of copyright or may provide assistance in defending the interests of its members. Also, collectives may act as a lobbying group with the government, for example, with respect to the revision of the copyright law.

Collectives are also advantageous to users of copyright materials. They provide users with a specific place from which to obtain copyright permission. Often, the collective is the only place where the user must go to clear the rights. (When new collectives are in their initial stages, they might not represent all rights holders whose permissions are required, so users may have to consult more than one source.) Collectives are experts at clearing copyright; that is their role. Thus, permission can be obtained quickly and easily. The costs of royalties are usually set in advance and there is certainty of these costs that can be helpful in planning budgets. Permission can often be obtained on a blanket basis, thereby eliminating the time and effort of obtaining permission for each individual use and/or type of material.

Although each collective may have a different mandate and operate differently, they all share some common ground. Basically, copyright holders join the appropriate collective, that is, the collective that exercises the particular right(s) that concern their creations. The collectives then establish a royalty rate to be paid by various users of the copyright materials in their repertoire. In the case of the performing rights collective and the retransmission ones, for example, the Copyright Board, a specialized tribunal dealing only with specific copyright matters, determines this rate. In the case of other collectives like the photocopying ones, the Copyright Board will only help set the rate and terms and conditions if so requested by either the collective or the person or user with whom the royalty rate is being negotiated. Once the rates are set, users are able to buy blanket licences or to obtain access to individual copyright materials, upon paying the appropriate fee. The collective collects all these fees, applies some of it to administration costs and distributes the remaining monies to copyright holders, based upon a suitable formula.

Collectives do not, in general, deal with moral rights.

Although collectives are regulated by the *Copyright Act*, the day-to-day operations and rules of each collective are established on an individual basis; no two collectives will operate in exactly the same manner. If you are interested in joining a collective, or accessing works within a collective's repertoire, you should contact the collective that deals with your type of rights and/or creations. Contact information for many collectives is in Chapter 14: Using Copyright Materials.

SUMMARY

A copyright holder, or representative, can assign or license, on an individual basis or through a copyright collective, the economic and neighbouring rights set out in the *Copyright Act*. These rights can be divided by right, time and territory. The assignment or license of copyrights has no effect on the transfer of ownership of moral rights. In fact, moral rights cannot be assigned or licensed, but the exercise of them may be waived by an author. Copyrights and moral rights may be dealt with in a will.

Chapter 12

HOW IS COPYRIGHT VIOLATED?

"Anything they take off my record is mine," says the soul music pioneer [James Brown], speaking from his Augusta, Ga., office. "Is it all right if I take some paint off your house and put it on mine? Can I take a button off your shirt and put it on mine? Can I take a toenail off your foot—is that all right with you?"
Michael Miller, "The questionable ethics of modern creativity," *The Wall Street Journal*, as printed in *The Globe and Mail*, Sept. 7, 1987, p. B4

WHAT IS A VIOLATION OF COPYRIGHT?

Violation of copyright means a breach of the copyright law. "Infringement" is the legal term used to denote this violation.

Under the Canadian copyright law, there are two types of violations. Direct violation occurs where a right in the *Act* is directly violated, and indirect violation occurs through dealings with infringing copies. These dealings must normally be of a commercial nature. Each type of violation is described below.

To fully understand this chapter, you should read Chapter 9: Rights Protected by Copyright as well as Chapter 10: Limitations on Rights. Chapter 13 will discuss the remedies for violations of copyright.

TERMS USED TO DESCRIBE VIOLATIONS OF COPYRIGHT

So far, any breaches of the *Copyright Act* have been referred to as violations or infringements. Infringement is the term used in the copyright statute. Violation means infringement and is the term used in lay language. There are a number of other terms the public uses in connection with copyright violation or related activities. These terms include plagiarism, piracy, bootlegging and counterfeiting. These are not legal expressions found in the copyright statute, but may include activities that are referred to in the *Act*. These words are explained below in terms of their actual meaning and also in terms of the copyright law. Where aspects of these activities are not covered by copyright law, they may be unlawful under other areas of the law.

Plagiarism

Plagiarism is a term often used in association with literary works. According to *Black's Law Dictionary*, plagiarism is "the act of appropriating the literary composition of another, or parts or passages or his writings, or the ideas or language of the same, and passing them off as the product of one's own mind." As such, plagiarism may violate the right to reproduce a copyright work and may also violate the moral right of the author to have his or her name associated with his or her work. Where plagiarism is an appropriation of ideas, without the appropriation of the actual expression of those ideas, it is not a violation of copyright since copyright does not protect ideas.

Piracy

Piracy is the illicit duplication of legitimate works or other subject-matter. For instance, reprinted books, videos, computer software and CD-ROMs may be pirated versions. Pirated goods are usually recognized because of substandard packaging and labels, as well as quality of the copied materials. Piracy is a violation of the right of reproduction and may also involve plagiarism. Piracy is also used to refer to "stealing" copyright materials from the Internet.

Bootlegging

Bootlegging is the unauthorized recording of a live event, such as a concert. Bootlegging (i.e., making an unauthorized audio or video recording) is a violation of the right in a performer's performance, and if copyright works are being performed, a violation of the right in that underlying work.

Counterfeiting

Counterfeiting is making a copy of something without authority and deceiving or defrauding the public by passing that copy off as original or genuine. Where you have a counterfeit product—for instance, a tape containing music or computer software—that item as well as any affixed labels and packaging are illegally reproduced. Counterfeiting involves a violation of the right of reproduction.

Moral Rights Violation

In all of the above cases, the copy may be an inferior reproduction of the original product resulting, for example, in poor sound quality in the case of a sound recording, in poor picture quality in the case of an audio-visual recording, or containing bugs in the case of computer software—these are all arguably violations of moral rights. There is no moral rights protection in a performer's performance, a sound recording or a communication signal.

COPYRIGHT

Direct Infringement (Directly Violating a Right)

In basic terms, copyright is violated by doing any of the things or exercising any of the rights that only the copyright owner may do, without the consent of the copyright owner. Thus, you cannot reproduce a book, show a film to the public, perform a musical work in public, or record a live performance without violating copyright, unless you have obtained permission from the copyright holder. Also, you cannot authorize the use of any of the exclusive rights of the copyright holder.

Like other areas of the law, ignorance of the law is no excuse for the direct violation of copyright. Further, it is irrelevant whether the work or other subject-matter is marked as being protected by copyright, whether copying is done in good faith, whether the violater had any intention of making money, or whether the violation was for commercial or noncommercial purposes.[1] What is relevant is that the work or other subject-matter was performed, published, recorded, etc., without the consent of the copyright owner.

Violation of copyright is a question of fact and the circumstances of each alleged copyright violation must be examined based upon its own facts. The facts of each individual case of copyright violation must be applied to the definition of each right set out in the *Act*. The section below is an illustration of some of the considerations a court may take into account when hearing a copyright violation case.

VIOLATION OF THE RIGHT TO PRODUCE OR REPRODUCE

An author has the right "to produce or reproduce the work or any substantial part thereof." Anyone who uses this right without the permission of the copyright holder is infringing copyright. Thus, only an author may reproduce or authorize a reproduction of his or her work, or make any "colourable imitation" of the work (i.e., a disguised reproduction). Whether something is a colourable imitation is a question of fact. "Colourable imitation" has been found in a modified Popeye character,[2] a radio broadcast of a sketch,[3] and in substantial borrowed parts of a compilation, rearranged and published in a different format.[4]

As is included in the definition of the right to reproduce a work, the reproduction right applies to a "substantial" reproduction of the original work. The infringing work, then, need not be a work copied in its entirety. It is only illegal when a substantial part of a work has been appropriated. This is a question of fact that depends upon many factors including the quality and the quantity of the portions used from the original work, the degree of competition with the original work, and the nature of the reproduction.

It is fairly straightforward that a violation occurs when a work is copied word-for-word. However, where portions are added and omitted, the violation is a question of fact and each case must be examined on its own to see the substantiality of the reproduction or the degree of the amount taken.

Remember that there is no copyright in ideas and therefore the use of an idea cannot be a violation of copyright. However, when the form or expression of ideas is copied, there may be a copyright violation. It is not a violation where two people create similar works, based on similar ideas or facts, as long as each work is created on its own, and the creators did not have access to the other's work, thereby each used information from the original sources.

Subconscious copying may be illegal. For example, if someone hears a tune on the radio, then later "composes" a very similar tune, there may be a copyright violation. For example, George Harrison was found to have subconsciously copied elements of the music from the Chiffons' hit "He's so Fine" in his song "My Sweet Lord."[5] In a subconscious copying claim, the copyright holder must prove substantial similarity to his or her work as well as access to it, and of course, that a substantial portion was copied.

Reproducing a copy of a work may also be a violation of this right.

In determining copyright infringement, a court will look at similarities between the two works, and not the differences. Witnesses may give evidence in their analysis of the two works in question on the similarity of the two works.

Indirect Infringement

Indirect infringement concerns certain activities such as selling infringing copies of copyright protected material. It also involves acts to which the copyright owner does not have exclusive rights, but that nevertheless violate copyright. The *Copyright Act* states that copyright is violated by any person who does the following activities with any work, sound recording or fixation of a performer's performance or communication signal, that to the knowledge of that person infringes copyright (or he or she should have known that it would infringe copyright), or that it would infringe copyright if it had been made within Canada:

- sells or rents it, or by way of trade exposes or offers it for sale or rent
- distributes to such an extent as to affect prejudicially the owner of the copyright
- exhibits in public by way of trade
- possesses a work, sound recording or fixation of a performer's performance or communication signal for purposes of doing any of the three above things with it
- imports it into Canada for sale or rent

Unlike direct infringement, when there is indirect infringement, the violator may plead ignorance. Where, however, copyright is marked on the protected material, it will be difficult for a violator to succeed with a defence of ignorance since it is obvious that copyright probably exists in the item.

Further, there is indirect copyright infringement where any person who, for profit, permits a theatre or other place of entertainment to be used for the performance in public of a work or other subject-matter without the consent of the owner of the copyright, unless that person was not aware, and had no reasonable ground for suspecting, that the performance would be an infringement of copyright. Therefore, any owner of an entertainment establishment should be careful in contracting out the use of his or her establishment.

MORAL RIGHTS

A violation of moral rights occurs where any act or omission is done contrary to any of the moral rights in the absence of consent by the author. For instance, a violation may be omitting the author's name on his or her work. Also, a violation may be modifying a work in a manner prejudicial to the honour or reputation of a creator; for example, colourizing or digitally manipulating a photograph. Further, a violation may be associating a work with a cause or product, resulting in prejudice to the honour or reputation of the author.

There is nothing in the *Act* that says that a single act cannot be both a violation of copyright and moral rights. For example, an adaptation of a play without permission may be a violation of both copyright and moral rights if the adaptation is prejudicial to the honour or reputation of the author.

SUMMARY

Copyright may be violated directly, by using one of the exclusive rights of the copyright holder without permission, or indirectly through certain dealings with an infringing copy of a work or other subject-matter. Moral rights can be violated through any act or omission that is contrary to any of the moral rights.

Chapter 13

WHAT ARE THE REMEDIES FOR THE VIOLATION OF COPYRIGHT?

Unauthorized reproduction/sampling is a violation of
applicable laws and subject to criminal prosecution.
Frank Zappa's album cover, *Jazz from Hell*

REMEDIES IN GENERAL

When the rights of a copyright holder are violated, that copyright holder is entitled to certain remedies for the violation. These remedies could be preventing further violation, and/or seeking compensation or redress for the violating acts. Remedies for the violation of copyright can be divided into three categories: border, civil and criminal.

The violation of copyright may involve additional violations of areas of law other than copyright; for instance, *Criminal Code* offences, trade-mark violation, privacy rights and so on. This chapter merely sets out those remedies specifically referring to copyright, and specifically found in the *Copyright Act* since these are the most prominent and most obvious remedies employed in copyright violation cases. If you consult a lawyer, he or she will discuss whether there is a violation of copyright and the full range of remedies in copyright law or other areas of the law. Your lawyer will also discuss the time and expense involved in copyright litigation, as well as realistic expectations with respect to your likely outcome.

BORDER REMEDIES

"Border remedies" allow allegedly infringing or pirated copyright materials being imported into Canada to be detained at the border. The rationale behind these remedies is that it is easier to stop infringing copies at the border than after they are dispersed throughout the country. Since January 1, 1994, the Canadian *Copyright Act* has had more comprehensive provisions dealing with the importation of infringing copyright works or other subject-matter into Canada. The most notable change in 1994 is that Canadian Customs officials can now act on copyright materials other than books.

In order to get Canadian Customs officers at the border to detain suspected infringing copies of your work, you must obtain a court order. This is done by making an application to the Federal Court of Canada or to a superior court of law in any of the provinces. The person who makes the application, the "applicant," must be the copyright owner or exclusive licensee of the copyright (or a lawyer representing such people). The applicant must notify the Minister of Revenue of the court action.

The application must provide the following information:

1. that the copyright material is about to be imported into Canada or has been imported into Canada but has not yet been released, either
   (a) in the jurisdiction where the material was made and it was made without the consent of the person who then owned the copyright in that jurisdiction, or
   (b) the material was made elsewhere than in a country to which the Act applies, and
2. the material, to the knowledge of the importer, would have infringed copyright if made in Canada by the importer.

If the court is satisfied that the above conditions have been made, it may issue a court order. This court order will direct the Minister of National Revenue to take reasonable measures to detain the work or other subject-matter (i.e., Customs officials may detain the work at the border). The order will direct the Minister of National Revenue to notify the applicant and the importer once the works or other subject-matter have been detained and provide reasons for the detention. The court may provide for any other matters it considers appropriate.

Before making an order, the court may require some security from the applicant. The court will fix the amount of the security based on covering duties, storage, handling charges and other amounts that may become chargeable against the works or other subject-matter. The security amount may also reflect any other reimbursement for expenses incurred by the owner, importer or consignee of the materials.

The applicant or the importer may be given an opportunity by the Minister of Revenue to inspect the detained materials in order to substantiate or refuse, as appropriate, the applicant's claim.

The applicant must commence a court action for copyright infringement within two weeks of the goods being detained by Customs officials. Otherwise, the allegedly infringing materials will be released without notice to the applicant. This will happen if the applicant does not notify the Minister of Revenue that he or she has commenced a court action for a final determination by the court on the issues set out in the initial application (see above).

If the court makes a final determination in favour of the applicant, the court may make any order it considers appropriate. This includes an order that the works or other subject-matter be destroyed, or be delivered to the applicant as the applicant's "property absolutely."

Whether or not the applicant is successful in his application, he is still able to pursue other remedies in the *Copyright Act*. The border remedies specifically included in the *Copyright Act* are in addition to any other rights a copyright owner may have under the *Customs Act*.

There are also border measures against parallel imports of books as described in Chapter 9: Rights Protected by Copyright.

Further information on border remedies can be obtained from:

> Canada Customs and Revenue Agency
> c/o Manager, Prohibited Importations Unit
> 10th Floor, 191 Laurier Avenue West
> Ottawa, Ontario K1A 0L8

> T: 613.954.7049
> F: 613.957.4653
> E: **Shelley.Hoye@ccra-adrc.gc.ca**
> W: n/a

Printed Matter

In addition to, and separate from, the above border remedies, are distinct remedies for the importation of "reprints" of certain copyright works, "reprints of Canadian copyrighted works, and reprints of British copyrighted works which have been copyrighted in Canada."[1] Reprints basically means reprints of books, though calendars were once stopped at the border under this provision.

If an author or publisher or other copyright owner wishes to stop books from entering the country, they must state so in writing to Revenue Canada. Any request to the Department would require certain information like the name and nationality of the author, publisher, title of book and the place of publication. Contact the Department for specifics of the requirements. Once satisfied with the request, the Department will include the book in Tariff Item 9897.00.00 of the Customs Tariff Schedule and will stop all books at the border bearing that title. No court order is required for books, although it is possible to proceed by obtaining a court order and to follow the procedures set out above for all copyright works. Further information can be obtained from Revenue Canada at the above address.

Once a book is deemed to be in the Customs Tariff Schedule, no one, including the copyright owner, can import it (unless there is an explicit provision allowing such importation as discussed in previous chapters).

CIVIL REMEDIES

A civil remedy allows a copyright holder to take direct action against a person (or company, etc.) who violates his or her copyright. A copyright owner whose rights have been violated is entitled to a number of civil remedies such as an injunction, damages, accounts of profits, delivery up and "otherwise that are or may be conferred by law for the infringement of a right." Unless copyright is registered at the Canadian Copyright Office, a plaintiff is only entitled to an injunction (and no damages, etc.) if the defendant proves that, at the date of the infringement, the defendant was "not aware and had no reasonable grounds for suspecting that copyright subsisted in the work or other subject-matter." The same is true for any authors whose moral rights have been infringed. In certain circumstances, copyright owners whose rights have been violated may join together and sue the alleged infringer as a class action.[2] The available civil remedies are described below.

Although a court of law awards civil remedies, equivalent remedies may be obtained by individuals without going through lengthy and complete court proceedings. Once an alleged violator has been notified by a copyright holder that copyright is being violated, there are many opportunities for an out-of-court settlement. For instance, the parties might settle after a warning letter is issued to the alleged violator, or after the copyright holder initiates a lawsuit with documents that have been filed with the court and that have been delivered to the alleged violator. As well, mediation and alternative dispute resolution is an increasingly popular method of settling out-of-court.

Mediation is a negotiation-like procedure that generally involves both the plaintiff and the defendant, their lawyers and a mediator who is professionally trained to conduct the negotiations with a view to achieving a resolution satisfactory to both sides. Mediation allows for quicker, less expensive and less formal ways of settling a dispute. This is an alternative both parties to the dispute would have to agree upon, and a lawyer could advise you on how to proceed by way of mediation. Like any other body of law, the copyright statute gives direction to disputing parties as to what damages and other measures are appropriate for an out-of-court settlement.

Provisions for summary proceedings have recently been added to the *Copyright Act* to help speed up the court procedures for certain infringements. As of October 1, 1999, these summary procedures are available for copyright or moral rights infringement cases, and in relation to tariffs set by the Board including the private copying tariff. Unless the court determines otherwise, it will hear and determine these cases "without delay and in a summary way." The same remedies as those available for infringement of copyright are available for infringements of moral rights.[3]

Limitation Period on Civil Actions

A copyright holder must sue an alleged violator within three years of the commencement of the infringement. The three-year limit may start to run from the discovery of the infringement, instead of from the commencement of the violation, if the copyright holder can prove that he or she had no way of knowing about the infringing activity through "reasonable diligence." Also, allowing some infringement in one part of a work or other subject-matter may not bar a copyright holder from suing for violation in the same or different work or other subject-matter after the limitation period in the infringement in that one part has expired.

This limitation period applies to violation of copyright and moral rights.

Who May Sue?

Any person, author or owner of copyright, or anyone having a title, right or interest in writing in the copyright, may institute a court action for violation of that copyright. The interest may be in the form of a written assignment or licence. Thus, a person who has mere permission (e.g., verbal permission) to use copyright material cannot sue to stop others from using the material in the same manner. Whether an interest has been granted depends on the circumstances in each case and on the wording of the licence. If a person has an interest, that interest must relate to the one for which the lawsuit is being instituted. For example, if a person is granted the exhibition right in a painting, that person may not sue for violation of the reproduction right in the painting.

Although persons with a non-exclusive licence may not sue under the *Copyright Act*, they may sue for breach of contract under contract law. For instance, if Adam licenses the use of an image for his Web site from the copyright owner Kyle, and Kyle breaches the agreement, for example, by not providing the image to Adam in a timely fashion, then Adam may enforce his rights against Kyle for breach of contract.

The person who commences a court action is called a "plaintiff."

Who Can Be Sued?

Any person who allegedly uses a copyright work or other subject-matter in a manner that only the copyright owner may use it, may be sued. This includes any person who authorizes the infringing use of copyright material. It may also include persons legally responsible for the alleged violator, such as a parent or employer. In essence, all parties involved could be sued since the *Act* does not specifically state who may be named as a party in a lawsuit.

The issue of who is liable on the Internet (e.g., Web site owners, Bulletin Board operators, online services like AOL or Sympatico) has been the focus of much discussion around the world. When the two new digital copyright treaties were being discussed in December, 1996 (see Chapter 5: How Does International Copyright Protection Work?), it was agreed by WIPO member countries that this should be a matter for each country to decide on its own and that it should not be included in the new treaties. To date, countries like the United States and Australia have limited the liability of certain parties in their own copyright laws as opposed to explicitly setting out who is liable. In most situations, liability has to be decided based on each particular set of circumstances. There have been no Canadian court cases on this point. However, in late 1999, the Copyright Board issued a decision, in relation to liability for music broadcast on the Internet, that an Internet service provider (ISP) is not liable if it acts as a mere conduit regarding musical works that are posted or transmitted using the ISP's facilities. However, the ISP could be liable if it posts content itself, associates itself with others who post content, creates embedded links or moderates a newsgroup.

The person being sued, or the person defending or denying an action commenced by the plaintiff, is called the "defendant." The defendant is sometimes referred to as the alleged violator or infringer. Despite the wording used here, which may state, for example, that the plaintiff or defendant must prove something, it is usually the lawyer representing the plaintiff or defendant who will do these things on behalf of his or her client, the plaintiff or defendant.

Costs

In civil law matters, the costs of retaining a lawyer are the responsibility of the client, or the person who engages that lawyer. Once the matter goes to court, it is possible that the successful party recovers some of these costs, and that the unsuccessful party is responsible for the costs of both parties. It is also possible that legal costs are a part of a negotiated out-of-court settlement.

There are no absolute rules on the recovery of costs. The *Copyright Act* specifically provides that the expense or cost of a lawsuit is in the discretion of the court. Thus, it is up to a judge to decide whether costs are recoverable in a court case and in what amount. Since costs are in the discretion of the court, a court could refuse, for example, to make an order regarding costs where a plaintiff is successful in a copyright infringement suit where the infringed work or other subject-matter is considered obscene.

Where to Sue

The *Copyright Act* states that the federal court or any provincial court (including small claims court) may hear an action for copyright violation and enforce any civil remedies. Thus, you have the option of the venue in which to commence an action.

If the amount of damages being claimed is within the limits allowed in small claims court, you may want to pursue the action on your own (but note that your claim might then be limited to damages and no injunction). The advantage of small claims court is that it is often speedier than other courts and costs can be minimized since plaintiffs often represent themselves without the aid of a lawyer. You are only eligible to sue in small claims court if the monetary compensation being claimed is within a certain limit. For example, at the time of writing this edition, this amount is $6,000 in Ontario.

If you begin your action in a court other than small claims court, a choice will have to be made between commencing it in federal or provincial court. There are certain advantages and disadvantages of proceeding in either the federal or provincial court that your lawyer will outline to you. One of the main advantages of proceeding in the federal court as opposed to a provincial court is that the federal court is more specialized, having jurisdiction to deal only with specific matters, and as such is believed by some to have a greater expertise in intellectual property matters. Other advantages are that the federal court may give you an earlier trial date than a provincial court; there may be monetary ceilings for the claiming of damages in certain provincial courts; and the federal court may grant a restraining order that is valid throughout Canada whereas provincial courts have power only within their own province.

Description of Civil Remedies

PRE-JUDGEMENT ORDERS
There is always a danger that once a legal suit is commenced against an alleged violator of copyright that that alleged violator will quickly dispose of illegal copies of a work or other subject-matter or plates used to make it in order to eliminate any evidence of infringement. Because of this, a plaintiff may ask the court for an "Anton Pillar order," which is essentially a civil search warrant. An Anton Pillar order will order the alleged violator to allow the plaintiff or a representative to enter and inspect the defendant's premises and seize any infringing copies or to take pictures of them prior to any court hearing. This is done without warning to the defendant.

In general, an Anton Pillar order will be granted where the harm done to the plaintiff without such an order is greater than the harm done to the defendant with the order. This remedy is quite extreme and will only be granted under certain conditions, that is, where there is strong circumstantial evidence of copyright infringement, there is very serious actual or potential damage accruing to the plaintiff, and there is very good reason to believe that the defendant has incriminating evidence and might, if warned, destroy these items before trial. The plaintiff must undertake to reimburse the defendant for any damages to the defendant caused by the granting of the order. The issuance of an order is decided on the facts of each case.

In November, 1993, an Ontario Court awarded the co-plaintiffs CANCOPY and McGraw-Hill Ryerson Ltd., an Anton Pillar Order against the copy shop Ink Copy Inc., which was then allegedly photocopying a book published by McGraw-Hill Ryerson. The co-plaintiffs have since won the case.

INJUNCTIONS

An injunction is an order made by a court, on behalf of a complainant, ordering someone to refrain from, or continuing, a particular activity. For example, an injunction could prevent the further showing of a film or a television program, or require certain content to be removed from a Web site. Injunctions are a common type of remedy for copyright violations because they can be obtained relatively quickly and provide an immediate solution. However, they can also be costly to obtain. Injunctions can be granted either at the commencement of an action or at the end of it. There are interim, interlocutory and permanent injunctions.

Interim Injunction

An interim injunction is granted for a short period of time, usually without notice to the alleged infringer, as part of an Anton Pillar order (as discussed above). It is granted in cases of extreme urgency where there is strong evidence that the alleged offender will abscond or destroy evidence if notified about the injunction. Generally, the interim injunction lasts for ten days (for example, under the Rules of the Federal Court), and is continued as an interlocutory injunction, if warranted, pending the outcome of the trial.

Interlocutory Injunction

An interlocutory injunction is the continuation of an interim injunction. The alleged offender is notified about the request for an interlocutory injunction and there is a hearing to determine whether the interlocutory should be granted. The purpose of an interlocutory injunction is to prevent irreparable harm to a plaintiff awaiting the outcome of a trial. As such, an interlocutory injunction is limited in time to the end of the trial in question or can be otherwise limited in time to a date earlier than the trial.

A plaintiff may ask a court for an interlocutory injunction at the commencement of a court action if he or she can prove that continuing the infringing activity will cause serious, irreparable harm to the plaintiff, which cannot be compensated in damages (if blatant copying, irreparable harm need not necessarily be proven, as long as there is a serious question to be tried). Whether or not an interlocutory injunction is ordered by a court depends on the facts of each case. A judge must examine the position of both parties and the possible damages to each of them. It is up to the copyright owner to satisfy the court that the interim injunction should be continued as an interlocutory injunction until the trial is completed. The alleged infringer will have an opportunity at the hearing for the interlocutory injunction to argue that the interim injunction should not have been granted at all and should not be continued as an interlocutory injunction.

Over the past few years, it has become increasingly difficult to obtain an interlocutory or interim injunction in Canada. It is almost impossible, even in the case of blatant copying, unless there is clear and compelling evidence of irreparable harm meaning that the plaintiff will either be put out of business in short order or the application for an *ex parte* interim injunction is made part of an Anton Pillar application (and therefore there is strong evidence that the defendant will abscond). In most federal court cases, the court is prepared to award damages at the end of the trial. As a result, applications for summary judgement prior to trial have become the proceeding of choice in order to shorten an action.

Permanent Injunction

A permanent injunction is awarded by a court at the end of a trial to order an infringer to "permanently" stop the infringing activity. It may be ordered by a court once it has been established that copyright violation has taken place.

Where a defendant proves that he or she was not aware of copyright and had no reasonable grounds for suspecting that copyright subsisted in the work or other subject-matter, he or she may only be subject to an injunction, and not to the other remedies listed below. If, at the date of infringement, the copyright in the work or other subject-matter was registered under the *Act* with the Canadian Copyright Office, the defendant may be subject to all remedies (since this would be reasonable grounds for suspecting that copyright existed). Keep in mind that copyright need not be registered at the time of its creation, but may be registered, for instance, at the time when a lawsuit is being contemplated.

Injunctions with Respect to Buildings

Where a building or other structure is either built or in the process of being constructed, and it infringes or may infringe copyright when completed, an injunction cannot be obtained to stop construction or to order its demolition. The same may not be true if an injunction is obtained prior to the building or structure being built.[4] For example, an injunction may be obtained to stop a house from being built from plans where copyright has not been cleared in those plans, but once building has commenced the copyright owner will have to look at remedies other than an injunction.

Wide injunction

Generally, an injunction will apply to specific work or other subject-matter being infringed at a specific time. However, a "wide injunction" was recently introduced into Canadian copyright law that allows a court to grant an injunction not only in relation to a specific work or other subject-matter, but also with respect to preventing infringement of copyright in any of the works or other subject-matter in which the plaintiff currently has or will in the future have a copyright interest.

DAMAGES

A copyright owner may claim monetary "damages" from a violator of copyright, and that part of the profits made from the infringement decided by a court to be "just and proper." Damages are monetary compensation recovered in a court proceeding by a person whose copyright has been violated. *Black's Law Dictionary* defines damages in the following manner: "A pecuniary compensation or indemnity, which may be recovered in the courts by any person who has suffered loss, detriment, or injury, whether to his person, property, or rights, through the unlawful act or omission or negligence of another."

A court may award damages to a plaintiff even if no profit was made by the infringer. In fact, it is not necessary to prove or to suffer real damages in order for an award of damages to be made: violation is sufficient.

The amount of damages that a court may order is not set out in the *Copyright Act*. Thus, the court will determine this amount on a case-by-case basis. Assessing the amount of appropriate damages is a "matter of common sense."[5] Damages are determined on a "rough" basis, taking into account the amount of sales lost to the plaintiff and the amount of profit derived by the defendant.[6] Also, see the discussion below on statutory damages.

Damages should be high enough to act as a deterrent to the violation of copyright, as opposed to a measure of damages that merely convinces a potential infringer that, from a commercial point of view, copying a work or other subject-matter is a risk worth taking. A court may base the amount of damages on the cost for the licensed use of the work or other subject-matter, or on the loss of profits in the commercial markets where the work or other subject-matter would have otherwise been exploited. Monetary losses that can be proven can also be recovered.

The discussion so far has focused on what is called compensatory or actual damages. There are, however, different kinds of damages that a court may award a plaintiff. Another type of damages is called "punitive or exemplary" damages. The purpose of these types of damages is to punish a person for flagrant misbehaviour or to set an example of the consequences of breaking the law. Although the *Act* does not specifically refer to exemplary or punitive damages, Canadian copyright law has been interpreted to allow the awarding of such damages.[7] Such damages may be awarded where there is "blatant infringement, accompanied by total disregard for the rights of others,"[8] "fraud or malice"[9] or where there is "some form of wilful or reckless disregard of the rights of the plaintiff, or a very deliberate scheme to infringe copyright."[10] Thus, the conduct and motives of the infringer will be taken into account with respect to punitive or exemplary damages.

In an April, 1994 case where CANCOPY and the publisher McGraw-Hill Ryerson won a civil suit against a copy shop, an Ontario court ordered the copy shop to pay more than $133,000 for illegal photocopying. Fifty thousand dollars was awarded to McGraw-Hill Ryerson, $31,063 to CANCOPY, $30,000 in punitive damages to both plaintiffs and $22,000 in costs.

Special provision for schools, libraries, archives and museums
A copyright owner whose works are not licensed by a collective such as CANCOPY or COPIBEC (and is eligible to be) is limited in what he may collect for illegal photocopying by educational institutions, libraries, archives and museums. The copyright owner is limited to the amount of royalties he or she would have received if he or she were a member of a collective such as CANCOPY or COPIBEC.

Statutory damages
Statutory damages were recently introduced into Canadian copyright law. Statutory damages allow a copyright holder to collect specified damages as set out in the *Copyright Act* as opposed to actual damages resulting from the infringing activities. Statutory damages guarantee a minimum award once the infringement is proven without having to prove the actual loss suffered, and they also act as a deterrent to future infringements.

Under the statutory damages regime, a copyright owner may request at any time before a final judgement in a court case, in lieu of damages and profits, statutory damages of $500 to $20,000, in respect of each work or other subject-matter infringed by the defendant, as the court considers just. The court will take in account the good or bad faith of the defendant, the parties' conduct before and during the court proceedings, and the need to prevent other infringements of the copyright in question. This may be lowered to $200 where the infringer was not aware and had no reasonable grounds to believe that he/she had infringed copyright. There are specific circumstances set out in the *Act* to which the statutory damages provisions do not apply.

Copyright collectives, as defined in the *Act*, are also entitled to certain statutory damages for non-payment of royalties. By foregoing other monetary damages, the collective may claim an award of statutory damages not less than three, and not more than ten, times the amount of the applicable royalties, as the court considers just.

Statutory damages do not apply to parallel importation. Also, statutory damages probably do not apply to moral rights infringement.

ACCOUNTS OF PROFITS
The notion of accounts of profits denotes the principle that an infringer has illegally made use of another's property—the copyright protected material—making profits therefrom and should "account" for these profits. The *Act* states that in addition to a court awarding damages for the violation of copyright, it may award "such part of the profits that the infringer has made from the infringement as the court may decide to be just and proper." The account of profits would be in addition to "regular" damages.

The general rule is that an infringer must pay to the copyright owner any and all profits associated with the violation. There is no method set out in the *Act* for calculating these profits. The term "profits" is not defined, but the *Act* states that "the plaintiff shall be required to prove only receipts or revenues derived from the infringement" and the defendant shall be required to prove "every element of cost" that he claims.

RETURNING ILLEGAL COPIES ("DELIVERY UP")
A copyright violator must give the copyright owner all infringing copies of a work or other subject-matter, and all plates used to produce the infringing copies.

Matters to Prove
When a court case commences for the violation of copyright, a number of things must be proven. For instance, it must be established that copyright exists in a work or other subject-matter, that the author is the owner of the work or other subject-matter (or that the owner has the right to sue), that

there is a violation of copyright, and that the defendant is responsible for that violation.

There are two presumptions set out in the *Copyright Act* to help a plaintiff prove a case of copyright violation. First, there is a presumption that copyright subsists in a work or other subject-matter. This presumption means that a copyright work or other subject-matter in which infringement is claimed is automatically presumed to be protected by copyright, or in other words, a plaintiff need not prove this point. Thus, a defendant who wishes to prove otherwise—that is, that copyright does not exist in the work or other subject-matter—has the burden of proof of doing so.

A burden of proof simply means that one of the parties, i.e., the defendant, must prove a fact or prove a fact in dispute. In order for a defendant to prove that copyright does not exist in the work, he would present evidence to the contrary, for example, that proves that the work is not original (in the copyright sense of the word), or is in the public domain.

Second, there is a presumption of ownership. The author of a work, or performer, maker or broadcaster of other subject-matter, is presumed to be the owner of the copyright in that work or other subject-matter. The defendant may prove the contrary of this presumption. For example, the defendant may produce a written assignment or other evidence that a written assignment exists and that the author, performer, maker or broadcaster is not the owner of the copyright.

There are two further subsections relating to the presumption of ownership. The first presumption relates to the situation where an author's name appears on a work, or the name of a performer, maker or broadcaster is indicated on the other subject-matter. This provision provides that if a name is on a work or other subject-matter in such a manner as to indicate that he or she is the author of the work, or performer, maker or broadcaster of other subject-matter, then that person is presumed to be the author, performer, maker or broadcaster, unless the contrary is proven. Notice that there is no requirement that the copyright symbol appear on the work or other subject-matter, or that there be a statement expressing that copyright belongs to the author, performer, maker or broadcaster indicated on the work or other subject-matter. The second presumption relates to the situation where a name other than the author's name appears on a work, or performer's, maker's or broadcaster's name appears on other subject-matter. This section provides that where no name is indicated on a work, or other subject-matter, as its author, performer, maker or broadcaster, or the name is not the real name of the author, performer, maker or broadcaster, or one by which he or she is commonly known, and a name purporting to be that of the publisher or proprietor of the work or other subject-matter is listed, their name will be presumed to be the owner of the copyright for infringement proceedings unless the contrary is proven.

Once the existence of copyright and proper ownership of the work or other subject-matter are established, the plaintiff must prove that a violation took place; for example, that the defendant reproduced a substantial part of the work or other subject-matter in question (and did not go to a common source in doing so). The plaintiff must prove the infringement. In order to do so, the court may look at direct and indirect (circumstantial) evidence, can hear parties' testimony and the testimony of other witnesses including experts, can compare the two works or other subject-matter, looking for similarities and dissimilarities, examine the repetition of errors (unless it can be proven that errors existed in a common source consulted by the parties), and consider if it was possible for the defendant to complete the work within the given time frame. Note that violation of copyright is not measured by assessing the harm to a copyright owner—either the violation occurs or it does not occur.

Once the plaintiff has presented the case, it is up to the defendant to prove that he or she has not infringed copyright. For example, if two works are very similar but not exact, the defendant may bring evidence that his or her work was created independently, using common sources. Alternatively, the defendant may bring evidence showing that any similarity is coincidental and that, in fact, the defendant had no access to the allegedly violated work. Also, the defendant may prove that his use of the work or other subject-matter was within one of the exceptions in the *Copyright Act* and therefore does not constitute a violation of copyright. Although innocence is not generally a defence with relation to copyright violation, it may be claimed with respect to indirect violation (or commercial uses of copyright materials). If the defendant is successful in the defence, he will not be found liable for copyright violation.

If the defendant is unsuccessful in defending a copyright violation case, the plaintiff is entitled to a number of remedies. These remedies will be included in the claim against the defendant when the lawsuit commences and are discussed above under the heading: Description of Civil Remedies.

CRIMINAL REMEDIES

The criminal sanctions that relate to copyright violations are found in the *Copyright Act* and not in the *Criminal Code*. These sanctions are available in specific circumstances set out in the *Act*. Criminal sanctions may be more appropriate than civil remedies where the extent of the infringement makes it too costly for an individual to sue, or where the nature of the illegal conduct should be set as an example in order to deter others from engaging in the same or similar activities. However, with criminal sanctions, the complainant has no absolute right to proceed as the ultimate decision whether to charge an individual rests with the police, and the ultimate decision whether to proceed rests with the Crown (i.e., the government). The police and Crown must make their decisions independent of factors that may be of interest to a complainant and may not be influenced by private interests. All a victim can do is file a complaint with the police. It is then up to the police to investigate the alleged crime. There are RCMP across Canada seeking out only copyright offenders.

The complainant receives no direct monetary compensation where criminal charges are laid.

A criminal proceeding is not a bar to a civil proceeding.

Historically, the police have sought to charge large-scale operators under the criminal provisions, for commercial dealings of copyright goods, for example, video or software piracy on a large-scale. The law does not, however, limit the criminal remedies to such cases.

By calling the RCMP, provincial or city police, an investigation may be undertaken to substantiate a claim of a criminal offence.

Activities that Constitute a Criminal Offence

INFRINGING COPIES

The following activities knowingly done with illegal copies (copies of copyright works or other subject-matter made without the permission of the copyright owner) may come within the criminal sanctions of the *Copyright Act*:

- making for sale or rent
- selling or renting , or by way of trade exposing or offering for sale or hire
- distributing for the purpose of trade, or to such an extent as to affect prejudicially the owner of the copyright

- exhibiting in public, by way of trade
- importing for sale or rent into Canada

Whether one of these activities is done with knowledge is a matter of fact for the courts to decide upon examination of all the facts of the case.

Where any of the above activities take place, the violator may be subject to a maximum fine and to a maximum prison term. Both the fine and imprisonment may be simultaneously imposed. There are two sets of maximum fines and imprisonment terms set out in the *Act* depending on how the Crown decides to proceed in the particular case. The Crown has the choice to proceed by summary conviction or by indictment. Generally, offences punishable on summary conviction are less serious crimes and are subject to a lesser penalty than those tried by indictment. A first offence of copyright violation may, for example, proceed by way of summary conviction. In the case of a summary conviction, the violator may be subject to a maximum fine of $25,000 or to imprisonment for a term up to six months, or to both. In the case of a conviction on indictment, the violator may be subject to a fine of up to $1 million or to imprisonment for a term of up to five years, or to both. Note that the fine and imprisonment periods are maximum amounts. The court may choose appropriate fines and/or imprisonment periods within these limitations, depending upon the facts of the particular cases. The different procedures for proceeding, summary conviction procedure and the procedure on indictment, are set out in the *Criminal Code*. On summary conviction proceedings, there is a limitation period. For example, in Ontario, the charge must be laid within two years of the discovery of the offence. There is no limitation period for matters the Crown elects to proceed on by way of indictment.

INFRINGING PLATES AND PERFORMANCES

Further, it is an offence to knowingly make or possess any plate for making infringing copies, or to cause a work or other subject-matter to be performed in public for private profit, without authorization. The fines and imprisonment terms are the same as above.

Even before criminal remedy proceedings begin (i.e., a trial) with respect to infringing plates, the court may order that all apparent infringing copies of the work or other subject-matter or all plates in the possession of the alleged violator that may be used to make illegal copies be destroyed or delivered to the copyright owner, or otherwise dealt with as the court may think fit.

Additionally, a person who, without written consent, knowingly performs or causes to be performed in public for private profit an infringing work or other subject-matter that is a part or whole of any dramatic or operatic work or music composition, may be subject to a fine on summary conviction not exceeding $250, and in a second or subsequent offence, to a $250 fine or imprisonment for two months, or both.

Finally, any person "who makes or causes to be made any change in or suppression of the title, or the name of the author, of any dramatic or operatic work or musical composition. . . . or who makes or causes to be made any change in the work or composition itself" without written consent, in order to perform a whole or part of the work or composition in public for private profit, may be subject on summary conviction to a maximum fine of $500, or in a second or subsequent offence, to the $500 fine and imprisonment up to four months, or both.

SPOTTING ILLEGAL WORKS

From time-to-time, you may come across what appears to be illegal reproductions of copyright works or other subject-matter. For instance, you may rent a video that has photocopied labels, or one that has poor picture quality and plays in mono as opposed to stereo. Or you may purchase software where the packaging, labelling, instruction manuals and purchase price lead you to suspect that you have not purchased a legal copy. Also, you may come across an audio cassette with a label indicating a certain artist who is, in fact, different from the artist performing on the tape. As piracy has become more rampant, many associations that represent particular groups of copyright holders have instituted "anti-piracy" units that are equipped to make investigations on such claims. If you encounter suspicious goods, you may want to contact one of the associations that represents such goods, for example, the Canadian Recording Industry Association or the Canadian Motion Picture Distributors Association, or alternatively, the police, who may institute an investigation.

SUMMARY

A copyright holder whose creations have been used without permission is entitled to certain remedies including border, civil and criminal ones.

Chapter 14

USING COPYRIGHT MATERIALS

> *Pirates issued their own Chinese version of the*
> *Encyclopedia Britannica in Taiwan before the*
> *legitimate edition could be published, kept selling it*
> *despite court rulings and, with amazing chutzpa,*
> *warned consumers to "watch out for fakes."*
>
> Gary M. Hoffman and George T. Marcou,
> "Who's Stealing America's Ideas," *The Washington Post*,
> November 5, 1989, p. C3

THE "USE" OF COPYRIGHT MATERIALS

People who want to use copyright materials often think that because a certain work is protected by copyright, that work cannot be used. This is a false assumption. When a work is protected by copyright, that work may be used in a variety of ways; however any use (at least those covered by the *Copyright Act*) must be authorized by the copyright owner, or by a representative of the copyright owner (unless that right is subject to an exception or a compulsory licence). This chapter will deal with obtaining authorization to use materials protected by copyright. When the term "use" is seen in this book, it refers to the use of copyright material in the copyright sense of the word. For instance, use may refer to a reproduction of a work or a public performance of a sound recording. It does not refer to, for example, lending a copy of a book to a friend.

WHEN IS PERMISSION REQUIRED?

General Rule

Every time you use copyright material in a manner that only the copyright owner has the right to do, you must obtain permission from the copyright owner. As you now know, owning the tangible aspect of a work protected by copyright does not exempt you from obtaining permission, since ownership of the tangible work does not necessarily mean that you own copyright in that work. For example, owning a painting does not necessarily mean that you own copyright in that painting. If you own the "physical property"— that is, the painting—you cannot reproduce it or exhibit it in public without authorization from the copyright holder. The same is true with other subject-matter such as sound recordings.

Except for commercial rentals of sound recordings and computer software, the copyright law does not distinguish between commercial and non-commercial uses of a copyright work. Generally, if copyright exists in a work, and if there is no specific exception for that particular use, then permission of the copyright owner must be obtained in order to use the work. Even amateurs who are dealing with a copyright work, such as a theatre group performing a play, must get permission to perform a copyright work. This general rule applies to works on the Internet (see Chapter 16: Digital Copyright and Electronic Rights, for further discussion on this issue).

Using copyright works in Canada—even foreign works provided they are protected in Canada—is always according to the provisions in the Canadian copyright law. The use of Canadian copyright works in other countries would be under the copyright laws of that country (provided that country and Canada have copyright relations). This chapter deals with the use of copyright materials in Canada.

See Figure 14.1 for some questions to ask when using a creation.

OBTAINING PERMISSION

Once you have established that the use of a work or other subject-matter requires permission from its copyright owner, you must obtain the necessary permission. Unfortunately, there is no one-stop clearance centre for copyright in Canada. This fact, however, does not absolve users of copyright materials from obtaining permission. Tracking down a copyright owner may depend upon common sense, ingenuity, resourcefulness and contacts. This chapter will list some of the numerous sources where you

Figure 14.1: When Using A Creation

If you plan to use a creation, these are some of the questions you should ask yourself:

☐ Are you using a work or other subject-matter protected by copyright?

☐ Is the duration of copyright still running or is it in the public domain?

☐ Is it an adaptation or translation of a public domain piece?

☐ Are you using a substantial portion of that work or other subject-matter?

☐ Are you using it in the copyright sense by reproducing it, perhaps electronically, performing it in public, adapting it, broadcasting it, etc.?

☐ Is there an exception in the law that permits you to use that work or other subject-matter without obtaining permission?

☐ Are you modifying the work in a manner that may be prejudicial to the honour or reputation of the creator?

☐ Does the author's name appear in association with the work?

can go to obtain permission for specific types of copyright materials or specific rights.

Only a copyright owner (or his or her representative) can give you permission to use copyright protected material. Chapter 7: Who Owns Copyright? will help you determine ownership in copyright materials. Keep in mind that the ownership of copyright can be transferred in whole or in part. If you have direct access to a copyright holder, you may want to contact that person for copyright clearance. However, you should be aware that in many instances it is a representative or heir of the copyright owner who may give you permission or guide you to the person who can give permission. Representatives of the author may include lawyers, agents and so on. A representative may also be a copyright collective, whose primary job is to clear copyright and who acts on behalf of many copyright holders. Copyright collectives are discussed in general in Chapter 10: Limitations on Rights and Chapter 11: How Can Rights Be Exploited?, and specific copyright collectives are discussed below.

Finding the owner of a copyright work or other subject-matter is not always straightforward. You should contact one of the copyright collectives if one exists with respect to that type of work, other subject-matter, or the relevant rights. In the case of a published work, you may wish to contact the publisher or producer to help you establish the whereabouts of the owner of copyright. You may also want to contact any associations or organizations who might have some contact with, or knowledge of, the copyright owner. The Internet may also be a helpful aid in locating a copyright owner.

Further, you should search through the Copyrights Registers at the Canadian Copyright Office, or hire someone to undertake a search on your behalf. At the time of writing this edition of the book, computer access is only available for works registered on or after October 1, 1991. With respect to copyright in other subject-matter, searches are available as of September 1, 1997. A manual search must be undertaken for any works registered before October 1, 1991 and any assignments made prior to this date. These searches can only be done in the Copyright Office in Hull, Quebec.

Since copyright registration is not mandatory in Canada, not all copyright owners will be listed there. One should not assume that because a work is not registered, that it is not protected by copyright. Nevertheless, the Registers do contain information about many copyright holders and authors. The records of the Copyright Office are open to the public and are free of charge. Assistance is available to use the search facilities and copies of or extracts from the Registers, or copies of certificates, licences or other documents can be obtained for a fee. If you do not check the Registers at the Copyright Office, you may be subject to heavier remedies (damages and not just an injunction) in a copyright violation court case.

For further information, contact the Copyright Office at:

> Canadian Intellectual Property Office
> Client Service Centre
> Copyright Office
> Industry Canada
> Place du Portage, Phase I
> 450 Victoria Street, Room C-229, 2nd Floor
> Hull, Quebec KIA 0C9
> Business hours: 8:00 - 16:45
>
> T: 819.997.1936
> F: 819.997.6357
> E: **cipo.contact@ic.gc.ca**
> 🌐 **cipo.gc.ca**

Depending on the circumstances, you may wish to check foreign copyright offices, such as the one in the United States. Online searches are available for American registrations made after January 1, 1978. Further information on searching the files of the American Copyright Office is available by contacting:

> Reference and Bibliography Section, LM-451
> Copyright Office
> Library of Congress
> Washington, D.C. 20559-6000 U.S.A.
>
> T: 202.707.6850
> F: 202.707.6859 (indicate person or section)
> E: **copyinfo@loc.gc**
> 🌐 **www.loc.gov/copyright**
> For online searches: 🌐 **www.loc.gov/copyright/rb.html**

Further, a lawyer may be able to assist you in locating a copyright holder. Lastly, there are specialized companies whose job it is to search for copyright owners in Canada and abroad.

COPYRIGHT COLLECTIVES

One "representative" of a copyright owner may be a copyright collective. Where a copyright owner is a member of a collective, the collective may be contacted in order to obtain permission to use his or her copyright materials. Collectives provide users of copyright materials with quick and easy access to a large repertoire. They are an excellent source for those seeking permission to use copyright materials. Even if the creator is not represented by the collective you contact, the collective may be able to provide you with information to help you locate a copyright owner.

OBTAINING PERMISSION FOR SPECIFIC WORKS

Below is a list of organizations and collectives that operate in certain areas. Since new organizations and collectives are being formed from time to time and the mandate of existing ones may change, the information mentioned herein should not be taken as being conclusive. The collectives mentioned below may not necessarily be "collectives" as defined in the *Copyright Act* and therefore may not be under the jurisdiction of the Copyright Board. The organizations and collectives listed below, however, are places that creators and users should be aware of with respect to giving or obtaining permission to use copyright materials. In addition, a helpful list of copyright-related organizations, and a list of collectives, appear on the Copyright Board's Web site at: **WEB** **www.cb-cda.gc.ca/collectives-e.html**.

Many of the listed organizations and collectives have agreements with similar organizations and collectives in different countries and can provide permission to use foreign works in Canada. For instance, if you wish to use images by Swiss artists, the rights may be cleared through the Canadian collective that represents those Swiss artists in Canada. If you want to perform a song by a British composer, contact the Canadian collective that represents British composers in Canada.

Depending on the nature of the copyright collective or organization, you may be able to obtain an individual or transactional licence for a specific work for use one time only, or a blanket licence that provides the access to a large repertoire of works for multiple copying over a specified period of time. Some collectives and organizations allow for requests for permissions to be made online from their Web site.

The list below has been updated in this edition of the book and, among other changes, now includes information on clearing rights for electronic uses. However, you will see that clearing electronic rights through an organization or collective is in its infancy and it may be necessary in many situations to contact the copyright owner directly for electronic uses. It will be interesting to see how this develops in the future.

Literary Works

The Canadian Copyright Licensing Agency, also known as CANCOPY, administers the rights in published print materials in Canada, with the exception of Quebec. These rights include a variety of forms of reprographic reproduction including photocopying. A licence from CANCOPY may allow you to reproduce print materials containing a short story, essay, poem, artistic work (not an original) or play. It may also allow you to copy a chapter from a book, an article from a newspaper, magazine or other publication, or an entry from a collective work such as an encyclopedia or dictionary. CANCOPY has a special service to license educational institutions that need to copy print sheet music on a job-by-job basis. CANCOPY may issue licences for the making of multiple copies of works in its repertoire as long as there is no systematic or cumulative copying and the copying does not substitute for the purchase of the original work. You can obtain an individual licence or a blanket licence from CANCOPY.

CANCOPY has recently begun to license certain digital reproductions of published works. In the Fall of 1999, CANCOPY announced that it had concluded a licence with the University of Calgary for CANCOPY's "first digital pilot project." Under the pilot project, the university may use specific copyright materials in an electronic reserve reading room for two courses for a period of one year. Students enrolled in the courses access the digital materials through a password protected, user-controlled network developed by the university. The project includes materials from ten copyright owners in Canada and the United States. Permissions for the project were cleared with the owners, and their terms and conditions of use were incorporated into the licence. CANCOPY has since finalized four other similar licences and has launched a service, Post Secondary Electronic Course Content Services (PECCS) specifically for this type of use.

In addition, CANCOPY offers individual digital licences on a case-by-case basis, where requested, for educational, and other uses such as K-12 schools, Web sites, and Intranets. At the time of writing, CANCOPY has other digital licensing projects in the works that they expect to finalize in the near future.

Further, it was announced on June 29, 2000, that CANCOPY would take on the digital licensing activities of The Electronic Rights Licensing Agency (TERLA) whose membership consists of almost 700 freelance writers, illustrators and photographers.

For further information, contact:
CANCOPY
Canadian Copyright Licensing Agency
One Yonge Street, Suite 1900
Toronto, Ontario M5E 1E5

T: 416.868.1620 or 1.800.893.5777
F: 416.868.1621
E: **admin@cancopy.com**
WEB **www.cancopy.com**

If you have a licence with CANCOPY, you have access to print materials in the province of Quebec because of an arrangement it has with COPIBEC. COPIBEC, the Société Québécoise de Gestion Collective des Droits de Reproduction, administers the right for the reprography of print materials in Quebec. In addition to licensing similar materials to CANCOPY, COPIBEC's repertoire includes the various publications of the different ministries of Quebec. COPIBEC was founded in 1997 by the l'union des écrivaines et écrivains québécois (UNEQ) and the Association nationale des éditeurs de livres (ANEL).

Regarding digital licensing, COPIBEC deals with these permissions on a case-by-case basis, in consultation with the rights holders concerned and has not yet established a licensing tariff structure for these uses. Also, COPIBEC is involved with some specific digital rights projects. For further information, contact:

COPIBEC
1290, rue Saint-Denis, 7th floor
Montreal, PQ H2X 3J7

T: 514.288.1664 or 1.800.717.2022
F: 514.288.1669
E: **info@copibec.qc.ca**
WEB **www.copibec.qc.ca**

Both COPIBEC and CANCOPY have reciprocal agreements with various collectives around the world. You can obtain permission from them to reproduce literary works from countries such as Australia, Denmark, France, Germany, Iceland, Ireland, Italy, Liechtenstein, Malta, Netherlands, New Zealand, Norway, South Africa, Spain, United Kingdom, United States, and Switzerland.

Dramatic Works

The Playwrights Union of Canada (PUC) clears copyright with respect to the public performance of English language plays for amateur and educational performances. Sometimes they can also clear rights for professional performances. With respect to the reproduction of plays, PUC is a member of CANCOPY as are many of PUC's individual members. Thus, CANCOPY should be contacted with respect to the reproduction of plays. PUC also reproduces its members' scripts for sale and distribution.

For further information, contact:

> The Playwrights Union of Canada
> 54 Wolseley Street, 2nd Floor
> Toronto, Ontario M5T 1A5
>
> T: 416.947.0201
> F: 416.703.0059
> E: **info@puc.ca**
> WEB **www.puc.ca**

La société des auteurs et compositeurs dramatiques (SACD) clears copyright with respect to the public performance, both amateur and professional, in French language scripts for plays, television programs and movies.

For further information, contact:

> Société des Auteurs et Compositeurs Dramatiques (SACD)
> 5186, Chemin de la Côte-des-Neiges
> Bureau 3
> Montreal, Quebec H3T 1X8
>
> T: 514.738.8877
> F: 514.342.4615
> E: **e.schlittler@sympatico.ca**
> WEB **www.sacd.fr**

Musical Works

As you know, the copyright in a musical work is separate and distinct from the copyright in a sound recording embodying that musical work.

Like most copyright works, copyright holders of musical works enjoy a bundle of rights in these works. The most commonly used rights with respect to musical works are the rights of public performance and reproduction.

PUBLIC PERFORMING RIGHT

Performing rights societies have been in existence in Canada for more than seventy years. The Society of Composers, Authors and Music Publishers of Canada (SOCAN) is the name of the copyright collective for performing rights in musical works. Its members are music composers, lyricists, songwriters and their publishers from across Canada and around the world. SOCAN is a result of a merger of two separate performing rights societies, CAPAC and PROCAN. It licenses virtually the world's repertoire of commercially exploited musical works in Canada.

SOCAN administers non-dramatic performing rights or "small rights." If you need to clear rights for live performances such as those given by bands, by the playing of compact discs, and music at bars, school dances, offices, stores, or for television and radio, SOCAN can help you. SOCAN issues blanket licences. Dramatic performing rights or "grand rights" for complete performances of operas, ballets, musicals and other dramatic works must be obtained directly from the copyright owner.

The list of situations and venues where performing rights for musical works must be cleared is quite extensive. The Copyright Board sets royalty rates for a variety of situations. Some of these rates are approved annually. Rates are set for such categories of performance including:

- radio
- television
- live entertainment in cabarets, cafes, clubs, cocktail bars, dining rooms, lounges, restaurants, roadhouses, taverns and similar establishments
- live performances at theatres or other places of entertainment
- exhibitions and fairs
- cinemas
- skating rinks
- receptions, conventions, assemblies and fashion shows

- sports events
- public parks, streets or squares and parades
- circuses, ice shows, comedy shows, magic shows, fireworks displays and sound and light shows
- theme parks (e.g., Canada's Wonderland, Ontario Place Corporation)
- public conveyances such as aircraft, passenger ships, railroad trains, buses
- performance of an individual work at any single event
- background music in establishments
- background music suppliers
- transmitters of non-broadcast services (e.g., cable television and cable radio)
- recorded music for dancing in discos, dance halls, ballrooms and hotels
- fitness activities (e.g., dancercize and aerobics)
- Karaoke bars

If your use of music falls into any of the above categories or a related category, you should obtain a licence from SOCAN.

The Copyright Board of Canada recently ruled that music made available on the Internet is protected under Canadian copyright law, and entitled SOCAN to collect royalties from the person who posted it because it determined that it is that person who communicates the work, and that other intermediaries such as Internet service providers only provide the tools required for the transmission of the work to occur. The decision was released on October 27, 1999 and a copy of it is available on the Web site of the Copyright Board. Questions relating to the amount of royalties to be paid under the tariff are to be determined in separate proceedings by the Board. At the time of writing, a final decision had not been rendered, and therefore there is no mechanism for clearing rights for the public performance of music on the Internet. However, if you are playing music on your Web site, you may want to contact SOCAN to see whether a decision has been rendered and/or to advise them of the details relating to your use of music, and to determine whether the tariff is applicable to you.

For further information, contact:

SOCAN
41 Valleybrook Drive
Don Mills, Ontario M3B 2S6

T: 416.445.8700 or 1.800.55SOCAN (76226)
F: 416.445.7108
E: **socan@socan.ca**
 www.socan.ca

REPRODUCTION RIGHT

A musical work can be reproduced in a number of ways: by audio reproduction, by audio-visual reproduction, and by reprographic reproduction.

You have to clear the reproduction right whether you are a record producer cutting a new CD, or a choir taping a song still protected by copyright, or if you are using music on a television program.

The reproduction right in a musical work is usually assigned to a music publisher. The music publisher will try to maximize the copyright royalties for the song composer and lyricist. It is not unusual for a songwriter to act as his or her own publisher. A publisher and songwriter usually make an arrangement to share equally in the proceeds from the exploitation of a song. If you want to reproduce a song, you can deal with the music publisher, as it is safe to assume that the music publisher will give the songwriter his or her share.

There are tens of thousands of music publishers, from large conglomerates to individual songwriters, with varying size repertoires. The Canadian Musical Reproduction Rights Agency Limited (CMRRA) is an organization that represents a large number of them in Canada and abroad. CMRRA is a nonexclusive agent. Thus, music publishers represented by CMRRA can enter into licensing arrangements through CMRRA, or directly with users.

For further information, contact:

Canadian Musical Reproduction Rights Agency Limited
56 Wellesley Street West, Suite 320
Toronto, Ontario M5S 2S3

T: 416.926.1966
F: 416.926.7521
E: **inquiries@cmrra.ca**
 www.cmrra.ca

The Society for Reproduction Rights of Authors, Composers and Publishers in Canada (Sodrac) Inc. represents a large number of authors, composers and music publishers in Quebec. It also represents music publishers from France, Spain, Italy, Portugal, South America and many other countries.

For further information, contact:

Society for Reproduction Rights of Authors, Composers
and Publishers in Canada Inc.
759, Victoria Square, Suite 420
Montreal, Quebec H2Y 2J7

T: 514.845.3268
F: 514.845.3401
E: **sodrac@mlink.net**
(WEB) www.sodrac.com

Audio Reproduction

Rates for the reproduction right in a musical work are settled by negotiation between the record industry and the music publisher and, as a result, there is an industry standard rate. From January 1, 2000 to December 31, 2001, the industry standard rate is 7.4 cents per musical work of five minutes or less and 1.48 cents for each additional minute. If you want to reproduce a six-minute song, the rate would be 7.4 + 1.48 or 8.88 cents. Beginning January 1, 2002, the rates are 7.7 cents per music works of five minutes or less and 1.54 cents for each additional minute. For licences issued at a lower rate, you are obliged, as the rates increase, to pay the new higher rate if your recording is still on the market when the increase applies. If you need to clear rights in order to make an audio recording of a musical work, contact the music publisher, CMRRA or SODRAC.

Audio-visual Reproduction

Each time you include a musical work in a film, television program or commercial, you must negotiate a royalty rate with the music publisher, CMRRA or SODRAC.

Reprography

With respect to the reproduction of sheet music from books, contact the music publisher.

Sound Recordings

REPRODUCTION RIGHT

Since copyright clearance to use a musical work does not include the use of a recording of that work, separate copyright permission must be obtained to "reproduce" a sound recording.

The Audio Video Licensing Agency (AVLA) administers the reproduction right in audio and music video recordings. If you need to reproduce a master audio recording, you may be able to obtain permission to do so from AVLA.

For further information, contact:

> The Audio Video Licensing Agency
> 890 Yonge Street, Suite 1200
> Toronto, Ontario M4W 3P4
>
> T: 416.922.8727 or 1.800.668.8820
> F: 416.922.9610
> E: **info@avla.ca**
> **www.cria.ca/relate.html**

Neighbouring rights

PUBLIC PERFORMANCE AND BROADCAST OF SOUND RECORDINGS

Sound recording performers and producers are now entitled to receive royalty payments from those who use their sound recordings for public performance or broadcast on radio. The responsible parties for paying royalties are the radio broadcasting industry and commercial and non-commercial establishments that use sound recordings. The statement of royalties that has been approved by the Copyright Board for payment by commercial radio stations is available on the Web site of the Copyright Board at: **www.cb-cda.gc.ca**.

The royalties are collected by a single copyright collective established in 1997, the Neighbouring Rights Collective of Canada (NRCC). However, NRCC will not distribute these royalties to individuals, but rather to its five member collectives.

In addition, NRCC is a member of the CPCC (see below) and will receive revenues from manufacturers and importers of blank audio recording media to distribute to performers and producers.

If you are a radio broadcaster or commercial or non-commercial establishment that publicly performs or broadcasts sound recordings, contact:

> NRCC
> 920 Yonge Street, Suite 502
> Toronto, ON M4W 3C7
>
> T: 416.968.8870
> F: 416.962.7797
> E: **info@nrdv.ca**
> **site under construction**

LEVY ON BLANK AUDIO RECORDING MEDIA

Certain copyright holders are now entitled to collect compensation for private copying of sound recordings via a levy on blank audio recording media like cassettes and certain digital formats (CDs and CDRs), made or imported, and sold in Canada. The beneficiaries of this levy are eligible composers, lyricists, performers and producers of sound recordings, which they may collect through their professional associations or collectives.

The Copyright Board sets this levy. The first decision on private copying was issued on December 17, 1999 (**www.cb-cda.gc.ca/index-e.html**) and is valid for 1999 and 2000. The decision sets the amount of the levy on analog audio cassette tapes (of forty minutes or longer) and certain recordable and re-writeable digital formats. Consumers do not directly pay the levy although the levy is likely to be recognized in the price of recording media. Manufacturers and importers will pay the levy on leviable media that they sell or otherwise dispose of in Canada.

For further information, contact:

> CPCC/SCPCP
> 150 Eglinton Avenue East, Suite 403
> Toronto, Ontario M4P 1E8
>
> T: 416.486.6832
> F: 416.485.4373
> E: n/a
> **www.cpcc.ca**

Music Videos

AVLA also licenses the rights in music videos. If you are reproducing a music video or showing it in public or on television, AVLA can help you obtain copyright permission.

Artistic Works

There are two copyright collectives that represent artistic works. Many visual or graphic artists, designers, craftspeople, cartoonists, illustrators, printmakers, illustration artists, sculptors, video artists and architects belong to one of these collectives.

If you want to exhibit an artistic work of a Canadian artist outside of Quebec, or reproduce the work, for instance, on the cover of a book or in a calendar, photocopy it, use it in a television program, or include it on a CD-ROM or Web page, you should contact:

> CARfac Copyright Collective
> Box 172
> Christopher Lake, Saskatchewan S0J 0N0
>
> T: 306.982.4784
> F: 306.982.4784
> E: **collective@carfac.ca**
> 📧 **www.carfac.ca/collective/**

For permission to use works of Quebec artists, contact SODRAC (see above), or:

> SODART
> 640 Côte d'Abraham
> Québec, Québec G1R 1A1
>
> T: 418.640.7464
> F: 418.640.2567
> E: **sodart@mlink.net**
> 📧 **www.raav.org/sodart**

These collectives also have reciprocal agreements with various collectives in other countries.

Retransmitted Works

There are a number of copyright collectives that represent various Canadian copyright holders. There are also a number of collectives representing American rights holders whose works are retransmitted in Canada. Lastly, some collectives that represent other rights are members of one of the retransmission collectives; for instance, CANCOPY is a member of the Canadian Retransmission Collective.

Independent Canadian film and television producers, and all non-North American producers and all owners of programs broadcast on PBS, can obtain royalties for retransmission from the Canadian Retransmission Collective (CRC). For further information, contact:

> Canadian Retransmission Collective
> 20 Toronto St., Suite 830
> Toronto, Ontario M5V 2B8
>
> T: 416.304.0290
> F: 416.304.0496
> E: **info@crc-scrc.ca**
> ⓦ **www.crc-scrc.ca**

Private Canadian broadcasters including privately owned affiliates of the CBC and Radio-Canada networks should contact:

> Canadian Broadcasters Rights Agency Inc.
> 280 Albert Street, Suite 1000
> Ottawa, Ontario K1P 5G8
>
> T: 613.232.4370
> F: 613.236.9241
> E: n/a
> ⓦ **www.cbra.ca**

The Canadian Broadcasting Corporation (CBC)/Société Radio-Canada (SRC) and Radio-Quebec belong to a separate retransmission collective (along with ABC, CBS and NBC). For further information contact:

> Canadian Retransmission Right Association
> 250 Lanark Avenue
> Ottawa, Ontario K1Z 6R5

T: 613.724.5362
F: 613.724.5453
E: n/a
W: n/a

Rights holders not mentioned under any of the above categories could visit the Web site of the Copyright Board for further information about retransmission collectives.

Online Clearance Mechanisms

There are a number of interesting Internet initiatives, both non-profit and for-profit, that are "privatising" what in the past would have been considered the domain of copyright collectives. The Internet and software developments make it much easier for rights holders to license their own works without the help of a collective, or to work with one of the many e-commerce companies or clearing houses to do so. It is now very easy to access the Web site of a number of newspaper or magazine publishers and directly purchase an article online from them. It will be interesting to watch over the next few years how collectives and other Internet initiatives define their roles.

USING CROWN WORKS (I.E., GOVERNMENT MATERIAL)

Federal Government Materials

STATUTES, DECISIONS, ETC.
Anyone may, without charge or request for permission, reproduce enactments and consolidations of enactments of the Government of Canada, and decisions and reasons for decisions of federally-constituted courts and administrative tribunals, provided due diligence is exercised in ensuring the accuracy of the materials reproduced and the reproduction is not represented as an official version.

OTHER FEDERAL MATERIALS
Other than statutes, decisions, etc., as discussed above, all other federal government material, in any format, whether distributed or disseminated

for free, or for a fee, requires permission from the government to reproduce, adapt or translate, in whole or in part, or to use in any other copyright manner.

In order to obtain permission to reproduce, adapt or translate Government of Canada materials, in whole or in part, you must send a written
request to the Crown Copyright Officer at Public Works and Government
Services Canada, or complete the Crown Copyright Clearance Form. Either
way, you must provide descriptive information about the government material to be used, and the percentage proportion of the document being reproduced, as well as descriptive information about your publication. A fee may
be applied for the use of the copyright material for commercial purposes. A
copy of the Application for Crown Copyright Clearance Form is included
in Appendix II.

For more information on obtaining copyright clearance to use
Government of Canada materials, contact:

> Crown Copyright Officer
> Canadian Government Publishing
> Public Access Programs Sector
> Ottawa, Ontario K1A 0S5
>
> T: 613.990.2210
> F: 613.998.1450
> E: **copyright.droitsdauteur@pwgsc.gc.ca**
> 🌐 **publications.pwgsc.gc.ca/publishing/copyright/
> crownis-e.html**

Copyright materials of Crown corporations must be cleared through the
specific Crown corporation. For instance, the Canadian Broadcasting
Corporation (CBC) and the National Film Board (NFB) can give permission to use works in which they own the copyright. Also, the House of
Commons, the Senate, Statistics Canada and the National Research Council
can clear the copyright in copyright materials owned by them.

Provincial and Territorial Government Materials

Following the Canadian federal government's lead, the province of Ontario
now allows use of certain materials without prior permission. As stated on
its site:

Although the Queen's Printer for Ontario claims copyright in Ontario statutes, regulations and judicial decisions, the Queen's Printer permits any person to reproduce the text and images contained in the statutes, regulations and judicial decisions without seeking permission and without charge. The materials must be reproduced accurately and the reproduction must not be represented as an official version.

In addition, the Queen's Printer requires that Crown copyright in the legal materials continue to be acknowledged in a manner specified on its site. See **www.gov.on.ca/MBS/english/common/copypolicy.html** or e-mail: **copyright@gov.on.ca** for further information.

The use of other Ontario government materials, and copyright materials of any other provincial government, with the exception of Quebec, must be cleared through the particular provincial department responsible for the administration of copyright. COPIBEC's repertoire includes the various publications of the different ministries of Quebec.

Municipal Government Materials

Municipal government materials must be cleared through the particular municipal department responsible for the administration of copyright.

UNLOCATABLE COPYRIGHT OWNERS

If you have used all your resources to identify or locate a copyright owner and have been unsuccessful, you may be allowed to use the copyright material in question without directly obtaining permission from the copyright holder. In 1988, a provision was added to the law to set up a procedure for users of copyright materials to access the works of copyright owners who cannot be located. As a result of this provision, the Copyright Board now has the power to issue licences for the use of published works where the copyright owner cannot be located.

In order to use works of unlocatable copyright holders, you must apply to the Copyright Board and satisfy it that the copyright owner cannot be located. In order to satisfy the Copyright Board, you must convince it that every reasonable effort has been made to locate the copyright holder. Proof may include evidence of correspondence and phone calls with the rights holder or a representative including any copyright collectives or estate executors, as well as associations or organizations relevant to the work or copyright holder, contacting publishing houses, libraries, universities and museums. If the Board is not satisfied that sufficient research has been undertaken to locate the copyright holder, it may advise you to continue your efforts, and may even suggest how to go about locating a copyright holder.

If the Board is satisfied by your efforts, it may, at its discretion, give permission (i.e., issue a licence) to use the work. This permission is non-exclusive; that is, others may be given the same permission for the same work. The permission is valid only in Canada; it does not protect you from infringement proceedings for things done outside the country, even if the author is Canadian. The licence is subject to any terms and conditions, including royalty payments, which the Board may establish.

The copyright owner may, within five years after expiration of the licence, collect the royalties that are set out in the licence. If the royalties are uncollectible, the copyright owner may start a court action to recover them. In many cases, this money will be held in trust by a copyright collective during the five-year period and will revert to the collective if it is not claimed within five years by the copyright holder. A copyright owner cannot terminate a licence granted by the Copyright Board.

The unlocatable copyright owner provision is open to anyone trying to access a particular copyright work, including librarians, teachers, students, curators, archivists, publishers, sound recording and film producers, and business people. The unlocatable copyright owner provision only applies to published works. There is no equivalent provision for unpublished works.

To apply for a licence, you must submit an application in writing to the Copyright Board with the following information.

- the description of the work (type, title, year of publication, and any other related information)
- the names and nationalities of the author, copyright owner and publisher/producer, etc.
- if the author is dead, the date of death
- your intended use of the work. Be specific and provide as much detail as possible

For example, if you want to reproduce written material to include in a book, indicate the length of the written material, a description of the book including its length, the purpose of the book, whether it is for free distribution or for sale (if for sale, include the suggested sale price). It is also helpful if you include with your application:

- the material you want to reproduce
- the period of time in which you want to use the work
- a full description of your efforts to locate the copyright holder. Include copies of any relevant material such as letters, faxes and copies of e-mail correspondence
- the name, title, address, telephone and fax numbers of the licence applicant

Based on the above information, the Board will issue you a licence if it considers that you have done everything possible to locate the copyright owner. If you provide sufficient information, the Board can respond as quickly as thirty days from the date of your application, but it will not guarantee such a quick response. Because each application has to be carefully examined, it is best to make your application to the Board as soon as you can and not to wait until the last minute.

If the Board issues a licence, the licence will indicate the authorized use (e.g., how many reproductions are permitted for what distribution and for what purpose), the length of the licence, the licence fee (which the copyright owner can claim within five years of the licence's expiry date), and any other terms and conditions the Board considers appropriate.

As an example of an unlocatable copyright owner licence issued by the Board, on February 21, 2000, the Copyright Board issued a non-exclusive licence to the Canadian Institute for Historical Microreproductions authorizing the reproduction of 560 works in a variety of formats. Figure 14.2 shows a reproduction of the licence, with the Board's reasons.

For more information on using the unlocatable copyright owner provision, contact:

Copyright Board
56 Sparks Street, Suite 800
Ottawa, Ontario K1A 0C9

T: 613.952.8621
F: 613.952.8630
E: **cb-cda@smtp.gc.ca**
www.cb-cda.gc.ca/

MORAL RIGHTS

Obtaining permission to use a copyright work licenses you for the "economic" right, however, it does not give you any permission regarding

Figure 14.2: Sample of Non-exclusive Licence

Ottawa, February 21, 2000	Ottawa, le 21 février 2000

FILE: 2000-UO/TI-1

UNLOCATABLE COPYRIGHT OWNERS

Non-exclusive licence issued to the Canadian Institute for Historical Microreproductions authorizing the reproduction of 560 works

Pursuant to the provisions of subsection 77(1) of the *Copyright Act*, the Copyright Board issues the following licence to the Canadian Institute for Historical Microreproductions:

(1) The licence authorizes the reproduction, in print form, microfiches or CD-ROMs, of the works listed in the appendices to the January 17, 2000 application (of which 28 titles have been removed by the applicant on January 21, 2000). The total number of copies of each work shall not exceed 75.

(2) The licence expires on December 31, 2001. The authorized reproduction must be completed by that date.

(3) The licence is non-exclusive and valid only in Canada.

(4) The Institute shall pay 10¢ per work reproduced in print form or microfiche and 15¢ per work reproduced on CD-ROM (multiplied by the number of copies made in each case), to any person who establishes, before December 31, 2006, ownership of the copyright in a work covered by this licence.

(5) This licence is conditional on the applicant's filing with the Board an undertaking to comply with the conditions set out in paragraph (4) above.

DOSSIER : 2000-UO/TI-1

TITULAIRES DE DROITS D'AUTEUR INTROUVABLES

Licence non exclusive délivrée à l'Institut canadien de microreproductions historiques autorisant la reproduction de 560 œuvres

Conformément aux dispositions du paragraphe 77(1) de la *Loi sur le droit d'auteur*, la Commission du droit d'auteur délivre la licence qui suit à l'Institut canadien de microreproductions historiques :

1) La licence autorise la reproduction, sous forme d'imprimés, de microfiches ou de CD-ROM, des œuvres énumérées aux annexes de la requête du 17 janvier 2000. De ces œuvres, 28 ont été retirées par la requérante le 21 janvier 2000. Le nombre total d'exemplaires de chaque œuvre ne peut dépasser 75.

2) La licence expire le 31 décembre 2001. La reproduction autorisée devra être complétée d'ici cette date.

3) La licence est non exclusive et valide seulement au Canada.

4) L'Institut versera 10 ¢ par œuvre reproduite sous forme d'imprimés ou de microfiches et 15 ¢ par œuvre reproduite sur CD-ROM (multipliés par le nombre de copies produites dans chacun des cas) à toute personne qui établit, avant le 31 décembre 2006, qu'elle détient le droit d'auteur sur toute œuvre faisant l'objet de la présente licence.

5) Cette licence est conditionnelle au dépôt auprès de la Commission d'un engagement de la requérante de se conformer aux conditions stipulées au paragraphe 4) ci-dessus.

Le secrétaire de la Commission,

Claude Majeau
Secretary to the Board

moral rights. In other words, clearing copyright does not mean that you have cleared the moral rights in a work. By obtaining permission to use a work, you can use that work "as is." You may not modify or adapt or "morph" the work. According to the *Copyright Act*, you cannot distort, mutilate or otherwise modify a copyright work if that would be prejudicial to the honour or reputation of the author. If the work is a painting, sculpture or engraving, you cannot change the work whatsoever, that is, prejudice to honour or reputation of the author is not a condition. Keep in mind that a change in the location of a work, the physical means by which a work is exposed or the physical structure containing a work, and steps taken in good faith to restore or preserve a work, do not by themselves constitute a distortion, mutilation or other modification of a copyright work.

Further, even if you have permission to use a copyright work, the author has the right to have his or her name appear in association with the work, to use a pseudonym or to remain anonymous. Lastly, someone who has permission to use a copyright work does not have the right to use the work in association with a product, service, cause or institution if that use is prejudicial to the honour or reputation of the author.

As discussed earlier, moral rights belong to the author of a work. This is true even if the owner of a work is someone other than the author of a work. For example, an employer may own copyright in a staff written script, however, the writer of that script owns the moral rights in it. Unlike copyright rights, moral rights cannot be licensed or assigned. Moral rights, however, may be waived and may be passed on upon death. This is discussed in Chapter 11: How Can Rights Be Exploited?.

SUMMARY

If you are planning to use a work or other subject-matter protected by copyright, you must obtain permission, and/or pay a royalty, prior to that use. There are a number of sources to clear copyright permission, including the copyright owner and the various copyright collectives.

Chapter 15

CANADIAN AND AMERICAN COPYRIGHT LAWS: A COMPARISON

The Congress shall have Power . . . To promote the Progress of Science and useful arts, by securing for limited Times to Authors and Inventors the exclusive Right to their respective Writings and Discoveries.

United States Constitution, Article I, Section 8

THE RELEVANCY OF AMERICAN COPYRIGHT LAW TO CANADIANS

The underlying principles of the Canadian and American copyright laws, and perhaps copyright laws around the world, are basically the same; that is, to provide creators with adequate protection in their creations and provide users with reasonable access to these creations. Notwithstanding this fact, there remain many differences in the philosophies behind, and practical effects of, the Canadian and American copyright laws.

If your work is being used in the United States, this chapter is pertinent since you are protected in the United States under the American copyright law. Even where your work is not being used in the United States, the American Copyright Office may be of some assistance with respect to registering and depositing your works and searching for owners of copyright materials.

WORKS PROTECTED IN THE UNITED STATES

Canada and the United States generally protect the same types of works and grant similar rights to creators, though the terminology used in the respective legislations may differ. For example, works explicitly protected under the American copyright legislation include the following:

- literary works
- musical works (including any accompanying words)
- dramatic works (including any accompanying music)
- pantomimes and choreographic works
- pictorial, graphic and sculptural works
- motion pictures and other audio-visual works
- sound recordings

RIGHTS GRANTED IN THE UNITED STATES
Exclusive rights granted to copyright holders under the American Copyright Act include the following:

- to reproduce a copyright work in copies or phonorecords
- to prepare derivative works based upon the copyright work
- to distribute copies or phonorecords of the work to the public by sale or other transfer of ownership, or by rental, lease or lending
- to publicly perform literary, musical, dramatic, and choreographic works, pantomimes, and motion pictures and other audio-visual works
- to publicly display literary, musical, dramatic, and choreographic works, pantomimes, and pictorial, graphic, or sculptural works, including the individual images of a motion picture or other audio-visual work
- to perform a sound recording by digital audio transmission

In addition, copyright holders may authorize others to use any of the rights listed above.

FAIR USE AND EXCEPTIONS
There are wider allowances for the free use of copyright materials under the American law than under Canadian law. This is true for uses subject to fair use, as well as for the provisions specifically for user groups like teachers, librarians and archivists. For example, fair use in the United States, unlike the fair dealing provision in Canada, allows for the making of multiple copies for classroom use under certain limited circumstances.

You should not assume that an act constituting a copyright violation under Canadian law is a violation in the United States. Always keep in mind that when a work is being used in the United States, it is subject to the fair use provision and the exceptions set out in the American *Copyright Act*. Likewise, when American material is used in Canada, it is subject to the fair dealing provision and the exceptions set out in the Canadian *Copyright Act*.

LENGTH OF PROTECTION

Until October, 1998, the general duration of copyright protection in the United States was life-plus-fifty. On October 27, 1998, President Clinton signed into law the Sonny Bono Copyright Term Extension Act, which immediately extended the term of copyright an additional twenty years, making the term for most works the life of the author plus 70 years. Therefore, under current American copyright law, works created on or after January 1, 1978 enjoy the general term of copyright protection of life-plus-seventy. Copyright expires at the end of the calendar on the seventieth year, i.e., December 31 of that year. As such, Canadian works are protected in the United States for life-plus-seventy years whereas American works are protected in Canada for life-plus-fifty (since you apply the copyright law where the work is being used).

The duration of protection for works created, but not published or registered, before January 1, 1978 is life-plus-seventy, but the duration never expires before December 31, 2002. If the work is published before December 31, 2002, the duration will not expire before December 31, 2047.

The duration for pre-1978 works that are in their original or renewal term of copyright is ninety-five years from the date the copyright was originally secured.[1]

Like the Canadian law, there are specific provisions in the American law for the duration of copyright in specific circumstances. For example, where there is a "work made for hire," that is, a work was prepared by an employee within the scope of his or her employment, or where a certain work is specially ordered or commissioned for use in particular works (for example, a contribution to a motion picture or other audio-visual work), the term of copyright protection is ninety-five years from the date of publication or one hundred and twenty years from the date of creation of the work, or whichever expires first. Further, where there is an anonymous or pseudonymous work, the duration of copyright is ninety-five years from first publication or one hundred and twenty years from creation, whichever is shorter. This is provided the author's identity is not revealed in the American Copyright Office records.

REGISTRATION, AND COPYRIGHT NOTICE REQUIREMENTS

Similar to Canadian law, copyright protection is automatic in the United States when the work is created and in some fixed form. At one time, such things as publication, registration and using proper copyright notices were necessary for protection in the United States. For works first published on or after March 1, 1989, registration or inclusion of any form of copyright notice is not required to preserve the life-plus-seventy protection. Before March 1, 1989, the use of the copyright notice was necessary on all published works and omitting it could result in loss of copyright protection. However, there are corrective steps that may be followed to ensure that copyright was not lost for this reason.

Despite the absence of formal requirements in the current law for registering certain works, the law provides many incentives for doing so, even for non-American originated creations. For instance, registering before or within five years of first publication provides *prima facie* evidence of copyright validity and of the truth of the statements contained in the registration certificate. Also, registering published works before or within three months of publication, or before infringement, permits successful plaintiffs in infringement suits to seek special statutory damages and lawyers' fees in virtually all cases (otherwise, only an order of actual damages and profits is available to the copyright owner of a published work). Furthermore, registration establishes a public record of the copyright claim. Thus, an infringer cannot claim that he or she had no way of knowing a copyright existed and therefore cannot claim to be an innocent infringer to seek a reduction in damages payable to the copyright owner. Registration may be made at any time. Both published and unpublished works may be registered.

For copyright owners of works of American origin, registering a work may be necessary in order to file an infringement suit in an American court. As a general rule, under American law, the prelitigation registration does not apply to foreign (i.e., non-American) authors including persons or companies who initially acquired copyright protection under the Canadian *Copyright Act*, and by virtue of the international copyright conventions, acquired copyright protection in the United States (unless publication occurred simultaneously in the Canada and the United States). You should check into the details of this if you think your work may be of American origin.

If you do register in the United States, you might want to take advantage of other American Copyright Office benefits, for instance, voluntary recording of transfers of copyright ownership.

EMPLOYMENT SITUATIONS AND ASSIGNMENTS OF COPYRIGHT

If you are working in the United States or for an American individual or company, be aware that the United States has different laws and industry standards than Canada for works created in the course of employment as well as for commissioned works. Also, in certain industries in the United States, you may automatically be asked to assign, as oppose to license, your copyrights as a precondition of employment. For instance, American movie and television producers may require an assignment of the publishing rights to a musical score. Similarly, if you write a spec script for a film, you will initially own the copyright in the script, however, if you sell the script to an American production company or studio, they will require an assignment of the copyright. Even if the assignment of rights is not obvious, be on guard for American contracts that automatically vest copyright ownership in the party specially ordering or commissioning certain types of works, such as collections and audio-visual works, including motion pictures and certain computer software. Also, keep in mind that contractual arrangements can override the statutory law and you may be able to negotiate better terms in a contract than those initially offered to you.

In the United States, copyright generally belongs to the author. However, in employment or what is referred to as "work made for hire" situations, the employer or other person for whom the work was prepared is considered the author and owner of the copyright. This is true unless the parties have expressly agreed otherwise in writing. Recall that in Canada, even in employment situations, the original creator of the work remains the author of the work for copyright purposes notwithstanding the fact that the employer is the owner of the copyright. This has important consequences for such things as moral rights protection.

Examples of works made for hire include a video game created by a staff game creator for Video Game Corporation, a newspaper article written by a staff journalist for publication in *The L.A. Times*, and a musical arrangement written for ZZZ Music Company by a salaried staff arranger. It also includes a script commissioned for a film or CD-ROM even where no salaried employment relationship exists, if the scriptwriter and film/

CD-ROM producer sign an agreement to the effect that it is a work made for hire.

MORAL RIGHTS

Moral rights protection under American federal and state laws is not the same as moral rights protection under the Canadian *Copyright Act*. The explicit moral rights protection that exists in the American *Copyright Act* (through an amendment made to it by the *Visual Artists Rights Act* of 1990) is for one group of creators—visual artists, or more accurately, those who create "works of visual art." The law gives certain visual artists the right to claim authorship in their work, and to prevent the use of their name in association with a work. In addition, the law grants artists the right to prevent the intentional distortion, mutilation or other objectionable modification of certain works of "recognized stature." Artists who qualify for federal moral rights protection can also prevent any destruction of certain works. Some states such as New York and California also have moral rights protection for visual artists.

NEW AMERICAN DIGITAL LEGISLATION

On October 28, 1998, President Clinton signed into law the *Digital Millennium Copyright Act* of 1998 (DMCA) to update the American *Copyright Act*. Among other things, the DMCA helps copyright owners protect their digital content through its anticircumvention and copyright management information provisions. At the current time, there are no similar provisions in the Canadian *Copyright Act*, however this new American legislation may serve as an example in Canada and around the world as we begin to determine how copyright law applies in the digital world.

Regarding anticircumvention, the DMCA protects against the tampering of copyright protection technologies and rights management systems. The DMCA prohibits unauthorized circumvention of technological measures controlling access to or restricting use of a copyright protected work, as well as certain devices and services used for such unauthorized circumvention. The types of technological measures protected include passwords, serial numbers and encryption that copyright owners use to control or restrict access to their works. For example, the law might be infringed by using a bootleg password to gain unauthorized access to a sound recording or video clip.

In addition, the DMCA prohibits deliberate tampering with copyright management information, including knowingly providing false copyright management information, or distributing false copyright management information, "with the intent to induce, enable, facilitate or conceal infringement." Copyright management information includes the title of a work, the name of its author and the copyright owner, other identifying information, and terms and conditions for use of the work, provided they are "conveyed in connection with" copies, phonorecords, performances or displays of the work. It also prohibits intentionally removing or altering copyright management information, or knowingly distributing or publicly performing works from which the copyright management information has been removed or altered.

Further, the DMCA provides a limitation on the potential liability of Internet service providers (ISPs) for certain copyright infringements by their customers and others (e.g., employees and agents). Under specified circumstances, ISPs with infringing copyright materials on their systems will not be liable for monetary relief such as "damages, costs, attorneys' fees, and any other form of monetary payment," or for certain injunctions or other equitable relief for infringement of copyright.

HOW TO OBTAIN FURTHER INFORMATION ON AMERICAN COPYRIGHT LAW

The American Copyright Office has extensive information on many aspects of its law. The best place to begin your search would be in the Office's Web site. Contact information is:

> Copyright Office
> Publications Section, LM-455
> Library of Congress
> Washington, D.C. 20559-6000 U.S.A.

> T: 202.707.3000 (information specialists are on duty 8:30 a.m. to 5:00 p.m., Eastern Time, Monday – Friday)
> Forms hotline (24 hours) T: 202.707.9100
> F. 202.707.6859 (indicate person or section)
> Fax-on-demand: 202.707.3000
> E: **copyinfo@loc.gov**
> **www.loc.gov/copyright**

SUMMARY

Copyright holders who are protected under the Canadian *Copyright Act* are protected when their creations are used in the United States and such protection is governed by the rights and remedies set out in the American *Copyright Act*. Although there are many similarities with respect to the copyright laws in the two countries, there are differences with respect to the registration system, maintaining and enforcing copyright protection and exceptions from the law, all of which should be taken into account when exploiting copyright works in the United States.

Chapter 16

DIGITAL COPYRIGHT AND ELECTRONIC RIGHTS

In the classic American film, "The Graduate," a drunk tycoon gave Dustin Hoffman a famous word of career advice: "Plastics." In an eerie replay of that scene, a certified Hollywood mogul gave a member of my staff another one-word bit of advice. He leaned forward conspiratorially and uttered the magic word: "Digital."

Ralph Oman, Register of Copyrights of the United States of America, "Reflections on Digital Technology: The Shape of Things to Come," WIPO Worldwide Symposium on the Impact of Digital Technology on Copyright and Neighboring Rights, Harvard University, Cambridge, Massachusetts, USA, March 31 to April 2, 1993

INTRODUCTION

Throughout this third edition, references have been added, and information provided, to deal with digital copyright issues and electronic rights. However, because of the hype, novelty and lack of material on copyright law in this area, it seemed appropriate and important to devote a chapter solely to it.

In general, the laws and principles of copyright applicable to digital media are no different from those applicable to works in traditional formats; this chapter is based on the presumption that Canadian copyright law is generally flexible enough to meet the challenges of new technology, and it sets out specific examples and the application of law to particular and new fact situations arising from digital media. The discussion of these issues could easily fill a book and it is assumed that you will have read and/or will have to return to earlier chapters where necessary to get a fuller understanding of the copyright law and principles discussed here.

When writing the second edition of this book in 1994-95, there was much discussion among individuals, lawyers, governments and Internet users about whether intellectual property laws would survive the Internet, and if so, in what form. The focus of this discussion has shifted and most discussions now centre on the form of protection that is appropriate.

Although various areas of intellectual property deal with aspects of digital media, copyright is the most prominent area and the only one dealt with here. In addition to intellectual property law, other areas of the law, especially privacy, rights in domain names, and patent law are relevant on the Internet and should not be overlooked. Contract law or licensing is also playing a growing role regarding the use of digital media. A later section in this chapter provides information on licensing digital media.

When examining digital copyright issues, there is discussion both on the copyright protection of the content itself, as well as on copyright implications from the distribution of that content. For example, posting content on a Web site includes issues of protection of that content as well as legalities in accessing that content and distributing it to others.

Be aware that all of the information in this book reflects both the copyright law and the technology as it exists at the time of writing this edition.

OLD LAW, NEW TECHNOLOGY

Copyright law originated because of technology and the need to control copying by printing presses. The law has evolved in order to meet the copying challenges presented by "new" technologies that once included photocopying machines, VCRs, tape recorders and computers. In discussing the application of current Canadian copyright law and principles, it is assumed that the Canadian law will be flexible enough to apply to the most recent, as well as future, technologies. However, in some instances, the law may be vague in its application to new technology, or the *Act* might require some amendments. In other cases, the law is clear, however, the administration, compliance, and enforcement of the law creates a new perspective, requiring new challenges to be confronted. As such, this chapter will both answer, and raise, questions about the applicability of copyright law to digital media.

TERMINOLOGY

What Is Digital Media?

There is no definitive definition of digital media. For purposes of this book, digital media refers to any content in a digital form. Some refer to digital media as new media or multimedia. Basically, it is the content we find on the Internet as well as in "containers" like CD-ROMs and DVDs. This content may be text, data, images, sound or combinations of any of these elements. One unique aspect of digital media is that it is found in various different types of containers and disseminated through a large variety of ways, from being accessible (i.e., for sale) in a CD-ROM in a "traditional" store, to being accessible via telephone lines, cable and satellite.

All content on the Internet or the World Wide Web (the Web) is in a digital form. Although the Internet goes beyond what is the Web, this book interchangeably uses these two terms.

What Is "Digital" Technology?

Digital technology means the storage, reproduction and transmission of any piece of information—data, sound, video, text, graphics—in the form of digits, in binary code consisting of zeros and ones. The digital pattern can be transmitted by satellite, optical fibre or co-axial cable, microwave link and conventional phone lines, and can then be converted back to its original format. Digital information is usually only machine-readable and must be converted by the machine into some other form before it can be understood by human beings.

The terms digital and electronic are used interchangeably in this book. Electronic copies are in a digital format. With future technology, digital works may include but also go beyond being electronic works. Because digital and electronic do not have exactly the same meaning, ensure that any agreements assigning or licensing digital or electronic rights are specific about defining these rights.

What Are Electronic Rights?

Rights attaching to digital media are generally referred to as "electronic rights," "e-rights" or "digital rights." Other terms used to describe related rights are "database rights," "multimedia rights," "CD-ROM rights," "Web site rights," and "Internet rights." However described, electronic rights constitute the "bundle of rights" over which a copyright owner has sole and exclusive control. These rights are reproduction, public performance, adaptation, telecommunication to the public, and all the other rights specified in the current *Copyright Act*. Each right is separate and distinct from the other rights and can be separately exploited by the copyright owner, usually in exchange for monetary compensation. In addition, an author has moral rights in a digital work.

CURRENT COPYRIGHT LAW AND DIGITAL MEDIA

This section of the chapter applies the current copyright law to issues that are pertinent to digital media.

Works Protected By Copyright

In order for a digital work to be protected by copyright, it must meet the general requirements concerning originality, fixation and nationality of creator and place of publication that are discussed in Chapter 3: Is Your Creation Eligible for Copyright Protection?

If the work meets these requirements, it will be protected like any other literary, artistic, dramatic and musical work since the *Copyright Act* protects all works in any mode or form of expression.

Works protected include an electronic book, a digital recording and a compilation of works. A compilation of works could be a multimedia work like a CD-ROM encyclopedia. Online material is protected if it is fixed in some form, for example, as a print-out, or if it is saved on a floppy disk, hard drive or other back-up mechanism. In the United States, courts have determined that this condition of fixation can be met by interactive works (i.e., works in which the user participates and makes choices as to the order of the access to the material), and Canadian courts are likely to come to the same conclusion.

Ownership and Duration of Copyright

The rules concerning the ownership and duration of copyright equally pertain to digital works as to works in traditional formats.

If you are involved with the adaptation of a pre-existing work into an electronic format, you should carefully review all prior agreements made with respect to that work to determine any contractual arrangements regarding the ownership of digital rights. For instance, if your previous work is a published book or film script, you must check the original contract with the book publisher or film producer. In the best circumstances, the contract will clearly specify whether the author of the book or script—or the publisher or the producer—owns the electronic rights. Some contracts may refer to certain electronic rights, such as a CD-ROM, but may not refer to other electronic media or future media. It is also possible that the contract is unclear or silent regarding electronic rights. Many older contracts, and even some not so old, do not specifically mention electronic rights and it is sometimes unclear as to who owns them. In this situation, discussions may need to be re-opened between the parties who signed the original contract. The American courts have given the benefit of the doubt to authors where there is ambiguity in the scope of rights licensed in a contract and have thereby not allowed an unintended benefit to a person to whom copyright has been licensed. It is likely that Canadian courts would follow the American example. Two pending court cases in Canada have encouraged copyright owners to specify all licensed or assigned rights in writing in order to avoid future disputes or lawsuits. Determining your rights before entering new contractual arrangements will help clarify your situation and possibly also avoid having the courts interpret any ambiguity in your contracts.

Keep in mind that the owner or licensee of a copyright work who is not the author does not have the moral rights in that work. Unless an appropriate waiver has been obtained from the author of the work, the work cannot be modified or used in any other manner that would infringe an author's moral rights.

Economic Rights

THE RIGHT OF REPRODUCTION

The right of reproduction includes digital reproductions. If you make an electronic version of a photograph, you are making an electronic reproduction of it and must obtain permission to do so. Likewise, if you download an article from the Internet to your hard drive or a floppy disk, or you print an article from the Internet, you are making a reproduction of a work.

Electronic products are sometimes verbatim reproduction of text, but often the electronic products change or enhance the original work. Examples of enhancements are "A Hard Days' Night CD-ROM" in which text, sound and images were added to the original movie and book, respectively. Where original work is reproduced verbatim, adapted, or enhanced, it may raise rights other than reproduction—for instance, the right of adaptation, and moral rights like the rights of integrity and association. These rights are discussed below.

Browsing

The question of whether every instance of "browsing" on the Web constitutes or should constitute a reproduction of a work for copyright purposes is much discussed among governments, copyright scholars and laypeople. This is in part because there is no one definition of browsing, and browsing can constitute a variety of activities. For instance, browsing an electronic library can mean accessing an entire periodical article on your computer monitor. It can also mean accessing a database listing various periodicals on a certain subject, or accessing the first page of a periodical article. In some cases of browsing, entire works are accessed, and in other cases, portions are accessed. Also, in some cases, the results of the browsing is analogous to walking through the aisles of a library while in other cases, it is analogous to photocopying entire copyright works found in that library. Further, current technology invariably involves a reproduction of a work in order for it to be accessed through many of the browsing activities set out above, which would also constitute a reproduction for copyright purposes. In sum, browsing does involve the right of reproduction in all or most circumstances.

Although most browsing may be protected by Canadian copyright law, content on Web sites may still be reproduced without permission in a number of situations:

- if the content on the Web site is in the public domain
- if you are using information, facts or ideas from a Web site without reproducing any copyright works
- where a copyright notice is posted on the Web site permitting certain uses. These notices often permit reproducing content for personal or non-commercial purposes, and for educational, non-profit, research purposes. (However, the lack of a copyright notice/warning does not mean that you may use the work without permission.)
- if you may "imply" a licence to use the copyright materials in the Web site where explicit permission is not given. This "implied licence" means that in particular circumstances you may imply that the copyright owner is permitting you to use the materials in certain manners. For instance, I may imply that I can print out a copyright protected article I read on someone's Web site, although I would probably not imply that I may make fifty print copies to distribute to colleagues or to provide to students in a class I am teaching

Browsing may be addressed in future amendments to the Canadian *Copyright Act*.

Caching

Similar to browsing, caching may be an infringement of the right of reproduction. Caching involves your browser (the computer software you use to browse or surf the Internet) storing in its memory copies of certain pages you visit on the Web on a temporary basis. Caching may also be done by an Internet service provider (in which case, there may be issues of who is liable if the caching is not legal). Caching may be addressed in future amendments to the Canadian *Copyright Act*.

Linking

A link is a spot on a Web site on which a user may click and is then taken either to a different page in the same site or to a different Web site. A copyright issue arises when that link is to a different Web site. For example, is permission needed to include a link from one Web site to another Web site? There are no Canadian cases on this point, however, non-Canadian cases that have been settled out of court seem to indicate that you may link to the first or home page of a Web site, but before linking to an internal or deeper page (usually called "deep linking"), you should obtain advance permission. Some Web site owners, however, do ask for permission prior to including any links on their site; some consider this netiquette (or net manners). The reason many Web site owners oppose deep linking is that they want to better control, or direct, the user on their Web site, and prefer the user to enter their site on its home page.

Framing

Framing involves putting a frame around the content in another Web site that often appears as if that content belongs to the Web site containing the frames. Similar to linking, no answers have yet been provided by the courts as to whether framing is legal. The key in using frames is to use them in a way that does not mislead the viewer in terms of who the creator/originator of the site/content is, so as to avoid possible moral rights infringement and therefore copyright infringement. Many Web site owners are using frames with content in their own sites, but not with content from other sites, as a way to avoid any possible legal problems.

Listservs, Bulletin Boards and Newsgroups

A listserv is a program that distributes a message to a list of e-mail addresses. Listserv messages automatically appear when you collect your e-mail. An electronic bulletin board is accessible via the Internet for collecting and relaying electronic messages; it requires the computer user to obtain or send the message. A newsgroup is a discussion group on a specific topic, maintained on a computer network. The main difference between a listserv and a bulletin board is how the information is relayed or acquired. To be part of a listserv, one must have subscribed and information/e-mail is sent to the subscriber. A bulletin board, on the other hand, is open to anyone who is interested in acquiring information and therefore a person would have to seek out the information on their own. A newsgroup can operate in both of these manners. In all of these situations, copyright material may be distributed and permission may be required in advance (unless a licence may be implied from the specific circumstances). Note that it is arguable that there is a copyright in the collection/compilation of messages on a listserv, bulletin board or newsgroup. Also, see the discussion below on the right of telecommunication to the public.

THE RIGHT OF PUBLIC PERFORMANCE

The right to perform in public applies to digital works. The display of a CD-ROM or content on a Web site to people in a restaurant, store or classroom are examples of the application of this right.

THE RIGHT OF PUBLICATION

The right of publication, or the right to first make copies of a work available to the public, applies to digital works. This means that only the copyright holder of an electronic book has the right to first sell or freely distribute copies of the electronic book to the public. Note that this is only true where there is no underlying work, for example, in a print format. If there is a print work, the right of publication, first making copies of a work available to the public, would apply to that print format or to any other initial format.

THE RIGHT OF ADAPTATION

Any adaptation of a work in a digital format requires the clearance of the right of adaptation. An adaptation may be an enhancement to an underlying work, or manipulation of images or text. Even if you have the right to adapt a copyright work, you must still respect the author's moral rights (unless they have been waived in your favour).

THE RIGHT OF TELECOMMUNICATION TO THE PUBLIC

In order for the right of telecommunication to be infringed, there must be a telecommunication to the public. It is likely that if one person sends a copyright work by electronic mail to another person, the right of telecommunication need not be cleared (although an illegal copy may result at the other end if there is a print out or if it is saved on a diskette). However, if that same work is posted on an electronic bulletin board where anyone can dial in with his computer and by pressing the right buttons can access it, then this would probably be considered use of the right of telecommunication to the public. In this latter example, the work is being transmitted to the public notwithstanding the fact that each member of the public is receiving the transmission at different times, and on-demand or at his or her own convenience.

If you are creating digital works for distribution in "physical" retail outlets, for example, creating a CD-ROM for sale in a computer or book store, then the right of telecommunication may be irrelevant to you. However, considering many digital products are being distributed electronically (for example, on the Internet) and the fact that electronic stores may soon replace "physical stores," you should carefully consider whether you need to obtain a licence for the right to telecommunicate.

THE RIGHT TO PROHIBIT IMPORTATION

The right to prohibit importation of copyright works includes works in a digital format. Customs Canada may be empowered through a court order to detain pirated digital copies, for example, CD-ROMs, at the border. It is less clear how this right will prevent infringing electronically distributed works from entering Canada. This is further explored below.

THE EXHIBITION RIGHT IN ARTISTIC WORKS

The right of exhibition applies only with respect to artistic works including artistic works in an electronic format. Because issues of exhibition and the display of works may become more prevalent on the Web, this is an issue that may attract further discussion with respect to all electronic works, not just artistic works. Note that the current Canadian *Copyright Act*, unlike the American *Act*, does not have a right of display.

THE RIGHT OF AUTHORIZATION

The copyright owner of a digital copyright work has the right to authorize any of his or her rights.

THE COMMERCIAL RENTAL RIGHT

The *Copyright Act* provides a commercial rental right in computer programs, and sound recordings of musical works and of performers' performances.

The commercial rental right applies to computer programs on floppy disks, CD-ROMs, DVDs and other hardware, and to digital sound recordings and sound recordings of musical works and performers' performances. Thus, rental stores must obtain permission from copyright holders to rent these works and other subject-matter. The commercial rental right applies where there is a "motive of gain" in the overall operations of the person who rents the work or other subject-matter. Thus, a public library would probably not be considered to have a motive of gain if it were to rent computer programs, CD-ROMs and sound recordings without the permission of the copyright owner, even if an administrative fee or other cost is charged.

Keep in mind that only certain computer programs are subject to the rental right—stand-alone computer programs like word processors and accounting programs, and other computer programs that can be reproduced in the ordinary course of their use other than by a reproduction during their execution in conjunction with a machine, device or computer, such as might be found in an elevator or car. Also, "copy-protected" software, that is, software that cannot be reproduced in the ordinary course of its use is not covered under the rental right. Since most cartridge-type computer games currently being sold are copy-protected, they would not enjoy a rental right.

When you rent copyright works or other subject-matter, you must still respect the rights of the copyright holder. For instance, you cannot reproduce any rented copyright work or show it in public without the permission of the copyright holder.

RIGHT TO MAKE A SOUND RECORDING

Both the mechanical right and synchronization rights will have to be cleared when making a digital recording.

Mechanical right

A copyright holder has the right to make an audio recording of a work, or authorize others to do so. Whether this is an analog or digital recording, the mechanical right to make the recording must be cleared from the copyright owner of the literary, dramatic or musical work from which the recording is made.

Where a work is in the public domain, anyone may make a sound recording of that work without obtaining permission. Thus, anyone may make a recording of "Overture of 1812." However, this does not mean that anyone else's recording of a performance may be freely copied.

Synchronization right

The synchronization right must be cleared when including music in the making of a film or television program, multimedia work, CD-ROM or DVD where music is synchronized with the visuals in these products. Basically, whenever sound is matched with pictures, this right must be cleared from the copyright holder of the music.

The synchronization right is usually dealt with by a contract and separate permissions must be obtained for the use of the mechanical and synchronization rights.

Moral Rights

All moral rights, the rights of paternity, integrity and association, apply to digital works. Non-attribution of copyright material in an electronic magazine (affecting the right of paternity), manipulating a photograph (affecting the right of integrity), and pornographic images associated with a copyright work (affecting the right of association) are all examples of possible infringements of moral rights on the Internet. In fact, moral rights could occupy a more significant role on the Internet. This is because "digital" activities like morphing (i.e., computer manipulation of images), sampling ("borrowing" small portions of works for use in new works), and other digital manipulation of images, sound and text means that more works can easily be manipulated, modified and appropriated and thereby infringe moral rights.

Under the current Canadian law, moral rights cannot be assigned or licensed but may be waived, that is, the author of a work can agree not to exercise his or her moral rights. This, however, is not automatic upon the licensing or assigning of the economic rights in a copyright work. If an author chooses or is required to waive some or all of his or her moral rights, then he or she will not be able to prevent any changes or manipulations to images, text, music or other works or insist on a credit. Because the significance of waiving moral rights, especially for digital uses of copyright works, is so great, creators, licensees and assignees of copyright works should express any waiver clearly in writing. Also, note that where an author waives moral rights in favour of an assignee or licensee, the waiver may be valid for any person authorized by the owner or licensee to use the work, unless the original waiver indicated something to the contrary, i.e., that the waiver does not extend any further than the owner or licensee on behalf of whom the waiver was originally made.

Neighbouring Rights

The rights in performers' performances, sound recordings and broadcast signals would apply equally to analogue and digital recordings, public performances, and broadcasts.

Limitations on Rights

Fair dealing and exceptions in the law are theoretically applicable to digital works. Under the current law, fair dealing may be claimed if a small portion of a copyright work or other subject-matter is used, and if that use would be considered "fair" by a court of law, and if the use is for one of the following purposes: research, private study, criticism, review or news reporting (and in the latter three cases, the source, if given in the original material, is included in the reproduced, performed, etc. portion of it). In addition, the *Copyright Act* has a number of exceptions to the rights of copyright owners that apply in very specific circumstances. In some circumstances, the limitations are technologically neutral and could apply to uses of copyright materials in a digital form, however, many of the new exceptions, for libraries, for example, specifically exclude their application to digital media or digital uses. Specifically, in some exceptions, a library may not provide copies of a work to a patron in digital form although the work may be photocopied.

HOW CAN DIGITAL RIGHTS BE EXPLOITED?

Who Wants Electronic Rights?

Online services such as Sympatico and AOL need as much content as possible to make their services attractive and useful to their customers ("subscribers"). Multimedia producers/developers/publishers who make off-line and online products also need as much content as possible. In addition, traditional publishers of magazines and books are converting certain text and print materials into digital formats. In fact, some traditional trade publishers will insist upon having certain of the electronic rights (generally rights that compete with their own scope of business) if they are publishing a print format of your work. Further, with present and future technology, more owners of intellectual property may choose to publish their own works and distribute them on the Internet.

Licensing Electronic Rights

Licensing electronic rights is complicated. It is complicated because electronic rights are new and there are few precedents on which to rely. It is complicated because technology is continuously redefining the meaning of electronic rights. Some of the copyright issues you should consider when acquiring or licensing electronic rights are set out below. These issues apply to the acquiring and licensing of rights for off-line and online products. They also apply with respect to ancillary rights. For example, if you grant a licence to a book publisher to publish your book in print format, you may grant "ancillary" rights for sound recordings, motion pictures, specific electronic media, etc.

In your negotiations and contracts, you must first determine the nature and scope of the rights being acquired or licensed. An electronic publisher will require rights to allow him to reproduce and distribute the digital product. But will it be reproduced verbatim or manipulated in some manner, and will the right of adaptation be an issue—and what about moral rights? Another consideration is how the copyright work will be incorporated into the electronic product. Will the underlying work constitute the entire electronic product? Or is the licence for the inclusion of the work in an electronic magazine or a CD-ROM encompassing hundreds of other works, and if so, do the copyright holders get the right to approve the other material in the CD-ROM?

Second, you must consider the platform(s) or nature of the electronic product that will embody your copyright materials. Platforms include various forms of media such as CD-ROM and DVD. Because it is impossible to forecast future media, copyright holders should specify each kind of platform to which they agree and should also specify in the agreement that they are reserving all rights not granted. Copyright holders should not sign agreements that use wording like "all future technology in existence now or in the future." That way, when a new platform comes into existence, copyright holders will have the opportunity to re-negotiate the terms and conditions, including compensation, under which their works can be used on that new platform. Developers/producers/publishers acquiring rights should ensure that they have the necessary rights to each kind of platform in which their product will appear.

Third, you should consider how the digital product will be distributed. Will it be sold in stores and/or via the Internet? Electronic media transcends conventional marketplace and physical stores may not necessarily exist for electronic media in the future. Works can be "sold" and distributed electronically and need never take on a physical form.

For electronic distributions, you have to consider the rights of the end user, the consumer using the electronic work. The end user will need the right to read and view the electronic version, but what about the right to make digital copies and the right to redistribute it to others? And is the end user to be permitted to adapt the original work?

Fourth, consider the duration of the grant of electronic rights. With technology changing so rapidly, copyright holders may be hesitant to grant rights for the full term of copyright since they may want to later exploit their work in the newest media.

Fifth, consider whether the grant of rights need be exclusive or not. If a copyright holder grants exclusive rights, he or she may be able to obtain greater compensation than when granting non-exclusive rights. However, if the grant is non-exclusive, the copyright holder may have further avenues of exploiting the same work to different licensees in present and future technologies.

Whether negotiating rights or platforms or distribution, each item is separate and distinct from all other items. Further, although not practical for most of your licensing agreements, it is possible that for each item you negotiate, you have a different length of time and geographic boundary. For example, you could license the CD-ROM rights in Canada for thirty years, and license the Web site rights worldwide for fifteen years. Like other arrangements relating to copyright, it is important to have a written agreement to define the relationship.

The Value of Rights

Compensation for electronic rights is a matter of negotiation between the contracting parties. Industry standards for the value of electronic rights have not yet been established. In addition, certain "non-linear" works that do not have beginnings and endings *per se* and in which the material can be accessed and used by consumers in a variety of ways and for a variety of lengths of time, make it difficult to measure the "length" of a work and determine appropriate remuneration. The value of rights is a matter of negotiation between a copyright owner and potential licensee of those rights.

In establishing a value for electronic rights, you will also have to negotiate the structure of payment. Will there be a lump sum fee or a royalty based on a percentage of sales? If the electronic product is distributed electronically, will the compensation be defined by the number of people who access the work and/or amount of time people access the digital works? This is all negotiable. Because it is difficult to predict the size of the market for an electronic product, it is best for both parties to fully understand the position of the other party and to negotiate a licence that takes into account both of their interests.

Clearing Rights

Clearing rights for the use of online and off-line digital products is similar to clearing rights for the use of non-digital works. However, getting the appropriate clearances for multimedia products can be a massive undertaking. A single compact disc (CD-ROM) can store over 650 megabytes of information, roughly equivalent to 250,000 pages of text. And the data is usually much more than text; it can consist of anything capable of being digitized such as text, sound, images and full motion video. Rights clearance can be a nightmare from an administrative point of view.

In addition, the multimedia developer/producer/publisher requires rights not only to use copyright works in the multimedia project or Web site, but because of the end-use of multimedia works, they may want to sub-license these rights to end users for such things as online use, making hard copies, interactive use, etc.

Rights can be cleared directly from rights holders and often from copyright collectives and other licensing agencies who represent them. The role of copyright collectives has recently grown from licensing rights of public performance in music to reprography and retransmission. Existing copyright collectives already have infrastructures that could be used with respect to rights on the Internet. In fact, some collectives assist with clearing digital rights. If collectives could license for digital works, then that would allow for a one-stop clearance centre. However, it may be too early to predict the role of copyright collectives regarding e-rights.

ENFORCING COPYRIGHT ON THE INTERNET

As can be seen, the copyright law is generally flexible enough to apply to new technology—at least in principle. However, the administration of copyright is a major problem. In this context, administration refers to clearing rights in, and monitoring illegal uses of, copyright materials.

Piracy

The Internet is, in many ways, a mecca for copyright infringement. Like a high speed printing press, the Internet makes it easy, quick and virtually cost-free to reproduce copyright materials. A scanner can quickly input a large document into a computer, as compared to the time and expense of typesetting a manuscript for publication in print format; it is relatively easy to download copyright works from the Internet and copy them without permission and without compensating the copyright holder. Also, the copies are virtually identical to the originals.

Further, e-mail and bulletin boards, and the Internet make it possible to distribute, with the touch of a button, electronic information to large groups, thereby adding to the greater potential for illegal reproduction of digital works. It is easier for a person who obtains an electronic document to forward it to a large group than it is for a person who receives a paper copy of the same document.

Lastly, because of the nature of digital works, which are easy to manipulate and change, it becomes a greater challenge for creators to preserve their moral right of integrity. And with greater copying, there is a greater chance for creators not being credited for their work.

Modes of Enforcement

Effective mechanisms for monitoring and preventing illegal access, reproduction, distribution, manipulation, and the like, of copyright materials on the Internet, are just getting their feet wet in Cyberspace. There are a number of technological mechanisms in both software and hardware, such as encryption (similar to scrambled satellite signals), tagging (the incorporation of a copyright notice or other message into the protected work to make it obvious that an illegal copy has been made and distributed), watermarking (a work has a unique watermark and the original can be detected from a counterfeit copy), conversion/anti-copying (a digital work is transformed into an intermediary form so that the raw information or content cannot be edited or altered and the quality of the work diminishes with each successive copy), and employing market forces (pricing originals inexpensively so people will be willing to buy them).

In addition, licensing content for digital uses, whether for use in a Web site or to access an online database, has become more commonplace. E-commerce is also playing a significant role by allowing copyright holders, or representative copyright collectives or for-profit companies, to directly sell access to their online content. And, of course, education of creators and consumers about copyright laws as well as greater enforcement of rights and precedent-setting legal cases help deter potential copyright infringers.

COPYRIGHT PROTECTION IN OTHER COUNTRIES

Copyright protection in foreign countries is governed by the laws of each individual country. As discussed in Chapter 5, this may raise some complex international law questions as to where the infringement takes place on the Internet and which country's laws apply. For instance, which country has jurisdiction when a work is uploaded to the Internet from a computer in country A, downloaded in country B, and the host server is in country C? Where the laws in the two countries provide different protection and remedies for infringement, these issues become even more important, for instance, if there was an allegedly moral rights infringement in a work transmitted from the United States to France (and only France's law would protect the moral rights of the author).

OLD LAW, NEW TECHNOLOGY REVISITED

At the time of writing, the Canadian and American governments and governments around the world, as well as the World Intellectual Property Organization (WIPO), are studying the application of current copyright laws and principles as they apply to digital media, as well as the administration and enforcement of digital rights. As discussed in Chapter 5, there are two recent WIPO treaties that deal with digital copyright media. And, as discussed in Chapter 15, the United States passed legislation in 1998 to specifically deal with some digital copyright issues. As Ralph Oman, former Register of Copyrights of the United States recently said, "For the last 50 years, copyright scholars have built whole careers around 'the challenge of new technology.' Well, that new break-through technology is finally here, and it's knocking at the door."[1]

Appendix I

Chapter C-42

COPYRIGHT ACT

An Act respecting copyright

SHORT TITLE

Short title **1.** This Act may be cited as the *Copyright Act. R.S., c. C-30, s. 1.*

INTERPRETATION

Definitions **2.** In this Act,

"architectural work" means any building or structure or any model of a building or structure;

"architectural work of art" *[Repealed, 1993, c. 44, s. 53]*

"artistic work" includes paintings, drawings, maps, charts, plans, photographs, engravings, sculptures, works of artistic craftsmanship, architectural works, and compilations of artistic works;

"Berne Convention country" means a country that is a party to the Convention for the Protection of Literary and Artistic Works concluded at Berne on September 9, 1886, or any one of its revisions, including the Paris Act of 1971;

"Board" means the Copyright Board established by subsection 66(1);

"book" means a volume or a part or division of a volume, in printed form, but does not include

(a) a pamphlet,

(b) a newspaper, review, magazine or other periodical,

(c) a map, chart, plan or sheet music where the map, chart, plan or sheet music is separately published, and

(d) an instruction or repair manual that accompanies a product or that is supplied as an accessory to a service;

"broadcaster" means a body that, in the course of operating a broadcasting undertaking, broadcasts a communication signal in accordance with the law of the country in which the broadcasting undertaking is carried on, but excludes a body whose primary activity in relation to communication signals is their retransmission;

"choreographic work" includes any work of choreography, whether or not it has any story line;

"cinematograph" [Repealed, 1997, c. 24, s. 1]

"cinematographic work" includes any work expressed by any process analogous to cinematography, whether or not accompanied by a soundtrack;

"collective society" means a society, association or corporation that carries on the business of collective administration of copyright or of the remuneration right conferred by section 19 or 81 for the benefit of those who, by assignment, grant of licence, appointment of it as their agent or otherwise, authorize it to act on their behalf in relation to that collective administration, and

(a) operates a licensing scheme, applicable in relation to a repertoire of works, performer's performances, sound recordings or communication signals of more than one author, performer, sound recording maker or broadcaster, pursuant to which the society, association or corporation sets out classes of uses that it agrees to authorize under this Act, and the royalties and terms and conditions on which it agrees to authorize those classes of uses, or

(b) carries on the business of collecting and distributing royalties or levies payable pursuant to this Act;

"collective work" means

(a) an encyclopaedia, dictionary, year book or similar work,

(b) a newspaper, review, magazine or similar periodical, and

(c) any work written in distinct parts by different authors, or in which works or parts of works of different authors are incorporated;

"commercially available" means, in relation to a work or other subject-matter,

(a) available on the Canadian market within a reasonable time and for a reasonable price and may be located with reasonable effort, or

(b) for which a licence to reproduce, perform in public or communicate

to the public by telecommunication is available from a collective society within a reasonable time and for a reasonable price and may be located with reasonable effort;

"communication signal" means radio waves transmitted through space without any artificial guide, for reception by the public;

"compilation" means

(a) a work resulting from the selection or arrangement of literary, dramatic, musical or artistic works or of parts thereof, or

(b) a work resulting from the selection or arrangement of data;

"computer program" means a set of instructions or statements, expressed, fixed, embodied or stored in any manner, that is to be used directly or indirectly in a computer in order to bring about a specific result;

"copyright" means the rights described in

(a) section 3, in the case of a work,

(b) sections 15 and 26, in the case of a performer's performance,

(c) section 18, in the case of a sound recording, or

(d) section 21, in the case of a communication signal;

"country" includes any territory;

"defendant" includes a respondent to an application;

"delivery" [Repealed, 1997, c. 24, s. 1]

"dramatic work" includes

(a) any piece for recitation, choreographic work or mime, the scenic arrangement or acting form of which is fixed in writing or otherwise,

(b) any cinematographic work, and

(c) any compilation of dramatic works;

"educational institution" means

(a) a non-profit institution licensed or recognized by or under an Act of

Parliament or the legislature of a province to provide pre-school, elementary, secondary or post-secondary education,

(b) a non-profit institution that is directed or controlled by a board of education regulated by or under an Act of the legislature of a province and that provides continuing, professional or vocational education or training,

(c) a department or agency of any order of government, or any non-profit body, that controls or supervises education or training referred to in paragraph (a) or (b), or

(d) any other non-profit institution prescribed by regulation;

"engravings" includes etchings, lithographs, woodcuts, prints and other similar works, not being photographs;

"every original literary, dramatic, musical and artistic work" includes every original production in the literary, scientific or artistic domain, whatever may be the mode or form of its expression, such as compilations, books, pamphlets and other writings, lectures, dramatic or dramatico-musical works, musical works, translations, illustrations, sketches and plastic works relative to geography, topography, architecture or science;

"exclusive distributor" means, in relation to a book, a person who

(a) has, before or after the coming into force of this definition, been appointed in writing, by the owner or exclusive licensee of the copyright in the book in Canada, as

  (i) the only distributor of the book in Canada or any part of Canada, or

  (ii) the only distributor of the book in Canada or any part of Canada in respect of a particular sector of the market, and

(b) meets the criteria established by

regulations made under section 2.6, and, for greater certainty, if there are no regulations made under section 2.6, then no person qualifies under this definition as an "exclusive distributor";

"Her Majesty's Realms and Territories" *[Repealed, 1997, c. 24, s. 1]*

"infringing" means

(a) in relation to a work in which copyright subsists, any copy, including any colourable imitation, made or dealt with in contravention of this Act,

(b) in relation to a performer's performance in respect of which copyright subsists, any fixation or copy of a fixation of it made or dealt with in contravention of this Act,

(c) in relation to a sound recording in respect of which copyright subsists, any copy of it made or dealt with in contravention of this Act, or

(d) in relation to a communication signal in respect of which copyright subsists, any fixation or copy of a fixation of it made or dealt with in contravention of this Act.

The definition includes a copy that is imported in the circumstances set out in paragraph 27(2)(e) and section 27.1 but does not otherwise include a copy made with the consent of the owner of the copyright in the country where the copy was made;

"lecture" includes address, speech and sermon;

"legal representatives" includes heirs, executors, administrators, successors and assigns, or agents or attorneys who are thereunto duly authorized in writing;

"library, archive or museum" means

(a) an institution, whether or not incorporated, that is not established or conducted for profit or that does not form a part of, or is not administered or directly or indirectly controlled by, a body that is established or conducted for profit, in which is held and maintained a collection of documents and other materials that is open to the public or to researchers, or

(b) any other non-profit institution prescribed by regulation;

"literary work" includes tables, computer programs, and compilations of literary works;

"maker" means

(a) in relation to a cinematographic work, the person by whom the arrangements necessary for the making of the work are undertaken, or

(b) in relation to a sound recording, the person by whom the arrangements necessary for the first fixation of the sounds are undertaken;

"Minister", except in section 44.1, means the Minister of Industry;

"moral rights" means the rights described in subsection 14.1(1);

"musical work" means any work of music or musical composition, with or without words, and includes any compilation thereof;

"perceptual disability" means a disability that prevents or inhibits a person from reading or hearing a literary, musical, dramatic or artistic work in its original format, and includes such a disability resulting from

(a) severe or total impairment of sight or hearing or the inability to focus or move one's eyes,

(b) the inability to hold or manipulate a book, or

(c) an impairment relating to comprehension;

"performance" means any acoustic or visual representation of a work, performer's performance, sound recording or communication signal, including a representation made by means of any mechanical instrument, radio receiving set or television receiving set;

"performer's performance" means any of the following when done by a performer:

(a) a performance of an artistic work, dramatic work or musical work, whether or not the work was previously fixed in any material form, and whether or not the work's term of copyright protection under this Act has expired,

(b) a recitation or reading of a literary work, whether or not the work's term of copyright protection under this Act has expired, or

(c) an improvisation of a dramatic work, musical work or literary work, whether or not the improvised work is based on a pre-existing work;

"photograph" includes photo-lithograph and any work expressed by any process analogous to photography;

"plaintiff" includes an applicant;

"plate" includes

(a) any stereotype or other plate, stone, block, mould, matrix, transfer or negative used or intended to be used for printing or reproducing copies of any work, and

(b) any matrix or other appliance used or intended to be used for making or reproducing sound recordings, performer's performances or communication signals;

"premises" means, in relation to an educational institution, a place where education or training referred to in the definition "educational institution" is provided, controlled or supervised by the educational institution;

"receiving device" [Repealed, 1993, c. 44, s. 79]

"Rome Convention country" means a country that is a party to the International Convention for the Protection of Performers, Producers of Phonograms and Broadcasting

Organisations, done at Rome on October 26, 1961;

"sculpture" includes a cast or model;

"sound recording" means a recording, fixed in any material form, consisting of sounds, whether or not of a performance of a work, but excludes any soundtrack of a cinematographic work where it accompanies the cinematographic work;

"telecommunication" means any transmission of signs, signals, writing, images or sounds or intelligence of any nature by wire, radio, visual, optical or other electromagnetic system;

"treaty country" means a Berne Convention country, UCC country or WTO Member;

"UCC country" means a country that is a party to the Universal Copyright Convention, adopted on September 6, 1952 in Geneva, Switzerland, or to that Convention as revised in Paris, France on July 24, 1971;

"work" includes the title thereof when such title is original and distinctive;

"work of joint authorship" means a work produced by the collaboration of two or more authors in which the contribution of one author is not distinct from the contribution of the other author or authors;

"work of sculpture" [Repealed, 1997, c. 24, s. 1]

"WTO Member" means a Member of the World Trade Organization as defined in subsection 2(1) of the World Trade Organization Agreement Implementation Act. R.S., 1985, c. C-42, s. 2; R.S., 1985, c. 10 (4th Supp.), s. 1; 1988, c. 65, s. 61; 1992, c. 1, s. 145(F); 1993, c. 23, s. 1, c. 44, ss. 53, 79; 1994, c. 47, s. 56; 1995, c. 1, s. 62; 1997, c. 24, s. 1.

Compilations **2.1** (1) A compilation containing two or more of the categories of literary, dramatic, musical or artistic works shall be deemed to be a compilation of the category making up the most substantial part of the compilation.

Idem (2) The mere fact that a work is included in a compilation does not increase, decrease or otherwise affect the protection conferred by this Act in respect of the copyright in the work or the moral rights in respect of the work. 1993, c. 44, s. 54.

Definition of "maker" **2.11** For greater certainty, the arrangements referred to in paragraph (b) of the definition "maker" in section 2, as that term is used in section 19 and in the definition "eligible maker" in section 79, include arrangements for entering into contracts with performers, financial arrangements and technical arrangements required for the first fixation of the sounds for a sound recording. 1997, c. 24, s. 2.

Definition of "publications" **2.2** (1) For the purposes of this Act, "publication" means

(a) in relation to works,

(i) making copies of a work available to the public,

(ii) the construction of an architectural work, and

(iii) the incorporation of an artistic work into an architectural work, and

(b) in relation to sound recordings, making copies of a sound recording available to the public, but does not include

(c) the performance in public, or the communication to the public by telecommunication, of a literary, dramatic, musical or artistic work or a sound recording, or

(d) the exhibition in public of an artistic work.

Issue of photographs and engravings (2) For the purpose of subsection (1), the issue of photographs and engravings of sculptures and architectural works is not deemed to be publication of those works.

Where no consent of copyright owner (3) For the purposes of this Act, other than in respect of infringement of copyright, a work or other subject-matter is not deemed to be published or performed in public or communicated to the public by telecommunication if that act is done without the consent of the owner of the copyright.

Unpublished works

(4) Where, in the case of an unpublished work, the making of the work is extended over a considerable period, the conditions of this Act conferring copyright are deemed to have been complied with if the author was, during any substantial part of that period, a subject or citizen of, or a person ordinarily resident in, a country to which this Act extends. *1997, c. 24, s. 2.*

Telecommunication

2.3 A person who communicates a work or other subject-matter to the public by telecommunication does not by that act alone perform it in public, nor by that act alone is deemed to authorize its performance in public. *1997, c. 24, s. 2.*

Communication to the public by telecommunication

2.4 (1) For the purposes of communication to the public by telecommunication,

(a) persons who occupy apartments, hotel rooms or dwelling units situated in the same building are part of the public, and a communication intended to be received exclusively by such persons is a communication to the public;

(b) a person whose only act in respect of the communication of a work or other subject-matter to the public consists of providing the means of telecommunication necessary for another person to so communicate the work or other subject-matter does not communicate that work or other subject-matter to the public; and

(c) where a person, as part of

(i) a network, within the meaning of the Broadcasting Act, whose operations result in the communication of works or other subject-matter to the public, or

(ii) any programming undertaking whose operations result in the communication of works or other subject-matter to the public,

transmits by telecommunication a work or other subject-matter that is communicated to the public by another person who is not a retransmitter of a signal within the meaning of subsection 31(1), the transmission and communication of that work or other subject-matter by those persons constitute a single communication to the public for which those persons are jointly and severally liable.

Regulations

(2) The Governor in Council may make regulations defining "programming undertaking" for the purpose of paragraph (1)(c).

Exception

(3) A work is not communicated in the manner described in paragraph (1)(c) or 3(1)(f) where a signal carrying the work is retransmitted to a person who is a retransmitter to whom section 31 applies. *1997, c. 24, s. 2.*

What constitutes rental

2.5 (1) For the purposes of paragraphs 3(1)(h) and (i), 15(1)(c) and 18(1)(c), an arrangement, whatever its form, constitutes a rental of a computer program or sound recording if, and only if,

(a) it is in substance a rental, having regard to all the circumstances; and

(b) it is entered into with motive of gain in relation to the overall operations of the person who rents out the computer program or sound recording, as the case may be.

Motive of gain

(2) For the purpose of paragraph (1)(b), a person who rents out a computer program or sound recording with the intention of recovering no more than the costs, including overhead, associated with the rental operations does not by that act alone have a motive of gain in relation to the rental operations. *1997, c. 24, s. 2.*

Exclusive distributor

2.6 The Governor in Council may make regulations establishing distribution criteria for the purpose of paragraph (b) of the definition "exclusive distributor" in section 2. *1997, c. 24, s. 2.*

Exclusive licence

2.7 For the purposes of this Act, an exclusive licence is an authorization to do any act that is subject to copyright to the exclusion of all others including the copyright owner, whether the authorization is granted by the owner or an exclusive licensee claiming under the owner. *1997, c. 24, s. 2.*

PART I

COPYRIGHT AND MORAL RIGHTS IN WORKS

Copyright

Copyright in works

3. (1) For the purposes of this Act, "copyright", in relation to a work, means the sole right to produce or reproduce the work or any substantial part thereof in any material form whatever, to perform the work or any substantial part thereof in public or, if the work is unpublished, to publish the work or any substantial part thereof, and includes the sole right

(a) to produce, reproduce, perform or publish any translation of the work,

(b) in the case of a dramatic work, to convert it into a novel or other non-dramatic work,

(c) in the case of a novel or other non-dramatic work, or of an artistic work, to convert it into a dramatic work, by way of performance in public or otherwise,

(d) in the case of a literary, dramatic or musical work, to make any sound recording, cinematograph film or other contrivance by means of which the work may be mechanically reproduced or performed,

(e) in the case of any literary, dramatic, musical or artistic work, to reproduce, adapt and publicly present the work as a cinematographic work,

(f) in the case of any literary, dramatic, musical or artistic work, to communicate the work to the public by telecommunication,

(g) to present at a public exhibition, for a purpose other than sale or hire, an artistic work created after June 7, 1988, other than a map, chart or plan,

(h) in the case of a computer program that can be reproduced in the ordinary course of its use, other than by a reproduction during its execution in conjunction with a machine, device or computer, to rent out the computer program, and

(i) in the case of a musical work, to rent out a sound recording in which the work is embodied,

and to authorize any such acts.

(1.1) A work that is communicated in the manner described in paragraph (1)(f) is fixed even if it is fixed simultaneously with its communication. (1.2) to (4) *[Repealed, 1997, c. 24, s. 3] R.S., 1985, c. C-42, s. 3; R.S., 1985, c. 10 (4th Supp.), s. 2; 1988, c. 65, s. 62; 1993, c. 23, s. 2, c. 44, s. 55; 1997, c. 24, s. 3.*

Simultaneous fixing

4. *[Repealed, 1997, c. 24, s. 4]*

Works in which Copyright may Subsist

5. (1) Subject to this Act, copyright shall subsist in Canada, for the term hereinafter mentioned, in every original literary, dramatic, musical and artistic work if any one of the following conditions is met:

Conditions for subsistence of copyright

(a) in the case of any work, whether published or unpublished, including a cinematographic work, the author was, at the date of the making of the work, a citizen or subject of, or a person ordinarily resident in, a treaty country;

(b) in the case of a cinematographic work, whether published or unpublished, the maker, at the date of the making of the cinematographic work,

(i) if a corporation, had its headquarters in a treaty country, or

(ii) if a natural person, was a citizen or subject of, or a person ordinarily resident in, a treaty country; or

(c) in the case of a published work, including a cinematographic work,

(i) in relation to subparagraph 2.2 (1)(a)(i), the first publication in such a quantity as to satisfy the reasonable demands of the public, having regard to the nature of the work, occurred in a treaty country, or

(ii) in relation to subparagraph 2.2 (1)(a)(ii) or (iii), the first publication occurred in a treaty country.

Protection for older works　(1.01) For the purposes of subsection (1), a country that becomes a Berne Convention country or a WTO Member after the date of the making or publication of a work shall, as of becoming a Berne Convention country or WTO Member, as the case may be, be deemed to have been a Berne Convention country or WTO Member at the date of the making or publication of the work, subject to subsection (1.02) and section 29.

Limitation　(1.02) Subsection (1.01) does not confer copyright protection in Canada on a work whose term of copyright protection in the country referred to in that subsection had expired before that country became a Berne Convention country or WTO Member, as the case may be.

Application of subsections (1.01) and (1.02)　(1.03) Subsections (1.01) and (1.02) apply, and are deemed to have applied, regardless of whether the country in question became a Berne Convention country or a WTO Member before or after the coming into force of those subsections.

First publication　(1.1) The first publication described in subparagraph (1)(c)(i) or (ii) is deemed to have occurred in a treaty country notwithstanding that it in fact occurred previously elsewhere, if the interval between those two publications did not exceed thirty days.

Idem　(1.2) Copyright shall not subsist in Canada otherwise than as provided by subsection (1), except in so far as the protection conferred by this Act is extended as hereinafter provided to foreign countries to which this Act does not extend.

Minister may extend copyright to other countries　(2) Where the Minister certifies by notice, published in the Canada Gazette, that any country that is not a treaty country grants or has undertaken to grant, either by treaty, convention, agreement or law, to citizens of Canada, the benefit of copyright on substantially the same basis as to its own citizens or copyright protection substantially equal to that conferred by this Act, the country shall, for the purpose of the rights conferred by this Act, be treated as if it were a country to which this Act extends, and the Minister may give a certificate, notwithstanding that the remedies for enforcing the rights, or the restrictions on the importation of copies of works, under the law of such country, differ from those in this Act.

(2.1) [Repealed, 1994, c. 47, s. 57]

(3) to (6) [Repealed, 1997, c. 24, s. 5]

Reciprocity protection preserved　(7) For greater certainty, the protection to which a work is entitled by virtue of a notice published under subsection (2), or under that subsection as it read at any time before the coming into force of this subsection, is not affected by reason only of the country in question becoming a treaty country. R.S., 1985, c. C-42, s. 5; 1993, c. 15, s. 2, c. 44, s. 57; 1994, c. 47, s. 57; 1997, c. 24, s. 5.

Term of Copyright

Term of copyright　6. The term for which copyright shall subsist shall, except as otherwise expressly provided by this Act, be the life of the author, the remainder of the calendar year in which the author dies, and a period of fifty years following the end of that calendar year. R.S., 1985, c. C-42, s. 6; 1993, c. 44, s. 58.

Anonymous and pseudonymous works　6.1 Except as provided in section 6.2, where the identity of the author of a work is unknown, copyright in the work shall subsist for whichever of the following terms ends earlier:

(a) a term consisting of the remainder of the calendar year of the first publication of the work and a period of fifty years following the end of that calendar year, and

(b) a term consisting of the remainder of the calendar year of the making of the work and a period of seventy-five years following the end of that calendar year, but where, during that term, the author's identity becomes commonly known, the term provided in section 6 applies. *1993, c. 44, s. 58.*

Anonymous and pseudonymous works of joint authorship **6.2** Where the identity of all the authors of a work of joint authorship is unknown, copyright in the work shall subsist for whichever of the following terms ends earlier:

(a) a term consisting of the remainder of the calendar year of the first publication of the work and a period of fifty years following the end of that calendar year, and

(b) a term consisting of the remainder of the calendar year of the making of the work and a period of seventy-five years following the end of that calendar year,

but where, during that term, the identity of one or more of the authors becomes commonly known, copyright shall subsist for the life of whichever of those authors dies last, the remainder of the calendar year in which that author dies, and a period of fifty years following the end of that calendar year. *1993, c. 44, s. 58.*

Term of copyright in posthumous works **7.** (1) Subject to subsection (2), in the case of a literary, dramatic or musical work, or an engraving, in which copyright subsists at the date of the death of the author or, in the case of a work of joint authorship, at or immediately before the date of the death of the author who dies last, but which has not been published or, in the case of a lecture or a dramatic or musical work, been performed in public or communicated to the public by telecommunication, before that date, copyright shall subsist until publication, or performance in public or communication to the public by telecommunication, whichever may first happen, for the remainder of the calendar year of the publication or of the performance in public or

communication to the public by telecommunication, as the case may be, and for a period of fifty years following the end of that calendar year.

(2) Subsection (1) applies only where **Application of subsection (1)** the work in question was published or performed in public or communicated to the public by telecommunication, as the case may be, before the coming into force of this section.

(3) Where **Transitional provision**

(a) a work has not, at the coming into force of this section, been published or performed in public or communicated to the public by telecommunication,

(b) subsection (1) would apply to that work if it had been published or performed in public or communicated to the public by telecommunication before the coming into force of this section, and

(c) the relevant death referred to in subsection (1) occurred during the period of fifty years immediately before the coming into force of this section,

copyright shall subsist in the work for the remainder of the calendar year in which this section comes into force and for a period of fifty years following the end of that calendar year, whether or not the work is published or performed in public or communicated to the public by telecommunication after the coming into force of this section.

(4) Where **Transitional provision**

(a) a work has not, at the coming into force of this section, been published or performed in public or communicated to the public by telecommunication,

(b) subsection (1) would apply to that work if it had been published or performed in public or communicated to the public by telecommunication before the coming into force of this section, and

(c) the relevant death referred to in subsection (1) occurred more than fifty years before the coming into force of this section,

copyright shall subsist in the work for the remainder of the calendar year in which this section comes into force and for a period of five years following the end of that calendar year, whether or not the work is published or performed in public or communicated to the public by telecommunication after the coming into force of this section. *R.S., 1985, c. C-42, s. 7; 1993, c. 44, s. 58; 1997, c. 24, s. 6.*

8. *[Repealed, 1993, c. 44, s. 59]*

Cases of joint authorship **9.** (1) In the case of a work of joint authorship, except as provided in section 6.2, copyright shall subsist during the life of the author who dies last, for the remainder of the calendar year of that author's death, and for a period of fifty years following the end of that calendar year, and references in this Act to the period after the expiration of any specified number of years from the end of the calendar year of the death of the author shall be construed as references to the period after the expiration of the like number of years from the end of the calendar year of the death of the author who dies last.

Nationals of other countries (2) Authors who are nationals of any country, other than a country that is a party to the North American Free Trade Agreement, that grants a term of protection shorter than that mentioned in subsection (1) are not entitled to claim a longer term of protection in Canada. *R.S., 1985, c. C-42, s. 9; 1993, c. 44, s. 60.*

Term of copyright in photographs **10.** (1) Where the owner referred to in subsection (2) is a corporation, the term for which copyright subsists in a photograph shall be the remainder of the year of the making of the initial negative or plate from which the photograph was derived or, if there is no negative or plate, of the initial photograph, plus a period of fifty years.

Where author majority shareholder (1.1) Where the owner is a corporation, the majority of the voting shares of which are owned by a natural person who

would have qualified as the author of the photograph except for subsection (2), the term of copyright is the term set out in section 6.

(2) The person who

Author of photograph

(a) was the owner of the initial negative or other plate at the time when that negative or other plate was made, or

(b) was the owner of the initial photograph at the time when that photograph was made, where there was no negative or other plate,

is deemed to be the author of the photograph and, where that owner is a body corporate, the body corporate is deemed for the purposes of this Act to be ordinarily resident in a treaty country if it has established a place of business therein. *R.S., 1985, c. C-42, s. 10; 1993, c. 44, s. 60; 1994, c. 47, s. 69(F); 1997, c. 24, s. 7.*

11. *[Repealed, 1997, c. 24, s. 8]*

11.1 Except for cinematographic works in which the arrangement or acting form or the combination of incidents represented give the work a dramatic character, copyright in a cinematographic work or a compilation of cinematographic works shall subsist

Cinematographic works

(a) for the remainder of the calendar year of the first publication of the cinematographic work or of the compilation, and for a period of fifty years following the end of that calendar year; or

(b) if the cinematographic work or compilation is not published before the expiration of fifty years following the end of the calendar year of its making, for the remainder of that calendar year and for a period of fifty years following the end of that calendar year. *1993, c. 44, s. 60; 1997, c. 24, s. 9.*

12. Without prejudice to any rights or privileges of the Crown, where any work is, or has been, prepared or published by or under the direction or control of Her Majesty or any government department,

Where copyright belongs to Her Majesty

the copyright in the work shall, subject to any agreement with the author, belong to Her Majesty and in that case shall continue for the remainder of the calendar year of the first publication of the work and for a period of fifty years following the end of that calendar year. *R.S., 1985, c. C-42, s. 12; 1993, c. 44, s. 60.*

Ownership of Copyright

Ownership of copyright

13. (1) Subject to this Act, the author of a work shall be the first owner of the copyright therein.

Engraving, photograph or portrait

(2) Where, in the case of an engraving, photograph or portrait, the plate or other original was ordered by some other person and was made for valuable consideration, and the consideration was paid, in pursuance of that order, in the absence of any agreement to the contrary, the person by whom the plate or other original was ordered shall be the first owner of the copyright.

Work made in the course of employment

(3) Where the author of a work was in the employment of some other person under a contract of service or apprenticeship and the work was made in the course of his employment by that person, the person by whom the author was employed shall, in the absence of any agreement to the contrary, be the first owner of the copyright, but where the work is an article or other contribution to a newspaper, magazine or similar periodical, there shall, in the absence of any agreement to the contrary, be deemed to be reserved to the author a right to restrain the publication of the work, otherwise than as part of a newspaper, magazine or similar periodical.

Assignments and licences

(4) The owner of the copyright in any work may assign the right, either wholly or partially, and either generally or subject to limitations relating to territory, medium or sector of the market or other limitations relating to the scope of the assignment, and either for the whole term of the copyright or for any other part thereof, and may grant any interest in the right by licence, but no assignment or grant is valid unless it is in writing signed by the owner of the right in respect of which the assign-

ment or grant is made, or by the owner's duly authorized agent.

Ownership in case of partial assignment

(5) Where, under any partial assignment of copyright, the assignee becomes entitled to any right comprised in copyright, the assignee, with respect to the rights so assigned, and the assignor, with respect to the rights not assigned, shall be treated for the purposes of this Act as the owner of the copyright, and this Act has effect accordingly.

Assignment of right of action

(6) For greater certainty, it is deemed always to have been the law that a right of action for infringement of copyright may be assigned in association with the assignment of the copyright or the grant of an interest in the copyright by licence.

Exclusive licence

(7) For greater certainty, it is deemed always to have been the law that a grant of an exclusive licence in a copyright constitutes the grant of an interest in the copyright by licence. *R.S., 1985, c. C-42, s. 13; 1997, c. 24, s. 10.*

Limitation where author is first owner of copyright

14. (1) Where the author of a work is the first owner of the copyright therein, no assignment of the copyright and no grant of any interest therein, made by him, otherwise than by will, after June 4, 1921, is operative to vest in the assignee or grantee any rights with respect to the copyright in the work beyond the expiration of twenty-five years from the death of the author, and the reversionary interest in the copyright expectant on the termination of that period shall, on the death of the author, notwithstanding any agreement to the contrary, devolve on his legal representatives as part of the estate of the author, and any agreement entered into by the author as to the disposition of such reversionary interest is void.

Restriction

(2) Nothing in subsection (1) shall be construed as applying to the assignment of the copyright in a collective work or a licence to publish a work or part of a work as part of a collective work.

(3) *[Repealed, 1997, c. 24, s. 11]*

(4) *[Repealed, R.S., 1985, c. 10 (4th Supp.), s. 3]*
R.S., 1985, c. C-42, s. 14; R.S., 1985, c. 10 (4th

Supp.), s. 3; 1997, c. 24, s. 11.

14.01 [Repealed, 1997, c. 24, s. 12]

Moral Rights

Moral rights **14.1** (1) The author of a work has, subject to section 28.2, the right to the integrity of the work and, in connection with an act mentioned in section 3, the right, where reasonable in the circumstances, to be associated with the work as its author by name or under a pseudonym and the right to remain anonymous.

No assignment of moral rights (2) Moral rights may not be assigned but may be waived in whole or in part.

No waiver by assignment (3) An assignment of copyright in a work does not by that act alone constitute a waiver of any moral rights.

Effect of waiver (4) Where a waiver of any moral right is made in favour of an owner or a licensee of copyright, it may be invoked by any person authorized by the owner or licensee to use the work, unless there is an indication to the contrary in the waiver. R.S., 1985, c. 10 (4th Supp.), s. 4.

Term **14.2** (1) Moral rights in respect of a work subsist for the same term as the copyright in the work.

Succession (2) The moral rights in respect of a work pass, on the death of its author, to

(a) the person to whom those rights are specifically bequeathed;

(b) where there is no specific bequest of those moral rights and the author dies testate in respect of the copyright in the work, the person to whom that copyright is bequeathed; or

(c) where there is no person described in paragraph (a) or (b), the person entitled to any other property in respect of which the author dies intestate.

Subsequent succession (3) Subsection (2) applies, with such modifications as the circumstances require,

on the death of any person who holds moral rights. R.S., 1985, c. 10 (4th Supp.), s. 4; 1997, c. 24, s. 13.

PART II

COPYRIGHT IN PERFORMER'S PERFORMANCES, SOUND RECORDINGS AND COMMUNICATION SIGNALS

Performers' Rights

15. (1) Subject to subsection (2), a performer has a copyright in the performer's performance, consisting of the sole right to do the following in relation to the performer's performance or any substantial part thereof: Copyright in performer's performance

(a) if it is not fixed,

(i) to communicate it to the public by telecommunication,

(ii) to perform it in public, where it is communicated to the public by telecommunication otherwise than by communication signal, and

(iii) to fix it in any material form,

(b) if it is fixed,

(i) to reproduce any fixation that was made without the performer's authorization,

(ii) where the performer authorized a fixation, to reproduce any reproduction of that fixation, if the reproduction being reproduced was made for a purpose other than that for which the performer's authorization was given, and

(iii) where a fixation was permitted under Part III or VIII, to reproduce any reproduction of that fixation, if the reproduction being reproduced was made for a purpose other than one permitted under Part III or VIII, and

(c) to rent out a sound recording of it,

and to authorize any such acts.

Conditions (2) Subsection (1) applies only if the performer's performance

(a) takes place in Canada or in a Rome Convention country;

(b) is fixed in

(i) a sound recording whose maker, at the time of the first fixation,

(A) if a natural person, was a Canadian citizen or permanent resident of Canada within the meaning of the Immigration Act, or a citizen or permanent resident of a Rome Convention country, or

(B) if a corporation, had its headquarters in Canada or in a Rome Convention country, or

(ii) a sound recording whose first publication in such a quantity as to satisfy the reasonable demands of the public occurred in Canada or in a Rome Convention country; or

(c) is transmitted at the time of the performer's performance by a communication signal broadcast from Canada or a Rome Convention country by a broadcaster that has its headquarters in the country of broadcast.

Publication (3) The first publication is deemed to have occurred in a country referred to in paragraph (2)(b) notwithstanding that it in fact occurred previously elsewhere, if the interval between those two publications does not exceed thirty days. *R.S., 1985, c. C-42, s. 15; 1993, c. 44, s. 61; 1997, c. 24, s. 14.*

Contractual arrangements 16. Nothing in section 15 prevents the performer from entering into a contract governing the use of the performer's performance for the purpose of broadcasting, fixation or retransmission. *R.S., 1985, c. C-42, s. 16; 1994, c. 47, s. 59; 1997, c. 24, s. 14.*

Cinematographic works 17. (1) Where the performer authorizes the embodiment of the performer's performance in a cinematographic work, the performer may no longer exercise, in relation to the performance where embodied in that cinematographic work, the copyright referred to in subsection 15(1).

Right to remuneration (2) Where there is an agreement governing the embodiment referred to in subsection (1) and that agreement provides for a right to remuneration for the reproduction, performance in public or communication to the public by telecommunication of the cinematographic work, the performer may enforce that right against

(a) the other party to the agreement or, if that party assigns the agreement, the assignee, and

(b) any other person who

(i) owns the copyright in the cinematographic work governing the reproduction of the cinematographic work, its performance in public or its communication to the public by telecommunication, and

(ii) reproduces the cinematographic work, performs it in public or communicates it to the public by telecommunication,

and persons referred to in paragraphs (a) and (b) are jointly and severally liable to the performer in respect of the remuneration relating to that copyright.

Application of subsection (2) (3) Subsection (2) applies only if the performer's performance is embodied in a prescribed cinematographic work.

Exception (4) If so requested by a country that is a party to the North American Free Trade Agreement, the Minister may, by a statement published in the Canada Gazette, grant the benefits conferred by this section, subject to any terms and conditions specified in the statement, to performers who are nationals of that country or another country that is a party to the Agreement or are Canadian citizens or permanent residents within the meaning of the Immigration Act and whose performer's performances are embodied in works other than the prescribed cinematographic works referred to in subsection (3). *R.S., 1985, c. C-42, s. 17; 1994, c. 47, s. 59; 1997, c. 24, s. 14.*

Rights of Sound Recording Makers

Copyright in sound recordings

18. (1) Subject to subsection (2), the maker of a sound recording has a copyright in the sound recording, consisting of the sole right to do the following in relation to the sound recording or any substantial part thereof:

(a) to publish it for the first time,

(b) to reproduce it in any material form, and

(c) to rent it out,

and to authorize any such acts.

Conditions for copyright

(2) Subsection (1) applies only if

(a) the maker of the sound recording was a Canadian citizen or permanent resident of Canada within the meaning of the Immigration Act, or a citizen or permanent resident of a Berne Convention country, a Rome Convention country or a country that is a WTO Member, or, if a corporation, had its headquarters in one of the foregoing countries,

(i) at the date of the first fixation, or

(ii) if that first fixation was extended over a considerable period, during any substantial part of that period; or

(b) the first publication of the sound recording in such a quantity as to satisfy the reasonable demands of the public occurred in any country referred to in paragraph (a).

Publication

(3) The first publication is deemed to have occurred in a country referred to in paragraph (2)(a) notwithstanding that it in fact occurred previously elsewhere, if the interval between those two publications does not exceed thirty days. *R.S., 1985, c. C-42, s. 18; R.S., 1985, c. 10 (4th Supp.), s. 17(F); 1994, c. 47, s. 59; 1997, c. 24, s. 14.*

Provisions Applicable to both Performers and Sound Recording Makers

Right to remuneration.

19. (1) Where a sound recording has been published, the performer and maker are entitled, subject to section 20, to be paid equitable remuneration for its performance in public or its communication to the public by telecommunication, except for any retransmission

Royalties

(2) For the purpose of providing the remuneration mentioned in subsection (1), a person who performs a published sound recording in public or communicates it to the public by telecommunication is liable to pay royalties

(a) in the case of a sound recording of a musical work, to the collective society authorized under Part VII to collect them; or

(b) in the case of a sound recording of a literary work or dramatic work, to either the maker of the sound recording or the performer

Division of royalties

(3) The royalties, once paid pursuant to paragraph (2)(a) or (b), shall be divided so that

(a) the performer or performers receive in aggregate fifty per cent; and

(b) the maker or makers receive in aggregate fifty per cent. *R.S., 1985, c. C-42, s. 19; 1994, c. 47, s. 59; 1997, c. 24, s. 14*

Conditions

20. (1) The right to remuneration conferred by section 19 applies only if

(a) the maker was, at the date of the first fixation, a Canadian citizen or permanent resident of Canada within the meaning of the Immigration Act, or a citizen or permanent resident of a Rome Convention country, or, if a corporation, had its headquarters in one of the foregoing countries; or

(b) all the fixations done for the sound recording occurred in Canada or in a Rome Convention country.

Exception

(2) Notwithstanding subsection (1), if the Minister is of the opinion that a Rome Convention country does not grant a right to remuneration, similar in scope and duration to that provided by section 19, for the

performance in public or the communication to the public of a sound recording whose maker, at the date of its first fixation, was a Canadian citizen or permanent resident of Canada within the meaning of the Immigration Act or, if a corporation, had its headquarters in Canada, the Minister may, by a statement published in the Canada Gazette, limit the scope and duration of the protection for sound recordings whose first fixation is done by a maker who is a citizen or permanent resident of that country or, if a corporation, has its headquarters in that country.

Exception (3) If so requested by a country that is a party to the North American Free Trade Agreement, the Minister may, by a statement published in the Canada Gazette, grant the right to remuneration conferred by section 19 to performers or makers who are nationals of that country and whose sound recordings embody dramatic or literary works.

Application of section 19 (4) Where a statement is published under subsection (3), section 19 applies

(a) in respect of nationals of a country mentioned in that statement, as if they were citizens of Canada or, in the case of corporations, had their headquarters in Canada; and

(b) as if the fixations made for the purpose of their sound recordings had been made in Canada. R.S., 1985, c. C-42, s. 20; 1994, c. 47, s. 59; 1997, c. 24, s. 14

Rights of Broadcasters

Copyright in communication signals **21.** (1) Subject to subsection (2), a broadcaster has a copyright in the communication signals that it broadcasts, consisting of the sole right to do the following in relation to the communication signal or any substantial part thereof:

(a) to fix it,

(b) to reproduce any fixation of it that was made without the broadcaster's consent,

(c) to authorize another broadcaster to retransmit it to the public simultaneously with its broadcast, and

(d) in the case of a television communication signal, to perform it in a place open to the public on payment of an entrance fee, and to authorize any act described in paragraph (a), (b) or (d).

Conditions for copyright (2) Subsection (1) applies only if the broadcaster

(a) at the time of the broadcast, had its headquarters in Canada, in a country that is a WTO Member or in a Rome Convention country; and

(b) broadcasts the communication signal from that country.

Exception (3) Notwithstanding subsection (2), if the Minister is of the opinion that a Rome Convention country or a country that is a WTO Member does not grant the right mentioned in paragraph (1)(d), the Minister may, by a statement published in the Canada Gazette, declare that broadcasters that have their headquarters in that country are not entitled to that right. R.S., 1985, c. C-42, s. 21; 1994, c. 47, s. 59; 1997, c. 24, s. 14

Reciprocity

Reciprocity **22.** (1) Where the Minister is of the opinion that a country other than a Rome Convention country grants or has undertaken to grant

(a) to performers and to makers of sound recordings, or

(b) to broadcasters that are Canadian citizens or permanent residents of Canada within the meaning of the Immigration Act or, if corporations, have their headquarters in Canada, as the case may be, whether by treaty, convention, agreement or law, benefits substantially equivalent to those conferred by this Part, the Minister may, by a statement published in the Canada Gazette,

(c) grant the benefits conferred by this Part

(i) to performers and to makers of sound recordings, or

(ii) to broadcasters as the case may be, that are citizens, subjects or permanent residents of or, if corporations, have their headquarters in that country, and

(d) declare that that country shall, as regards those benefits, be treated as if it were a country to which this Part extends.

Reciprocity   (2) Where the Minister is of the opinion that a country other than a Rome Convention country neither grants nor has undertaken to grant

(a) to performers, and to makers of sound recordings, or

(b) to broadcasters

that are Canadian citizens or permanent residents of Canada within the meaning of the Immigration Act or, if corporations, have their headquarters in Canada, as the case may be, whether by treaty, convention, agreement or law, benefits substantially equivalent to those conferred by this Part, the Minister may, by a statement published in the Canada Gazette,

(c) grant the benefits conferred by this Part to performers, makers of sound recordings or broadcasters that are citizens, subjects or permanent residents of or, if corporations, have their headquarters in that country, as the case may be, to the extent that that country grants those benefits to performers, makers of sound recordings or broadcasters that are Canadian citizens or permanent residents of Canada within the meaning of the Immigration Act or, if corporations, have their headquarters in Canada, and

(d) declare that that country shall, as regards those benefits, be treated as if it were a country to which this Part extends.

Application of Act   (3) Any provision of this Act that the Minister specifies in a statement referred to in subsection (1) or (2)

(a) applies in respect of performers,

makers of sound recordings or broadcasters covered by that statement, as if they were citizens of or, if corporations, had their headquarters in Canada; and

(b) applies in respect of a country covered by that statement, as if that country were Canada

(4) Subject to any exceptions that the   Application Minister may specify in a statement referred   of Act to in subsection (1) or (2), the other provisions of this Act also apply in the way described in subsection. (3) R.S., 1985, c. C-42, s. 22; 1994, c. 47, s. 59; 1997, c. 24, s. 14.

Term of Rights

23. (1) Subject to this Act, the rights con-   Term of ferred by sections 15, 18 and 21 terminate   rights fifty years after the end of the calendar year in which

(a) in the case of a performer's performance,

(i) its first fixation in a sound recording, or

(ii) its performance, if it is not fixed in a sound recording, occurred;

(b) in the case of a sound recording, the first fixation occurred; or

(c) in the case of a communication signal, it was broadcast.

(2) The rights to remuneration con-   Term of ferred on performers and makers by section   right to 19 have the same terms, respectively, as   remunera-   tion those provided by paragraphs (1)(a) and (b).

(3) Subsections (1) and (2) apply whether   Application the fixation, performance or broadcast   of subsections occurred before or after the coming into   (1) and (2) force of this Part.

(4) Where the performer's performance,   Berne sound recording or communication signal   Convention   countries, meets the requirements set out in section   Rome 15, 18 or 21, as the case may be, a country   Convention   countries, that becomes a Berne Convention country,   WTO a Rome Convention country or a WTO   Members Member after the date of the fixation, performance or broadcast is, as of becoming a Berne Convention country, Rome

Convention country or WTO Member, as the case may be, deemed to have been such at the date of the fixation, performance or broadcast.

Vhere term protection expired

(5) Subsection (4) does not confer any protection in Canada where the term of protection in the country referred to in that subsection had expired before that country became a Berne Convention country, Rome Convention country or WTO Member, as the case may be. *R.S., 1985, c. C-42, s. 23; 1994, c. 47, s. 59; 1997, c. 24, s. 14.*

Ownership of Copyright

Owner-
ship of
copyright

24. The first owner of the copyright

(a) in a performer's performance, is the performer;

(b) in a sound recording, is the maker; or

(c) in a communication signal, is the broadcaster that broadcasts it. *R.S., 1985, c. C-42, s. 24; 1994, c. 47, s. 59; 1997, c. 24, s. 14.*

Assign-
ment of
rights

25. Subsections 13(4) to (7) apply, with such modifications as the circumstances require, in respect of the rights conferred by this Part on performers, makers of sound recordings and broadcasters. *R.S., 1985, c. C-42, s. 25; 1993, c. 44, s. 62; 1994, c. 47, s. 59; 1997, c. 24, s. 14.*

Performers' Rights – WTO Countries

Performer's
perfor-
mance in
WTO
country

26. (1) Where a performer's performance takes place on or after January 1, 1996 in a country that is a WTO Member, the performer has, as of the date of the performer's performance, a copyright in the performer's performance, consisting of the sole right to do the following in relation to the performer's performance or any substantial part thereof:

(a) if it is not fixed, to communicate it to the public by telecommunication and to fix it in a sound recording, and

(b) if it has been fixed in a sound recording without the performer's authorization, to reproduce the fix-

ation or any substantial part thereof,

and to authorize any such acts.

Where
country
joins WTO
after Jan. 1,
1996

(2) Where a performer's performance takes place on or after January 1, 1996 in a country that becomes a WTO Member after the date of the performer's performance, the performer has the copyright described in subsection (1) as of the date the country becomes a WTO Member.

Performer's
perfor-
mances
before Jan. 1,
1996

(3) Where a performer's performance takes place before January 1, 1996 in a country that is a WTO Member, the performer has, as of January 1, 1996, the sole right to do and to authorize the act described in paragraph (1)(b).

Where
country
joins WTO
after Jan. 1,
1996

(4) Where a performer's performance takes place before January 1, 1996 in a country that becomes a WTO Member on or after January 1, 1996, the performer has the right described in subsection (3) as of the date the country becomes a WTO Member.

Term of
performer's
rights

(5) The rights conferred by this section subsist for the remainder of the calendar year in which the performer's performance takes place and a period of fifty years following the end of that calendar year.

Assignment
of rights

(6) Subsections 13(4) to (7) apply, with such modifications as the circumstances require, in respect of a performer's rights conferred by this section.

Limitation

(7) Notwithstanding an assignment of a performer's right conferred by this section, the performer, as well as the assignee, may

(a) prevent the reproduction of

(i) any fixation of the performer's performance, or

(ii) any substantial part of such a fixation,

where the fixation was made without the performer's consent or the assignee's consent; and

(b) prevent the importation of any fixation of the performer's performance, or any reproduction of such a fixation, that the importer knows or ought to have known was made without the performer's consent or the assignee's consent. *R.S., 1985, c. C-42, s. 26; R.S., 1985, c. 10 (4th Supp.), s. 17(F); 1993, c. 44, s. 63; 1994, c. 47, s. 59; 1997, c. 24, s. 14.*

PART III

INFRINGEMENT OF COPYRIGHT AND MORAL RIGHTS AND EXCEPTIONS TO INFRINGEMENT

Infringement of Copyright

General

Infringement generally **27.** (1) It is an infringement of copyright for any person to do, without the consent of the owner of the copyright, anything that by this Act only the owner of the copyright has the right to do.

Secondary infringement (2) It is an infringement of copyright for any person to

(a) sell or rent out,

(b) distribute to such an extent as to affect prejudicially the owner of the copyright,

(c) by way of trade distribute, expose or offer for sale or rental, or exhibit in public,

(d) possess for the purpose of doing anything referred to in paragraphs (a) to (c), or

(e) import into Canada for the purpose of doing anything referred to in paragraphs (a) to (c),

a copy of a work, sound recording or fixation of a performer's performance or of a communication signal that the person knows or should have known infringes copyright or would infringe copyright if it had been made in Canada by the person who made it.

Knowledge of importer (3) In determining whether there is an infringement under subsection (2) in the case of an activity referred to in any of paragraphs (2)(a) to (d) in relation to a copy that was imported in the circumstances referred to in paragraph (2)(e), it is irrelevant whether the importer knew or should have known that the importation of the copy infringed copyright.

Plates (4) It is an infringement of copyright for any person to make or possess a plate that has been specifically designed or adapted for the purpose of making infringing copies of a work or other subject-matter.

Public performance for profit (5) It is an infringement of copyright for any person, for profit, to permit a theatre or other place of entertainment to be used for the performance in public of a work or other subject-matter without the consent of the owner of the copyright unless that person was not aware, and had no reasonable ground for suspecting, that the performance would be an infringement of copyright. *R.S., 1985, c. C-42, s. 27; R.S., 1985, c. 1 (3rd Supp.), s. 13, c. 10 (4th Supp.), s. 5; 1993, c. 44, s. 64; 1997, c. 24, s. 15.*

Parallel Importation of Books

Importation of books **27.1** (1) Subject to any regulations made under subsection (6), it is an infringement of copyright in a book for any person to import the book where

(a) copies of the book were made with the consent of the owner of the copyright in the book in the country where the copies were made, but were imported without the consent of the owner of the copyright in the book in Canada; and

(b) the person knows or should have known that the book would infringe copyright if it was made in Canada by the importer.

Secondary infringement (2) Subject to any regulations made under subsection (6), where the circumstances described in paragraph (1)(a) exist, it is an infringement of copyright in an imported book for any person who knew or should have known that the book would infringe copyright if it was made in Canada by the importer to

(a) sell or rent out the book;

(b) by way of trade, distribute, expose

or offer for sale or rental, or exhibit in public, the book; or

(c) possess the book for the purpose of any of the activities referred to in paragraph (a) or (b).

imitation   (3) Subsections (1) and (2) only apply where there is an exclusive distributor of the book and the acts described in those subsections take place in the part of Canada or in respect of the particular sector of the market for which the person is the exclusive distributor.

Exclusive   (4) An exclusive distributor is deemed, stributor   for the purposes of entitlement to any of the remedies under Part IV in relation to an infringement under this section, to derive an interest in the copyright in question by licence.

Notice   (5) No exclusive distributor, copyright owner or exclusive licensee is entitled to a remedy under Part IV in relation to an infringement under this section unless, before the infringement occurred, notice has been given within the prescribed time and in the prescribed manner to the person referred to in subsection (1) or (2), as the case may be, that there is an exclusive distributor of the book.

:gulations   (6) The Governor in Council may, by regulation, establish terms and conditions for the importation of certain categories of books, including remaindered books, books intended solely for re-export and books imported by special order. *1997, c. 24, s. 15.*

28. *[Repealed, 1997, c. 24, s. 15]*

28.01 *[Repealed, 1997, c. 24, s. 16]*

28.02 *and 28.03 [Repealed, 1997, c. 24, s. 17]*

Moral Rights Infringement

ingement   **28.1** Any act or omission that is contrary to generally   any of the moral rights of the author of a work is, in the absence of consent by the author, an infringement of the moral rights. *R.S., 1985, c. 10 (4th Supp.), s. 6.*

Nature of   **28.2** (1) The author's right to the integrity right of   of a work is infringed only if the work is, integrity

to the prejudice of the honour or reputation of the author,

(a) distorted, mutilated or otherwise modified; or

(b) used in association with a product, service, cause or institution.

(2) In the case of a painting, sculpture   Where or engraving, the prejudice referred to in   prejudice subsection (1) shall be deemed to have   deemed occurred as a result of any distortion, mutilation or other modification of the work.

(3) For the purposes of this section,   When work not

(a) a change in the location of a work,   distorted, the physical means by which a work   etc. is exposed or the physical structure containing a work, or

(b) steps taken in good faith to restore or preserve the work

shall not, by that act alone, constitute a distortion, mutilation or other modification of the work. *R.S., 1985, c. 10 (4th Supp.), s. 6.*

Exceptions

Fair Dealing

29. Fair dealing for the purpose of research   Research or private study does not infringe copy-   or private right. *R.S., 1985, c. C-42, s. 29; R.S., 1985, c. 10*   study *(4th Supp.), s. 7; 1994, c. 47, s. 61; 1997, c. 24, s. 18.*

29.1 Fair dealing for the purpose of criti-   Criticism cism or review does not infringe copyright   or review if the following are mentioned:

(a) the source; and

(b) if given in the source, the name of the

(i) author, in the case of a work,

(ii) performer, in the case of a performer's performance,

(iii)maker, in the case of a sound recording, or

(iv)broadcaster, in the case of a communication signal. *1997, c. 24, s. 18.*

29.2 Fair dealing for the purpose of news   News reporting does not infringe copyright if the   reporting following are mentioned:

(a) the source; and

(b) if given in the source, the name of the

　(i) author, in the case of a work,

　(ii) performer, in the case of a performer's performance,

　(iii) maker, in the case of a sound recording, or

　(iv) broadcaster, in the case of a communication signal. *1997, c. 24, s. 18.*

Acts Undertaken Without Motive of Gain

Motive of gain **29.3** (1) No action referred to in section 29.4, 29.5, 30.2 or 30.21 may be carried out with motive of gain.

Cost recovery (2) An educational institution, library, archive or museum, or person acting under its authority does not have a motive of gain where it or the person acting under its authority, does anything referred to in section 29.4, 29.5, 30.2 or 30.21 and recovers no more than the costs, including overhead costs, associated with doing that act. *1997, c. 24, s. 18.*

Educational Institutions

Reproduction for instruction **29.4** (1) It is not an infringement of copyright for an educational institution or a person acting under its authority

　(a) to make a manual reproduction of a work onto a dry-erase board, flip chart or other similar surface intended for displaying handwritten material, or

　(b) to make a copy of a work to be used to project an image of that copy using an overhead projector or similar device

for the purposes of education or training on the premises of an educational institution.

Reproduction for examinations, etc. (2) It is not an infringement of copyright for an educational institution or a person acting under its authority to

　(a) reproduce, translate or perform in public on the premises of the educational institution, or

(b) communicate by telecommunication to the public situated on the premises of the educational institution

a work or other subject-matter as required for a test or examination.

(3) Except in the case of manual reproduction, the exemption from copyright infringement provided by paragraph (1)(b) and subsection (2) does not apply if the work or other subject-matter is commercially available in a medium that is appropriate for the purpose referred to in that paragraph or subsection, as the case may be. *1997, c. 24, s. 18.* Where work commercially available

29.5 It is not an infringement of copyright for an educational institution or a person acting under its authority to do the following acts if they are done on the premises of an educational institution for educational or training purposes and not for profit, before an audience consisting primarily of students of the educational institution, instructors acting under the authority of the educational institution or any person who is directly responsible for setting a curriculum for the educational institution: Performan

　(a) the live performance in public, primarily by students of the educational institution, of a work;

　(b) the performance in public of a sound recording or of a work or performer's performance that is embodied in a sound recording; and

　(c) the performance in public of a work or other subject-matter at the time of its communication to the public by telecommunication. *1997, c. 24, s. 18.*

29.6 (1) Subject to subsection (2) and section 29.9, it is not an infringement of copyright for an educational institution or a person acting under its authority to News and commenta

　(a) make, at the time of its communication to the public by telecommunication, a single copy of a news program or a news commentary program, excluding documentaries, for the purposes of performing the copy for the students of the educational institution for educational or training purposes; and

(b) perform the copy in public, at any time or times within one year after the making of a copy under paragraph (a), before an audience consisting primarily of students of the educational institution on its premises for educational or training purposes.

Royalties for reproduction and performance

(2) The educational institution must

(a) on the expiration of one year after making a copy under paragraph (1)(a), pay the royalties and comply with any terms and conditions fixed under this Act for the making of the copy or destroy the copy; and

(b) where it has paid the royalties referred to in paragraph (a), pay the royalties and comply with any terms and conditions fixed under this Act for any performance in public of the copy after the expiration of that year. *1997, c. 24, s. 18.*

production of broadcast

29.7 (1) Subject to subsection (2) and section 29.9, it is not an infringement of copyright for an educational institution or a person acting under its authority to

(a) make a single copy of a work or other subject-matter at the time that it is communicated to the public by telecommunication; and

(b) keep the copy for up to thirty days to decide whether to perform the copy for educational or training purposes.

Royalties for reproduction

(2) An educational institution that has not destroyed the copy by the expiration of the thirty days infringes copyright in the work or other subject-matter unless it pays any royalties, and complies with any terms and conditions, fixed under this Act for the making of the copy.

Royalties for performance

(3) It is not an infringement of copyright for the educational institution or a person acting under its authority to perform the copy in public for educational or training purposes on the premises of the educational institution before an audience

consisting primarily of students of the educational institution if the educational institution pays the royalties and complies with any terms and conditions fixed under this Act for the performance in public. *1997, c. 24, s. 18.*

29.8 The exceptions to infringement of copyright provided for under sections 29.5 to 29.7 do not apply where the communication to the public by telecommunication was received by unlawful means. *1997, c. 24, s. 18.*

Unlawful reception

29.9 (1) Where an educational institution or person acting under its authority

Records and marking

(a) makes a copy of a news program or a news commentary program and performs it pursuant to section 29.6, or

(b) makes a copy of a work or other subject-matter communicated to the public by telecommunication and performs it pursuant to section 29.7,

the educational institution shall keep a record of the information prescribed by regulation in relation to the making of the copy, the destruction of it or any performance in public of it for which royalties are payable under this Act and shall, in addition, mark the copy in the manner prescribed by regulation.

(2) The Board may, with the approval of the Governor in Council, make regulations

Regulations

(a) prescribing the information in relation to the making, destruction, performance and marking of copies that must be kept under subsection (1),

(b) prescribing the manner and form in which records referred to in that subsection must be kept and copies destroyed or marked, and

(c) respecting the sending of information to collective societies referred to in section 71. *1997, c. 24, s. 18.*

30. The publication in a collection, mainly composed of non-copyright matter, intended for the use of educational institutions, and so described in the title and in any advertisements issued by the publisher, of

Literary collections

short passages from published literary works in which copyright subsists and not themselves published for the use of educational institutions, does not infringe copyright in those published literary works if

(a) not more than two passages from works by the same author are published by the same publisher within five years;

(b) the source from which the passages are taken is acknowledged; and

(c) the name of the author, if given in the source, is mentioned. *R.S., 1985, c. C-42, s. 30; R.S., 1985, c. 10 (4th Supp.), s. 7; 1997, c. 24, s. 18.*

Libraries, Archives and Museums

Management and maintenance of collection

30.1 (1) It is not an infringement of copyright for a library, archive or museum or a person acting under the authority of a library, archive or museum to make, for the maintenance or management of its permanent collection or the permanent collection of another library, archive or museum, a copy of a work or other subject-matter, whether published or unpublished, in its permanent collection

(a) if the original is rare or unpublished and is

(i) deteriorating, damaged or lost, or

(ii) at risk of deterioration or becoming damaged or lost;

(b) for the purposes of on-site consultation if the original cannot be viewed, handled or listened to because of its condition or because of the atmospheric conditions in which it must be kept;

(c) in an alternative format if the original is currently in an obsolete format or the technology required to use the original is unavailable;

(d) for the purposes of internal record-keeping and cataloguing;

(e) for insurance purposes or police investigations; or

(f) if necessary for restoration.

(2) Paragraphs (1)(a) to (c) do not apply where an appropriate copy is commercially available in a medium and of a quality that is appropriate for the purposes of subsection (1). *Limitati*

(3) If a person must make an intermediate copy in order to make a copy under subsection (1), the person must destroy the intermediate copy as soon as it is no longer needed. *Destruc of intern ate copi*

(4) The Governor in Council may make regulations with respect to the procedure for making copies under subsection (1). *1997, c. 24, s. 18; 1999, c. 31, s. 59(E). Regulati*

30.2 (1) It is not an infringement of copyright for a library, archive or museum or a person acting under its authority to do anything on behalf of any person that the person may do personally under section 29 or 29.1. *Researcl or priva study*

(2) It is not an infringement of copyright for a library, archive or museum or a person acting under the authority of a library, archive or museum to make, by reprographic reproduction, for any person requesting to use the copy for research or private study, a copy of a work that is, or that is contained in, an article published in *Copies c articles f research*

(a) a scholarly, scientific or technical periodical; or

(b) a newspaper or periodical, other than a scholarly, scientific or technical periodical, if the newspaper or periodical was published more than one year before the copy is made.

(3) Paragraph (2)(b) does not apply in respect of a work of fiction or poetry or a dramatic or musical work. *Restricti*

(4) A library, archive or museum may make a copy under subsection (2) only on condition that *Conditic*

(a) the person for whom the copy will be made has satisfied the library, archive or museum that the person will not use the copy for a purpose other than research or private study; and

(b) the person is provided with a single copy of the work.

Patrons of other libraries, etc. (5) A library, archive or museum or a person acting under the authority of a library, archive or museum may do, on behalf of a person who is a patron of another library, archive or museum, anything under subsection (1) or (2) in relation to printed matter that it is authorized by this section to do on behalf of a person who is one of its patrons, but the copy given to the patron must not be in digital form.

Destruction of intermediate copies (5.1) Where an intermediate copy is made in order to copy a work referred to in subsection (5), once the copy is given to the patron, the intermediate copy must be destroyed.

Regulations (6) The Governor in Council may, for the purposes of this section, make regulations

(a) defining "newspaper" and "periodical";

(b) defining scholarly, scientific and technical periodicals;

(c) prescribing the information to be recorded about any action taken under subsection (1) or (5) and the manner and form in which the information is to be kept; and

(d) prescribing the manner and form in which the conditions set out in subsection (4) are to be met. *1997, c. 24, s. 18.*

Copying works deposited in archive **30.21** (1) It is not an infringement of copyright for an archive to make a copy, in accordance with subsection (3), of an unpublished work that is deposited in the archive after the coming into force of this section.

Notice (2) When a person deposits a work in an archive, the archive must give the person notice that it may copy the work in accordance with this section.

Conditions for copying of works (3) The archive may only copy the work if

(a) the person who deposited the work, if a copyright owner, does not, at the time the work is deposited, prohibit its copying;

(b) copying has not been prohibited by any other owner of copyright in the work; and

(c) the archive is satisfied that the

person for whom it is made will use the copy only for purposes of research or private study and makes only one copy for that person.

Regulations (4) The Governor in Council may prescribe the manner and form in which the conditions in subsection (3) may be met.

Where copyright owner cannot be found (5) Where an archive requires the consent of the copyright owner to copy an unpublished work deposited in the archive before the coming into force of this section but is unable to locate the owner, the archive may copy the work in accordance with subsection (3).

Notice (6) The archive must make a record of any copy made under subsection (5) and keep it available for public inspection, as prescribed.

Posthumous works (7) It is not an infringement of copyright for an archive to make a copy, in accordance with subsection (3), of any work to which subsection 7(4) applies if it was in the archive on the date of coming into force of this section. *1997, c. 24, s. 18; 1999, c. 31, s. 60(E).*

Machines Installed in Educational Institutions, Libraries, Archives and Museums

No infringement by educational institution, etc. **30.3** (1) An educational institution or a library, archive or museum does not infringe copyright where

(a) a copy of a work is made using a machine for the making, by reprographic reproduction, of copies of works in printed form;

(b) the machine is installed by or with the approval of the educational institution, library, archive or museum on its premises for use by students, instructors or staff at the educational institution or by persons using the library, archive or museum; and

(c) there is affixed in the prescribed manner and location a notice warning of infringement of copyright.

Application (2) Subsection (1) only applies if, in respect of a reprographic reproduction,

(a) the educational institution, library, archive or museum has entered into an agreement with a collective society that is authorized by copyright owners to grant licences on their behalf;

(b) the Board has, in accordance with section 70.2, fixed the royalties and related terms and conditions in respect of a licence;

(c) a tariff has been approved in accordance with section 70.15; or

(d) a collective society has filed a proposed tariff in accordance with section 70.13.

Order (3) Where a collective society offers to negotiate or has begun to negotiate an agreement referred to in paragraph (2)(a), the Board may, at the request of either party, order that the educational institution, library, archive or museum be treated as an institution to which subsection (1) applies, during the period specified in the order.

Agreement with copyright owner (4) Where an educational institution, library, archive or museum has entered into an agreement with a copyright owner other than a collective society respecting reprographic reproduction, subsection (1) applies only in respect of the works of the copyright owner that are covered by the agreement.

Regulations (5) The Governor in Council may, for the purposes of paragraph 1(c), prescribe by regulation the manner of affixing and location of notices and the dimensions, form and contents of notices. *1997, c. 24, s. 18.*

Libraries, Archives and Museums in Educational Institutions

Application to libraries, etc. within educational institutions **30.4** For greater certainty, the exceptions to infringement of copyright provided for under sections 29.4 to 30.3 and 45 also apply in respect of a library, archive or museum that forms part of an educational institution. *1997, c. 24, s. 18.*

National Archives of Canada

30.5 The National Archives of Canada may Copies for archival purposes

(a) make a copy of a recording, as defined in section 8 of the National Archives Act, for the purposes of that section; and

(b) at the time that a broadcasting undertaking, within the meaning of subsection 2(1) of the Broadcasting Act, communicates a work or other subject-matter to the public by telecommunication, make a copy for archival purposes of the work or other subject-matter that is included in that communication. *1997, c. 24, s. 18.*

Computer Programs

30.6 It is not an infringement of copyright Permitted acts in a computer program for a person who owns a copy of the computer program that is authorized by the owner of the copyright to

(a) make a single reproduction of the copy by adapting, modifying or converting the computer program or translating it into another computer language if the person proves that the reproduced copy is

(i) essential for the compatibility of the computer program with a particular computer,

(ii) solely for the person's own use, and

(iii) destroyed immediately after the person ceases to be the owner of the copy; or

(b) make a single reproduction for backup purposes of the copy or of a reproduced copy referred to in paragraph (a) if the person proves that the reproduction for backup purposes is destroyed immediately when the person ceases to be the owner of the copy of the computer program. *1997, c. 24, s. 18.*

Incidental Inclusion

Incidental use **30.7** It is not an infringement of copyright to incidentally and not deliberately

(a) include a work or other subject-matter in another work or other subject-matter; or

(b) do any act in relation to a work or other subject-matter that is incidentally and not deliberately included in another work or other subject-matter. *1997, c. 24, s. 18.*

Ephemeral Recordings

Ephemeral recordings **30.8** (1) It is not an infringement of copyright for a programming undertaking to fix or reproduce in accordance with this section a performer's performance or work, other than a cinematographic work, that is performed live or a sound recording that is performed at the same time as the performer's performance or work, if the undertaking

(a) is authorized to communicate the performer's performance, work or sound recording to the public by telecommunication;

(b) makes the fixation or the reproduction itself, for its own broadcasts;

(c) does not synchronize the fixation or reproduction with all or part of another recording, performer's performance or work; and

(d) does not cause the fixation or reproduction to be used in an advertisement intended to sell or promote, as the case may be, a product, service, cause or institution.

Record keeping (2) The programming undertaking must record the dates of the making and destruction of all fixations and reproductions and any other prescribed information about the fixation or reproduction, and keep the record current.

Right of access by copyright owners (3) The programming undertaking must make the record referred to in sub-section (2) available to owners of copyright in the works, sound recordings or performer's performances, or their representatives, within twenty-four hours after receiving a request.

Destruction (4) The programming undertaking must destroy the fixation or reproduction within thirty days after making it, unless

(a) the copyright owner authorizes its retention; or

(b) it is deposited in an archive, in accordance with subsection (6).

Royalties (5) Where the copyright owner authorizes the fixation or reproduction to be retained after the thirty days, the programming undertaking must pay any applicable royalty.

Archive (6) Where the programming undertaking considers a fixation or reproduction to be of an exceptional documentary character, the undertaking may, with the consent of an official archive, deposit it in the official archive and must notify the copyright owner, within thirty days, of the deposit of the fixation or reproduction.

Definition of "official archive" (7) In subsection (6), "official archive" means the National Archives of Canada or any archive established under the law of a province for the preservation of the official archives of the province.

Application (8) This section does not apply where a licence is available from a collective society to make the fixation or reproduction of the performer's performance, work or sound recording.

Telecommunications by networks (9) A broadcasting undertaking, as defined in the Broadcasting Act, may make a single reproduction of a fixation or reproduction made by a programming undertaking and communicate it to the public by telecommunication, within the period referred to in subsection (4), if the broadcasting undertaking meets the conditions set out in subsection (1) and is part of a prescribed network that includes the programming undertaking.

Limitations (10) The reproduction and communication to the public by telecommunication must be made

(a) in accordance with subsections (2) to (6); and

(b) within thirty days after the day on which the programming undertaking made the fixation or reproduction.

Definition of "programming undertaking" (11) In this section, "programming undertaking" means

(a) a programming undertaking as defined in subsection 2(1) of the Broadcasting Act;

(b) a programming undertaking described in paragraph (a) that originates programs within a network, as defined in subsection 2(1) of the Broadcasting Act; or

(c) a distribution undertaking as defined in subsection 2(1) of the Broadcasting Act, in respect of the programs that it originates.

The undertaking must hold a broadcasting licence issued by the Canadian Radio-television and Telecommunications Commission under the Broadcasting Act. *1997, c. 24, s. 18.*

Pre-recorded recordings **30.9** (1) It is not an infringement of copyright for a broadcasting undertaking to reproduce in accordance with this section a sound recording, or a performer's performance or work that is embodied in a sound recording, solely for the purpose of transferring it to a format appropriate for broadcasting, if the undertaking

(a) owns the copy of the sound recording, performer's performance or work and that copy is authorized by the owner of the copyright;

(b) is authorized to communicate the sound recording, performer's performance or work to the public by telecommunication;

(c) makes the reproduction itself, for its own broadcasts;

(d) does not synchronize the reproduction with all or part of another recording, performer's performance or work; and

(e) does not cause the reproduction to be used in an advertisement intended to sell or promote, as the case may be, a product, service, cause or institution.

Record keeping (2) The broadcasting undertaking must record the dates of the making and destruction of all reproductions and any other prescribed information about the reproduction, and keep the record current.

Right of access by copyright owners (3) The broadcasting undertaking must make the record referred to in subsection (2) available to owners of copyright in the sound recordings, performer's performances or works, or their representatives, within twenty-four hours after receiving a request.

Destruction (4) The broadcasting undertaking must destroy the reproduction when it no longer possesses the sound recording or performer's performance or work embodied in the sound recording, or at the latest within thirty days after making the reproduction, unless the copyright owner authorizes the reproduction to be retained.

Royalty (5) If the copyright owner authorizes the reproduction to be retained, the broadcasting undertaking must pay any applicable royalty.

Application (6) This section does not apply if a licence is available from a collective society to reproduce the sound recording, performer's performance or work.

Definition of "broadcasting undertaking" (7) In this section, "broadcasting undertaking" means a broadcasting undertaking as defined in subsection 2(1) of the Broadcasting Act that holds a broadcasting licence issued by the Canadian Radio-television and Telecommunications Commission under that Act. *1997, c. 24, s. 18.*

Retransmission

Interpretation **31.** (1) In this section,

"retransmitter" does not include a

person who uses Hertzian waves to retransmit a signal but does not perform a function comparable to that of a cable retransmission system;

"signal" means a signal that carries a literary, dramatic, musical or artistic work and is transmitted for free reception by the public by a terrestrial radio or terrestrial television station.

Retrans mission of local signals (2) It is not an infringement of copyright to communicate to the public by telecommunication any literary, dramatic, musical or artistic work if

(a) the communication is a retransmission of a local or distant signal;

(b) the retransmission is lawful under the Broadcasting Act;

(c) the signal is retransmitted simultaneously and in its entirety, except as otherwise required or permitted by or under the laws of Canada; and

(d) in the case of the retransmission of a distant signal, the retransmitter has paid any royalties, and complied with any terms and conditions, fixed under this Act.

Regulations (3) The Governor in Council may make regulations defining "local signal" and "distant signal" for the purposes of this section. *R.S., 1985, c. C-42, s. 31; R.S., 1985, c. 10 (4th Supp.), s. 7; 1988, c. 65, s. 63; 1997, c. 24, ss. 16, 52(F).*

Persons with Perceptual Disabilities

Reproduction in alternate format **32.** (1) It is not an infringement of copyright for a person, at the request of a person with a perceptual disability, or for a non-profit organization acting for his or her benefit, to

(a) make a copy or sound recording of a literary, musical, artistic or dramatic work, other than a cinematographic work, in a format specially designed for persons with a perceptual disability;

(b) translate, adapt or reproduce in sign language a literary or dramatic work, other than a cinematographic

work, in a format specially designed for persons with a perceptual disability; or

(c) perform in public a literary or dramatic work, other than a cinematographic work, in sign language, either live or in a format specially designed for persons with a perceptual disability.

(2) Subsection (1) does not authorize the making of a large print book. Limitation

(3) Subsection (1) does not apply where the work or sound recording is commercially available in a format specially designed to meet the needs of any person referred to in that subsection, within the meaning of paragraph (a) of the definition "commercially available". *R.S., 1985, c. C-42, s. 32; R.S., 1985, c. 10 (4th Supp.), s. 7; 1997, c. 24, s. 19.* Limitation

Statutory Obligations

32.1 (1) It is not an infringement of copyright for any person No infringe- ment

(a) to disclose, pursuant to the Access to Information Act, a record within the meaning of that Act, or to disclose, pursuant to any like Act of the legislature of a province, like material;

(b) to disclose, pursuant to the Privacy Act, personal information within the meaning of that Act, or to disclose, pursuant to any like Act of the legislature of a province, like information;

(c) to make a copy of an object referred to in section 14 of the Cultural Property Export and Import Act, for deposit in an institution pursuant to a direction under that section; and

(d) to make a fixation or copy of a work or other subject-matter in order to comply with the Broadcasting Act or any rule, regulation or other instrument made under it.

(2) Nothing in paragraph (1)(a) or (b) authorizes a person to whom a record or Limitation

information is disclosed to do anything that, by this Act, only the owner of the copyright in the record, personal information or like information, as the case may be, has a right to do.

Destruction of fixation or copy (3) Unless the Broadcasting Act otherwise provides, a person who makes a fixation or copy under paragraph (1)(d) shall destroy it immediately on the expiration of the period for which it must be kept pursuant to that Act, rule, regulation or other instrument. *1997, c. 24, s. 19.*

Miscellaneous

Permitted acts **32.2** (1) It is not an infringement of copyright

(a) for an author of an artistic work who is not the owner of the copyright in the work to use any mould, cast, sketch, plan, model or study made by the author for the purpose of the work, if the author does not thereby repeat or imitate the main design of the work;

(b) for any person to reproduce, in a painting, drawing, engraving, photograph or cinematographic work

  (i) an architectural work, provided the copy is not in the nature of an architectural drawing or plan, or

  (ii) a sculpture or work of artistic craftsmanship or a cast or model of a sculpture or work of artistic craftsmanship, that is permanently situated in a public place or building;

(c) for any person to make or publish, for the purposes of news reporting or news summary, a report of a lecture given in public, unless the report is prohibited by conspicuous written or printed notice affixed before and maintained during the lecture at or about the main entrance of the building in which the lecture is given, and, except while the building is being used for public worship, in a position near the lecturer;

(d) for any person to read or recite in public a reasonable extract from a published work; or

(e) for any person to make or publish, for the purposes of news reporting or news summary, a report of an address of a political nature given at a public meeting.

(2) It is not an infringement of copyright **Further permitted acts** for a person to do any of the following acts without motive of gain at any agricultural or agricultural-industrial exhibition or fair that receives a grant from or is held by its directors under federal, provincial or municipal authority:

(a) the live performance in public of a musical work;

(b) the performance in public of a sound recording embodying a musical work or a performer's performance of a musical work; or

(c) the performance in public of a communication signal carrying

  (i) the live performance in public of a musical work, or

  (ii) a sound recording embodying a musical work or a performer's performance of a musical work.

(3) No religious organization or insti- **Further permitted acts** tution, educational institution and no charitable or fraternal organization shall be held liable to pay any compensation for doing any of the following acts in furtherance of a religious, educational or charitable object:

(a) the live performance in public of a musical work;

(b) the performance in public of a sound recording embodying a musical work or a performer's performance of a musical work; or

(c) the performance in public of a communication signal carrying

  (i) the live performance in public of a musical work, or

  (ii) a sound recording embodying a

musical work or a performer's performance of a musical work. *1997, c. 24, s. 19.*

Interpretation

No right to equitable remuneration **32.3** For the purposes of sections 29 to 32.2, an act that does not infringe copyright does not give rise to a right to remuneration conferred by section 19. *1997, c. 24, s. 19.*

Compensation for Acts Done Before Recognition of Copyright of Performers and Broadcasters

Certain rights and interests protected **32.4** (1) Notwithstanding section 27, where a person has, before the later of January 1, 1996 and the day on which a country becomes a WTO member, incurred an expenditure or liability in connection with, or in preparation for, the doing of an act that would have infringed copyright under section 26 commencing on the later of those days, had that country been a WTO member, any right or interest of that person that

(a) arises from or in connection with the doing of that act, and

(b) is subsisting and valuable on the later of those days

is not prejudiced or diminished by reason only that that country has become a WTO member, except as provided by an order of the Board made under subsection 78(3).

Compensation (2) Notwithstanding subsection (1), a person's right or interest that is protected by that subsection terminates if and when the owner of the copyright pays that person such compensation as is agreed to between the parties or, failing agreement, as is determined by the Board in accordance with section 78.

Limitation (3) Nothing in subsections (1) and (2) affects any right of a performer available in law or equity. *1997, c. 24, s. 19.*

Certain rights and interests protected **32.5** (1) Notwithstanding section 27, where a person has, before the later of the coming into force of Part II and the day on which a country becomes a Rome Convention country, incurred an expenditure or liability in connection with, or in preparation for, the doing of an act that would have infringed copyright under section 15 or 21 commencing on the later of those days, had Part II been in force or had that country been a Rome Convention country, any right or interest of that person that

(a) arises from or in connection with the doing of that act, and

(b) is subsisting and valuable on the later of those days

is not prejudiced or diminished by reason only that Part II has come into force or that the country has become a Rome Convention country, except as provided by an order of the Board made under subsection 78(3).

Compensation (2) Notwithstanding subsection (1), a person's right or interest that is protected by that subsection terminates if and when the owner of the copyright pays that person such compensation as is agreed to between the parties or, failing agreement, as is determined by the Board in accordance with section 78.

Limitation (3) Nothing in subsections (1) and (2) affects any right of a performer available in law or equity. *1997, c. 24, s. 19.*

Compensation for Acts Done Before Recognition of Copyright or Moral Rights

Certain rights and interests protected **33.** (1) Notwithstanding subsections 27(1), (2) and (4) and sections 27.1, 28.1 and 28.2, where a person has, before the later of January 1, 1996 and the day on which a country becomes a treaty country, incurred an expenditure or liability in connection with, or in preparation for, the doing of an act that would have infringed a copyright owner's copyright or an author's moral rights had that country been a treaty country, any right or interest of that person that

(a) arises from or in connection with the doing of that act, and

(b) is subsisting and valuable on the latest of those days

is not prejudiced or diminished by reason only that that country has become a treaty country, except as provided by an order of the Board made under subsection 78(3).

Compensation (2) Notwithstanding subsection (1), a person's right or interest that is protected by that subsection terminates, as against the copyright owner or author, if and when that copyright owner or the author, as the case may be, pays that person such compensation as is agreed to between the parties or, failing agreement, as is determined by the Board in accordance with section 78. *R.S., 1985, c. C-42, s. 33; R.S., 1985, c. 10 (4th Supp.), s. 7; 1997, c. 24, s. 19.*

PART IV

REMEDIES

Civil Remedies

Copyright **34.** (1) Where copyright has been infringed, the owner of the copyright is, subject to this Act, entitled to all remedies by way of injunction, damages, accounts, delivery up and otherwise that are or may be conferred by law for the infringement of a right.

Moral rights (2) In any proceedings for an infringement of a moral right of an author, the court may grant to the author or to the person who holds the moral rights by virtue of subsection 14.2(2) or (3), as the case may be, all remedies by way of injunction, damages, accounts, delivery up and otherwise that are or may be conferred by law for the infringement of a right.

Costs (3) The costs of all parties in any proceedings in respect of the infringement of a right conferred by this Act shall be in the discretion of the court.

Summary proceedings (4) The following proceedings may be commenced or proceeded with by way of application or action and shall, in the case of an application, be heard and determined without delay and in a summary way:

(a) proceedings for infringement of copyright or moral rights;

(b) proceedings taken under section 44.1, 44.2 or 44.4; and

(c) proceedings taken in respect of

(i) a tariff certified by the Board under Part VII or VIII, or

(ii) agreements referred to in section 70.12.

Practice and procedure (5) The rules of practice and procedure, in civil matters, of the court in which proceedings are commenced by way of application apply to those proceedings, but where those rules do not provide for the proceedings to be heard and determined without delay and in a summary way, the court may give such directions as it considers necessary in order to so provide.

Actions (6) The court in which proceedings are instituted by way of application may, where it considers it appropriate, direct that the proceeding be proceeded with as an action.

Meaning of "application" (7) In this section, "application" means a proceeding that is commenced other than by way of a writ or statement of claim. *R.S., 1985, c. C-42, s. 34; R.S., 1985, c. 10 (4th Supp.), s. 8; 1993, c. 15, s. 3(E), c. 44, s. 65; 1994, c. 47, s. 62; 1997, c. 24, s. 20.*

Presumptions respecting copyright and ownership **34.1** (1) In any proceedings for infringement of copyright in which the defendant puts in issue either the existence of the copyright or the title of the plaintiff thereto,

(a) copyright shall be presumed, unless the contrary is proved, to subsist in the work, performer's performance, sound recording or communication signal, as the case may be; and

(b) the author, performer, maker or broadcaster, as the case may be, shall, unless the contrary is proved, be presumed to be the owner of the copyright.

Where no grant registered (2) Where any matter referred to in subsection (1) is at issue and no assignment of the copyright, or licence granting an interest in the copyright, has been registered under this Act,

(a) if a name purporting to be that of

(i) the author of the work,

(ii) the performer of the performer's performance,

(iii) the maker of the sound recording, or

(iv) the broadcaster of the communication signal

is printed or otherwise indicated thereon in the usual manner, the person whose name is so printed or indicated shall, unless the contrary is proved, be presumed to be the author, performer, maker or broadcaster;

(b) if

(i) no name is so printed or indicated, or if the name so printed or indicated is not the true name of the author, performer, maker or broadcaster or the name by which that person is commonly known, and

(ii) a name purporting to be that of the publisher or owner of the work, performer's performance, sound recording or communication signal is printed or otherwise indicated thereon in the usual manner,

the person whose name is printed or indicated as described in subparagraph (ii) shall, unless the contrary is proved, be presumed to be the owner of the copyright in question; and

(c) if, on a cinematographic work, a name purporting to be that of the maker of the cinematographic work appears in the usual manner, the person so named shall, unless the contrary is proved, be presumed to be the maker of the cinematographic work. *1997, c. 24, s. 20.*

Liability for infringement **35.** (1) Where a person infringes copyright, the person is liable to pay such damages to the owner of the copyright as the owner has suffered due to the infringement and, in addition to those damages, such part of the profits that the infringer

has made from the infringement and that were not taken into account in calculating the damages as the court considers just.

Proof of profits (2) In proving profits,

(a) the plaintiff shall be required to prove only receipts or revenues derived from the infringement; and

(b) the defendant shall be required to prove every element of cost that the defendant claims. *R.S., 1985, c. C-42, s. 35; 1997, c. 24, s. 20.*

Protection of separate rights **36.** (1) Subject to this section, the owner of any copyright, or any person or persons deriving any right, title or interest by assignment or grant in writing from the owner, may individually for himself or herself, as a party to the proceedings in his or her own name, protect and enforce any right that he or she holds, and, to the extent of that right, title and interest, is entitled to the remedies provided by this Act.

Where copyright owner to be made party (2) Where proceedings referred to in subsection (1) are taken by a person other than the copyright owner, the copyright owner must be made a party to those proceedings, except

(a) in respect of proceedings taken under section 44.1, 44.2 or 44.4;

(b) in respect of interlocutory proceedings unless the court is of the opinion that the interests of justice require the copyright owner to be a party; and

(c) in any other case, if the court is of the opinion that the interests of justice do not require the copyright owner to be a party.

Owner's liability for costs (3) A copyright owner who is made a party to proceedings pursuant to subsection (2) is not liable for any costs unless the copyright owner takes part in the proceedings.

Apportionment of damages, profits (4) Where a copyright owner is made a party to proceedings pursuant to subsection (2), the court, in awarding damages or profits, shall, subject to any agreement between the person who took the proceedings and the copyright owner, apportion the damages or profits referred to in subsection 35(1) between them as the court considers appropriate. *R.S., 1985, c. C-42, s. 36; 1994, c. 47, s. 63; 1997, c. 24, s. 20.*

Concurrent jurisdiction of Federal Court

37. The Federal Court has concurrent jurisdiction with provincial courts to hear and determine all proceedings, other than the prosecution of offences under section 42 and 43, for the enforcement of a provision of this Act or of the civil remedies provided by this Act. *R.S., 1985, c. C-42, s. 37; 1997, c. 24, s. 20.*

Recovery of possession of copies, plates

38. (1) Subject to subsection (2), the owner of the copyright in a work or other subject-matter may

(a) recover possession of all infringing copies of that work or other subject-matter, and of all plates used or intended to be used for the production of infringing copies, and

(b) take proceedings for seizure of those copies or plates before judgment if, under the law of Canada or of the province in which those proceedings are taken, a person is entitled to take such proceedings,

as if those copies or plates were the property of the copyright owner.

Powers of court

(2) On application by

(a) a person from whom the copyright owner has recovered possession of copies or plates referred to in subsection (1),

(b) a person against whom proceedings for seizure before judgment of copies or plates referred to in subsection (1) have been taken, or

(c) any other person who has an interest in those copies or plates,

a court may order that those copies or plates be destroyed, or may make any other order that it considers appropriate in the circumstances.

Notice to interested persons

(3) Before making an order under subsection (2), the court shall direct that notice be given to any person who has an interest in the copies or plates in question,

unless the court is of the opinion that the interests of justice do not require such notice to be given.

Circumstances court to consider

(4) In making an order under subsection (2), the court shall have regard to all the circumstances, including

(a) the proportion, importance and value of the infringing copy or plate, as compared to the substrate or carrier embodying it; and

(b) the extent to which the infringing copy or plate is severable from, or a distinct part of, the substrate or carrier embodying it.

Limitation

(5) Nothing in this Act entitles the copyright owner to damages in respect of the possession or conversion of the infringing copies or plates. *R.S., 1985, c. C-42, s. 38; 1997, c. 24, s. 20.*

Statutory damages

38.1 (1) Subject to this section, a copyright owner may elect, at any time before final judgment is rendered, to recover, instead of damages and profits referred to in subsection 35(1), an award of statutory damages for all infringements involved in the proceedings, with respect to any one work or other subject-matter, for which any one infringer is liable individually, or for which any two or more infringers are liable jointly and severally, in a sum of not less than $500 or more than $20,000 as the court considers just.

Where defendant unaware of infringement

(2) Where a copyright owner has made an election under subsection (1) and the defendant satisfies the court that the defendant was not aware and had no reasonable grounds to believe that the defendant had infringed copyright, the court may reduce the amount of the award to less than $500, but not less than $200.

Special case

(3) Where

(a) there is more than one work or other subject-matter in a single medium, and

(b) the awarding of even the minimum amount referred to in subsection (1) or (2) would result in a total award that, in the court's opinion, is grossly out of proportion to the infringement,

the court may award, with respect to each work or other subject-matter, such lower amount than $500 or $200, as the case may be, as the court considers just.

Collective societies

(4) Where the defendant has not paid applicable royalties, a collective society referred to in section 67 may only make an election under this section to recover, in lieu of any other remedy of a monetary nature provided by this Act, an award of statutory damages in a sum of not less than three and not more than ten times the amount of the applicable royalties, as the court considers just.

Factors to consider

(5) In exercising its discretion under subsections (1) to (4), the court shall consider all relevant factors, including

(a) the good faith or bad faith of the defendant;

(b) the conduct of the parties before and during the proceedings; and

(c) the need to deter other infringements of the copyright in question.

No award

(6) No statutory damages may be awarded against

(a) an educational institution or a person acting under its authority that has committed an act referred to in section 29.6 or 29.7 and has not paid any royalties or complied with any terms and conditions fixed under this Act in relation to the commission of the act;

(b) an educational institution, library, archive or museum that is sued in the circumstances referred to in section 38.2; or

(c) a person who infringes copyright under paragraph 27(2)(e) or section 27.1, where the copy in question was made with the consent of the copyright owner in the country where the copy was made.

Exemplary or punitive damages not affected

(7) An election under subsection (1) does not affect any right that the copyright

owner may have to exemplary or punitive damages. *1997, c. 24, s. 20.*

Maximum amount that may be recovered

38.2 (1) An owner of copyright in a work who has not authorized a collective society to authorize its reprographic reproduction may recover, in proceedings against an educational institution, library, archive or museum that has reproduced the work, a maximum amount equal to the amount of royalties that would have been payable to the society in respect of the reprographic reproduction, if it were authorized, either

(a) under any agreement entered into with the collective society; or

(b) under a tariff certified by the Board pursuant to section 70.15.

Agreements with more than one collective society

(2) Where agreements respecting reprographic reproduction have been signed with more than one collective society or where more than one tariff applies or where both agreements and tariffs apply, the maximum amount that the copyright owner may recover is the largest amount of the royalties provided for in any of those agreements or tariffs.

Application

(3) Subsections (1) and (2) apply only where

(a) the collective society is entitled to authorize, or the tariff provides for the payment of royalties in respect of, the reprographic reproduction of that category of work; and

(b) copying of that general nature and extent is covered by the agreement or tariff. *1997, c. 24, s. 20.*

Injunction only remedy when defendant not aware of copyright

39. (1) Subject to subsection (2), in any proceedings for infringement of copyright, the plaintiff is not entitled to any remedy other than an injunction in respect of the infringement if the defendant proves that, at the date of the infringement, the defendant was not aware and had no reasonable ground for suspecting that copyright subsisted in the work or other subject-matter in question.

Exception where copyright registered (2) Subsection (1) does not apply if, at the date of the infringement, the copyright was duly registered under this Act. *R.S., 1985, c. C-42, s. 39; 1997, c. 24, s. 20.*

Wide injunction **39.1** (1) When granting an injunction in respect of an infringement of copyright in a work or other subject-matter, the court may further enjoin the defendant from infringing the copyright in any other work or subject-matter if

(a) the plaintiff is the owner of the copyright or the person to whom an interest in the copyright has been granted by licence; and

(b) the plaintiff satisfies the court that the defendant will likely infringe the copyright in those other works or subject-matter unless enjoined by the court from doing so.

Application of injunction (2) An injunction granted under subsection (1) may extend to works or other subject-matter

(a) in respect of which the plaintiff was not, at the time the proceedings were commenced, the owner of the copyright or the person to whom an interest in the copyright has been granted by licence; or

(b) that did not exist at the time the proceedings were commenced. *1997, c. 24, s. 20.*

No injunction in case of a building **40.** (1) Where the construction of a building or other structure that infringes or that, if completed, would infringe the copyright in some other work has been commenced, the owner of the copyright is not entitled to obtain an injunction in respect of the construction of that building or structure or to order its demolition.

Certain remedies inapplicable (2) Sections 38 and 42 do not apply in any case in respect of which subsection (1) applies. *R.S., 1985, c. C-42, s. 40; 1997, c. 24, s. 21.*

Limitation period for civil remedies **41.** (1) Subject to subsection (2), a court may not award a remedy in relation to an infringement unless

(a) in the case where the plaintiff knew, or could reasonably have been expected to know, of the infringement at the time it occurred, the proceedings for infringement are commenced within three years after the infringement occurred; or

(b) in the case where the plaintiff did not know, and could not reasonably have been expected to know, of the infringement at the time it occurred, the proceedings for infringement are commenced within three years after the time when the plaintiff first knew, or could reasonably have been expected to know, of the infringement.

Restriction (2) The court shall apply the limitation period set out in paragraph (1)(a) or (b) only in respect of a party who pleads a limitation period. *R.S., 1985, c. C-42, s. 41; R.S., 1985, c. 10 (4th Supp.), s. 9; 1997, c. 24, s. 22.*

Criminal Remedies

Offences and punishment **42.** (1) Every person who knowingly

(a) makes for sale or rental an infringing copy of a work or other subject-matter in which copyright subsists,

(b) sells or rents out, or by way of trade exposes or offers for sale or rental, an infringing copy of a work or other subject-matter in which copyright subsists,

(c) distributes infringing copies of a work or other subject-matter in which copyright subsists, either for the purpose of trade or to such an extent as to affect prejudicially the owner of the copyright,

(d) by way of trade exhibits in public an infringing copy of a work or other subject-matter in which copyright subsists, or

(e) imports for sale or rental into Canada any infringing copy of a work or other subject-matter in which copyright subsists

is guilty of an offence and liable

(f) on summary conviction, to a fine not exceeding twenty-five thousand dollars or to imprisonment for a term not exceeding six months or to both, or

(g) on conviction on indictment, to a fine not exceeding one million dollars or to imprisonment for a term not exceeding five years or to both.

Possession and performance offences and punishment

(2) Every person who knowingly

(a) makes or possesses any plate that is specifically designed or adapted for the purpose of making infringing copies of any work or other subject-matter in which copyright subsists, or

(b) for private profit causes to be performed in public, without the consent of the owner of the copyright, any work or other subject-matter in which copyright subsists

is guilty of an offence and liable

(c) on summary conviction, to a fine not exceeding twenty-five thousand dollars or to imprisonment for a term not exceeding six months or to both, or

(d) on conviction on indictment, to a fine not exceeding one million dollars or to imprisonment for a term not exceeding five years or to both.

Power of court to deal with copies or plates

(3) The court before which any proceedings under this section are taken may, on conviction, order that all copies of the work or other subject-matter that appear to it to be infringing copies, or all plates in the possession of the offender predominantly used for making infringing copies, be destroyed or delivered up to the owner of the copyright or otherwise dealt with as the court may think fit.

Limitation period

(4) Proceedings by summary conviction in respect of an offence under this section may be instituted at any time within, but not later than, two years after the time when the offence was committed.

Parallel importation of books

(5) No person may be prosecuted under this section for importing a book or deal-ing with an imported book in the manner described in section 27.1. *R.S., 1985, c. C-42, s. 42; R.S., 1985, c. 10 (4th Supp.), s. 10; 1997, c. 24, s. 24.*

43. (1) Any person who, without the written consent of the owner of the copyright or of the legal representative of the owner, knowingly performs or causes to be performed in public and for private profit the whole or any part, constituting an infringement, of any dramatic or operatic work or musical composition in which copyright subsists in Canada is guilty of an offence and liable on summary conviction to a fine not exceeding two hundred and fifty dollars and, in the case of a second or subsequent offence, either to that fine or to imprisonment for a term not exceeding two months or to both.

Infringement in case of dramatic, operatic or musical work

(2) Any person who makes or causes to be made any change in or suppression of the title, or the name of the author, of any dramatic or operatic work or musical composition in which copyright subsists in Canada, or who makes or causes to be made any change in the work or composition itself without the written consent of the author or of his legal representative, in order that the work or composition may be performed in whole or in part in public for private profit, is guilty of an offence and liable on summary conviction to a fine not exceeding five hundred dollars and, in the case of a second or subsequent offence, either to that fine or to imprisonment for a term not exceeding four months or to both. *R.S., c. C-30, s. 26.*

Change or suppression of title or author's name

43.1 *[Repealed, 1997, c. 24, s. 25]*

Importation

44. Copies made out of Canada of any work in which copyright subsists that if made in Canada would infringe copyright and as to which the owner of the copyright gives notice in writing to the Canada Customs and Revenue Agency that the owner desires that the copies not be so imported into Canada, shall not be so imported and are deemed to be included in tariff item No. 9897.00.00 in the List of Tariff Provisions set out in the schedule to

Importation of certain copyright works prohibited

the Customs Tariff, and section 136 of that Act applies accordingly. *R.S., 1985, c. C-42, s. 44; R.S., 1985, c. 41 (3rd Supp.), s. 116; 1997, c. 36, s. 205; 1999, c. 17, s. 119.*

Definitions **44.1** (1) In this section and sections 44.2 and 44.3,

"court" means the Federal Court or the superior court of a province;

"duties" has the same meaning as in the Customs Act;

"Minister" means the Minister of National Revenue;

"release" has the same meaning as in the Customs Act.

Power of court (2) A court may make an order described in subsection (3) where the court is satisfied that

(a) copies of the work are about to be imported into Canada, or have been imported into Canada but have not yet been released;

(b) either

(i) copies of the work were made without the consent of the person who then owned the copyright in the country where the copies were made, or

(ii) the copies were made elsewhere than in a country to which this Act extends; and

(c) the copies would infringe copyright if they were made in Canada by the importer and the importer knows or should have known this.

Who may apply (2.1) A court may make an order described in subsection (3) on application by the owner or exclusive licensee of copyright in a work in Canada.

Order of court (3) The order referred to in subsection (2) is an order

(a) directing the Minister

(i) to take reasonable measures, on the basis of information reasonably required by the Minister

and provided by the applicant, to detain the work, and

(ii) to notify the applicant and the importer, forthwith after detaining the work, of the detention and the reasons therefor; and

(b) providing for such other matters as the court considers appropriate.

How application made (4) An application for an order made under subsection (2) may be made in an action or otherwise, and either on notice or ex parte, except that it must always be made on notice to the Minister.

Court may require security (5) Before making an order under subsection (2), the court may require the applicant to furnish security, in an amount fixed by the court,

(a) to cover duties, storage and handling charges, and any other amount that may become chargeable against the work; and

(b) to answer any damages that may by reason of the order be incurred by the owner, importer or consignee of the work.

Application for directions (6) The Minister may apply to the court for directions in implementing an order made under subsection (2).

Minister may allow inspection (7) The Minister may give the applicant or the importer an opportunity to inspect the detained work for the purpose of substantiating or refuting, as the case may be, the applicant's claim.

Where applicant fails to commence an action (8) Unless an order made under subsection (2) provides otherwise, the Minister shall, subject to the Customs Act and to any other Act of Parliament that prohibits, controls or regulates the importation or exportation of goods, release the copies of the work without further notice to the applicant if, two weeks after the applicant has been notified under subparagraph (3)(a)(ii), the applicant has not notified the Minister that the applicant has commenced a proceeding for a final determination by the court of the issues referred to in paragraphs (2)(b) and (c).

Where court finds in plaintiff's favour

(9) Where, in a proceeding commenced under this section, the court finds that the circumstances referred to in paragraphs (2)(b) and (c) existed, the court may make any order that it considers appropriate in the circumstances, including an order that the copies of the work be destroyed, or that they be delivered up to the plaintiff as the plaintiff's property absolutely.

Other remedies not affected

(10) For greater certainty, nothing in this section affects any remedy available under any other provision of this Act or any other Act of Parliament. *1993, c. 44, s. 66; 1997, c. 24, s. 27.*

Importation of books

44.2 (1) A court may, subject to this section, make an order described in subsection 44.1(3) in relation to a book where the court is satisfied that

(a) copies of the book are about to be imported into Canada, or have been imported into Canada but have not yet been released;

(b) copies of the book were made with the consent of the owner of the copyright in the book in the country where the copies were made, but were imported without the consent of the owner in Canada of the copyright in the book; and

(c) the copies would infringe copyright if they were made in Canada by the importer and the importer knows or should have known this.

Who may apply

(2) A court may make an order described in subsection 44.1(3) in relation to a book on application by

(a) the owner of the copyright in the book in Canada;

(b) the exclusive licensee of the copyright in the book in Canada; or

(c) the exclusive distributor of the book.

Limitation

(3) Subsections (1) and (2) only apply where there is an exclusive distributor of the book and the acts described in those subsections take place in the part of Canada or in respect of the particular sector of the market for which the person is the exclusive distributor.

Application of certain provisions

(4) Subsections 44.1(3) to (10) apply, with such modifications as the circumstances require, in respect of an order made under subsection (1). *1994, c. 47, s. 66; 1997, c. 24, s. 28.*

Limitation

44.3 No exclusive licensee of the copyright in a book in Canada, and no exclusive distributor of a book, may obtain an order under section 44.2 against another exclusive licensee of the copyright in that book in Canada or against another exclusive distributor of that book. *1997, c. 24, s. 28.*

Importation of other subject-matter

44.4 Section 44.1 applies, with such modifications as the circumstances require, in respect of a sound recording, performer's performance or communication signal, where a fixation or a reproduction of a fixation of it

(a) is about to be imported into Canada, or has been imported into Canada but has not yet been released;

(b) either

(i) was made without the consent of the person who then owned the copyright in the sound recording, performer's performance or communication signal, as the case may be, in the country where the fixation or reproduction was made, or

(ii) was made elsewhere than in a country to which Part II extends; and

(c) would infringe the right of the owner of copyright in the sound recording, performer's performance or communication signal if it was made in Canada by the importer and the importer knows or should have known this. *1997, c. 24, s. 28.*

Exceptions

45. (1) Notwithstanding anything in this Act, it is lawful for a person

(a) to import for their own use not more than two copies of a work or other subject-matter made with the consent of the owner of the copyright in the country where it was made;

(b) to import for use by a department of the Government of Canada or a province copies of a work or other subject-matter made with the consent of the owner of the copyright in the country where it was made;

(c) at any time before copies of a work or other subject-matter are made in Canada, to import any copies, except copies of a book, made with the consent of the owner of the copyright in the country where the copies were made, that are required for the use of a library, archive, museum or educational institution;

(d) to import, for the use of a library, archive, museum or educational institution, not more than one copy of a book that is made with the consent of the owner of the copyright in the country where the book was made; and

(e) to import copies, made with the consent of the owner of the copyright in the country where they were made, of any used books, except textbooks of a scientific, technical or scholarly nature for use within an educational institution in a course of instruction.

Satisfactory evidence (2) An officer of customs may, in the officer's discretion, require a person seeking to import a copy of a work or other subject-matter under this section to produce satisfactory evidence of the facts necessary to establish the person's right to import the copy. *R.S., 1985, c. C-42, s. 45; R.S., 1985, c. 41 (3rd Supp.), s. 117; 1993, c. 44, s. 67; 1994, c. 47, s. 67; 1997, c. 24, s. 28.*

PART V

ADMINISTRATION

Copyright Office

46. The Copyright Office shall be attached to the Patent Office. *R.S., c. C-30, s. 29.*

Copyright Office

47. The Commissioner of Patents shall exercise the powers conferred and perform the duties imposed on him by this Act under the direction of the Minister, and, in the absence of the Commissioner of Patents or if the Commissioner is unable to act, the Registrar of Copyrights or other officer temporarily appointed by the Minister may, as Acting Commissioner, exercise those powers and perform those duties under the direction of the Minister. *R.S., c. C-30, s. 30.*

Powers of Commissioner and Registrar

48. There shall be a Registrar of Copyrights. *R.S., c. C-30, s. 31.*

Registrar

49. The Commissioner of Patents, the Registrar of Copyrights or an officer, clerk or employee of the Copyright Office may sign certificates and certified copies of the Register of Copyrights. *R.S., 1985, c. C-42, s. 49; 1992, c. 1, s. 47; 1993, c. 15, s. 4.*

Register of Copyrights, certificates and certified copies

50. The Registrar of Copyrights shall perform such other duties in connection with the administration of this Act as may be assigned to him by the Commissioner of Patents. *R.S., c. C-30, s. 33.*

Other duties of Registrar

51. *[Repealed, 1992, c. 1, s. 48]*

52. The Commissioner of Patents shall, subject to the Minister, oversee and direct the officers, clerks and employees of the Copyright Office, have general control of the business thereof and perform such other duties as are assigned to him by the Governor in Council. *R.S., c. C-30, s. 35.*

Control of Business and Officials

53. (1) The Register of Copyrights is evidence of the particulars entered in it, and a copy of an entry in the Register is evidence of the particulars of the entry if it is certified by the Commissioner of Patents, the Registrar of Copyrights or an officer, clerk or employee of the Copyright Office as a true copy.

Register to be evidence

Owner of copyright

(2) A certificate of registration of copyright is evidence that the copyright subsists and that the person registered is the owner of the copyright.

Assignee

(2.1) A certificate of registration of an assignment of copyright is evidence that the right recorded on the certificate has been assigned and that the assignee registered is the owner of that right.

Licensee

(2.2) A certificate of registration of a licence granting an interest in a copyright is evidence that the interest recorded on the certificate has been granted and that the licensee registered is the holder of that interest.

Admissibility

(3) A certified copy or certificate appearing to have been issued under this section is admissible in all courts without proof of the signature or official character of the person appearing to have signed it. *R.S., 1985, c. C-42, s. 53; 1992, c. 1, s. 49; 1993, c. 15, s. 5; 1997, c. 24, s. 30.*

Registration

Register of Copyrights

54. (1) The Minister shall cause to be kept at the Copyright Office a register to be called the Register of Copyrights in which may be entered

(a) the names or titles of works and of other subject-matter in which copyright subsists;

(b) the names and addresses of authors, performers, makers of sound recordings, broadcasters, owners of copyright, assignees of copyright, and persons to whom an interest in copyright has been granted by licence; and

(c) such other particulars as may be prescribed by regulation.

(2) *[Repealed, 1997, c. 24, s. 31]*

Single entry sufficient

(3) In the case of an encyclopaedia, newspaper, review, magazine or other periodical work, or work published in a series of books or parts, it is not necessary to make a separate entry for each number or part, but a single entry for the whole work is sufficient.

Indices

(4) There shall also be kept at the Copyright Office such indices of the Register established under this section as may be prescribed by regulation.

Inspection and extracts

(5) The Register and indices established under this section shall at all reasonable times be open to inspection, and any person is entitled to make copies of or take extracts from the Register.

Former registration effective

(6) Any registration made under the Copyright Act, chapter 70 of the Revised Statutes of Canada, 1906, has the same force and effect as if made under this Act.

Subsisting copyright

(7) Any work in which copyright, operative in Canada, subsisted immediately before January 1, 1924 is registrable under this Act. *R.S., 1985, c. C-42, s. 54; 1992, c. 1, s. 50; 1997, c. 24, s. 31.*

Copyright in works

55. (1) Application for the registration of a copyright in a work may be made by or on behalf of the author of the work, the owner of the copyright in the work, an assignee of the copyright, or a person to whom an interest in the copyright has been granted by licence.

Application for registration

(2) An application under subsection (1) must be filed with the Copyright Office, be accompanied by the fee prescribed by or determined under the regulations, and contain the following information:

(a) the name and address of the owner of the copyright in the work;

(b) a declaration that the applicant is the author of the work, the owner of the copyright in the work, an assignee of the copyright, or a person to whom an interest in the copyright has been granted by licence;

(c) the category of the work;

(d) the title of the work;

(e) the name of the author and, if the author is dead, the date of the author's death, if known;

(f) in the case of a published work, the date and place of the first publication; and

(g) any additional information pre-scribed by regulation. *R.S., 1985, c. C-42, s. 55; 1997, c. 24, s. 32.*

Copyright in subject-matter other than works
56. (1) Application for the registration of a copyright in subject-matter other than a work may be made by or on behalf of the owner of the copyright in the subject-matter, an assignee of the copyright, or a person to whom an interest in the copyright has been granted by licence.

Application for registration
(2) An application under subsection (1) must be filed with the Copyright Office, be accompanied by the fee prescribed by or determined under the regulations, and contain the following information:

(a) the name and address of the owner of the copyright in the subject-matter;

(b) a declaration that the applicant is the owner of the copyright in the subject-matter, an assignee of the copyright, or a person to whom an interest in the copyright has been granted by licence;

(c) whether the subject-matter is a per-former's performance, a sound recording or a communication signal;

(d) the title, if any, of the subject-matter;

(e) the date of

(i) in the case of a performer's per-formance, its first fixation in a sound recording or, if it is not fixed in a sound recording, its first performance,

(ii) in the case of a sound recording, the first fixation, or

(iii) in the case of a communication signal, its broadcast; and

(f) any additional information pre-scribed by regulation. *R.S., 1985, c. C-42, s. 56; 1993, c. 15, s. 6; 1997, c. 24, s. 32.*

Recovery of damages
56.1 Where a person purports to have the authority to apply for the registration of a copyright under section 55 or 56 on behalf of another person, any damage caused by a fraudulent or erroneous assumption of such authority is recoverable in any court of competent jurisdiction. *1997, c. 24, s. 32.*

Registration of assign-ment or licence
57. (1) The Registrar of Copyrights shall register an assignment of copyright, or a licence granting an interest in a copyright, on being furnished with

(a) the original instrument or a certi-fied copy of it, or other evidence satisfactory to the Registrar of the assignment or licence; and

(b) the fee prescribed by or determined under the regulations.

(2) [Repealed, 1992, c. 1, s. 51]

When assign-ment or licence is void
(3) Any assignment of copyright, or any licence granting an interest in a copyright, shall be adjudged void against any subse-quent assignee or licensee for valuable consideration without actual notice, unless the prior assignment or licence is regis-tered in the manner prescribed by this Act before the registering of the instrument under which the subsequent assignee or licensee claims.

Rectification of Register by the Court
(4) The Federal Court may, on applica-tion of the Registrar of Copyrights or of any interested person, order the rectifica-tion of the Register of Copyrights by

(a) the making of any entry wrongly omitted to be made in the Register,

(b) the expunging of any entry wrongly made in or remaining on the Register, or

(c) the correction of any error or defect in the Register,

and any rectification of the Register under this subsection shall be retroactive from such date as the Court may order. *R.S., 1985, c. C-42, s. 57; 1992, c. 1, s. 51; 1993, c. 15, s. 7; 1997, c. 24, s. 33.*

Execution of instruments
58. (1) Any assignment of copyright, or any licence granting an interest in a copyright, may be executed, subscribed or acknowl-edged at any place in a treaty country or a Rome Convention country by the assignor, licensor or mortgagor, before any notary public, commissioner or other official or the judge of any court, who is authorized by law to administer oaths or perform notarial acts in that place, and who also subscribes their signature and affixes thereto or

impresses thereon their official seal or the seal of the court of which they are such judge.

Execution of instruments
(2) Any assignment of copyright, or any licence granting an interest in a copyright, may be executed, subscribed or acknowledged by the assignor, licensor or mortgagor, in any other foreign country before any notary public, commissioner or other official or the judge of any court of the foreign country, who is authorized to administer oaths or perform notarial acts in that foreign country and whose authority shall be proved by the certificate of a diplomatic or consular officer of Canada performing their functions in that foreign country.

Seals to be evidence
(3) The official seal or seal of the court or the certificate of a diplomatic or consular officer is evidence of the execution of the instrument, and the instrument with the seal or certificate affixed or attached thereto is admissible as evidence in any action or proceeding brought under this Act without further proof.

Other testimony
(4) The provisions of subsections (1) and (2) shall be deemed to be permissive only, and the execution of any assignment of copyright, or any licence granting an interest in a copyright, may in any case be proved in accordance with the applicable rules of evidence. *R.S., 1985, c. C-42, s. 58; 1997, c. 24, s. 34.*

Fees

Fees regulations
59. The Governor in Council may make regulations

(a) prescribing fees, or the manner of determining fees, to be paid for anything required or authorized to be done in the administration of this Act; and

(b) prescribing the time and manner in which the fees must be paid. *R.S., 1985, c. C-42, s. 59; 1993, c. 15, s. 8.*

PART VI

MISCELLANEOUS PROVISIONS

Substituted Right

Subsistence of substituted right
60. (1) Where any person is immediately before January 1, 1924 entitled to any right in any work that is set out in column I of Schedule I, or to any interest in such a right, he is, as from that date, entitled to the substituted right set out in column II of that Schedule, or to the same interest in the substituted right, and to no other right or interest, and the substituted right shall subsist for the term for which it would have subsisted if this Act had been in force at the date when the work was made, and the work had been one entitled to copyright thereunder.

Where author has assigned the right
(2) Where the author of any work in which any right that is set out in column I of Schedule I subsists on January 1, 1924 has, before that date, assigned the right or granted any interest therein for the whole term of the right, then at the date when, but for the passing of this Act, the right would have expired, the substituted right conferred by this section shall, in the absence of express agreement, pass to the author of the work, and any interest therein created before January 1, 1924 and then subsisting shall determine, but the person who immediately before the date at which the right would have expired was the owner of the right or interest is entitled at his option either

(a) on giving such notice as is hereinafter mentioned, to an assignment of the right or the grant of a similar interest therein for the remainder of the term of the right for such consideration as, failing agreement, may be determined by arbitration, or

(b) without any assignment or grant, to continue to reproduce or perform the work in like manner as theretofore subject to the payment, if demanded by the author within three years after the date at which the right would have expired, of such royalties to the author as, failing agreement, may be determined by arbitration, or, where the work is incorporated in a collective work and the owner of the right or interest is the proprietor of that collective work, without any payment,

and the notice referred to in paragraph (a) must be given not more than one year or less than six months before the date at which the right would have expired, and must be sent by registered post to the author, or, if he cannot with reasonable diligence be found, advertised in the Canada Gazette.

Definition of "author" (3) For the purposes of this section, "author" includes the legal representatives of a deceased author.

Works made before this Act in force (4) Subject to this Act, copyright shall not subsist in any work made before January 1, 1924 otherwise than under and in accordance with the provisions of this section. *R.S., 1985, c. C-42, s. 60; R.S., 1985, c. 10 (4th Supp.), s. 17(F); 1997, c. 24, s. 52(F).*

Clerical Errors

Clerical errors do not invalidate **61.** Clerical errors in any instrument of record in the Copyright Office do not invalidate the instrument, but they may be corrected under the authority of the Registrar of Copyrights. *R.S., 1985, c. C-42, s. 61; 1992, c. 1, s. 52; 1993, c. 15, s. 10.*

Regulations

Regulations **62.** (1) The Governor in Council may make regulations

(a) prescribing anything that by this Act is to be prescribed by regulation; and

(b) generally for carrying out the purposes and provisions of this Act.

Rights saved (2) The Governor in Council may make orders for altering, revoking or varying any order in council made under this Act, but any order made under this section does not affect prejudicially any rights or interests acquired or accrued at the date when the order comes into operation, and shall provide for the protection of those rights and interests. *R.S., 1985, c. C-42, s. 62; 1997, c. 24, s. 37.*

63. *[Repealed, 1997, c. 24, s. 38]*

64. (1) In this section and section 64.1,

"article" means any thing that is made by hand, tool or machine;

"design" means features of shape, configuration, pattern or ornament and any combination of those features that, in a finished article, appeal to and are judged solely by the eye;

"useful article" means an article that has a utilitarian function and includes a model of any such article;

"utilitarian function", in respect of an article, means a function other than merely serving as a substrate or carrier for artistic or literary matter.

Non-infringement re certain designs (2) Where copyright subsists in a design applied to a useful article or in an artistic work from which the design is derived and, by or under the authority of any person who owns the copyright in Canada or who owns the copyright elsewhere,

(a) the article is reproduced in a quantity of more than fifty, or

(b) where the article is a plate, engraving or cast, the article is used for producing more than fifty useful articles,

it shall not thereafter be an infringement of the copyright or the moral rights for anyone

(c) to reproduce the design of the article or a design not differing substantially from the design of the article by

(i) making the article, or

(ii) making a drawing or other reproduction in any material form of the article, or

(d) to do with an article, drawing or reproduction that is made as described in paragraph (c) anything that the owner of the copyright has the sole right to do with the design or artistic work in which the copyright subsists.

Exception (3) Subsection (2) does not apply in respect of the copyright or the moral rights in an artistic work in so far as the work is used as or for

(a) a graphic or photographic representation that is applied to the face of an article;

(b) a trade-mark or a representation thereof or a label;

(c) material that has a woven or knitted pattern or that is suitable for piece goods or surface coverings or for making wearing apparel;

(d) an architectural work that is a building or a model of a building;

(e) a representation of a real or fictitious being, event or place that is applied to an article as a feature of shape, configuration, pattern or ornament;

(f) articles that are sold as a set, unless more than fifty sets are made; or

(g) such other work or article as may be prescribed by regulation.

Idem (4) Subsections (2) and (3) apply only in respect of designs created after the coming into force of this subsection, and section 64 of this Act and the Industrial Design Act, as they read immediately before the coming into force of this subsection, as well as the rules made under them, continue to apply in respect of designs created before that coming into force. *R.S., 1985, c. C-42, s. 64; R.S., 1985, c. 10 (4th Supp.), s. 11; 1993, c. 44, s. 68; 1997, c. 24, s. 39.*

Non-infringement re useful article features **64.1** (1) The following acts do not constitute an infringement of the copyright or moral rights in a work:

(a) applying to a useful article features that are dictated solely by a utilitarian function of the article;

(b) by reference solely to a useful article, making a drawing or other reproduction in any material form of any features of the article that are dictated solely by a utilitarian function of the article;

(c) doing with a useful article having only features described in paragraph (a), or with a drawing or reproduction made as described in paragraph (b), anything that the owner of the copyright has the sole right to do with the work; and

(d) using any method or principle of manufacture or construction.

(2) Nothing in subsection (1) affects Exception

(a) the copyright, or

(b) the moral rights, if any,

in any sound recording, cinematograph film or other contrivance by means of which a work may be mechanically reproduced or performed. *R.S., 1985, c. 10 (4th Supp.), s. 11; 1997, c. 24, s. 40.*

64.2 (1) This Act does not apply, and shall be deemed never to have applied, to any topography or to any design, however expressed, that is intended to generate all or part of a topography. Application of Act to topographies

(2) For greater certainty, the incorporation of a computer program into an integrated circuit product or the incorporation of a work into such a computer program may constitute an infringement of the copyright or moral rights in a work. Computer programs

(3) In this section, "topography" and "integrated circuit product" have the same meaning as in the Integrated Circuit Topography Act. *1990, c. 37, s. 33.* Definitions

65. *[Repealed, 1993, c. 44, s. 69]*

PART VII

COPYRIGHT BOARD AND COLLECTIVE ADMINISTRATION OF COPYRIGHT

Copyright Board

66. (1) There is hereby established a Board, to be known as the Copyright Board, consisting of not more than five members, including a chairman and a vice-chairman, to be appointed by the Governor in Council. Establishment

Service   (2) The members of the Board shall be appointed to serve either full-time or part-time.

Chairman   (3) The chairman must be a judge, either sitting or retired, of a superior, county or district court.

Tenure   (4) Each member of the Board shall hold office during good behaviour for a term not exceeding five years, but may be removed at any time by the Governor in Council for cause.

Re-appointment   (5) A member of the Board is eligible to be re-appointed once only.

Prohibition   (6) A member of the Board shall not be employed in the Public Service within the meaning of the Public Service Staff Relations Act during the member's term of office.

Members deemed public service employees   (7) A full-time member of the Board, other than the chairman, shall be deemed to be employed in

(a) the Public Service for the purposes of the Public Service Superannuation Act; and

(b) the public service of Canada for the purposes of any regulations made pursuant to section 9 of the Aeronautics Act. R.S., 1985, c. C-42, s. 66; R.S., 1985, c. 10 (1st Supp.), s. 1, c. 10 (4th Supp.), s. 12.

Duties of chairman   **66.1** (1) The chairman shall direct the work of the Board and apportion its work among the members of the Board.

Absence or incapacity of chairman   (2) If the chairman is absent or incapacitated or if the office of chairman is vacant, the vice-chairman has all the powers and functions of the chairman during the absence, incapacity or vacancy.

Duties of vice-chairman   (3) The vice-chairman is the chief executive officer of the Board and has supervision over and direction of the Board and its staff. R.S., 1985, c. 10 (4th Supp.), s. 12.

Remuneration and expenses   **66.2** The members of the Board shall be paid such remuneration as may be fixed by the Governor in Council and are entitled to be paid reasonable travel and living

expenses incurred by them in the course of their duties under this Act while absent from their ordinary place of residence. R.S., 1985, c. 10 (4th Supp.), s. 12.

Conflict of interest prohibited   **66.3** (1) A member of the Board shall not, directly or indirectly, engage in any activity, have any interest in a business or accept or engage in any office or employment that is inconsistent with the member's duties.

Termination of conflict of interest   (2) Where a member of the Board becomes aware that he is in a conflict of interest contrary to subsection (1), the member shall, within one hundred and twenty days, terminate the conflict or resign. R.S., 1985, c. 10 (4th Supp.), s. 12.

Staff   **66.4** (1) Such officers and employees as are necessary for the proper conduct of the work of the Board shall be appointed in accordance with the Public Service Employment Act.

Idem   (2) The officers and employees referred to in subsection (1) shall be deemed to be employed in the Public Service for the purposes of the Public Service Superannuation Act.

Technical assistance   (3) The Board may engage on a temporary basis the services of persons having technical or specialized knowledge to advise and assist in the performance of its duties and the Board may, in accordance with Treasury Board directives, fix and pay the remuneration and expenses of those persons. R.S., 1985, c. 10 (4th Supp.), s. 12.

Concluding matters after membership expires   **66.5** (1) A member of the Board whose term expires may conclude the matters that the member has begun to consider.

Decisions   (2) Matters before the Board shall be decided by a majority of the members of the Board and the presiding member shall have a second vote in the case of a tie. R.S., 1985, c. 10 (4th Supp.), s. 12.

Interim decisions   **66.51** The Board may, on application, make an interim decision. R.S., 1985, c. 10 (4th Supp.), s. 12.

Variation of decisions   **66.52** A decision of the Board respecting royalties or their related terms and conditions that is made under subsection 68(3), sections 68.1 or 70.15 or or subsections 70.2(2), 70.6(1), 73(1) or 83(8) may, on application, be varied by the Board if, in its opinion, there has been a material change in circumstances since the decision was made. *R.S., 1985, c. 10 (4th Supp.), s. 12; 1988, c. 65, s. 64; 1997, c. 24, s. 42.*

Regulations **66.6** (1) The Board may, with the approval of the Governor in Council, make regulations governing

(a) the practice and procedure in respect of the Board's hearings, including the number of members of the Board that constitutes a quorum;

(b) the time and manner in which applications and notices must be made or given;

(c) the establishment of forms for the making or giving of applications and notices; and

(d) the carrying out of the work of the Board, the management of its internal affairs and the duties of its officers and employees.

Publication of proposed regulations (2) A copy of each regulation that the Board proposes to make under subsection (1) shall be published in the Canada Gazette at least sixty days before the proposed effective date thereof and a reasonable opportunity shall be given to interested persons to make representations with respect thereto.

Exception (3) No proposed regulation that has been published pursuant to subsection (2) need again be published under that subsection, whether or not it has been altered as a result of representations made with respect thereto. *R.S., 1985, c. 10 (4th Supp.), s. 12.*

General powers, etc. **66.7** (1) The Board has, with respect to the attendance, swearing and examination of witnesses, the production and inspection of documents, the enforcement of its decisions and other matters necessary or proper for the due exercise of its jurisdiction, all such powers, rights and privileges as are vested in a superior court of record.

Enforcement of decisions (2) Any decision of the Board may, for the purposes of its enforcement, be made an order of the Federal Court or of any superior court and is enforceable in the same manner as an order thereof.

Procedure (3) To make a decision of the Board an order of a court, the usual practice and procedure of the court in such matters may be followed or a certified copy of the decision may be filed with the registrar of the court and thereupon the decision becomes an order of the court.

Effect of variation of decision (4) Where a decision of the Board that has been made an order of a court is varied by a subsequent decision of the Board, the order of the court shall be deemed to have been varied accordingly and the subsequent decision may, in the same manner, be made an order of the court. *R.S., 1985, c. 10 (4th Supp.), s. 12.*

Distribution, publication of notices **66.71** Independently of any other provision of this Act relating to the distribution or publication of information or documents by the Board, the Board may at any time cause to be distributed or published, in any manner and on any terms and conditions that it sees fit, any notice that it sees fit to be distributed or published. *1997, c. 24, s. 43.*

Studies **66.8** The Board shall conduct such studies with respect to the exercise of its powers as are requested by the Minister. *R.S., 1985, c. 10 (4th Supp.), s. 12.*

Report **66.9** (1) The Board shall, not later than August 31 in each year, submit to the Governor in Council through the Minister an annual report on the Board's activities for the preceding year describing briefly the applications made to the Board, the Board's decisions and any other matter that the Board considers relevant.

Tabling (2) The Minister shall cause a copy of each annual report to be laid before each House of Parliament on any of the first fifteen days on which that House is sitting after the Minister receives the report. *R.S., 1985, c. 10 (4th Supp.), s. 12.*

Regulations **66.91** The Governor in Council may make regulations issuing policy directions to the Board and establishing general criteria to be applied by the Board or to which the Board must have regard

(a) in establishing fair and equitable royalties to be paid pursuant to this Act; and

(b) in rendering its decisions in any matter within its jurisdiction. *1997, c. 24, s. 44.*

Collective Administration of Performing Rights and of Communication Rights

Public access to repertoires **67.** Each collective society that carries on

(a) the business of granting licences or collecting royalties for the performance in public of musical works, dramatico-musical works, performer's performances of such works, or sound recordings embodying such works, or

(b) the business of granting licences or collecting royalties for the communication to the public by telecommunication of musical works, dramatico-musical works, performer's performances of such works, or sound recordings embodying such works, other than the communication of musical works or dramatico-musical works in a manner described in subsection 31(2),

must answer within a reasonable time all reasonable requests from the public for information about its repertoire of works, performer's performances or sound recordings, that are in current use. *R.S., 1985, c. C-42, s. 67; R.S., 1985, c. 10 (1st Supp.), s. 1, c. 10 (4th Supp.), s. 12; 1993, c. 23, s. 3; 1997, c. 24, s. 45.*

Filing of proposed tariffs **67.1** (1) Each collective society referred to in section 67 shall, on or before the March 31 immediately before the date when its last tariff approved pursuant to subsection 68(3) expires, file with the Board a proposed tariff, in both official languages, of all royalties to be collected by the collective society.

(2) A collective society referred to in subsection (1) in respect of which no tariff has been approved pursuant to subsection 68(3) shall file with the Board its proposed tariff, in both official languages, of all royalties to be collected by it, on or before the March 31 immediately before its proposed effective date.

Where no previous tariff

(3) A proposed tariff must provide that the royalties are to be effective for periods of one or more calendar years.

Effective period of tariffs

(4) Where a proposed tariff is not filed with respect to the work, performer's performance or sound recording in question, no action may be commenced, without the written consent of the Minister, for

Prohibition of enforcement

(a) the infringement of the rights, referred to in section 3, to perform in public or to communicate to the public by telecommunication, the work, performer's performance or sound recording; or

(b) the recovery of royalties referred to in section 19.

(5) As soon as practicable after the receipt of a proposed tariff filed pursuant to subsection (1), the Board shall publish it in the Canada Gazette and shall give notice that, within sixty days after the publication of the tariff, prospective users or their representatives may file written objections to the tariff with the Board. *R.S., 1985, c. 10 (4th Supp.), s. 12; 1997, c. 24, s. 45.*

Publication of proposed tariffs

67.2 and **67.3** *[Repealed, 1997, c. 24, s. 45]*

68. (1) The Board shall, as soon as practicable, consider a proposed tariff and any objections thereto referred to in subsection 67.1(5) or raised by the Board, and

Board to consider proposed tariffs and objections

(a) send to the collective society concerned a copy of the objections so as to permit it to reply; and

(b) send to the persons who filed the objections a copy of any reply thereto.

(2) In examining a proposed tariff for the performance in public or the communication to the public by telecommunication of performer's performances of musical works, or of sound recordings embodying

Criteria and factors

such performer's performances, the Board

(a) shall ensure that

   (i) the tariff applies in respect of performer's performances and sound recordings only in the situations referred to in subsections 20(1) and (2),

   (ii) the tariff does not, because of linguistic and content requirements of Canada's broadcasting policy set out in section 3 of the Broadcasting Act, place some users that are subject to that Act at a greater financial disadvantage than others, and

   (iii) the payment of royalties by users pursuant to section 19 will be made in a single payment; and

(b) may take into account any factor that it considers appropriate.

Certification (3) The Board shall certify the tariffs as approved, with such alterations to the royalties and to the terms and conditions related thereto as the Board considers necessary, having regard to

(a) any objections to the tariffs under subsection 67.1(5); and

(b) the matters referred to in subsection (2).

Publication of approved tariffs (4) The Board shall

(a) publish the approved tariffs in the Canada Gazette as soon as practicable; and

(b) send a copy of each approved tariff, together with the reasons for the Board's decision, to each collective society that filed a proposed tariff and to any person who filed an objection. *R.S., 1985, c. C-42, s. 68; R.S., 1985, c. 10 (4th Supp.), s. 13; 1993, c. 23, s. 5; 1997, c. 24, s. 45.*

Special and transitional royalty rates **68.1** (1) Notwithstanding the tariffs approved by the Board under subsection 68(3) for the performance in public or the communication to the public by telecommunication of performer's performances of musical works, or of sound recordings

embodying such performer's performances,

(a) wireless transmission systems, except community systems and public transmission systems, shall pay royalties as follows:

   (i) in respect of each year, $100 on the first 1.25 million dollars of annual advertising revenues, and

   (ii) on any portion of annual advertising revenues exceeding 1.25 million dollars,

     (A) for the first year following the coming into force of this section, thirty-three and one third per cent of the royalties set out in the approved tariff for that year,

     (B) for the second year following the coming into force of this section, sixty-six and two thirds per cent of the royalties set out in the approved tariff for that year, and

     (C) for the third year following the coming into force of this section, one hundred per cent of the royalties set out in the approved tariff for that year;

(b) community systems shall pay royalties of $100 in respect of each year; and

(c) public transmission systems shall pay royalties, in respect of each of the first three years following the coming into force of this section, as follows:

   (i) for the first year following the coming into force of this section, thirty-three and one third per cent of the royalties set out in the approved tariff for that year,

   (ii) for the second year following the coming into force of this section, sixty-six and two thirds per cent of the royalties set out in the approved tariff for that year, and

(iii) for the third year following the coming into force of this section, one hundred per cent of the royalties set out in the approved tariff for that year.

Effect of paying royalties

(2) The payment of the royalties set out in subsection (1) fully discharges all liabilities of the system in question in respect of the approved tariffs.

Definition of "advertising revenues"

(3) The Board may, by regulation, define "advertising revenues" for the purposes of subsection (1).

Preferential royalty rates

(4) The Board shall, in certifying a tariff as approved under subsection 68(3), ensure that there is a preferential royalty rate for small cable transmission systems.

Regulations

(5) The Governor in Council may make regulations defining "small cable transmission system", "community system", "public transmission system" and "wireless transmission system" for the purposes of this section. *1997, c. 24, s. 45.*

Effect of fixing royalties

68.2 (1) Without prejudice to any other remedies available to it, a collective society may, for the period specified in its approved tariff, collect the royalties specified in the tariff and, in default of their payment, recover them in a court of competent jurisdiction.

Proceedings barred if royalties tendered or paid

(2) No proceedings may be brought for

(a) the infringement of the right to perform in public or the right to communicate to the public by telecommunication, referred to in section 3, or

(b) the recovery of royalties referred to in section 19

Continuation of rights

against a person who has paid or offered to pay the royalties specified in an approved tariff.

(3) Where a collective society files a proposed tariff in accordance with subsection 67.1(1),

(a) any person entitled to perform in public or communicate to the public by telecommunication those works, performer's performances or

sound recordings pursuant to the previous tariff may do so, even though the royalties set out therein have ceased to be in effect, and

(b) the collective society may collect the royalties in accordance with the previous tariff,

until the proposed tariff is approved. *1997, c. 24, s. 45.*

Public Performance in Places Other Than Theatres

69. (1) [Repealed, R.S., 1985, c. 10 (4th Supp.), s. 14]

Radio performances in places other than theatres

(2) In respect of public performances by means of any radio receiving set in any place other than a theatre that is ordinarily and regularly used for entertainments to which an admission charge is made, no royalties shall be collectable from the owner or user of the radio receiving set, but the Board shall, in so far as possible, provide for the collection in advance from radio broadcasting stations of royalties appropriate to the conditions produced by the provisions of this subsection and shall fix the amount of the same.

Expenses to be taken into account

(3) In fixing royalties pursuant to subsection (2), the Board shall take into account all expenses of collection and other outlays, if any, saved or savable by, for or on behalf of the owner of the copyright or performing right concerned or his agents, in consequence of subsection (2).

(4) *[Repealed, R.S., 1985, c. 10 (4th Supp.), s. 14] R.S., 1985, c. C-42, s. 69; R.S., 1985, c. 10 (4th Supp.), s. 14; 1993, c. 44, s. 73; 1997, c. 24, s. 52(F).*

70. *[Repealed, R.S., 1985, c. 10 (4th Supp.), s. 15]*

Collective Administration in Relation to Rights under Sections 3, 15, 18 and 21

Collective Societies

70.1 Sections 70.11 to 70.6 apply in respect of a collective society that operates

Collective societies

(a) a licensing scheme, applicable in relation to a repertoire of works of more than one author, pursuant to which the society sets out the classes of uses for which and the royalties and terms and conditions on which it agrees to authorize the doing of an act mentioned in section 3 in respect of those works;

(a.1) a licensing scheme, applicable in relation to a repertoire of performer's performances of more than one performer, pursuant to which the society sets out the classes of uses for which and the royalties and terms and conditions on which it agrees to authorize the doing of an act mentioned in section 15 in respect of those performer's performances;

(b) a licensing scheme, applicable in relation to a repertoire of sound recordings of more than one maker, pursuant to which the society sets out the classes of uses for which and the royalties and terms and conditions on which it agrees to authorize the doing of an act mentioned in section 18 in respect of those sound recordings; or

(c) a licensing scheme, applicable in relation to a repertoire of communication signals of more than one broadcaster, pursuant to which the society sets out the classes of uses for which and the royalties and terms and conditions on which it agrees to authorize the doing of an act mentioned in section 21 in respect of those communication signals. R.S., 1985, c. 10 (4th Supp.), s. 16; 1997, c. 24, s. 46.

Public information **70.11** A collective society referred to in section 70.1 must answer within a reasonable time all reasonable requests from the public for information about its repertoire of works, performer's performances, sound recordings or communication signals. 1997, c. 24, s. 46.

Tariff or agreement **70.12** A collective society may, for the purpose of setting out by licence the royalties and terms and conditions relating to classes of uses,

(a) file a proposed tariff with the Board; or

(b) enter into agreements with users. 1997, c. 24, s. 46.

Tariffs

70.13 (1) Each collective society referred to in section 70.1 may, on or before the March 31 immediately before the date when its last tariff approved pursuant to subsection 70.15(1) expires, file with the Board a proposed tariff, in both official languages, of royalties to be collected by the collective society for issuing licences. **Filing of proposed tariffs**

(2) A collective society referred to in subsection (1) in respect of which no tariff has been approved pursuant to subsection 70.15(1) shall file with the Board its proposed tariff, in both official languages, of all royalties to be collected by it for issuing licences, on or before the March 31 immediately before its proposed effective date. 1997, c. 24, s. 46. **Where no previous tariff**

70.14 Where a proposed tariff is filed under section 70.13, subsections 67.1(3) and (5) and subsection 68(1) apply, with such modifications as the circumstances require. 1997, c. 24, s. 46. **Application of certain provisions**

70.15 (1) The Board shall certify the tariffs as approved, with such alterations to the royalties and to the terms and conditions related thereto as the Board considers necessary, having regard to any objections to the tariffs. **Certification**

(2) Where a tariff is approved under subsection (1), subsections 68(4) and 68.2(1) apply, with such modifications as the circumstances require. 1997, c. 24, s. 46. **Application of certain provisions**

70.16 Independently of any other provision of this Act relating to the distribution or publication of information or documents by the Board, the Board shall notify persons affected by a proposed tariff, by **Distribution, publication of notices**

(a) distributing or publishing a notice, or

(b) directing another person or body to distribute or publish a notice, in such manner and on such terms and conditions as the Board sees fit. *1997, c. 24, s. 46.*

Prohibition of enforcement **70.17** Subject to section 70.19, no proceedings may be brought for the infringement of a right referred to in section 3, 15, 18 or 21 against a person who has paid or offered to pay the royalties specified in an approved tariff. *1997, c. 24, s. 46.*

Continuation of rights **70.18** Subject to section 70.19, where a collective society files a proposed tariff in accordance with section 70.13,

(a) any person authorized by the collective society to do an act referred to in section 3, 15, 18 or 21, as the case may be, pursuant to the previous tariff may do so, even though the royalties set out therein have ceased to be in effect, and

(b) the collective society may collect the royalties in accordance with the previous tariff,

until the proposed tariff is approved. *1997, c. 24, s. 46.*

Where agreement exists **70.19** If there is an agreement mentioned in paragraph 70.12(b), sections 70.17 and 70.18 do not apply in respect of the matters covered by the agreement. *1997, c. 24, s. 46.*

Agreement **70.191** An approved tariff does not apply where there is an agreement between a collective society and a person authorized to do an act mentioned in section 3, 15, 18 or 21, as the case may be, if the agreement is in effect during the period covered by the approved tariff. *1997, c. 24, s. 46.*

Fixing of Royalties in Individual Cases

Application to fix amount of royalty, etc. **70.2** (1) Where a collective society and any person not otherwise authorized to do an act mentioned in section 3, 15, 18 or 21, as the case may be, in respect of the works, sound recordings or communication signals included in the collective society's repertoire are unable to agree on the royalties to be paid for the right to do the act or on their related terms and conditions, either of them or a representative of either may, after giving notice to the other, apply to the Board to fix the royalties and their related terms and conditions.

Fixing royalties, etc. (2) The Board may fix the royalties and their related terms and conditions in respect of a licence during such period of not less than one year as the Board may specify and, as soon as practicable after rendering its decision, the Board shall send a copy thereof, together with the reasons therefor, to the collective society and the person concerned or that person's representative. *R.S., 1985, c. 10 (4th Supp.), s. 16; 1997, c. 24, s. 46.*

Agreement **70.3** (1) The Board shall not proceed with an application under section 70.2 where a notice is filed with the Board that an agreement touching the matters in issue has been reached.

Idem (2) An agreement referred to in subsection (1) is effective during the year following the expiration of the previous agreement, if any, or of the last period specified under subsection 70.2(2). *R.S., 1985, c. 10 (4th Supp.), s. 16.*

Effect of Board decision **70.4** Where any royalties are fixed for a period pursuant to subsection 70.2(2), the person concerned may, during the period, subject to the related terms and conditions fixed by the Board and to the terms and conditions set out in the scheme and on paying or offering to pay the royalties, do the act with respect to which the royalties and their related terms and conditions are fixed and the collective society may, without prejudice to any other remedies available to it, collect the royalties or, in default of their payment, recover them in a court of competent jurisdiction. *R.S., 1985, c. 10 (4th Supp.), s. 16; 1997, c. 24, s. 47.*

Examination of Agreements

Definition of "Commissi·" **70.5** (1) For the purposes of this section and section 70.6, "Commissioner" means the Commissioner of Competition appointed under the Competition Act.

Filing agreement with the Board (2) Where a collective society concludes an agreement to grant a licence authorizing a person to do an act mentioned in section 3, 15, 18 or 21, as the case may be, the collective society or the person may file a copy of the agreement with the Board within fifteen days after it is concluded.

Idem (3) Section 45 of the Competition Act does not apply in respect of any royalties or related terms and conditions arising under an agreement filed in accordance with subsection (2).

Access by missioner (4) The Commissioner may have access to the copy of an agreement filed in accordance with subsection (2).

quest for mination (5) Where the Commissioner considers that an agreement filed in accordance with subsection (2) is contrary to the public interest, the Commissioner may, after advising the parties concerned, request the Board to examine the agreement. *R.S., 1985, c. 10 (4th Supp.), s. 16; 1997, c. 24, s. 48; 1999, c. 2, ss. 45, 46.*

mination nd fixing ⌐f royalty **70.6** (1) The Board shall, as soon as practicable, consider a request by the Commissioner to examine an agreement and the Board may, after giving the Commissioner and the parties concerned an opportunity to present their arguments, alter the royalties and any related terms and conditions arising under the agreement, in which case section 70.4 applies with such modifications as the circumstances require.

Idem (2) As soon as practicable after rendering its decision, the Board shall send a copy thereof, together with the reasons therefor, to the parties concerned and to the Commissioner. *R.S., 1985, c. 10 (4th Supp.), s. 16; 1997, c. 24, s. 49(F); 1999, c. 2, s. 46.*

70.61 to 70.8 *[Repealed, 1997, c. 24, s. 50]*

Royalties in Particular Cases

Filing of proposed tariffs **71.** (1) Each collective society that carries on the business of collecting royalties referred to in subsection 29.6(2), 29.7(2) or (3) or paragraph 31(2)(d) shall file with the Board a proposed tariff, but no other person may file any such tariff.

Times for filing (2) A proposed tariff must be

(a) in both official languages; and

(b) filed on or before the March 31 immediately before the date that the approved tariff ceases to be effective.

⌐here no previous tariff (3) A collective society in respect of which no proposed tariff has been certified pursuant to paragraph 73(1)(d) shall file its proposed tariff on or before the March 31 immediately before its proposed effective date.

Effective period of tariffs (4) A proposed tariff must provide that the royalties are to be effective for periods of one or more calendar years. *R.S., 1985, c. C-42, s. 71; 1997, c. 24, s. 50.*

Publica-tion of proposed tariffs **72.** (1) As soon as practicable after the receipt of a proposed tariff filed pursuant to section 71, the Board shall publish it in the Canada Gazette and shall give notice that, within sixty days after the publication of the tariff, educational institutions and prospective retransmitters, or their representatives, may file written objections to the tariff with the Board.

Board to consider proposed tariffs and objections (2) The Board shall, as soon as practicable, consider a proposed tariff and any objections thereto referred to in subsection (1) or raised by the Board, and

(a) send to the collective society concerned a copy of the objections so as to permit it to reply; and

(b) send to the persons who filed the objections a copy of any reply thereto. *1997, c. 24, s. 50; 1999, c. 31, s. 61.*

Certification **73.** (1) On the conclusion of its consideration of proposed tariffs, the Board shall

(a) establish

(i) a manner of determining the royalties to be paid by educational institutions and retransmitters, and

(ii) such terms and conditions related to those royalties as the Board considers appropriate;

(b) determine the portion of the royalties referred to in paragraph (a) that is to be paid to each collective society;

(c) vary the tariffs accordingly; and

(d) certify the tariffs as the approved tariffs, whereupon the tariffs become for the purposes of this Act the approved tariffs.

No discrimination (2) For greater certainty, the Board, in establishing a manner of determining royalties under paragraph (1)(a) or in apportioning them under paragraph (1)(b), may not discriminate between owners of copyright on the ground of their nationality or residence.

Publication of approved tariffs

(3) The Board shall publish the approved tariffs in the Canada Gazette as soon as practicable and send a copy of each approved tariff, together with the reasons for the Board's decision, to each collective society that filed a proposed tariff and to any person who filed an objection. *1997, c. 24, s. 50; 1999, c. 31, s. 62.*

Special case

74. (1) The Board shall, in establishing a manner of determining royalties under paragraph 73(1)(a), ensure that there is a preferential rate for small retransmission systems.

Regulations

(2) The Governor in Council may make regulations defining "small retransmission systems" for the purpose of subsection (1). *1997, c. 24, s. 50.*

Effect of fixing royalties

75. Without prejudice to any other remedies available to it, a collective society may, for the period specified in its approved tariff, collect the royalties specified in the tariff and, in default of their payment, recover them in a court of competent jurisdiction. *1997, c. 24, s. 50.*

Claims by non-members

76. (1) An owner of copyright who does not authorize a collective society to collect, for that person's benefit, royalties referred to in paragraph 31(2)(d) is, if the work is communicated to the public by telecommunication during a period when an approved tariff that is applicable to that kind of work is effective, entitled to be paid those royalties by the collective society that is designated by the Board, of its own motion or on application, subject to the same conditions as those to which a person who has so authorized that collective society is subject.

Royalties that may be recovered

(2) An owner of copyright who does not authorize a collective society to collect, for that person's benefit, royalties referred to in subsection 29.6(2) or 29.7(2) or (3) is, if such royalties are payable during a period when an approved tariff that is applicable to that kind of work or other subject-matter is effective, entitled to be paid those royalties by the collective society that is designated by the Board, of its own motion or on application, subject to the same conditions as those to which a person who has so authorized that collective society is subject.

Exclusion of remedies

(3) The entitlement referred to in subsections (1) and (2) is the only remedy of the owner of the copyright for the payment of royalties for the communication, making of the copy or sound recording or performance in public, as the case may be.

Regulation

(4) The Board may, for the purposes of this section,

(a) require a collective society to file with the Board information relating to payments of royalties collected by it to the persons who have authorized it to collect those royalties; and

(b) by regulation, establish periods of not less than twelve months within which the entitlements referred to in subsections (1) and (2) must be exercised, in the case of royalties referred to in

(i) paragraph 29.6(2)(a), beginning on the expiration of the year during which no royalties are payable under that paragraph,

(ii) paragraph 29.6(2)(b), beginning on the performance in public,

(iii) subsection 29.7(2), beginning on the making of the copy,

(iv) subsection 29.7(3), beginning on the performance in public, or

(v) paragraph 31(2)(d), beginning on the communication to the public by telecommunication. *1997, c. 24, s. 50.*

Owners Who Cannot be Located

Circumstances in which licence may be issued by Board

77. (1) Where, on application to the Board by a person who wishes to obtain a licence to use

(a) a published work,

(b) a fixation of a performer's performance,

(c) a published sound recording, or

(d) a fixation of a communication signal

in which copyright subsists, the Board is satisfied that the applicant has made reasonable efforts to locate the owner of the copyright and that the owner cannot be located, the Board may issue to the applicant a licence to do an act mentioned in section 3, 15, 18 or 21, as the case may be.

Conditions of licence

(2) A licence issued under subsection (1) is non-exclusive and is subject to such terms and conditions as the Board may establish.

Payment to owner

(3) The owner of a copyright may, not later than five years after the expiration of a licence issued pursuant to subsection (1) in respect of the copyright, collect the royalties fixed in the licence or, in default of their payment, commence an action to recover them in a court of competent jurisdiction.

Regulations

(4) The Copyright Board may make regulations governing the issuance of licences under subsection (1).*1997, c. 24, s. 50.*

Compensation for Acts Done Before Recognition of Copyright or Moral Rights

Board may determine compensation

78. (1) Subject to subsection (2), for the purposes of subsections 32.4(2), 32.5(2) and 33(2), the Board may, on application by any of the parties referred to in one of those provisions, determine the amount of the compensation referred to in that provision that the Board considers reasonable, having regard to all the circumstances, including any judgment of a court in an action between the parties for the enforcement of a right mentioned in subsection 32.4(3) or 32.5(3).

Limitation

(2) The Board shall not

(a) proceed with an application under subsection (1) where a notice is filed with the Board that an agreement regarding the matters in issue has been reached; or

(b) where a court action between the parties for enforcement of a right referred to in subsection 32.4(3) or 32.5(3), as the case may be, has been commenced, continue with an application under subsection (1) until the court action is finally concluded.

Interim orders

(3) Where the Board proceeds with an application under subsection (1), it may, for the purpose of avoiding serious prejudice to any party, make an interim order requiring a party to refrain from doing any act described in the order until the determination of compensation is made under subsection (1). *1997, c. 24, s. 50.*

PART VIII

PRIVATE COPYING

Interpretation

79. In this Part,

Definitions

"audio recording medium" means a recording medium, regardless of its material form, onto which a sound recording may be reproduced and that is of a kind ordinarily used by individual consumers for that purpose, excluding any prescribed kind of recording medium;

"blank audio recording medium" means

(a) an audio recording medium onto which no sounds have ever been fixed, and

(b) any other prescribed audio recording medium;

"collecting body" means the collective society, or other society, association or corporation, that is designated as the collecting body under subsection 83(8);

"eligible author" means an author of a musical work, whether created before or after the coming into force of this Part, that is embodied in a sound recording, whether made before or after the coming into force of this Part, if copyright subsists in Canada in that musical work;

"eligible maker" means a maker of a sound recording that embodies a musical work, whether the first fixation of the sound recording occurred before or after the coming into force of this Part, if

(a) both the following two conditions are met:

(i) the maker, at the date of that first fixation, if a corporation, had its headquarters in Canada or, if a natural person, was a Canadian citizen or permanent resident of Canada within the meaning of the Immigration Act, and

(ii) copyright subsists in Canada in the sound recording, or

(b) the maker, at the date of that first fixation, if a corporation, had its headquarters in a country referred to in a statement published under section 85 or, if a natural person, was a citizen, subject or permanent resident of such a country;

"eligible performer" means the performer of a performer's performance of a musical work, whether it took place before or after the coming into force of this Part, if the performer's performance is embodied in a sound recording and

(a) both the following two conditions are met:

(i) the performer was, at the date of the first fixation of the sound recording, a Canadian citizen or permanent resident of Canada within the meaning of the Immigration Act, and

(ii) copyright subsists in Canada in the performer's performance, or

(b) the performer was, at the date of the first fixation of the sound recording, a citizen, subject or permanent resident of a country referred to in a statement published under section 85;

"prescribed" means prescribed by regulations made under this Part. *1997, c. 24, s. 50.*

Copying for Private Use

Where no infringement of copyright
80. (1) Subject to subsection (2), the act of reproducing all or any substantial part of

(a) a musical work embodied in a sound recording,

(b) a performer's performance of a musical work embodied in a sound recording, or

(c) a sound recording in which a musical work, or a performer's performance of a musical work, is embodied

onto an audio recording medium for the private use of the person who makes the copy does not constitute an infringement of the copyright in the musical work, the performer's performance or the sound recording.

(2) Subsection (1) does not apply if the act described in that subsection is done for the purpose of doing any of the following in relation to any of the things referred to in paragraphs (1)(a) to (c): Limitati

(a) selling or renting out, or by way of trade exposing or offering for sale or rental;

(b) distributing, whether or not for the purpose of trade;

(c) communicating to the public by telecommunication; or

(d) performing, or causing to be performed, in public. *1997, c. 24, s. 50.*

Right of Remuneration

81. (1) Subject to and in accordance with this Part, eligible authors, eligible performers and eligible makers have a right to receive remuneration from manufacturers and importers of blank audio recording media in respect of the reproduction for private use of Right of remuner

(a) a musical work embodied in a sound recording;

(b) a performer's performance of a musical work embodied in a sound recording; or

(c) a sound recording in which a musical work, or a performer's performance of a musical work, is embodied.

(2) Subsections 13(4) to (7) apply, with such modifications as the circumstances require, in respect of the rights conferred by subsection (1) on eligible authors, performers and makers. *1997, c. 24, s. 50.* Assignment of rights

Levy on Blank Audio Recording Media

82. (1) Every person who, for the purpose of trade, manufactures a blank audio recording medium in Canada or imports a blank audio recording medium into Canada Liability to pay levy

(a) is liable, subject to subsection (2) and section 86, to pay a levy to the collecting body on selling or otherwise disposing of those blank audio recording media in Canada; and

(b) shall, in accordance with subsection 83(8), keep statements of account of the activities referred to in paragraph (a), as well as of exports of those blank audio recording media, and shall furnish those statements to the collecting body.

No levy for exports (2) No levy is payable where it is a term of the sale or other disposition of the blank audio recording medium that the medium is to be exported from Canada, and it is exported from Canada. *1997, c. 24, s. 50.*

Filing of proposed tariffs **83.** (1) Subject to subsection (14), each collective society may file with the Board a proposed tariff for the benefit of those eligible authors, eligible performers and eligible makers who, by assignment, grant of licence, appointment of the society as their agent or otherwise, authorize it to act on their behalf for that purpose, but no person other than a collective society may file any such tariff.

Collecting body (2) Without limiting the generality of what may be included in a proposed tariff, the tariff may include a suggestion as to whom the Board should designate under paragraph (8)(d) as the collecting body.

Times for filing (3) Proposed tariffs must be in both official languages and must be filed on or before the March 31 immediately before the date when the approved tariffs cease to be effective.

Where no previous tariff (4) A collective society in respect of which no proposed tariff has been certified pursuant to paragraph (8)(c) shall file its proposed tariff on or before the March 31 immediately before its proposed effective date.

Effective period of levies (5) A proposed tariff must provide that the levies are to be effective for periods of one or more calendar years.

Publication of proposed tariffs (6) As soon as practicable after the receipt of a proposed tariff filed pursuant to subsection (1), the Board shall publish it in the Canada Gazette and shall give notice that, within sixty days after the publication of the tariff, any person may file written objections to the tariff with the Board.

Board to consider proposed tariffs and objections (7) The Board shall, as soon as practicable, consider a proposed tariff and any objections thereto referred to in subsection (6) or raised by the Board, and

(a) send to the collective society concerned a copy of the objections so as to permit it to reply; and

(b) send to the persons who filed the objections a copy of any reply thereto.

Duties of Board (8) On the conclusion of its consideration of the proposed tariff, the Board shall

(a) establish, in accordance with subsection (9),

(i) the manner of determining the levies, and

(ii) such terms and conditions related to those levies as the Board considers appropriate, including, without limiting the generality of the foregoing, the form, content and frequency of the statements of account mentioned in subsection 82(1), measures for the protection of confidential information contained in those statements, and the times at which the levies are payable,

(b) vary the tariff accordingly,

(c) certify the tariff as the approved tariff, whereupon that tariff becomes for the purposes of this Part the approved tariff, and

(d) designate as the collecting body the collective society or other society, association or corporation that, in the Board's opinion, will best fulfil the objects of sections 82, 84 and 86,

but the Board is not obligated to exercise its power under paragraph (d) if it has previously done so, and a designation under that paragraph remains in effect until the Board makes another designation, which it may do at any time whatsoever, on application.

Factors Board to consider

(9) In exercising its power under paragraph (8)(a), the Board shall satisfy itself that the levies are fair and equitable, having regard to any prescribed criteria.

Publication of approved tariffs

(10) The Board shall publish the approved tariffs in the Canada Gazette as soon as practicable and shall send a copy of each approved tariff, together with the reasons for the Board's decision, to the collecting body, to each collective society that filed a proposed tariff, and to any person who filed an objection.

Authors, etc., not represented by collective society

(11) An eligible author, eligible performer or eligible maker who does not authorize a collective society to file a proposed tariff under subsection (1) is entitled, in relation to

(a) a musical work,

(b) a performer's performance of a musical work, or

(c) a sound recording in which a musical work, or a performer's performance of a musical work, is embodied,

as the case may be, to be paid by the collective society that is designated by the Board, of the Board's own motion or on application, the remuneration referred to in section 81 if such remuneration is payable during a period when an approved tariff that is applicable to that kind of work, performer's performance or sound recording is effective, subject to the same conditions as those to which a person who has so authorized that collective society is subject.

Exclusion of other remedies

(12) The entitlement referred to in subsection (11) is the only remedy of the eligible author, eligible performer or eligible maker referred to in that subsection in respect of the reproducing of sound recordings for private use.

Powers of Board

(13) The Board may, for the purposes of subsections (11) and (12),

(a) require a collective society to file with the Board information relating to payments of moneys received by the society pursuant to section 84 to the persons who have authorized it to file a tariff under subsection (1); and

(b) by regulation, establish the periods, which shall not be less than twelve months, beginning when the applicable approved tariff ceases to be effective, within which the entitlement referred to in subsection (11) must be exercised.

Single proposed tariff

(14) Where all the collective societies that intend to file a proposed tariff authorize a particular person or body to file a single proposed tariff on their behalf, that person or body may do so, and in that case this section applies, with such modifications as the circumstances require, in respect of that proposed tariff. *1997, c. 24, s. 50.*

Distribution of Levies Paid

Distribution by collecting body

84. As soon as practicable after receiving the levies paid to it, the collecting body shall distribute the levies to the collective societies representing eligible authors, eligible performers and eligible makers, in the proportions fixed by the Board. *1997, c. 24, s. 50.*

Reciprocity

85. (1) Where the Minister is of the opinion that another country grants or has undertaken to grant to performers and makers of sound recordings that are Canadian citizens or permanent residents of Canada within the meaning of the Immigration Act or, if corporations, have their headquarters in Canada, as the case may be, whether by treaty, convention, agreement or law, benefits substantially equivalent to those conferred by this Part, the Minister may, by a statement published in the Canada Gazette,

(a) grant the benefits conferred by this Part to performers or makers of sound recordings that are citizens, subjects or permanent residents of or, if corporations, have their headquarters in that country; and

(b) declare that that country shall, as regards those benefits, be treated as if it were a country to which this Part extends.

Reciprocity

(2) Where the Minister is of the opin-

ion that another country neither grants nor has undertaken to grant to performers or makers of sound recordings that are Canadian citizens or permanent residents of Canada within the meaning of the Immigration Act or, if corporations, have their headquarters in Canada, as the case may be, whether by treaty, convention, agreement or law, benefits substantially equivalent to those conferred by this Part, the Minister may, by a statement published in the Canada Gazette,

(a) grant the benefits conferred by this Part to performers or makers of sound recordings that are citizens, subjects or permanent residents of or, if corporations, have their headquarters in that country, as the case may be, to the extent that that country grants those benefits to performers or makers of sound recordings that are Canadian citizens or permanent residents of Canada within the meaning of the Immigration Act or, if corporations, have their headquarters in Canada; and

(b) declare that that country shall, as regards those benefits, be treated as if it were a country to which this Part extends.

Application of Act (3) Any provision of this Act that the Minister specifies in a statement referred to in subsection (1) or (2)

(a) applies in respect of performers or makers of sound recordings covered by that statement, as if they were citizens of or, if corporations, had their headquarters in Canada; and

(b) applies in respect of a country covered by that statement, as if that country were Canada.

Application of Act (4) Subject to any exceptions that the Minister may specify in a statement referred to in subsection (1) or (2), the other provisions of this Act also apply in the way described in subsection (3). *1997, c. 24, s. 50.*

Exemption from Levy

Where no levy payable **86.** (1) No levy is payable under this Part where the manufacturer or importer of a

blank audio recording medium sells or otherwise disposes of it to a society, association or corporation that represents persons with a perceptual disability.

Refunds (2) Where a society, association or corporation referred to in subsection (1)

(a) purchases a blank audio recording medium in Canada from a person other than the manufacturer or importer, and

(b) provides the collecting body with proof of that purchase, on or before June 30 in the calendar year following the calendar year in which the purchase was made,

the collecting body is liable to pay forthwith to the society, association or corporation an amount equal to the amount of the levy paid in respect of the blank audio recording medium purchased.

If registration system exists (3) If regulations made under paragraph 87(a) provide for the registration of societies, associations or corporations that represent persons with a perceptual disability, subsections (1) and (2) shall be read as referring to societies, associations or corporations that are so registered. *1997, c. 24, s. 50.*

Regulations

Regulations **87.** The Governor in Council may make regulations

(a) respecting the exemptions and refunds provided for in section 86, including, without limiting the generality of the foregoing,

(i) regulations respecting procedures governing those exemptions and refunds,

(ii) regulations respecting applications for those exemptions and refunds, and

(iii) regulations for the registration of societies, associations or corporations that represent persons with a perceptual disability;

(b) prescribing anything that by this Part is to be prescribed; and

(c) generally for carrying out the purposes and provisions of this Part. *1997, c. 24, s. 50.*

Civil Remedies

Right of recovery **88.** (1) Without prejudice to any other remedies available to it, the collecting body may, for the period specified in an approved tariff, collect the levies due to it under the tariff and, in default of their payment, recover them in a court of competent jurisdiction.

Failure to pay royalties (2) The court may order a person who fails to pay any levy due under this Part to pay an amount not exceeding five times the amount of the levy to the collecting body. The collecting body must distribute the payment in the manner set out in section 84.

Order directing compliance (3) Where any obligation imposed by this Part is not complied with, the collecting body may, in addition to any other remedy available, apply to a court of competent jurisdiction for an order directing compliance with that obligation.

Factors to consider (4) Before making an order under subsection (2), the court must take into account

(a) whether the person who failed to pay the levy acted in good faith or bad faith;

(b) the conduct of the parties before and during the proceedings; and

(c) the need to deter persons from failing to pay levies. *1997, c. 24, s. 50.*

PART IX

GENERAL PROVISIONS

No copyright, etc., except by statute **89.** No person is entitled to copyright otherwise than under and in accordance with this Act or any other Act of Parliament, but nothing in this section shall be construed as abrogating any right or jurisdiction in respect of a breach of trust or confidence. *1997, c. 24, s. 50.*

Interpretation **90.** No provision of this Act relating to

(a) copyright in performer's performances, sound recordings or communication signals, or

(b) the right of performers or makers to remuneration

shall be construed as prejudicing any rights conferred by Part I or, in and of itself, as prejudicing the amount of royalties that the Board may fix in respect of those rights. *1997, c. 24, s. 50.*

Adherence to Berne and Rome Conventions **91.** The Governor in Council shall take such measures as are necessary to secure the adherence of Canada to

(a) the Convention for the Protection of Literary and Artistic Works concluded at Berne on September 9, 1886, as revised by the Paris Act of 1971; and

(b) the International Convention for the Protection of Performers, Producers of Phonograms and Broadcasting Organisations, done at Rome on October 26, 1961. *1997, c. 24, s. 50.*

Review of Act **92.** (1) Within five years after the coming into force of this section, the Minister shall cause to be laid before both Houses of Parliament a report on the provisions and operation of this Act, including any recommendations for amendments to this Act.

Reference to parliamentary committee (2) The report stands referred to the committee of the House of Commons, or of both Houses of Parliament, that is designated or established for that purpose, which shall

(a) as soon as possible thereafter, review the report and undertake a comprehensive review of the provisions and operation of this Act; and

(b) report to the House of Commons, or to both Houses of Parliament, within one year after the laying of the report of the Minister or any further time that the House of Commons, or both Houses of Parliament, may authorize. *1997, c. 24, s. 50.*

SCHEDULE I

(Section 60)

EXISTING RIGHTS

Column I	Column II
Existing Right	*Substituted Right*

Works other than Dramatic and Musical Works

Copyright	Copyright as defined by this Act.

Musical and Dramatic Works

Both copyright and performing right	Copyright as defined by this Act.
Copyright, but not performing right	Copyright as defined by this Act, except the sole right to perform the work or any substantial part thereof in public.
Performing right, but not copyright	The sole right to perform the work in public, but none of the other rights comprised in copyright as defined by this Act.

For the purposes of this Schedule the following expressions, where used in column I thereof, have the following meanings:

"Copyright" in the case of a work that according to the law in force immediately before January 1, 1924 has not been published before that date and statutory copyright wherein depends on publication, includes the right at common law, if any, to restrain publication or other dealing with the work;

"Performing right", in the case of a work that has not been performed in public before January 1, 1924, includes the right at common law, if any, to restrain the performance thereof in public.

In the case of an essay, article or portion forming part of and first published in a review, magazine or other periodical or work of a like nature, the right shall be subject to any right of publishing the essay, article or portion in a separate form to which the author is entitled on January 1, 1924 or would if this Act had not been passed have become entitled under section 18 of An Act to amend the Law of Copyright, being chapter 45 of the Statutes of the United Kingdom, 1842. *R.S., c. C-30, Sch. I; 1976-77, c. 28, s. 10.*

SCHEDULE II

[Repealed, 1993, c. 44, s. 74]

SCHEDULE III

[Repealed, 1997, c. 24, s. 51]

RELATED PROVISIONS

R.S., 1985, c. 10 (4th Supp.), ss. 23 to 27:

23. (1) The rights referred to in section 14.1 of the Copyright Act, as enacted by section 4, subsist in respect of a work even if the work was created before the coming into force of section 4. — Application re moral rights

(2) A remedy referred to in subsection 34(1.1) of the Copyright Act, as enacted by section 8, may only be obtained where the infringement of the moral rights of the author occurs after the coming into force of section 8. — Restriction

(3) Notwithstanding subsection (1) and the repeal by section 3 of subsection 14(4) of the Copyright Act, the rights referred to in section 14.1 of that Act, as enacted by section 4, are not enforceable against — Idem

(a) a person who, on the coming into force of this section, is the owner of the copyright in, or holds a licence in relation to, a work, or

(b) a person authorized by a person described in paragraph (a) to do an act mentioned in section 3 of that Act,

in respect of any thing done during the period for which the person described in paragraph (a) is the owner or for which the licence is in force, and the rights referred to in subsection 14(4) of that Act continue to be enforceable against a person described in paragraph (a) or (b) during that period as if subsection 14(4) of that Act were not repealed.

Application re computer programs **24.** Subsection 1(2), the definition "computer program" in subsection 1(3) and section 5 apply in respect of a computer program that was made prior to the day on which those provisions come into force but where, by virtue only of subsections 1(2) and (3) and this section, copyright subsists in a computer program that was made prior to May 27, 1987, nothing done in respect of the computer program before May 27, 1987 shall be construed to constitute an infringement of the copyright.

Making of records, perforated rolls, etc. **25.** It shall be deemed not to be an infringement of copyright in any musical, literary or dramatic work for any person to make within Canada during the six months following the coming into force of section 7 records, perforated rolls or other contrivances by means of which sounds may be reproduced and by means of which the work may be mechanically performed, if the person proves

(a) that before the coming into force of section 7, the person made such contrivances in respect of that work in accordance with section 29 or 30 of the Copyright Act and any regulation made under section 33 of that Act, as they read immediately before the coming into force of section 7; and

(b) that the making would, had it occurred before the coming into force of section 7, have been deemed not to have been an infringement of copyright by section 29 or 30 of the Copyright Act, as it read immediately before the coming into force of section 7.

Infringements before coming into force **26.** Subsection 64(1) and section 64.1 of the Copyright Act, as enacted by section 11, apply in respect of any alleged infringement of copyright occurring prior to, on or after the day on which section 11 comes into force.

Continuation in office **27.** Notwithstanding any other provision

of this Act, the members of the Copyright Appeal Board appointed pursuant to section 68 of the Copyright Act, as it read immediately before the coming into force of section 13, continue in office and may continue to perform their duties and exercise their powers to the extent necessary to consider and deal with any matter before it pursuant to section 69 of that Act before the coming into force of section 14.

1988, c. 65, s. 149:

First certified statements of royalties **149.** For greater certainty, the royalties in the first statements certified under paragraph 70.63(1)(d) of the Copyright Act become effective on January 1, 1990 regardless of when the statements are so certified."

1993, c. 23, ss. 6, 7:

Transitional: Statements o royalties **6.** (1) Notwithstanding section 67 of the Copyright Act, a statement filed with the Copyright Board pursuant to subsection 67(2) or (3) of that Act on or before September 1, 1992

(a) may provide, or

(b) may be amended with leave of the Board, if application therefor is made to the Board within twenty-eight days after the coming into force of this Act, to provide

for the payment of royalties, for the period beginning on the coming into force of this Act and ending at the end of 1993, in respect of the communication of dramatico-musical or musical works to the public by telecommunication, and a statement so filed or amended is effective for that period to the extent that the Board certifies it as approved pursuant to subsection 67.2(1) of the Copyright Act.

No duplication of royalties (2) Where a statement referred to in subsection (1) is certified as approved, the Board shall not certify as approved any other statement filed by the same applicant, to the extent that it provides for royalties in respect of the same act and for the same period as set out in the statement previously certified as approved.

Where this Act does not apply **7.** This Act does not apply in respect of statements filed with the Board pursuant to subsection 67(2) or (3) of the Copyright Act on or before September 1, 1991 that relate to any year before 1993.

1993, c. 44, ss. 60(2), (3):

Application of amendments to s. 10 (2) Subject to subsection 75(2) of this Act, section 10 of the Copyright Act, as enacted by subsection (1) of this section, applies to all photographs, whether made before or after the coming into force of this section.

Application of amendments to s. 11 (3) Except as provided by section 75 of this Act,

(a) section 11 of the Copyright Act, as enacted by subsection (1) of this section, applies only in respect of contrivances made after the coming into force of this section; and

(b) section 11 of the Copyright Act, as it read immediately before the coming into force of this section, continues to apply in respect of contrivances made before the coming into force of this section.

1993, c. 44, ss. 75 to 77:

Application of certain amendments **75.** (1) Subject to subsection (2), amendments to the Copyright Act made by this Act relating to the term of copyright apply in respect of all works, whether made before or after the coming into force of this section.

Idem (2) Where the term of the copyright in a work expires before the coming into force of this section, nothing in this Act shall be construed as extending or reviving that term.

Cinematographs **76.** (1) Except as provided by subsection (2) of this section, the Copyright Act, as amended by this Act, applies in respect of all cinematographs, whether made before or after the coming into force of this section, subject to subsection 75(2) of this Act.

Idem (2) Section 10 of the Copyright Act, as that section read immediately before the coming into force of this section and in so far as it governs who is the author of a photograph, continues to apply in respect of all cinematographs made before the coming into force of this section that were, before the coming into force of this section, protected as photographs.

Application of section 5 **77.** Nothing in section 5 of the Copyright Act, as amended by this Act, confers copyright on works made before the coming into force of this section that did not qualify for copyright under section 5 of the Copyright Act as it read immediately before the coming into force of this section.

1997, c. 24, s. 18(2):

(2) Section 30 of the Act, as enacted by subsection (1) of this section, does not apply in respect of collections referred to in section 30 that are published before the coming into force of section 30. Such collections continue to be governed by paragraph 27(2)(d) of the Act as it read before the coming into force of section 15 of this Act.

1997, c. 24, ss. 20(3), (4):

(3) Section 38.1 of the Copyright Act, as enacted by subsection (1) of this section, only applies

(a) to proceedings commenced after the date of the coming into force of that subsection; and

(b) where the infringement to which those proceedings relate occurred after that date.

(4) Section 39.1 of the Copyright Act, as enacted by subsection (1) of this section, applies in respect of

(a) proceedings commenced but not concluded before the coming into force of subsection (1) of this section; and

(b) proceedings commenced after the coming into force of subsection (1) of this section.

1997, c. 24, s. 22(2):

(2) Subsection (1) applies in respect of

(a) proceedings commenced but not concluded before this section comes into force; and

(b) proceedings commenced after this section comes into force.

1997, c. 24, ss. 53 to 58.1:

53. The levies in the first tariffs certified under paragraph 83(8)(c) of the Copyright Act, as enacted by section 50 of this Act, become effective at the beginning of the first calendar year following the coming into force of that paragraph, regardless of when the tariffs are so certified, and are effective for a period of two calendar years.

53.1 Notwithstanding subsection 67.1(2) and section 70.13 of the Copyright Act, as enacted by sections 45 and 46 of this Act, the date for the filing of the first proposed tariffs under those sections shall be on or before September 1 of the year of the coming into force of this section.

54. For greater certainty, all notices published under subsection 5(2) of the Copyright Act before the coming into force of this section are deemed to have been validly made and to have had force and effect in accordance with their terms.

54.1 Section 6 of the Copyright Act applies to a photograph in which copyright subsists on the date of the coming into force of this section, if the author is

(a) a natural person who is the author of the photograph referred to in subsection 10(2) of the Copyright Act, as enacted by section 7 of this Act; or

(b) the natural person referred to in subsection 10(1.1) of the Copyright Act, as enacted by section 7 of this Act.

55. (1) Part II of the Copyright Act, as enacted by section 14 of this Act, shall be construed as a replacement for subsections 5(3) to (6) and section 11 of the Copyright Act as those provisions read immediately before the coming into force of subsection 5(3) and section 8, respectively, of this Act.

(2) The rights conferred by Part II of the Copyright Act, as enacted by section 14 of this Act, shall not be construed as diminishing the rights conferred by subsections 5(3) to (6) and section 11 of the Copyright Act as those provisions read immediately before the coming into force of subsection 5(3) and section 8, respectively, of this Act, in relation to records, perforated rolls and other contrivances by means of which sounds may be mechanically reproduced that were made before the coming into force of subsection 5(3) and section 8, respectively, of this Act.

(3) Where an assignment of copyright or a grant of any interest therein

(a) was made before the coming into force of Part II of the Copyright Act, as enacted by section 14 of this Act, and

(b) was made by the maker of a sound recording who was a natural person,

subsections 14(1) and (2) of the Copyright Act continue to apply in respect of that assignment or grant, with such modifications as the circumstances require, as if the sound recording was the work referred to in those subsections and the maker of the sound recording was its author.

56. Nothing in this Act shall be construed as diminishing the right conferred by section 14.01 of the Copyright Act as that section read immediately before the coming into force of section 12 of this Act.

57. For greater certainty, the amendments to the Copyright Act that eliminate references to "British subject" and "Her Majesty's Realms and Territories" do not affect any copyright or moral rights that subsisted in Canada immediately before the coming into force of those amendments.

58. Nothing in this Act shall be construed as reviving a copyright that expired before the coming into force of this section.

58.1 No agreement concluded before April 25, 1996 that assigns a right or grants an interest by licence in a right that would be a copyright or a right to remuneration under this Act shall be construed as assigning or granting any rights conferred for the first time by this Act, unless the agreement specifically provides for the assignment or grant.

1997, c. 24, ss. 62, 63:

62. (1) The following provisions come into force or are deemed to have come into force on June 30, 1996: Coming into force

(a) the definitions "exclusive distributor", "educational institution" and "library, archive or museum" in section 2 of the Copyright Act, as enacted by subsection 1(5) of this Act;

(b) section 2.6 of the Copyright Act, as enacted by section 2 of this Act;

(c) section 27.1 of the Copyright Act, as enacted by section 15 of this Act; and

(d) section 45 of the Copyright Act, as enacted by section 28 of this Act.

(2) Notwithstanding subsection (1), the definition "exclusive distributor" referred to in paragraph (1)(a) shall be read as follows during the period beginning on June 30, 1996 and ending on the day that is sixty days after the day on which this Act is assented to:

"exclusive distributor" means, in relation to a book, a person who has, before or after the coming into force of this definition, been appointed in writing, by the owner or exclusive licensee of the copyright in the book in Canada, as

(a) the only distributor of the book in Canada or any part of Canada, or

(b) the only distributor of the book in Canada or any part of Canada in respect of a particular sector of the market.

(3) Notwithstanding paragraph (1)(d), paragraph 45(1)(e) of the Copyright Act, as enacted by section 28 of this Act, shall be read as follows for the period beginning on June 30, 1996 and ending on the day that is sixty days after the day on which this Act is assented to:

(e) to import copies, made with the consent of the owner of the copyright in the country where they were made, of any used books.

63. (1) No exclusive distributor, within the meaning assigned to that expression by subsection 62(2) of this Act, copyright owner or exclusive licensee is entitled to a remedy referred to in the Copyright Act in relation to an infringement referred to in subsection 27.1(1) or (2) of that Act, as enacted by section 15 of this Act, during the period beginning on June 30, 1996 and ending on the day on which this Act is assented to, unless

(a) before the infringement occurred, notice in writing has been given to the person referred to in subsection 27.1(1) or (2) of that Act, as enacted by section 15 of this Act, as the case may be, that

(i) there is an exclusive distributor of the book in Canada, and

(ii) section 27.1 of that Act came into force or was deemed to have come into force on June 30, 1996; and

(b) in the case of an infringement referred to in section 27.1 of that Act, as enacted by section 15 of this Act, the remedy is only in relation to a book that was imported during that period and forms part of the inventory of the person referred to in section 27.1 of that Act on the day on which this Act is assented to.

(2) No exclusive distributor, copyright owner or exclusive licensee is entitled to a remedy referred to in subsection (1) against an educational institution, library, archive or museum.

(3) For greater certainty, the expiration of the period referred to in subsection 62(2) of this Act does not affect the right of an exclusive distributor to continue, after the expiration of that period, legal proceedings validly commenced during that period.

AMENDMENT NOT IN FORCE

1997, c. 24, s. 20(2):

(2) Section 38 of the Copyright Act, as it read immediately before the coming into force of subsection (1) of this section, continues to apply in respect of proceedings commenced but not concluded before the coming into force of subsection (1) of this section.

Appendix II

APPLICATIONS FOR REGISTRATION OF COPYRIGHT AND CERTIFICATE OF REGISTRATION

❚✦❚ Canadian Intellectual Property Office
An Agency of Industry Canada

Office de la propriété Intellectuelle du Canada
Un organisme d'Industrie Canada

How your Copyright application is processed

The Copyright and Industrial Design Branch processes your application upon receipt.

You can obtain further information concerning your application for registration by:
Telephone: (819) 997-1725
Fax: (819) 997-6357

If you have already obtained a registration number from our office and you would like further information concerning your file, please indicate your registration

number when making any new request for service relating to your file.

Stage	Processing of your application	How you will be informed	Time limit	Fees
Formalities	Your application is considered complete when all the information is received and the fees are paid pursuant to the *Copyright Act* and *Regulations*. Applications are kept in the order received, files are created and assigned numbers whereupon they are forwarded to the copyright reviewer.	You are not informed at this point.	2 weeks	CAN$65
Revision 997-2334	A copyright reviewer checks the application to ensure that the information provided by the applicant is clear and accurate. If there are any questions, the reviewer will send a report to the applicant or their agent requesting clarification. Some corrections may be made by telephone.	Depending on the extent of the corrections and at the reviewer's discretion, the applicant is informed of the corrections by telephone or is sent a written report.	1 week	none
Registration	The copyright reviewer assigns a registration number by entering the information provided by the applicant in the automated register, prints the certificate, carries out a final quality control check and sends it to the client.	You will receive your Registration Certificate by mail.	1 week	none
Correcting certificate	At the client's request, a certificate of correction will be issued should a clerical error appear on an original registration certificate.	By mail or by telephone, depending on client's needs and fulfillment of requirements for the request.	2 days	Office error: none Client error: CAN$65
Request for accelerated action	Your application will be sent to revision and then to registration upon approval, on an accelerated basis.	The client will be informed of the approval by telephone.	3 days	CAN$65
Filing a licence, assignment or other document	Upon receipt of the original document or a certified true copy of the document to be registered, the Copyright Office staff verifies the authenticity of the documents, enters the information in the computer and issues a file number.	You are not informed unless certain details are missing.	4 weeks	CAN$65
Request for copies, extracts from the Register	Copies or extracts from the Register, or copies of certificates, licences or other documents will be provided.	By mail or by telephone, depending on client's need.	2 days	CAN$0.50 per page
Request for certified copy	The information in the Register will be verified, extracted and a certified copy will be issued.	By mail or by telephone, depending on client's need.	3 days	CAN$35 plus $0.50 per page attached

A more extensive *Guide to Copyrights* is available free of charge from:

IC no. 11372E
IC no. 11373F

Publications Centre
Canadian Intellectual Property Office
Industry Canada
Place du Portage 1
50 Victoria Street
Hull, Quebec
K1A 0C9

Telephone: (819) 953-5054
Fax: (819) 953-8998

Internet: http://cipo.gc.ca
E-mail: cipo.contact@ic.gc.ca

Canada

(000514-01-00)

CIPO ◆ OPIC

Canadian Intellectual Property Office	Office de la propriété intellectuelle du Canada	
An Agency of Industry Canada	Un organisme d'Industrie Canada	**Application for Registration of a Copyright**

Instructions

1. Title of the work
Enter the specific title of the work. Subtitles, alternative titles and descriptive matter are not permitted as part of the title. Titles are usually not protected by Copyright, but if a title is original and distinctive, it may be protected as part of the work it relates to. Please note that the application must refer to one work only.

2. Category of the work
Check the category that best describes your work. Please note that the description should apply to the work as it exists at the present time. It should not reflect what may be developed in the future. The following information may be helpful to you in selecting the appropriate description:

Literary:
Describes works consisting of text. This includes books, poems, song lyrics (without music), tables, compilations of literary works, catalogues, reports and translations of such works. Computer programs are also included in this category.

Note: Textual works in which a scenic arrangement or acting form is fixed in writing fall within the dramatic category (e.g. a screenplay).

Musical:
Describes any work of music or musical composition with or without words and includes any compilations thereof. This definition does not include song lyrics without music (literary).

Artistic:
Includes paintings, drawings, maps, charts, plans, photographs, engravings, sculptures, works of artistic craftsmanship, architectural works and compilations of artistic works.

Dramatic:
Includes any piece for recitation, choreographic work, or mime (action without speech) where the scenic arrangement or acting form is fixed in writing or otherwise. It also includes cinematographic productions such as films and videos. Examples of other dramatic works are: screenplays, scripts and plays.

Note: In some cases, a combination of these definitions may be required to accurately describe the nature of the work. For example, a book containing text and illustrations would be described as "literary and artistic," and a work which combines dramatic and musical elements, such as an opera, would be described as "dramatic and musical."

Short description and/or rights
In this space, you may enter a short description of the work you are seeking to register. Examples of such descriptions are: "computer program," "architectural plan," "book," "compilation," "choreographic work," "photograph," "sculpture," or "cinematograph."

If you are the owner of one or more particular rights, rather than the copyright in its entirety, you may use this space to identify the particular rights that you own. Examples are: "performing right," "reproduction right" or "publication right."

3. Publication
Check box A or B. If the work is published, enter the date and place of publication in the appropriate space. For the purposes of the *Copyright Act,* "publication" means "making copies of a work available to the public." This does not include the exhibition in public of an artistic work or the performance in public of a dramatic work.

4. Author
Insert the name and address of the author. In most cases, the term of copyright protection is based on the lifetime of the author. The name of the person or persons who actually created the work is required. If the author is dead, the exact date of the author's death should be added, if known. If more than one author, please attach a list of names and addresses of all the authors.

5. Owner
Complete parts A or B depending on whether ownership is to be in the name of an individual or a corporation. The copyright owner can be the author of the work, the employer of the author, or any person that has obtained ownership through a transfer of ownership, such as an assignment. Please note that a "licensee" should not register as the owner of the copyright. A copyright can be registered in the name of one or more individual(s) or corporation(s).

If there is more than one author or owner, copies of page 1 containing the additional owners names should be attached.

6. Applicant
Check box A or B or complete part C. The person who is making the application must complete this section. That person must be the author, legal representative, or agent of the author or legal representative, or the publisher or other person with an interest in the copyright. Please note that unless there is an agent named in section 8, the certificate will be sent to the person named in this section.

7. Declaration
Please check only one box.

8. Agent for applicant
This section is to be completed only if the application is being submitted by an agent. The certificate will be sent to the name and address given in this section. If this section is not completed, the certificate will be mailed to the applicant named in section 6.

Please note that payment may be made by cheque, by credit card (VISA or MasterCard), direct payment, deposit account or postal money order, payable in Canadian dollars to the Receiver General of Canada.

Please do not send copies of your work and do not add provincial or federal taxes.

Canadian Intellectual Property Office
An Agency of Industry Canada

Office de la propriété Intellectuelle du Canada
Un organisme d'Industrie Canada

Application for Registration of a Copyright

(please print)

1. Title of the work

2. Category of the work

☐ Literary   ☐ Musical   ☐ Artistic   ☐ Dramatic   ☐ Compilation

Short description of the work and/or rights being registered: (maximum 115 characters)

3. Publication

☐ A. The work is published   ☐ B. The work is unpublished

Date of first publication:
Y M D

Place of publication:
City/Town (optional)   Prov./State (optional)   Country

4. Author(s)   ☐ Same as owner(s) - (If more than one author, please attach a list of names and addresses of all the authors)

Family name   First name   Initial   Date of author's death, if known Y M D

Address

City/Town   Prov./State   Country   Postal/Zip Code

5. Owner(s) - (If more than one owner, please attach a list of names and addresses of all the owners)

A. Family name   First name   Initial

OR B. Name of corporation

Address

City/Town   Prov./State   Country   Postal/Zip Code

Canada   (000528-01-00)    CIPO   OPIC

6. Applicant(s)

☐ A. The applicant is the same as owner in section 5.　　☐ B. The applicant is the same as author in section 4.

OR

C. Family name　　　　　First name　　　　　Initial

OR D. Name of corporation

Address

City/Town　　Prov./State　　Country　　Postal/Zip Code

7. Declaration

The applicant is:

☐ A) author(s)　☐ B) owner(s)　☐ C) assignee(s)　☐ D) licensee(s) of the copyright in the work

8. Agent for applicant (if applicable)

A. Family name　　　　　First name　　　　　Initial

OR B. Name of firm

Address

City/Town　　Prov./State　　Country　　Postal/Zip Code

Telephone no.　　Fax no. (if available)　　E-mail address (if available)

(　)　　(　)

(For Canadian Intellectual Property Office use only)

All correspondence should be addressed to:
Copyright Office
Canadian Intellectual Property Office
Industry Canada
Place du Portage I
50 Victoria Street
Hull, Quebec K1A 0C9

Telephone: (819) 997-1725
Facsimile: (819) 997-6357

Internet address: http://cipo.gc.ca
E-mail: cipo.contact@ic.gc.ca

Please do not send copies of your work

Application for Registration of a Copyright in other Subject-matter

Instructions

Please complete the application form by providing the requested information in the appropriate white boxes. Kindly use a typewriter or print with a black pen, as your application will be electronically scanned. The following information should assist you in completing the form.

1. Title of the subject-matter
Enter the specific title of the subject-matter, if any. Please note that the application must refer to only one performer's performance, sound recording or communication signal.

2. Short description of the subject-matter (optional)
In this space you may enter a short description of the subject-matter you are seeking to register. Examples of public performance are the playing of recordings in shopping malls, bars, nightclubs, discotheques, hotels, airlines, skating rinks and restaurants. An example of the broadcasting of performances and sound recordings is radio airplay.

3. Type of subject-matter
Check the subject-matter and complete part A, B or C to which the application applies. The following definitions from the *Copyright Act* may be helpful.

Performer's performance:
Means any of the following when done by a performer:
(a) a performance of an artistic work, dramatic work or musical work, whether or not the work was previously fixed in any material form, and whether or not the work's term of copyright protection under this Act has expired;
(b) a recitation or reading of a literary work, whether or not the work's term of copyright protection under this Act has expired; or
(c) an improvisation of a dramatic work, musical work or literary work, whether or not the improvised work is based on a pre-existing work.

Sound recording:
Means a recording, fixed in any material form, consisting of sounds, whether or not of a performance of a work, but excludes any soundtrack of a cinematographic work where it accompanies the cinematographic work.

Communication signal:
Means radio waves transmitted through space without any artificial guide, for reception by the public.

4. Owner
Complete parts A and C or B and C depending on whether ownership is to be in the name of an individual or a corporation. The copyright owner is the performer in the case of a performer's performance, the maker in the case of a sound recording, or the broadcaster in the case of a communication signal or any person who has obtained ownership through a transfer of ownership such as an assignment. Copyright in other subject-matter can be registered in the name of one or more individuals or corporations. If there is more than one owner, copy(ies) of page 1 containing the additional owners' information should be attached.

5. Applicant
Check box A or complete B, C and D. The person who is making the application, not the agent, must complete this section. That person must be the owner, an assignee or a licensee. Please note that unless there is an agent named in section 7, the certificate of registration will be sent to the person named in this section.

6. Declaration
In this section, the applicant must identify himself by checking only one box, declaring that he/she is the owner, an assignee or a licensee of the copyright in the subject-matter.

7. Agent for applicant
This section is to be completed only if the application is being submitted by an agent. The certificate of registration will be sent to the name and address given in this section. If this section is not completed, the certificate will be mailed to the applicant named in section 5.

Please note that payment may be made by Visa, Mastercard, direct payment, deposit account, postal money order or cheque payable in Canadian dollars to the Receiver General of Canada.

Please do not send copies of your work and do not add provincial and federal taxes.

Visit CIPO on the Internet: http//cipo.gc.ca

Industry Canada
Industrie Canada

 Canada

Application for Registration of a Copyright in other Subject-matter

Please complete this application form by providing the requested information in the appropriate white boxes. Kindly use a typewriter or print with a black pen, as your application will be electronically scanned. For assistance in completing the form, please refer to the instruction sheet that is provided.

1. Title of the subject-matter (if any)

2. Short description of the subject-matter (optional)

3. Subject-matter

Type

			Date (yy/mm/dd)
☐ A. Performer's Performance	☐ 1st Fixation	☐ 1st Performance	
☐ B. Sound Recording — 1st Fixation			
☐ C. Communication Signal — 1st Broadcast			

4. Owner

A.   Family Name: Initial: First Name:

B.   Name of corporation (if applicable):

C.   Address:

    C/O:

    Street:

    City/Town: Prov./State:

    Country: Postal Code/ZIP:

    Telephone: (   )   Facsimile: (   )

    E-mail:

Industry Canada / Industrie Canada

Canada

5. Applicant

A. ☐ The applicant is the same as owner in section 4, or

B. Family Name: _____ Initial: ___ First Name: _____

C. Name of corporation or firm (if applicable): _____

D. Address:

C/O: _____

Street: _____

City/Town: _____   Prov./State: _____

Country: _____   Postal Code/ZIP: _____

Telephone: ( ) _____   Facsimile: ( ) _____

E-mail: _____

6. Declaration

I/We hereby declare that the applicant is:

☐ The Owner
of the copyright in the subject-matter

☐ An assignee
of the copyright in the subject-matter

☐ A licencee
of the copyright in the subject-matter

7. Agent

☐ The applicant is the same as owner in section 4, or

A. Family Name: _____ Initial: ___ First Name: _____

B. Name of corporation or firm (if applicable): _____

C. Address:

C/O: _____

Street: _____

City/Town: _____   Prov./State: _____

Country: _____   Postal Code/ZIP: _____

Telephone: ( ) _____   Facsimile: ( ) _____

E-mail: _____

All correspondence should be addressed to:

Canadian Intellectual Property Office
Copyright Office
50 Victoria Street, Place du Portage I
Hull, Quebec K1A 0C9

Telephone: (819) 997-1725, Facsimile: (819) 953-6977
Internet address: http://cipo.gc.ca

Please do not send copies of your work

Office de la propriété   Canadian
intellectuelle   Intellectual Property
du Canada   Office

Un organisme   An Agency of
d'Industrie Canada   Industry Canada

Droit d'auteur   *Copyright*

Certificat d'enregistrement   *Certificate of registration*

The copyright in the work described below has been registered as follows :
Le droit d'auteur sur l'oeuvre décrite ci-dessous a été enregistré comme suit :

Registration No. - Numéro d'enregistrement :   483588

Date of Registration - Date d'enregistrement :   March 10, 2000

First Published - Première publication :   unpublished

Title - Titre :   "Canadian Copyright Law, 3rd Edition"

Nature - Nature :   - Literary -

(manuscript/book on copyright law)

Owner(s) - Propriétaire(s):

Lesley E. Harris - Farragut Station, Box 33271 - Washington,
DC - U.S.A.

Author(s) - Auteur(s):

Lesley E. Harris - Washington, DC - U.S.A.

Bureau du droit d'auteur Copyright Office

Application for Crown Copyright Clearance

Applicant's File No.: _____   PWGSC File No.: _____

Application for Crown Copyright Clearance   ————————————————————————
This form is for obtaining permission to reproduce, translate and adapt Government of Canada information (in any format) only. For further instructions please contact the Public Works and Government Services Canada – Canadian Government Publishing (PWGSC-CGP), Crown Copyright Officer (613) 990-2210.

Title of Government Publication: _____

Cat. No.: _____   ISBN: _____

Copyright Date: _____ Vol. _____ No. _____

Author Department: _____ Copyright Holder: _____

Page # to be reproduced: _____

Intended Use
Commercial ☐   Educational ☐   Internal Use ☐
Tentative Title: _____

Format: _____
(paper – diskette – microfiche – faxLink – CD-ROM – Internet)

Language: English ☐   French ☐   Other ☐ _____
Territory: Canada ☐   U.S. ☐   Other ☐ _____
Tentative price: $ _____

Total pages of government work: _____ Total pages of your work: _____

Percentage of Crown copyright material: _____

Print or Production run: _____ Date to be published: _____

Translation: YES ☐ (specify) _____ NO ☐

Adaptation ☐   Revision ☐   N/A ☐

Should the government material be adapted or revised, the modified changes must be included with your request.

Braille ☐   Large Print ☐   N/A ☐

Other ☐ (specify) _____

Name and address: _____

———————————————————————————————————
(Name and address of Publishing House, if applicable)

I hereby certify that all the facts herein stated are true and correct to my knowledge and that I am fully aware of the implications regarding the Copyright Act, Section 12, of the Revised Statutes of Canada, 1985. N.B. Should you wish to purchase the Act and/or amendments, please contact our customer service at (819) 956-4802.

Signature: _____   Requester's Name (block letters): _____
Address: _____

———————————————————————————————————
Phone No.: _____ Fax No.: _____ Date: _____

Return to:
Crown Copyright Officer, Crown Copyright and Licensing
PWGSC-CGP, 350 Albert St., 4th Floor, Ottawa, Ontario K1A 0S5
Telephone: (613) 990-2210 • Fax: (613) 998-1450 • E-Mail: Copyright.Droitsdauteur@pwgsc.gc.ca

Reviewed 2000-07-141 8ØØ O-Canada. Maintained by Communications Coordination Services Branch of Public Works and Government Services CanadaCopyright & Disclaimers

Appendix III

MEMBER COUNTRIES OF BERNE CONVENTION, THE UCC AND THE WTO AND WIPO DIGITAL TREATIES

Countries belonging to the Berne Convention for the Protection of Literary and Artistic Works (as of July 19, 2000)

Albania	Colombia	Guinea
Algeria	Congo	Guinea-Bissau
Antigua and Barbuda	Costa Rica	Guyana
Argentina	Côte d'Ivoire	Haiti
Armenia	Croatia	Holy See
Australia	Cuba	Honduras
Austria	Cyprus	Hungary
Azerbaijan	Czech Republic	Iceland
Bahamas	Democratic Republic	India
Bahrain	of the Congo	Indonesia
Bangladesh	Denmark	Ireland
Barbados	Dominica	Israel
Belarus	Dominican Republic	Italy
Belgium	Ecuador	Jamaica
Belize	Egypt	Japan
Benin	El Salvador	Jordan
Bolivia	Equatorial Guinea	Kazakhstan
Bosnia and Herzegovina	Estonia	Kenya
Botswana	Fiji	Kyrgyzstan
Brazil	Finland	Latvia
Bulgaria	France	Lebanon
Burkina Faso	Gabon	Lesotho
Cameroon	Gambia	Liberia
Canada	Georgia	Libyan Arab Jamahiriya
Cape Verde	Germany	Liechtenstein
Central African Republic	Ghana	Lithuania
Chad	Greece	Luxembourg
Chile	Grenada	Madagascar
China	Guatemala	Malawi

Malaysia	Philippines	Swaziland
Mali	Poland	Sweden
Malta	Portugal	Switzerland
Mauritania	Qatar	Tajikistan
Mauritius	Republic of Korea	Thailand
Mexico	Republic of Moldova	The former Yugoslav
Monaco	Romania	Republic of Macedonia
Mongolia	Russian Federation	Togo
Morocco	Rwanda	Trinidad and Tobago
Namibia	Saint Kitts and Nevis	Tunisia
Netherlands	Saint Lucia	Turkey
New Zealand	Saint Vincent and the	Ukraine
Nicaragua	Grenadines	United Kingdom
Niger	Senegal	United Republic of Tanzania
Nigeria	Singapore	United States of America
Norway	Slovakia	Uruguay
Oman	Slovenia	Venezuela
Pakistan	South Africa	Yugoslavia
Panama	Spain	Zambia
Paraguay	Sri Lanka	Zimbabwe
Peru	Suriname	

(Total: 146 States)

Countries belonging to the Universal Copyright Convention (as of January 27, 2000)

Algeria	Germany	Saint Vincent and the
Australia	Guinea	Grenadines
Austria	Holy See	Saudi Arabia
Bahamas	Hungary	Senegal
Bangladesh	India	Slovakia
Barbados	Italy	Slovenia
Bolivia	Japan	Spain
Bosnia and Herzegovina	Kenya	Sri Lanka
Brazil	Liechtenstein	Sweden
Bulgaria	Mexico	Switzerland
Cameroon	Monaco	The former Yugoslav
China	Morocco	Republic of Macedonia
Colombia	Netherlands	Trinidad and Tobago
Costa Rica	Niger	Tunisia
Croatia	Norway	United Kingdom of Great
Cyprus	Panama	Britain and Northern
Czech Republic	Peru	Ireland
Denmark	Poland	United States of America
Dominican Republic	Portugal	Uruguay
Ecuador	Republic of Korea	Venezuela
El Salvador	Russian Federation	Yugoslavia
Finland	Rwanda	(Total: 62 countries)
France		

Memberships in World Trade Organization
(as of September 8, 2000)

Albania	Germany	New Zealand
Agola	Ghana	Nicaragua
Antigua and Barbuda	Greece	Niger
Argentina	Grenada	Nigeria
Australia	Guatemala	Norway
Austria	Guinea Bissau	Pakistan
Bahrain	Guinea	Panama
Bangladesh	Guyana	Papua New Guinea
Barbados	Haiti	Paraguay
Belgium	Honduras	Peru
Belize	Hong Kong, China	Philippines
Benin	Hungary	Poland
Bolivia	Iceland	Portugal
Botswana	India	Qatar
Brazil	Indonesia	Romania
Brunei Darussalam	Ireland	Rwanda
Bulgaria	Israel	Saint Kitts and Nevis
Burkina Faso	Italy	Saint Lucia
Burundi	Jamaica	Saint Vincent & the
Cameroon	Jordan	Grenadines
Canada	Japan	Senegal
Central African Republic	Kenya	Sierra Leone
Chad	Korea, Republic of	Singapore
Chile	Kuwait	Slovak Republic
Colombia	The Kyrgyz Republic	Slovenia
Congo	Latvia	Solomon Islands
Costa Rica	Lesotho	South Africa
Côte d'Ivoire	Liechtenstein	Spain
Cuba	Luxembourg	Sri Lanka
Cyprus	Macau, China	Suriname
Czech Republic	Madagascar	Swaziland
Democratic Republic of the	Malawi	Sweden
Congo	Malaysia	Switzerland
Denmark	Maldives	Tanzania
Djibouti	Mali	Thailand
Dominica	Malta	Togo
Dominican Republic	Mauritania	Trinidad and Tobago
Ecuador	Mauritius	Tunisia
Egypt	Mexico	Turkey
El Salvador	Mongolia	Uganda
Estonia	Morocco	United Arab Emirates
European Communities	Mozambique	United Kingdom
Fiji	Myanmar	United States
Finland	Namibia	Uruguay
France	Netherlands – For the	Venezuela
Gabon	Kingdom in Europe and	Zambia
The Gambia	for The Netherlands	Zimbabwe
Georgia	Antilles	

(Total: 138 members)

WIPO Copyright Treaty (as of July 15, 2000)

Ratifications and Accessions

Argentina
Belarus
Burkina Faso
Costa Rica
Croatia
Ecuador
El Salvador
Hungary
Indonesia

Japan
Kyrgyzstan
Latvia
Mexico
Panama
Republic of Moldova
Saint Lucia
Slovakia
Slovenia
United States of America (19)

WIPO Performances and Phonograms Treaty (as of July 15, 2000)

Ratifications and Accessions

Argentina
Belarus
Burkina Faso
Costa Rica
Croatia
Ecuador
El Salvador
Hungary

Latvia
Mexico
Panama
Republic of Moldova
Saint Lucia
Slovakia
Slovenia
United States of America (16)

# ENDNOTES

Introduction

1 Zachariah Chafee, " Reflections on the Law of Copyright" 45 *Columbia Law Review* 719, as quoted in Stewart, S.M., *International Copyright and Neighbouring Rights* 2nd. ed., (London: Butterworths 1989), p. 305.

Chapter 1

1 Industry Canada, *A Guide to Patents*, Supply and Services Canada, 1994.

Chapter 2

1 R.S.C. 1985, c. C-42, as amended. This citation refers to the 1924 *Copyright Act*. The amendments to the *Act* must also be referred to when examining the current Canadian copyright law.

Chapter 3

1 *University of London Press Ltd. v. University Tutorial Press Ltd.*, [1916] 2 Ch. 601.

2 *Canadian Admiral Corporation Ltd. v. Rediffusion Inc.* (1954), Ex. C.R. 382, 20 C.P.R. 75.

3 *Apple Computer, Inc. v. MacKintosh Computers Ltd.*, [1988] 1 F.C. 673 (C.A.), aff'd (1990), 30 C.P.R. 257 (S.C.C.).

4 Note that this reflects a relatively recent change. Prior to January 1, 1996, the term "treaty country" would have been restricted to a Berne Convention country. If a work is subject to copyright as of January 1, 1996 in any treaty country and is not in the public domain, it will be eligible for protection in Canada. In other words, the work need not be created or published after January 1, 1996. To illustrate this change in the *Act*, prior to January 1, 1996, there was a difference in the way protection was extended to UCC countries. This difference related to the scope of protection and which works were protected, but for all practical purposes, UCC works now get full protection before and after January 1, 1996.

Chapter 4

1 This does not in fact presume that publication on the Web is considered publication under the Canadian *Copyright Act*. The current law is unclear on this point.

2 Poor man's copyright is downplayed by the American Copyright Office and perhaps even discouraged as being a waste of time and money. In one New York state case, *Smith v. Berlin*, 141 N.Y.S. 2d 110 (1955), the Court dismissed evidence of a work mailed to oneself because of the ease of possible tampering with the envelope and replacing its contents. The Court held that the evidence did not prove anything. No other American case, state or federal, has considered such evidence. Poor man's copyright may have a different perspective in Canada due to the nature of our registration system and the lack of a government depository for works protected by copyright. In fact, poor man's copyright may be looked upon as providing further proof where registration of a work has been made with the Canadian Copyright Office.

Chapter 5

1 For information on Canada's position on these treaties, see 📖 **www.pch.gc.ca**, as well as
📖 **www.pch.gc.ca/culture/cult_ind/wctppt_e.htm.**

Chapter 6

1 *University of London Press Ltd. v. University Tutorial Press Ltd.*, [1916] 2 Ch. 601.

2 *Ibid.*

3 *Flamand v. Société Radio-Canada* (1967), 53 C.P.R. 217 (Que. S.C.).

4 There is some thought that the lecture need not be fixed to be protected as a literary work. Also, it may be possible for a "non-fixed" lecture to be protected as a performer's performance.

5 *Kantel v. Frank E. Grant, Nisbet and Auld Ltd.*, [1933] Ex. C.R. 84.

6 *Ludlow Music Inc. v. Canint Music Corp. Ltd.* (1967), 35 Fox. Pat. C. 114 (Ex. Ct.).

7 *Wood v. Boosey* (1868), L.R. 3 Q.B. 223.

8 *George Hensher Ltd. v. Restawile Upholstery (Lancs) Ltd.*, [1974] 2 All E.R. 420 (H.L.).

9 *King Features Syndicate, Inc. v. O. & M. Kleeman Ltd.*, [1941] A.C. 417 (H.L.).

10 *Bulman Group Ltd. v. "One-Write" Accounting Systems Ltd.* (1982), 62 C.P.R. (2d) 149 (F.C.).

11 *Neudorf v. Nettwerk Productions Ltd.*, [1999] B.C.J. No. 2831 (B.C.S.C.).

12 *Kantel v. Frank E. Grant, Nisbet and Auld Ltd., supra*, note 5.

Chapter 9

1 *National Breweries, Ltd. v. A. Paradis*, [1925] S.C.R. 666.

2 *Hawkes & Son (London), Ltd. v. Paramount Film Service, Ltd.*, [1934] Ch. 593 (C.A.).

3 Report of the Sub-Committee on the Revision of Copyright, Standing Committee on Communications and Culture, *A Charter of Rights for Creators*, October, 1985, recommendation 48 at p. 37. In responding to this report, the government stated that it agreed in principle and would consider the definition: Government of Canada, *Government Response to the Report of the Sub-Committee on the Revision of Copyright*, February, 1986.

4 Also, a legitimate copy of a work may be kept out of Canada if it is made in a country to which the *Act* does not apply. For example, if a computer program diskette is manufactured in Taiwan with the consent of the copyright owner, the Canadian exclusive licensee of that copyright owner could keep the work out of Canada. If someone wanted their exclusive licensee to be able to keep a parallel import out of Canada, it would be better to manufacture it in a non-treaty rather than in a treaty country.

5 For further reading on the exhibition right, see Wanda Noel, *The Right of Public Presentation: A Guide to the Exhibition Right* (Ottawa: Canadian Conference of the Arts, 1990).

6 *Millar v. Taylor* (1769), 4 Burr. 2303, 98 E.R. 201 (C.A.).

7 *Morang v. Lusueur* (1911), 45 S.C.R. 95.

8 However, since the right of paternity applies only in relation to uses covered by the economic rights, if author "A" used a pseudonym on an article, nothing prevents Author "B" from stating the real name of A in a subsequent article where there is no reproduction or other copyright use of A's work.

9 *Snow v. The Eaton Centre Ltd.* (1982), 70 C.P.R. (2d) 105 (Ont. H.C.).

10 *A Charter of Rights for Creators, Supra* at 20.

Chapter 10

1 *Hubbard v. Vosper*, [1972] 2 Q.B. 95 (Eng. C.A.).

2 *Hager v. ECW Press Ltd.*, (unreported, December 21, 1999, Doc. No. T-9-98, Fed. T.D.).

3 *Zamacois v. Douville and Marchand*, [1943] 2 D.L.R. 257 (Ex. Ct).

4 *Allen v. Toronto Star Newspaper Ltd.* (1995), 63 C.P.R. (3d) 517 (Ont. Ct. (Gen. Div.)).

5 *Les Rotisseries St.-Hubert Ltée c. Le Syndicat des Travailleurs(euses) de la Rotisserie St.-Hubert de Drummondville (C.S.N.)* (1987), 12 C.I.P.R. 89 (Qué. C.S.).

6   *MCA Canada Ltd.-MCA Canada Lté v. Gillberry & Hawke Advertising Agency Ltd.* (1976), 28 C.P.R. (2d) 52 (Fed. T.D.).
7   *Composers, Authors & Publishers Assn. of Canada Ltd. v. Kiwanis Club of West Toronto*, [1953] 2 S.C.R. 111.
8   *Composers, Authors, and Publishers Assn. v. Western Fair Assn.*, [1951] S.C.R. 596.

Chapter 11

1   *Fly by Nite Music Co. v. Record Warehouse Ltd.* (1975), 20 C.P.R. (2d) 263 (Fed. T.D.).
2   *Ward, Lock & Co. v. Long*, [1906] 2 Ch. 550.
3   See David Vaver, *Copyright Law* (Toronto: Irwin Law, 2000), at pp. 165, 231.

Chapter 12

1   The exception to this rule is the "commercial" rental right in sound recordings and computer programs, as discussed in Chapter 9: Rights Protected by Copyright.
2   *King Features Syndicate Inc. v. Benjamin H. Lechter*, [1950] Ex. C.R. 297.
3   *Kantel v. Frank E. Grant, Nisbet & Auld Ltd.*, [1933] Ex. C.R. 84.
4   *British Columbia Jockey Club v. Standen* (1985), 8 C.P.R. (3d) 283 (B.C.C.A.).
5   *Bright Tunes Music Corp. v. Harrisongs Music, Ltd.*, 420 F. Supp. 177 (1976) (U.S. District Court, S.D.N.Y.). In the Canadian case of *Gondos v. Hardy* (1982), 64 C.P.R. (2d) 145 (Ont. H.C.), the plaintiff claimed that "The Homecoming" by Hagood Hardy and "Moment of Love" by Rudy and Jerry Toth, violated his composition "Variations on a Theme in A Minor."

Chapter 13

1   See Code 9959 of Schedule VII to the Customs Tariff. Also, "copyrighted in Canada" means a work with a Canadian Copyright Office certificate, but the remedy is not limited to works with a Canadian author or publisher. The words "Canadian copyrighted works" are interpreted to mean any printed material protected by copyright in Canada, which would include works protected from all Berne countries and not just those works of Canadian citizens.
2   For information on an on-going class action suit on behalf of freelance writers, see: ⬛ www.pwac.ca.
3   This is only true with respect to moral rights infringements after June 8, 1988. The remedies for moral rights infringements on or prior to that date are generally limited to an injunction.
4   *Randall Homes Ltd. v. Hardwood Homes Ltd.* (1987), 17 C.P.R. (3d) 372 (Man. Q.B.).
5   *Kaffka v. Mountain Side Developments Ltd.* (1982), 62 C.P.R. (2d) 157 (B.C.S.C.).
6   *Slumber-Magic Co. Ltd. v. Sleep-King Adjustable Bed Co.* (1984), 3 C.P.R. (3d) 81 (B.C.S.C.).
7   Subsection 34(1) allows a court to give any remedies for the violation of copyright. In *R. v. James Lorimer and Co. Ltd.*, [1984] 1 F.C. 1065 (C.A.), exemplary damages were held to be appropriate in copyright infringement cases.
8   *M.C.A. v. Gillberry & Hawke Advertising Agency Ltd.* (1976), 28 C.P.R. (2d) 52 (Fed. T.D.).
9   *Zamacois v. Douville*, [1943] 2 D.L.R. 257.
10   *Bishop v. Stevens* (1990), 72 D.L.R. (4th) 97 (S.C.C.).

Chapter 15

1   Unlike Canada, renewal of copyright used to be permitted in the United States.

Chapter 16

1   "Reflections on Digital Technology: The Shape of Things to Come," WIPO Worldwide Symposium on the Impact of Digital Technology on Copyright and Neighboring Rights, Harvard University, Cambridge, Massachusetts, U.S.A., March 31 to April 2, 1993.

INDEX

Acceptance of offer, 160
Access to Information Act, 149
Accounting of profits, 184
Adaptation right, 111
Adaptations, 67, 87, 102
Addresses, 60
Agricultural fairs, 149
Allen, Woody, 105
American system. *See* United States
Anonymity, 119
Anti-piracy units, 189
Anton Pillar order, 179
Any material form whatever, 108
Apprenticeship, 91
Architectural works, 70
Archives, 142-147
Arrangements, 67, 87, 102
Artistic works
   architectural works, 70
   comic strips, 71
   engravings, 68, 69
   fictional characters, 71
   industrial designs, 71-73
   maps/charts/plans, 70
   paintings/drawings, 68
   permissions, 205, 206
   photographs, 69
   plastic works, 70
   sculptures, 70
   sketches/illustrations, 70

Assignments, 153-162
   future works, 158
   moral rights, 161, 162
   neighbouring rights, 162
   reversionary interest, 156
   rights, by, 155
   territory, by, 156
   time, by, 155, 156
   writing requirement, 159-161
Audio Video Licensing Agency (AVLA),
   203, 205
Audio-visual works, 64, 65, 83, 84, 100
Author. *See* Ownership of copyright
Authorization right, 111
Authorizations. *See* Using
   copyright materials
Automatic protection, 27-43
AVLA, 203, 205

Back-up copy, 130
Berne Convention, 46, 47, 312-316
Bill C-32, 13
Bill C-60, 13
Blank audio recording media levy,
   123, 204
Blank forms, 76
Blanket licences, 163
Books, 58, 59
Bootlegging, 167
Border remedies, 172-175
Broadcasting Act, 150

Broadcasts, 25, 26, 79, 123
  assignment, 162
  duration of copyright, 103, 104
  limitation on rights, 147, 148
  ownership of copyright, 93
Browsing, 227
Brussels Satellite Convention, 50
Bulletin board, 229

Caching, 228
Canadian Broadcasters Rights
  Agency Inc., 206
Canadian Copyright Licensing
  Agency, 137
Canadian Heritage, 15
Canadian Intellectual Property
  Office (CIPO), 10, 11, 15
Canadian ISBN Agency, 33
Canadian Musical Reproduction Rights
  Agency Limited (CMRRA), 201
Canadian Retransmission Collective
  (CRC), 206
Canadian Retransmission
  Right Association, 206-207
CANCOPY, 137, 141, 196-198
CARfac Copyright Collective, 205
Cartoon characters, 71
Certification marks, 5
Character merchandising, 72
Charts, 70
Choreographic works, 66
CIPO, 10, 11, 15
Civil actions, 175-186. *See also*
  Violation of copyright
Click-through licence, 131
CMRRA, 201
Co-authorship, 76-78, 91, 100, 101
Collective works, 73, 74, 86, 87, 100
Collectives
  exploitation of rights, 162-165
  obtaining permissions, 193-207
  schools, 136-142
Colourable imitation, 169
Comedies, 64
Comic strips, 71
Commercial rental right, 115-117
Commissioned works, 88, 89
Communication signals. *See* Broadcasts

Compensatory damages, 182
Compilations, 74-76, 87
Computer programs, 61, 62
  limitation of rights, 130, 131
  media, 62
  public domain software, 62
  shareware, 62
Confidential information, 7, 8, 11
Consideration, 160
Consultants, 91
Contracts, 90, 94, 160, 161
COPIBEC, 137, 141, 197, 198
Copyright
  moral rights, distinguished, 106, 152
  physical object, and, 152
Copyright Act, 12-14, 239-301
Copyright Board, 15, 195, 211
Copyright collectives. *See* Collectives
Copyright executor, 157
Copyright notice, 28, 29
Copyright Office, 15, 37
Copyright revision process, 13, 14
Copyright symbol, 28
Corporations, 92, 99, 103
Counterfeiting, 168
CPCC/SCPCP, 205
CRC, 206
Criminal remedies, 187-189
Criteria for protection, 17-26
  fixation, 20-23
  nationality/place of publication, 23-25
  originality, 18-20
Crown Copyright Officer, 208
Crown works, 73
Cultural Property Export and Import Act,
  149

Damages, 182-184
Databases, 20, 75, 76
Deep linking, 228
Defendant, 177
Delivery up, 184
Deposit of copyright material, 32, 36
Designs, 71, 72
Dictionary, 73
Digital copyright treaties, 49, 319
Digital media, 222-238
  clearing rights, 236

commercial rental right, 231
enforcing copyright on Internet,
  236-238
exhibition right, 230
exploitation of rights, 233-236
international law issues, 238
licenses, 196, 197, 234, 235
limitation on rights, 233
moral rights, 232
neighbouring rights, 233
ownership/duration of copyright,
  225, 226
protected works, 225
right of adaptation, 229
right of authorization, 230
right of public performance, 229
right of publication, 229
right of reproduction, 226-229
right of telecommunication to
  public, 230
right to make sound recording,
  231, 232
right to prohibit importation, 230
terminology, 224, 225
treaties, 49, 319
U.S. legislation, 219, 220
value of rights, 235, 236
Digital Millennium Copyright Act
  of 1998 (DMCA), 219, 220
Direct infringement, 168-170
DMCA, 219, 220
Dramatic works
  fixation, 21
  operas/musicals/comedies, 64
  permissions, 198
  plays, 64
  radio programs, 64
  scripts, 63
Drawings, 68
Droit de suite, 125
Duration of copyright, 95-104
  arrangements/adaptations, 102
  audio-visual works, 100
  author vs. owner, 96
  calculation of duration, 96
  collective works, 100
  communication signals, 103
  corporations, 99, 103

employment relationship, 101
general rule, 95, 96
government materials, 101
moral rights, 98
performer's performance, 103
photographs, 99
posthumous works, 101
public domain works, 103, 104
reversionary interest, 102
sound recordings, 102, 103
translations, 102
unexploited works, 97, 98
unknown authors, 101
works of joint authorship, 100, 101

Economic rights
  commercial rental right, 115-117
  exhibition right, 113, 114
  right of adaptation, 111
  right of authorization, 113
  right of public performance, 108, 109
  right of publication, 109-111
  right of reproduction, 107, 108
  right of telecommunication to
    public, 111, 112
  right of translation, 111
  right to make sound recording, 117
  right to prohibit importation, 112, 113
Editions, 60
Education. See Schools
Electronic bulletin board, 229
Electronic rights, 224, 225.
  See also Digital media
Employment relationship, 89-91
Encyclopedia, 73
Engravings, 68, 83
Ephemeral recordings, 147
Etchings, 68
Exceptions. See Limitations on rights
Exemplary damages, 183
Exhibition right, 113, 114
Exploitation of rights, 151-165
  collectives, 162-165
  digital media, 233-236
  licences/assignments.
    See Assignments
  who can exploit, 153
Expression of ideas, 16

Facts, 55
Fair dealing, 126-129
Fictional characters, 71
Fixation, 20-23
Fixed works, 22, 23
Flight Stop, 119
Folklore, 73
Foreign creators/countries. *See*
   International copyright protection
Formalities, 27-43
   automatic protection, 27, 28
   marking your creations, 28, 29
   registration. *See* Registration
Foster, George G., 1
Framing, 228
Free use, 215
Freelancers, 86

Games, 62, 63
Geneva Phonograms Convention, 49
Government departments, 14, 15
Government materials
   duration of copyright, 101
   ownership of copyright, 91
   permissions, 207-209
   protected works, as, 207-209

Hager, Barbara, 128
Harrison, George, 170
Hoffman, Gary M., 190
Home videos, 65

Ideas, 7, 16, 54, 55
Illustrations, 70
Importing
   border remedies, 172-175
   limitation on rights, 132, 133
   right to prohibit importation, 112, 113
Improvised work, 65
Incidental uses, 132
Independent contractors, 89-91
Indirect infringement, 170
Individual licences, 163
Industrial design, 6, 11
Industrial designs, 71-73
Industry Canada, 15
Information, 55

Infringement. *See* Violation of copyright
Injunctions, 180-182
Intangible aspect of creation, 15, 16
Integrated circuit topography protection,
   9-11
Intellectual property, 1-11
   confidential information, 7, 8, 11
   copyright, 8, 9, 11
   industrial design, 6, 11
   integrated circuit topography protection, 9-11
   patents, 3-5, 11
   trade marks, 5, 6, 11
Interim injunction, 180, 181
Interlocutory injunction, 180, 181
International copyright conventions,
   45-50, 312-319
International copyright protection, 44-53
   conventions, 45-50, 312-319
   enforcement (which country?), 50, 51
   enforcement in foreign countries,
   51, 52
   protection of foreigners in Canada, 53
   trade agreements, 50
International standard book number
   (ISBN), 32, 33
International standard music number
   (ISMN), 33
International standard serial number
   (ISSN), 33
International trade agreements, 50
Internet. *See also* Digital media
   enforcing copyright, 236-238
   jurisdiction, 51
   online clearance mechanisms, 207
   piracy, 237
   who is liable, 177
Irreparable harm, 181
ISBN, 32, 33
ISMN, 33
ISSN, 33

John, Elton, 12
Joint authorship, 76-78, 91, 100, 101
Journalist, 86

Koskinen, Tarja, 44

LAM provisions, 142-147
Lectures, 60, 147
Legislative/judicial/administrative
    proceedings, 129
Letters, 59, 82
Libraries/archives/museums, 142-147
Licenses, 153, 154. *See also* Assignments
Licensing bodies. *See* Collectives
Limitation period, 176
Limitations on rights, 126-150
    agricultural fairs, 149
    broadcasters, 147, 148
    collectives, 136-142
    computer programs, 130, 131
    fair dealing, 126-129
    importation of works, 132, 133
    incidental uses, 132
    LAM provisions, 142-147
    legislative/judicial/administrative
        proceedings, 129
    moral rights, 150
    news reporting/summary, 147
    non-profit organizations, 149
    other statutes, 149, 150
    parody, 129
    persons with perceptual
        disabilities, 149
    places of worship, 149
    public recitation of extracts, 129
    re-using moulds, 132
    schools, 133-136
    sound recordings, 131
    time-shifting of television
        broadcasts, 132
    works permanently situated in
        public place, 132
Limited edition, 69
Linking, 228
Listserv, 228, 229
Literary works
    books, 58, 59
    computer programs, 61, 2
    editions, 60
    games, 62, 63
    lectures/addresses/speeches/
        sermons, 60
    letters, 59
    names, 59

news, 60
permissions, 196-198
tables, 62
translations, 61
Lithographs, 68
Litigation. *See* Violation of copyright
Lyrics, 67

MacDonald, Flora, 151
Mailing copy to yourself, 39
Mann, Charles C., 80
Maps, 70
Marcou, George T., 190
Marking your creations, 28, 29
Material form, 108
Materials, 54
Mechanical right, 117
Mediation, 176
Member countries (international
    conventions), 312-318
Memoranda, 58, 59
Microchips, 9
Miller, Michael, 166
Moral rights, 117-121
    assigning, 161
    copyright, distinguished, 106
    digital media, 232
    duration of copyright, 98
    limitation of rights, 150
    ownership of copyright, 93, 94
    permissions, 211-212
    right of association, 120
    right of paternity, 118, 119
    testamentary dispositions, 162
    U.S., 219
    violation, 168, 171
    waiving, 161
Museums, 142-147
Music videos, 79
Musical works, 66-68
    arrangements/adaptations, 67
    fixation, 22
    ownership of copyright, 85
    permissions, 199-202
    sheet music, 67
    sound recordings. *See* Sound
        recordings

Names, 59
National Archives of Canada, 147
National Library legal deposit, 32
National Library of Canada, 32, 33
National treatment, 45
Nationality of creator, 24
Neighbouring rights, 121-123.
     See also Broadcasts, Performer's
     performances, Sound recordings
Neighbouring Rights Collective of
     Canada (NRCC), 203-204
News, 60
News reports and summaries, 147
News summary, 147
Newsgroup, 229
Non-profit organizations, 149
Non-scripted works, 65, 84, 100
NRCC, 203-204

Offer, 160
Oman, Ralph, 222, 238
Online clearance mechanisms, 207
Online registration, 35
Operas, 64
Originality, 18-20
Other subject-matter, 78, 79
Out-of-court settlement, 175, 176
Ownership of copyright, 80-94
     adaptations/arrangements, 87
     audio-visual works, 83, 84
     collective works, 86, 87
     commissioned work, 88, 89
     communication signals, 93
     compilations, 87
     corporations, 92
     employment relationship, 89-91
     engravings, 83
     finding the owner, 193-195
     general rule, 81, 82
     government materials, 91
     letters, 82
     moral rights, 93, 94
     musical works, 85
     newspaper/magazine/periodical
         contributions, 85, 86
     performer's performances, 93
     photographs, 83
     portraits, 83

school work, 88
second/subsequent owners, 82
sound recordings, 93
translation, 88
work of joint authorship, 91, 92
works generated by computer
     software, 92

Paintings, 68
Pamphlet, 59
Pan-Canadian licence, 137-139
Parallel imports, 111, 112
Parody, 129
Patent Cooperation Treaty (PCT), 4
Patents, 3-5, 11
PECCS, 197
Performer's performances, 25, 26, 78,
     121, 122
     assignment, 162
     duration of copyright, 103
     enforcing contractual obligations, 122
     ownership of copyright, 93
Permanent injunction, 181
Permissions. *See* Using copyright
     materials
Persons with perceptual disabilities, 149
Photographs, 69, 83, 99
Physical property law, 1
Piracy, 167
Place of publication, 24, 25
Places of worship, 149
Plagiarism, 167
Plaintiff, 177
Plans, 70
Plastic works, 70
Plays, 64
Playwrights Union of Canada
     (PUC), 198
PLR Commission, 124
Political speeches, 147
Poor man's copyright, 39
Portraits, 83
Pre-judgment orders, 179
Presumption of ownership, 185
Prints, 69
Privacy Act, 150
Protected works, 54-79
     artistic works, 68-73

audio-visual materials, 64, 65
choreographic works, 66
collective works, 73, 74
compilations, 74-76
dramatic works, 63, 64
folklore, 73
general rule, 56, 57
government materials, 73
literary works, 57-63
musical works, 66-68
other subject-matter, 78, 79
works of joint authorship, 76-78
Pseudonyms, 59, 119
Public domain software, 62
Public domain works, 103, 104
Public lecture, 147
Public lending right, 123, 124
Public Lending Right (PLR)
    Commission, 124
Public performance right, 108, 109
Public recitation of extracts, 129
Publication, 109-111
PUC, 198
Punitive damages, 183

Radio programs, 64
Raymond, W. G., 126
Re-using moulds/casts of artistic works,
    132
Real-life events, 55
Registering grant in interest, 157
Registers of Copyrights, 37
Registrar of Copyrights, 37
Registration, 30-43
    advantages, 30, 31
    American Copyright Office, with,
        40, 41
    application form, 35, 36, 302-311
    change of address, 38
    fees, 33
    final draft, 38
    further information (contact person),
        35
    how long does it take, 38
    in whose name, 34
    larger bodies of work, 36
    mailing copy to yourself, 39
    multimedia, 36

online, 35
procedure, 34, 35
Registers of Copyrights, 37
specialized registration/depositories,
    41-43
unpublished works, 38
who can register, 34
Rental right, 115-117
Reproduction right, 107, 108
Retransmission right, 112
Reversionary interest, 102, 156
Right of adaptation, 111
Right of association, 120
Right of authorization, 113
Right of integrity, 119, 120
Right of paternity, 118, 119
Right of public performance, 108, 109
Right of publication, 109-111
Right of reproduction, 107, 108
Right of resale, 125
Right of telecommunication to
    public, 111, 112
Right of translation, 111
Right to prevent changes to work, 119
Right to prohibit importation, 112, 113
Rights, 105-125
    defined, 105
    distinct/exclusive, 152
    droit de suite, 125
    economic. *See* Economic rights
    exploiting. *See* Exploitation of rights
    limitations. *See* Limitations on rights
    moral. *See* Moral rights
    neighbouring, 121-123
    public lending right, 123, 124
    right to resale, 125
    value of, 158, 159
Rome Convention, 48, 49
Royalty advance, 159
Rule of the shorter term, 45

Schools, 133-142
    copyright collectives, 136-142
    copyright warning, 144, 145
    instruction, 134
    ownership of copyright, 88
    performances, 134

Schools (*continued*)
  public performance of musical works,
    135, 136
  publication of short passages in
    collection, 136
  taping radio/TV programs, 135
  tests/exams, 134
Scripted works, 65, 84, 100
Scripts, 63, 64
Sculptures, 70
Sermons, 60
Shareware, 62
Sheet music, 67
Shrinkwrap licence, 131
Site licence, 130
Sketches, 63, 70
Slogans, 59
Small claims court, 178
Snow, Michael, 119
SOCAN, 85, 199-201
Société des auteurs et compositeurs
    dramatiques (SACD), 198
Societies. *See* Collectives
Society for Reproduction Rights of
    Authors, Composers and Publishers
    in Canada (Sodrac) Inc., 201-202
SODART, 205
SODRAC, 201-202
Sonny Bono Copyright Term Extension
    Act, 216
Sound recording symbol, 29
Sound recordings, 78, 79
  assignment, 162
  duration of copyright, 102, 103
  methods of protection, 25
  notice, 29
  ownership of copyright, 93
  permissions, 203-205
  private copying, 123, 131, 204
  public performance/broadcast, 122, 123
  right to make, 117, 231, 232
Sound tracks, 65
Specialized registration/depositories,
    41-43
Specific use licences, 163
Speeches, 60
Staff journalist, 86
Statutory damages, 183, 184

Subconscious copying, 169
Substantial part, 107, 108
Suspicious goods, 189
Synchronization right, 117

Tables, 62
Talk shows, 64
Telecommunications rights, 111, 112
TERLA, 197
Term of copyright. *See* Duration of
    copyright
Testamentary dispositions, 157, 162
Text of *Copyright Act*, 239-301
Time-shifting of television
    broadcasts, 132
Titles, 59, 60
Topography, 9
Trade agreements, 50
Trade marks, 5, 6, 11
Trade name, 5
Trade secrets, 7, 8, 11
Transactional licences, 163
Translation right, 111
Translations, 61, 88, 102
Treaty country, 24
Trollope, Anthony, 17
Twain, Shania, 128

UCC, 47, 48
Unexploited works, 97, 98
United States, 214-221
  assignment, 218
  digital legislation, 219, 220
  employment situations, 218
  free use, 215
  further information, 221
  length of protection, 216
  moral rights, 219
  protected works, 215
  registration, 40, 41, 217, 218
  rights, 215
Universal Copyright Convention
    (UCC), 47, 48
Unlocatable copyright owner provision,
    209-211
Using copyright materials, 190-213
  artistic works, 205, 206
  collectives, 195-207

dramatic works, 198
finding the owner, 191-195
general rule, 191
government material, 207-209
literary works, 196-198
moral rights, 211-213
music videos, 205
musical works, 199-202
neighbouring rights, 203-204
online clearance mechanisms, 207
retransmitted works, 206, 207
sound recordings, 203
unlocatable copyright owners, 209-211

Value of rights, 158, 159
Violation of copyright, 166-189
accounting of profits, 184
Anton Pillar order, 179
bootlegging, 167
border remedies, 172-175
burden of proof, 185
costs, 178
counterfeiting, 168
criminal remedies, 187-189
damages, 182-184
delivery up, 184
direct infringement, 168-170
indirect infringement, 170
injunctions, 180-182
limitation period, 176
matters to prove, 184-186
mediation, 176
moral rights, 168, 171
out-of-court settlement, 175, 176

piracy, 167
plagiarism, 167
pre-judgment orders, 179
presumption of ownership, 185
summary procedures, 176
where to sue, 178, 179
who can be sued, 177, 178
who may sue, 176, 177

Web-wrap licence, 131
WGAw Registration Service, 42, 43
WGC Registration Service, 42, 43
Wide injunction, 182
Will, 157, 162
WIPO, 46
WIPO Copyright Treaty, 49, 319
WIPO Performances and Phonograms
    Treaty, 49, 319
Words, 59
Work, 54
Work made for hire, 218
Works of artistic craftsmanship, 69
Works of joint authorship, 76-78, 91,
    100, 101
Works permanently situated in public
    place, 132
World Intellectual Property
    Organization (WIPO), 46
Writers Guild of America, West, 42, 43
Writers Guild of Canada, 42, 43
Written documents, 59

Year book, 73

ABOUT
THE AUTHOR

Lesley Ellen Harris began her career in copyright in 1984 working with a lobbying group (the Canadian Copyright Institute) interested in revising Canada's copyright laws. She went on to work with the Department of Communications (now Canadian Heritage) from 1987 to 1991, where she helped revise the country's copyright laws.

Recognized as a Copyright and Licensing expert, Lesley frequently speaks at conferences and seminars in Canada and the U.S., and has also spoken in Mexico, Denmark and England. Her articles and papers are published internationally, too, and she continues to be involved in copyright education.

Lesley's work focuses on copyright, licensing and e-commerce legal issues in publishing, information, entertainment, computers, the Internet and other media. And her clients range from individual creators to governments, associations, unions and corporations.

In 1998, she moved to Washington, D.C., where her husband works. With her virtual office established, Lesley is truly a citizen of the global village. You can visit her at **www.copyrightlaws.com**.

Lesley continues to reside in Washington, with her husband and their golden retriever, NAFTA.

OTHER PUBLICATIONS BY LESLEY ELLEN HARRIS

Lesley Ellen Harris is involved with a number of publications which may interest you.

The Copyright & New Media Law Newsletter: For Libraries, Archives & Museums is a unique international publication edited by Lesley Ellen Harris. It has been published since 1997. This print newsletter is designed to keep readers informed of the latest developments in copyright law, with contributors and subscribers from 20 countries. Geared towards those who work in libraries, archives, museums, corporations, educational institutions, governments and law firms, this Newsletter will keep you informed of copyright issues and provide practical solutions for everyday activities. Subscribers receive a 12-page print newsletter four times a year. In between issues of the print newsletter, subscribers receive frequent e-mail alerts.

Previous issues of the Newsletter have examined such topics as copyright collectives, liability for illegal content on the Internet, distance learning and copyright, international copyright treaties, copyright law developments in Canada and other countries, recent court cases on copyright law, licensing electronic resources, and reviews of helpful resources such as books, videos, list servs and Web sites.

The *E-LAM REPORTS* are a one-of-a-kind series of four electronic reports written by Lesley Ellen Harris that deal with online and e-commerce issues specifically for libraries, archives and museums. The reports provide the most recent information in this area and supply relevant tips, tools and trends to make e-commerce activities stand out. Each report features case studies and evaluations of libraries, archives and museums with interesting and successful e-commerce sites. Additionally, each report features analysis, providing up-to-the-moment information, as well as tips and advice for libraries, archives and museums. The topics of the four reports are: Developing your Online and E-Commerce Strategy; Options for Collecting Payment on the Internet; Marketing your Web Site and E-Commerce Activities; and Understanding Developments in Copyright Privacy and Other Legal Issues.

Lesley also prepares an e-letter *Copyright, New Media Law & E-Commerce News*. This e-letter provides the latest news on upcoming legislation and conventions related to copyright law and e-commerce in Canada and throughout the world, updates on relevant legal cases such as Napster and MP3.com, as well as recent developments in digital licensing.

For further information on the above publications, go to (WEB) **http:// copyrightlaws.com** or email (WEB) **lesley@copyrightlaws.com.**